PENGUIN BOOKS

ISTANBUL

John Freely was born in New York in 1926. He joined the US Navy at the age of seventeen and served with a commando unit in Burma and China during the last months of the Second World War. He received a Ph.D. in physics from New York University in 1960, and since then he has lived in New York, Boston, London, Athens, Istanbul and Venice. His first book was *Strolling Through Istanbul* (1972, with Hilary Sumner-Boyd). Since then he has written twenty other travel books, most of them about Greece and Turkey. Also published by Penguin are *Classical Turkey*, *Strolling Through Athens* and *Strolling Through Venice*.

ISTANBUL

THE IMPERIAL CITY

John Freely

PENGUIN BOOKS

PENGUIN BOOKS

Published by the Penguin Group
Penguin Books Ltd, 27 Wrights Lane, London w8 5tz, England
Penguin Putnam Inc., 375 Hudson Street, New York, New York 10014, USA
Penguin Books Australia Ltd, Ringwood, Victoria, Australia
Penguin Books Canada Ltd, 10 Alcorn Avenue, Toronto, Ontario, Canada m4v 3b2
Penguin Books (NZ) Ltd, Private Bag 102902, NSMC, Auckland, New Zealand

Penguin Books Ltd, Registered Offices: Harmondsworth, Middlesex, England

First published by Viking 1996
Published in Penguin Books 1998
5 7 9 10 8 6 4

Printed in England by Clays Ltd, St Ives plc

For Toots
Istanbul Memories

Contents

List of Colour Plates and Picture
    Acknowledgements   ix
Maps   xi
Preface   xv
Turkish Spelling and Pronunciation   xvii

PART I – BYZANTIUM

1 The Strait and the City, up to *c.* 658 BC   3
2 The Greek City-State of Byzantium,
     c. 658 BC–AD 196   13
3 Roman Byzantium, 196–330   25

PART II – CONSTANTINOPLE

4   The City of Constantine, 330–337   37
5   The Imperial Capital, 337–395   48
6   The Theodosian Walls, 395–450   58
7   The Late Roman City, 450–527   69
8   The Age of Justinian, 527–565   79
9   The Struggle for Survival, 565–717   90
10 The Iconoclastic Crisis, 717–845   101
11 Born in the Purple, 845–1056   114
12 The Dynasty of the Comneni, 1056–1185 129
13 The Latin Conquest, 1185–1261   143

CONTENTS

14 Renaissance and Civil War, 1261–1354   153
15 The Fall of Byzantium, 1354–1453   164

PART III – ISTANBUL

16 Istanbul, Capital of the Ottoman Empire,
      1453–1520   181
17 The Age of Süleyman the Magnificent,
      1520–1566   194
18 The House of Felicity, 1566–1623   206
19 The Procession of the Guilds, 1623–1638   221
20 Decline and Gilded Decadence, 1638–1730 237
21 In the Days of the Janissaries, 1730–1826 253
22 The Age of Reform, 1826–1876   268
23 The Fall of the Ottoman Empire,
      1876–1923   281
24 Istanbul under the Turkish Republic,
      1923–1995   299

PART IV – NOTES ON MONUMENTS AND MUSEUMS
317

APPENDICES

Glossary   383
List of Emperors and Sultans   387
Bibliography   390

Index   396

Colour Plates and Picture Acknowledgements

COLOUR PLATES

1. A youth feeding his donkey
2. & 3. Justinian I (527–65) and his wife, the empress Theodora
4. Orhan Gazi (1326–62); anonymous portrait
5. Murat I (1362–89)
6. Beyazit I (1389–1402); anonymous portrait
7. Mehmet II (1451–81); portrait by Sinan Bey, c. 1480
8. Beyazit I comes to the rescue of Niğbolu; miniature by Lokman in a *Hünername*, or *Book of the Sultan's Exploits*
9. Beyazit II (1481–1512); anonymous portrait
10. Selim I (1512–20); anonymous portrait
11. Roxelana, wife of Süleyman the Magnificent and mother of Selim II; anonymous portrait
12. Mihrimah Sultan, daughter of Süleyman and Roxelana; anonymous portrait
13. Süleyman's funeral procession; miniature in the *Süleymanname* of Lokman, 1579/80
14. Procession with musicians; anonymous miniature in a *Surname*, or *Book of Festivals*
15. Selim II (1566–74); miniature painting by Nigâri
16. Murat IV (1623–40); anonymous painting
17. Selim III (1789–1807); painting by Constantine Kapıdağlı
18. Mustafa II (1695–1703); miniature painting by Levni
19. Mahmut I (1730–54); anonymous portrait
20. Foreign ambassador presenting his credentials to Koca Yusuf Pasha, grand vezir of Selim III; anonymous painting

PICTURE ACKNOWLEDGEMENTS

Colour: nos. 4–12 and 14–20 are from the Topkapı Sarayı Museum, Istanbul; no. 1 is from the Mosaic Museum, Istanbul; nos. 2–3 © SCALA; no. 13 is © Chester Beatty Library, Dublin.

Black and white: pages 7, 17, 33, 39, 53, 63, 66, 72 (top), 81, 84, 136 (bottom), 158, 186, 200, 205, 217, 241, 250, 270, 285 are from Julia Pardoe, *Beauties of the Bosphorus* (1839); 9, Deutsche Archaelogisches Institut, Istanbul; 11, 23, 190, Edwin A. Grosvenor, Constantinople (2 vols.; Boston, 1900); 19, Capitoline Museum, Rome; 21 Department of Medical Illustration, University of Manchester; 32 (left), 56, 72 (left), 105, 136 (top), 149, 154, 307, 311, photographs by Anthony E. Baker; 32 (right), 59, Istanbul Archaeological Museum; 32 (left), Museo di Conservatori, Rome; 42, O. Panvinio, *De Ludis Circensibus* (Venice, 1600); 43, August Heisenberg, *Grabeskirche und Apostlekirche: Zwei Basiliken Konstantius* (2 vols.; Leipzig, 1908); 54, 93, Anselmo Banduri, *Imperium Orientale*; 72 (right), Ny Carlsberg Glyptotek, Copenhagen; 83, 117, 123, Dumbarton Oaks Center for Byzantine Studies; 92, 195, British Museum, London; 98, Biblioteca National, Turin/Bridgeman Art Library; 107, American Numismatic Society; 108, Biblioteca Apostolica Vaticana, Rome; 115, 118, Biblioteca Nacional, Madrid; 132, 166, Bibliothèque Nationale, Paris; 144, Biblioteca Estense, Modena; 151, 156 (left), Staatsbibliothek, Munich; 156 (right), Landsbibliothek, Stuttgart; 168, Albert Gabriel, *Châteaux Turcs du Bosphore* (Paris, 1943); 170, Charles du Fresne di Cange, *Constantinopolis Christiana* (Paris, 1680); 172, Alexander W. Hidden, *The Ottoman Dynasty* (New York, 1912); 182, Private collection, photograph from Franz Babinger collection; 209, W. Miller, *The Costume of Turkey* (1802); 212, 246, Fazıl Hüscyin, *Hubanname ve Zenanname* ('Book of Beauties and Women') (1793), Istanbul University Library; 218, 230, 268, Topkapı Sarayı Museum; 255, 272, Thomas Allom and Robert Walsh, *Constantinople and the Scenery of the Seven Churches of Asia Minor* (1839); 258, Istanbul University Library; 265, I. M. D'Ohsson, *Tableu Général de l'Empire Ottoman* (7 vols.; Paris, 1788–1824); 275, 292, Çelik Gülersoy; 293, Imperial War Museum, London; 295, 301, Turkish Ministry of Tourism; 296, Mustafa Erem Çalıkoğlu.

The Notes on Monuments and Museums section on pages 317–79 is illustrated by Arlene Brill.

The maps on pages xii–xiv are drawn by Nigel Andrews.

0   0.5 Miles

0   800 Metres

I–VII: The Seven Hills

Lycus River

Blachernae Palace

Tekfursarayı

VI

St Saviour in Chora

Cistern of Aetius

V

Cistern of Aspar

GOLDEN HORN

Galata Tower

Sycae (Galata)

BOSPHORUS

Wall of Constantine

Sea Wall

Holy Apostles

St Saviour Pantocrator

IV

Neorion

Prosphorion

Promontorium Bosphorium

Column of Marcian

Valens Aqueduct

Goth's Column

Lycus River

Forum Amastrianum

III

Philadelphaeum

Wall of Septimius Severus

Wall of Byzantium

I

Acropolis

Palace of Magnaura

Cistern of St Mocius

Forum Bovis

Mese

Forum of Constantine

Stoa Basilica

Haghia Eirene

Pege

VII

Mese

Forum Tauri, or of Theodosius

II

Milion

Augustaeum

Haghia Sophia

Theodosian Walls

Forum of Arcadius

Great Palace

SS. Sergius and Bacchus

Hippodrome

Sea Walls

Harbour of Theodosius (Port of Eleutherius)

Kontoskalion

Psamathia

Golden Gate

St John the Baptist of Studius

S E A   O F   M A R M A R A

BYZANTINE CONSTANTINOPLE

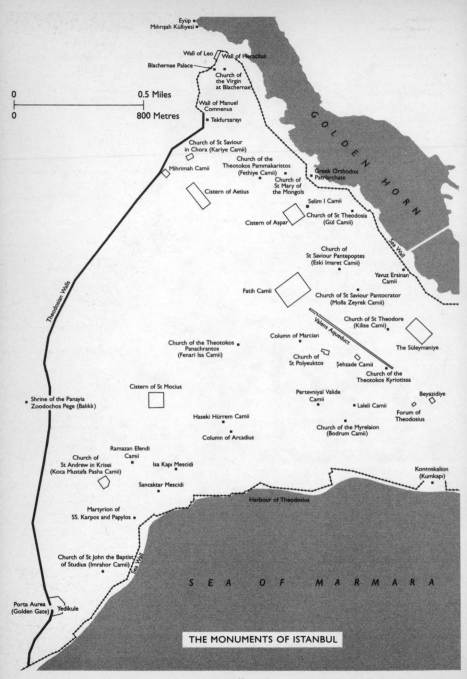

THE MONUMENTS OF ISTANBUL

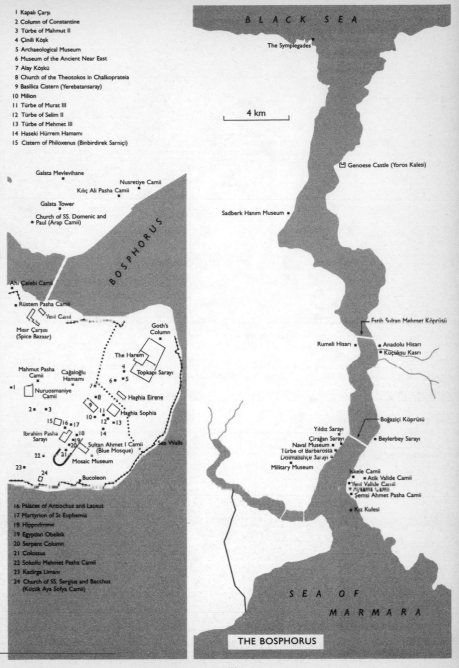

1 Kapalı Çarşı
2 Column of Constantine
3 Türbe of Mahmut II
4 Çinili Köşk
5 Archaeological Museum
6 Museum of the Ancient Near East
7 Alay Köşkü
8 Church of the Theotokos in Chalkoprateia
9 Basilica Cistern (Yerebatansaray)
10 Milion
11 Türbe of Murat III
12 Türbe of Selim II
13 Türbe of Mehmet III
14 Haseki Hürrem Hamamı
15 Cistern of Philoxenus (Binbirdirek Sarniçi)

BLACK SEA

The Symplegades

4 km

Genoese Castle (Yoros Kalesi)

Galata Mevlevihane

Nusretiye Camii

Kılıç Ali Pasha Camii

Galata Tower

Church of SS. Domenic and
Paul (Arap Camii)

Sadberk Hanım Museum

Ahi Çelebi Camii

BOSPHORUS

Rüstem Pasha Camii

Yeni Camii

Misir Çarşısı
(Spice Bazaar)

Goth's
Column

Fatih Sultan Mehmet Köprüsü

Rumeli Hisarı   Anadolu Hisarı
Küçüksu Kasrı

The Harem

Mahmut Pasha
Camii

Cağaloğlu
Hamamı

Topkapı Sarayı

4

6   5

Nuruosmaniye
Camii

1

7

8

Haghia Eirene

2   3

9

11

10

Haghia Sophia

12   13

15 16 17

10

İbrahim Pasha
Sarayı

18

19

14

Boğaziçi Köprüsü

Yıldız Sarayı
Çırağan Sarayı
Naval Museum
Türbe of Barbarossa
Dolmabahçe Sarayı

Beylerbey Sarayı

11

21

20

Sultan Ahmet I Camii
(Blue Mosque)

Sea Walls

Military Museum

23

Mosaic Museum

İskele Camii
Atik Valide Camii
Yeni Valide Camii
Ayazma Camii
Şemsi Ahmet Pasha Camii

24

Bucoleon

Kız Kulesi

16 Palaces of Antiochus and Lausus
17 Martyrion of St Euphemia
18 Hippodrome
19 Egyptian Obelisk
20 Serpent Column
21 Colossus
22 Sokollu Mehmet Pasha Camii
23 Kadirga Limanı
24 Church of SS. Sergius and Bacchus
   (Küçük Aya Sofya Camii)

SEA OF
MARMARA

THE BOSPHORUS

Preface

This is intended to be a well-illustrated introduction to the history of
the imperial city that has been known successively as Byzantium,
Constantinople and Istanbul, capital in turn of the Byzantine and
Ottoman empires. The book is not a formal history of these two world
empires, but rather a biography of the city itself and an account of
the social life of its people from the earliest settlements up to the
present day. It is also a guide to Istanbul's monuments, which are
described in the context of the city's living history, particularly with
regard to the role that they have played in its political, religious, intellectual, artistic and social life. The book will thus, I hope, be of prac-
tical use to all those who intend to visit Istanbul. Modern visitors can
compare their impressions with those of earlier travellers quoted in
the book, whose comments cover a span of more than 2,000 years,
and all of whom, even when they complain of the difficulties and
frustrations of living here, eventually reveal that they have fallen under
the spell of this most ancient of the world's great cities.

I am grateful to those who have helped me in many ways during my
research and writing of this book, particularly Ender Altuğ, librarian
of Boğaziçi Universitesi (University of the Bosphorus); Richard Dewey,
librarian of Robert College; Dr Anthony Greenwood, director of the
American Research Institute in Turkey; Çelik Gülersoy, director of the
Turkish Touring and Automobile Club; Dr Alpay Pasinli, director of
the Istanbul Archaeological Museum; and the staff of the library at
the German Archaeological Society in Istanbul; also Professor Behin
Aksoy, Professor Ahmet Çakmak, Godfrey Goodwin, Professor
Robert Osterhout, and Professor Lee Striker. I am grateful to Anthony

E. Baker for his photographs, to Arlene Brill for her drawings of the city's monuments, to Türe Özer for providing the Thomas Allom engravings, and to Eleo Gordon for invaluable advice in editing my manuscript.

I am also indebted to the late Professor Hilary Sumner-Boyd, my senior co-author in writing *Strolling through Istanbul* (Istanbul, 1972), which forms the basis for the section on Monuments and Museums in the present book. He found his last resting-place here and is now part of the city that he loved, his life forming part of its civic memory, so that as long as it endures he will not be forgotten.

Istanbul, 1996

Turkish Spelling and Pronunciation

Throughout this book, modern Turkish spelling has been used for Turkish proper names and for things that are specifically Turkish, with a few exceptions for Turkish words that have made their way into English. Modern Turkish is rigorously logical and phonetic, and the few letters that are pronounced differently from in English are indicated below. All letters have but a single sound, and none is totally silent. Turkish is very slightly accented, most often on the last syllable, but all syllables should be clearly and almost evenly accented.

Vowels are accentuated as in French or German; i.e. *a* as in f*a*ther (the rarely used *â* sounds rather like *ay*), *e* as in m*e*t, *i* as in mach*i*ne, *o* as in *o*h, *u* as in m*u*te. In addition there are three other vowels that do not occur in English; these are *ı* (undotted), pronounced as the *u* in b*u*t, *ö* as in German or as the *oy* in anno*y*, *ü* as in German or as the *ui* in s*ui*t.

Consonants are pronounced as in English, except the following:
c as *j* in *j*am; e.g. cami (mosque) = jahmy
ç as *ch* in *ch*at; e.g. çorba (soup) = chorba
g as in *g*et; never as in *g*em
ğ is almost silent and tends to lengthen the preceding vowel
ş as in *s*ugar; e.g. çeşme (fountain) = cheshme

PART I

BYZANTIUM

CHAPTER I

The Strait and the City

up to *c.* 658 BC

We should ideally approach Istanbul from the sea, as most travellers did for the first twenty-six centuries of its existence, coming to visit the city known in antiquity as Byzantium and later as Constantinople. The ship first passes from the Aegean through the Dardanelles, the Greek Hellespont, and then crosses the Sea of Marmara, the ancient Propontis. As we approach the eastern end of the Marmara we suddenly see the imperial city dramatically taking form between the pale blues of sea and sky, its domes and minarets rising from the hills on either side of the entrance to the Bosphorus, the incomparably beautiful strait that separates Europe and Asia between the Marmara and the Black Sea, the Pontus Euxinus of antiquity. This is indeed the imperial city, the capital in turn of two world empires over a period of nearly sixteen centuries. Monuments and ruins of the Byzantine and Ottoman empires crown the hills on either side of the strait as the ship makes its way into the port, crossing the mouth of the Golden Horn to its pier at the lower end of the Bosphorus on the European shore. We have come at last to the ancient metropolis that the Greeks refer to when they say '*stin polis*', meaning 'in the city' or 'to the city', needing no other name to identify it, for this is truly The City beyond compare.

Istanbul is the only city in the world that stands astride two continents. The main part of the city, which forms the south-easternmost extremity of Europe, is separated from its suburbs in Asia by the Bosphorus, which flows through a deep cleft that separates the two continents in the north-western corner of Turkey. The European part of the city is further divided by the Golden Horn, a scimitar-shaped estuary fed at its upper end by two streams known as the Sweet Waters of Europe, the Greek Cydaros and Barbyzes. The Horn, known to the Greeks as Chrysokeras, is some eight kilometres in length from the Sweet Waters to the point where it enters the Bosphorus, its width averaging about 500 metres. Over the last five kilometres of its course the Horn divides the European side of the city into two parts, with the medieval port quarter of Galata on the north and on the south the ancient imperial capital itself, the old city that some prefer to call Stamboul, though for Greeks it will always be Constantinopolis, or in English Constantinople.

The city was originally known as Byzantium, which was a thousand years old when Constantine the Great made it the capital of the Roman Empire in the year AD 330, whereupon it was called Constantinople, the City of Constantine. Then in 1453 Constantinople was captured by the Turks under Sultan Mehmet II, becoming the capital of the Ottoman Empire under its present name. The Ottoman Empire came to an end in 1923 with the founding of the modern Republic of Turkey, whose capital was then established in Ankara. Thus for the first time since late antiquity Istanbul was no longer the capital of a world empire, though in the years since then it has continued to be the most important city in Turkey, with a population that now exceeds 12 million, its European and Asian suburbs spreading on either side of the Bosphorus to within sight of the Black Sea.

Ancient Constantinople forms a roughly triangular peninsula, bounded on the north by the Golden Horn, on the south by the Marmara, and on the west by the Theodosian Walls built by Theodosius II in the first half of the fifth century AD, stretching for more than seven kilometres across the downs of Thrace. The area enclosed by the Theodosian Walls includes seven hills, six of them rising from the ridge that parallels the Golden Horn and the seventh with two peaks in the south-western corner of the old city. A river known as the Lycus, now canalized beneath the streets of Istanbul, enters the city and flows in the valley that separates the Seventh Hill from the Fifth and Sixth Hills, finally emptying into the Marmara in the Bay of Eleutheriou. The French scholar Petrus Gyllius, writing in the mid sixteenth century, used these seven hills as landmarks in his pioneering study of the topography of the ancient city. He numbered the First Hill as the eminence at the tip of the Constantinopolitan peninsula, the present Saray Burnu, or Palace Point, known in antiquity as the Promentorium Bosphorium.

The Byzantine historian Procopius described Constantinople as being 'surrounded by a garland of waters'. The city still owes much of its beauty to its unique setting, standing astride the strait at the confluence of the Bosphorus and the Golden Horn, whose waters meet off the Promentorium Bosphorium to flow together into the Marmara.

Gyllius called the Bosphorus the 'strait that surpasses all straits, because with one key it opens and closes two worlds, two seas'. The two seas to which Gyllius refers are the Aegean and the Euxine, and the two worlds are Europe and Asia, for the Bosphorus and the Hellespont have throughout history been the principal crossing-places between the two continents. And just as Troy controlled the straits in the prehistoric era through its position on the Hellespont, so did the imperial city on the Bosphorus hold the key to the two worlds and two seas from just before the dawn of history up until modern times.

Any description of the Bosphorus involves the names Rumeli and Anadolu, with reference, respectively, to places on the European and Asian shores of the strait. The first of these toponyms derives from that of the old Ottoman province of Rumeli, or Eastern Thrace, where 'Rum' refers to the eastern Roman dominions that later came to be called the Byzantine Empire. 'Anadolu' is the Turkish for Anatolia, the Asian part of Turkey, where 93 per cent of the country's land mass is located, a subcontinent also known as Asia Minor. 'Anatolia' is the Greek word for 'east', more literally the 'land of sunrise'. The name 'Asia' may originally have had the same meaning as this in both the Indo-European and Semitic families of languages, while 'Europe' may have meant 'sunset', or the 'land of darkness'. The distinction between these two names would have been dramatically evident to ancient navigators making their way up the Bosphorus from the Propontis to the Euxine, with the sun rising above one shore of the strait and then setting below the other, the deep waters of the channel clearly dividing the 'land of sunrise' from the 'land of darkness'.

The Bosphorus is about 35 kilometres long, measured along a line running down the centre of its channel, which changes direction nine times between the Black Sea and the Marmara, flowing generally north to south. The depth of the strait at the middle of its channel ranges from 50 to 75 metres for the most part, but at one point about halfway along its course it suddenly deepens to 110 metres. Its maximum width is some 3,500 metres, measured between Rumeli Feneri and Anadolu Feneri, the Lighthouses (in Turkish, '*fener*') of Europe and Asia, which mark the entrance to the strait from the Black Sea. The narrowest stretch of the Bosphorus begins about 20 kilometres from the Black Sea, where for about 3 kilometres the opposing continental shores are only about 700 metres apart. At the middle of this stretch the Bosphorus passes between Rumeli Hisarı and Anadolu Hisarı, the Castles (in Turkish, '*hisar*') of Europe and Asia, two fortresses built by the Turks before their capture of Constantinople. The fortress of Anadolu Hisarı stands at the mouth of one of the two streams called the Sweet Waters of Asia, the ancient Arete and Azarion, known in Turkish as Göksu and Küçüksu.

Both shores of the Bosphorus are indented with numerous bays and harbours, and in general it will be found that an indentation in one shore corresponds to a promontory on the other side of the strait. Most of the harbours shelter villages, almost all of them dating back to antiquity, with those on the upper Bosphorus inhabited up until recent years mostly by fishermen and their families. Despite the rapidly increasing urbanization of the Bosphorus shores, which has amalgamated all of the seaside villages on the lower strait into the urban mass of Istanbul, the hills and valleys along the waterway are still well-wooded, especially with cypresses, umbrella-pines, plane-trees, horse-chestnuts, terebinths and Judas-trees. The magenta to pink blossoms of the Judas-trees in spring, mingled with the mauve flowers of the ubiquitous wisteria and the red and white candles of the chestnuts, make the Bosphorus surpassingly beautiful at that season – painfully so in late April and early May, when nightingales serenade one another nocturnally in bowers along the strait, their songs echoing in our dreams.

The casual visitor to Istanbul, particularly if one comes in winter, might find it difficult to believe that the Bosphorus can be a perverse and dangerous body of water. Seen from the hills above its shores as it curves and successively narrows and widens, it often looks like a

View of the Bosphorus looking north from the Asian shore above the summer palace at Beylerbey.

long lake or a series of lakes, while its rapid flow from the Black Sea to the Marmara gives it the appearance of a river. Yet anyone who has ever observed its erratic currents and counter-currents, its various winds that encourage or hinder navigation in the heavy traffic of this international waterway, the impenetrable fogs that envelop it, even occasionally the icebergs that choke it, will realize that it is part of the ungovernable sea. Here Justinian's general Belisarius fought the invincible whale Porphyry, that Moby Dick who wrecked all shipping in the Bosphorus for months; and here Gyllius observed the largest shark he had ever seen. And on halcyon days in mid-winter schools of dolphins can be seen frolicking in its waves as they make their way through the strait, reminding us that the dolphin was represented on some of the earliest coins of Byzantium. Apollo sometimes took the form of a dolphin in Greek mythology, leading Hellenic navigators towards the sites of new colonies overseas, and it was supposedly his oracle at Delphi that first directed settlers here.

The earliest Greek myths about the Bosphorus probably date from the end of the Bronze Age, the latter part of the second millennium BC, when the Hellenes first came in contact with the world beyond the Hellespontine end of the Aegean. One of these stories tells the myth of Zeus and his mistress Io, daughter of the river-god Inachus, whom he changed into a heifer to conceal her from his jealous wife Hera. But Hera was not deceived and drove Io away, pursuing her with a relentless gadfly that forced her to swim this strait between Europe and Asia. Thenceforth the strait bore the name Bosphorus, or 'Cow's Ford', commemorating Io, the 'Inachean daughter, beloved of Zeus'.

The legend of Jason's search for the Golden Fleece is perhaps a folk-memory of the first Greek voyages through the strait, which expanded far to the north-east the bounds of the Hellenic *oecumene*, or inhabited world. Homer placed Jason's voyage a generation before the Trojan War, which both ancient and modern scholars have dated to *c*. 1200 BC. When Jason decided to embark on his expedition he commissioned a ship called *Argo*, in whose bow Athena inserted a piece of wood from the oracular oak at Dodona, giving it the power of speech. After the launching of *Argo*, whose name means 'swift', heroes from all over the Greek world volunteered to fill the fifty seats on its rowing-benches, including Orpheus and Heracles. These were the Argonauts, the crew of the vessel that Spenser in the *Faerie Queene* called 'The wondred *Argo*, which, in venturous peece/First through the *Euxine* seas bore all the flowr of *Greece*'. The only account of the voyage of *Argo* that has survived is the *Argonautica* of Apollonius of Rhodes, written in the mid third century BC. But Jason and the Argonauts are mentioned by sources as early as Homer, who in the *Odyssey* has Odysseus speak of '*Argo*, who is in all men's minds'. Pindar refers to the Argonauts in one of his Pythian Odes, where he writes of how 'Hera kindled sweet desire in the sons of God for the ship *Argo*. So that none should be left behind to nurse a life without danger at his mother's side, but rather he should find even against death the fairest antidote in his courage along with the others of his age.'

Gyllius imaginatively identified a number of sites along the Bosphorus associated with the legend of Jason and the Argonauts. These places can still be identified today, the most notable being the Symplegades,[1] also known as the Cyanean islets or Clashing Rocks,

*Pompey's Column on the Clashing Rocks;
early-seventeenth-century drawing.*

at Rumeli Feneri, where *Argo* barely made its way through into the
Euxine before the narrow passage closed behind it. The shores of the
upper Bosphorus approaching Rumeli Feneri and Anadolu Feneri
preserve their natural beauty more than anywhere else along the strait,
for they are situated in a military zone beyond the city limits of
Istanbul. The only evidences of modern civilization along the upper
Bosphorus are the argosies of oil-tankers and freighters that pass
through the strait on their way to and from the Black Sea, successors
of a commerce that began with the establishment of the first Greek
colonies on the shores of the Euxine.

The first of these colonies was Sinope (Sinop), founded in the mid
eighth century BC by the Ionian city of Miletus. During the following
century Miletus founded some thirty colonies around the shores
of the Euxine and the Propontis, while other Greek cities added a
few more foundations there and also along the Hellespont and the

Bosphorus. The first Greek colony on the Bosphorus was Chalcedon, founded by Megara c. 675 BC on the Asian side of the strait where it flows into the Propontis. This colony continues in existence as Kadıköy, an Asian suburb of Istanbul, long ago eclipsed by the imperial city across the strait. This latter began its existence as the Greek colony of Byzantium. According to Herodotus, Byzantium was founded seventeen years after the establishment of Chalcedon. Because of the later fame of the imperial city, many other states claimed credit for playing some role in the foundation of Byzantium, but scholars both ancient and modern generally agree that Megara was the principal founder.

The original site of Byzantium was on the First Hill, the acropolis above the Promentorium Bosphorium. The principal monuments on the First Hill are Haghia Sophia, the great church erected by Justinian; Topkapı Sarayı, the imperial residence of the Ottoman sultans for four centuries after the Turkish Conquest; and the Blue Mosque, built by Sultan Ahmet I in the early seventeenth century – three edifices spanning more than a thousand years in the history of the imperial city. Archaeological excavations on the First Hill have unearthed pottery and other artefacts dating as far back as the late sixth millennium BC, probably coming from settlements by the early Thracian tribes, including the Phrygians. But the acropolis on the First Hill has never been studied systematically by archaeologists, for much of the plateau is taken up with the courtyards and pavilions of Topkapı Sarayı. The saray is built over part of the site of the Great Palace of the Byzantine emperors, and that in turn was erected on the ruins of the ancient Greek city of Byzantium, making the First Hill a veritable palimpsest of history.

According to tradition, Byzantium was founded by Byzas the Megarian, who in one version of the myth is identified as the son of Poseidon and the nymph Keroessa, daughter of Zeus and Io. The foundation myth also says that before Byzas set out on his voyage he consulted the oracle of Apollo at Delphi, who advised him to settle 'opposite the land of the blind'. The meaning of this, according to Herodotus, quoting the Persian general Megabazus, was that 'the men of Chalcedon must have been blind at that time, for if they had any eyes, they would not have chosen an inferior site when a much finer one lay ready to hand'.

Byzas the Megarian, the eponymous founder of Byzantium;
from a coin of Byzantium, c. 230–220 BC.

One of the advantages offered by the site of Byzantium compared to that of Chalcedon was its greater defensibility, for the steep acropolis hill at the confluence of the Bosphorus and the Golden Horn was protected by the sea on all sides except to the west, where a defence wall could be erected. Another advantage was that the Golden Horn provided a superb natural harbour, shielded from storms by the heights that enclose it on all sides except where it opens into the Bosphorus, and there the promontory below the First Hill curves around to the north to shield the inner port. This promontory also acts as a barrier to divert the shoals of tunny that swim down the Bosphorus from the Black Sea, forcing them into the port and creating an abundant fishery that became one of the principal sources of income for the people of Byzantium. Other important sources of income were the tolls and harbour fees paid by the ships that passed through the strait, for Byzantium controlled the Bosphorus from the beginning of its history, and this was the principal reason for its subsequent rise to greatness. As Gyllius pointed out, 'The Bosphorus is the first creator of Byzantium, greater and more important than Byzas, the first founder of Byzantium.'

Such were the beginnings of the Greek colony of Byzantium, which in time became 'the city of all cities', still imperial in its splendour though the empires of which it was once the capital have now vanished.

CHAPTER 2

The Greek City-State of Byzantium
c. 658 BC–AD 196

Byzantium and Chalcedon were among a dozen Greek colonies along the shores of the Propontis. Closest to Byzantium on the European shore was Selymbria, and beyond that Perinthus, while Chalcedon's principal neighbours on the Asian coast of the Marmara were Dascylium and Cyzicus. Among the Greek colonies around the Black Sea the closest to the Bosphorus were Mesembria, on the European coast, and on the Asian shore Heraclea Pontica. The hinterland of the European colonies in this group was part of Thrace, while the Asian side was in Bithynia. The lands outside the cities on both sides of the straits were at that time inhabited by the barbarous Thracian tribes described by Herodotus in Book V of his *Histories*, where he writes that among them 'The most reputable sources of income are war and plunder.'

Thus Byzantium and the other Greek colonies on the coasts of Thrace and Bithynia were little islands of Hellenic civilization surrounded by barbarians, from whom they protected themselves by walling in their cities. The original walls[1] of Byzantium enclosed the acropolis hill on all sides, including the precipitous slopes leading down to the Bosphorus and the Golden Horn. The defence walls were restored on several occasions to make use of advances in military engineering. Many of these advances were made by Philon of Byzantium, who in the third century bc wrote the first treatise on military engineering. The walls of Byzantium were so strong that on several occasions the city withstood invaders who captured Chalcedon and other towns in the region.

The first settlers of Byzantium were principally Dorian Greeks from

Megara, and so the political institutions of the city were Spartan rather than Athenian. One of the Spartan traditions adopted in Byzantium was the enslavement of the local Thracian population and their reduction to helot-like serfs whom the Byzantines called prounikoi, or bearers of burdens. The cultural traditions of Byzantium in its early years were inherited from Megara, including its calendar, alphabet and religious cults, as evidenced by inscriptions and reliefs on archaic tombstones.

Byzantium, along with all other Greek colonies, was a *polis*, or city-state, its government usually democratic, though at times it was controlled by oligarchies and sometimes by tyrants. The Byzantines had the usual Council and People's Assembly of the Greek *polis*, with officials called polemarchs, or generals. They worshipped the Olympian gods of Greece, and ancient sources mention temples in Byzantium dedicated to more than a dozen of these deities, as well as shrines of the Anatolian goddess Cybele and the Egyptian god Serapis. At some of their religious festivals the most notable event was a torch-race, in which naked youths ran from the Promentorium Bosphorium up to the acropolis to light a sacrificial fire there.

The ancient sources seldom write of daily life in the city of Byzantium, but when they do they usually mention its ancient traditions of democracy and commerce, as well as the sybaritic ways of the Byzantines and Chalcedonians, who established a close alliance in the classical period. The historian Theopompus of Chios writes thus of their ways in the latter half of the fourth century BC:

The Byzantines had by this time long had a democratic government; also their city was situated at a trading-place, and the entire population spent their time in the market-place and by the water side; hence they had accustomed themselves to amours and drinking in the taverns. As for the Chalcedonians, before they all came to have a share with the Byzantines in the government, they devoted themselves unceasingly to the better pursuits of life; but after they had once tasted of the democratic liberties of the Byzantines they sank utterly into corrupt luxury, and in their daily lives, from having been the most sober and restrained, they became wine-bibbers and spendthrifts.

The merchants of Byzantium had a reputation for being sots, as the Athenian playwright Menander has one of his characters remark in a surviving fragment of one of his lost comedies, *The Flute Girl*: 'Byzantium makes all of her merchants drunkards. The whole night through for your sake we were drinking, and methinks, 'twas very strong wine too. At any rate I got up with a head for four.' Athenaeus of Naucratis quotes a Byzantine poet in referring to the proverbial drunkenness of the merchants of Byzantium in his *Deipnosophists*, or *The Learned Banquet*: 'For a man who guzzles wine as a horse does water, speaks gibberish and cannot recognize a single letter, speechless he lies immersed in his sleep like one who drinks the poppy drug.' Athenaeus elsewhere quotes the playwright Diphilus of Sinope, who has one of his characters describe a drunken merchant of Byzantium:

But another man has sailed into the port of Byzantium; only a two-day voyage, without a scratch; he has made money, and is overjoyed that he has made a profit of 12 per cent. He is full of talk about his fares, he belches forth his loans, celebrating a debauch with the help of rough panders. Up to him I sidle purring, the moment he disembarks: I put my hand in his, I remind him of Zeus the Saviour, I am all engrossed in the act of serving him. That's my way.

Athenaeus, in still another reference to Byzantine alcoholism and general decadence, refers to the historian Phylarchus of Athens:

Phylarchus, in the sixth book, says that the Byzantines are all besotted with wine and live in the wine-shop; they let out their own marriage-chambers, along with their wives, to strangers, and cannot bear to hear the sound of a war-trumpet even in their dreams. Hence on one occasion, when war was made on them, their general Leonides ordered tents for the wine-dealers to be set up on the walls and they at last reluctantly stopped leaving the ranks: this is recorded by Damon in his book on Byzantium.

The dissolute ways of the Byzantines are often mentioned by the city's poets, most notably Antiphilus of Byzantium, who flourished in the first century AD. Antiphilus satirizes the immorality of his fellow Byzantines in a poem entitled 'On a Ship built from the Profits of a Bordello', in which the whore-launched vessel speaks for itself:

I was formerly, too, my master's partner in his lucrative trade, when the crew he collected consisted of public votaries [prostitutes] from Cyprus. From these profits he built my keel that Cyprus might see me, a product of this land, tossing in the sea. My rig befits a lady of pleasure; I wear dainty white linen, and my timbers are tinted with a delicate dye. Come sailors, confidently mount on my stern. I can take any number of rowers.

Other poems by Antiphilus are addressed to the various women to whom he was paying court, such as this epigram apparently written in his latter days:

I am a quince of last year kept fresh in my young skin, unspoiled, unwrinkled, as downy as newly-born ones, still attached to my leafy stalk, a rare gift in the winter season; but for such as thou, my queen, even the cold and snow bear fruit.

Byzantium produced one of the few women poets of ancient Greece other than the immortal Sappho. She was the epic poetess Moero of Byzantium, who flourished *c.* 300 BC, her best-known work being a volume entitled *Arai*, or *Curses*. One of Moero's few surviving verses is a poem in honour of Dionysus and Aphrodite, the deities of wine and love, whose cults were evidently very popular in Byzantium:

Cluster, full of the juice of Dionysus, thou restest under the roof of Aphrodite's golden chamber; no longer shall the vine, thy mother, cast her lovely branch around thee, and put forth above thy head her sweet leaves.

Such are the last surviving echoes of the poetry of the ancient Greek city of Byzantium, whose remains are buried under the monuments and ruins of Byzantine Constantinople and Ottoman Istanbul.

Byzantium and the Greek cities of Asia Minor came under Persian domination soon after 546 BC, when Cyrus the Great captured Sardis. Cyrus and his successors, the first three being Cambyses II, Darius and Xerxes, organized the Persian kingdom into twenty provinces called satrapies, each ruled by a royal governor known as a satrap. The Greek cities in Asia Minor had governors from among their own citizens appointed by the satraps, who under the aegis of Persia dispensed with democratic assemblies and ruled as dictators, whom the Greeks in their own language called tyrants. Byzantium was part of the satrapy governed from Dascylium, and its earliest known tyrant is identified by Herodotus as Ariston, who was in control of the city when Darius set out on his great expedition against the Scythians in 513 BC.

The following year Darius reached the Bosphorus, where he had Mandrocles of Samos build a bridge of boats across the strait. Herodotus describes this incident in Book IV of the *Histories*, in which Byzantium makes its first appearance in recorded history. His description indicates that the bridge was constructed between Anadolu Hisarı and Rumeli Hisarı, the narrowest point of the strait. He writes that Darius 'had two marble columns erected on one of which is an inscription in Assyrian characters showing the various nations which were serving in the campaign; the other had a similar inscription in Greek'. After enumerating the Persian forces, he goes on to say that 'Years afterwards the people of Byzantium removed these columns and used them in their own city to build the altar of Artemis the Protector; a single plinth was left lying near the temple of Dionysus in Byzantium.'

During the remaining years of the sixth century BC Byzantium and the other Greek cities in the east remained under the rule of tyrants

*View of the Bosphorus looking south from the Asian shore above
the fortress of Anadolu Hisarı, the Castle of Asia.*

appointed by Darius. Then in 499 BC the Ionian cities of western Asia Minor revolted against Persian rule, led by Aristagoras, the tyrant of Miletus. After some initial successes, including the liberation of Byzantium and Chalcedon, the revolt was crushed in 494 BC. The Persians then utterly destroyed Miletus and enslaved its surviving inhabitants, after which they subdued all of the other Ionian cities. When that campaign was complete the Persians sent their Phoenician fleet to attack the remaining Greek cities along the straits. According to Herodotus, 'The people of Byzantium, and their opposite neighbours in Chalcedon, instead of awaiting the attack of the Phoenicians by sea, abandoned their homes and fled to the Black Sea coast, where they established themselves at Mesembria.' Herodotus goes on to say that the Phoenicians 'destroyed by fire' all of the Greek cities along the straits, presumably including Byzantium and Chalcedon.

Byzantium and the other cities along the straits were apparently soon rebuilt, for when Xerxes invaded Greece in 481 BC they contributed a hundred ships to the Persian fleet, according to Herodotus. After the Persians were defeated at Plataea in 479 BC by the Greeks under Pausanias, the survivors made their way home under the command of Artabazus, who had them ferried across the Bosphorus at Byzantium.

Two years later the Greek League sent off a fleet under Pausanias, who forced the Persian garrison in Byzantium to surrender. While he was in Byzantium, Pausanias began to intrigue with Xerxes with the aim of setting himself up as ruler of all Greece. When rumours of his plot reached Sparta, Pausanias was recalled home and put on trial, but he was acquitted and soon returned on his own to Byzantium. There he immediately resumed his intrigues, leading to his expulsion from the city in c. 475 BC. During his years as tyrant of Byzantium, Pausanias built a stadium in the city, as evidenced by an inscription bearing his name set into the outer defence-walls of Topkapı Sarayı.

Byzantium soon afterwards became a member of the Athenian League. Athens completely dominated the League, imposing annual tributes on the member states, who were assessed according to their resources. The number of states was about 300, and the total annual tribute ranged from 400 to 600 talents, of which the initial contribution of Byzantium was 15 talents, one of the highest quotas in the League, a measure of the city's wealth at that time.

Pausanias (c. 510–c. 468 BC).

Byzantium and Samos revolted against Athenian domination in the summer of 440 BC. The Athenians immediately sent a fleet under the command of Pericles to besiege Samos, which surrendered in May of the following year, with Byzantium capitulating shortly afterwards.

When the Peloponnesian War began in 431 BC Byzantium was forced to join the Athenian League against Sparta, an alliance that lasted for two decades. But then in 413 BC, after the failure of the Athenian expedition against Syracuse, Byzantium and many other allies of Athens defected to the Spartans.

The Athenians mounted a naval expedition against Byzantium and Chalcedon in 409 BC. When they reached the Bosphorus they built a fortified settlement on the Asian shore opposite Byzantium, naming it Chrysopolis, the City of Gold, now known in Turkish as Üsküdar. Using Chrysopolis as their base, the Athenians, led by Alcibiades, besieged Byzantium. At the height of the siege the anti-Spartan party admitted the Athenian troops into the city by letting down ladders from the walls. The Athenians then captured Byzantium, returning the city to its citizens on condition that they entered into an alliance with Athens.

The Peloponnesian War came to an end in 404 BC, when the

Spartans decisively defeated the Athenians at Aegospotami on the Hellespont. The following year the Byzantines, racked both by internal strife and by a war with the Thracian tribes, petitioned the Spartans to reassume control of the city. The Spartans sent them the general Clearchus, who recruited a force of mercenaries and established himself as the tyrant of Byzantium, executing a number of the wealthiest citizens. The cruelty of Clearchus finally led Sparta to remove him from power in 403 BC.

Clearchus was eventually replaced by the Spartan general Anaxibius, who was tyrant of Byzantium when the Greek mercenaries known as the Ten Thousand arrived at the Bosphorus in 400 BC, at the end of their epic journey back from service in Persia, immortalized by Xenophon in his *Anabasis*, or the *March Up Country*. Anaxibius reluctantly provided ships to ferry the mercenaries across the Bosphorus to Byzantium, and then soon afterwards tricked them through false promises into marching off into Thrace, barring the gates of the city behind them. When the Ten Thousand realized that they had been cruelly duped they turned back and began to attack the city, but Xenophon persuaded them to desist, telling them that they would be disgraced for ever if they sacked a Greek city.

The Spartans continued to hold Byzantium until 390 BC, when the democratic faction took control and allowed the city to be taken by an Athenian fleet commanded by Thrasybulus. Then in March 377 BC Athens announced the formation of the Second Athenian Alliance, of which Byzantium was a charter member. The democratic faction seized power again in 363 BC with the aid of the Theban leader Epaminondas, and Byzantium severed its alliance with Athens. An anti-Athenian coalition was formed in 357 BC by King Mausolus of Caria, who allied himself with Byzantium and the islands of Rhodes, Chios and Cos. The Athenians sent a fleet to attack Chios, beginning a conflict known as the Social War. The war dragged on until the summer of 355 BC, when Athens made peace with the allies and recognized the independence of Byzantium and the three island states.

Meanwhile Macedon had risen as a new power under Philip II, who came to the throne in 359 BC. The Byzantines at first were allies of Philip, but when he invaded Thrace in 341 BC, leaving his son Alexander to serve as regent in Pella, they and their neighbours allied

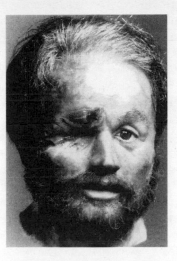

*Philip II of Macedon (reigned 359–336 BC); head as
reconstructed by Richard Neave of the Department of Medical
Illustration, University of Manchester.*

themselves with Athens and prepared their defences against the
Macedonians. Philip attacked Byzantium in 340 BC, beginning a
memorable siege in which the Byzantines were assisted by the
Athenians. Philip finally broke off the siege in the spring of 339 BC,
whereupon the citizens of Byzantium erected a monument in honour
of Athens for having come to their aid.

Byzantium retained its independence throughout the Hellenistic
period, which began with the death of Alexander the Great in 323 BC.
The city withstood an invasion by the Gauls beginning in 279 BC,
a siege by the Seleucid king Antiochus II in 246 BC, and another
siege by the Rhodians and the Bithynian king Prusias I in 220 BC.
The Hellenistic period effectively ended in western Asia Minor in
129 BC, when the Romans organized their province of Asia.
Byzantium had by then entered into a formal alliance with Rome, in
which it enjoyed the protection of the Romans and, though paying
tribute, retained its status as a free city. The Romans linked the new
province to Italy through the Via Egnatia, a high-road leading from

the Adriatic coast to Thrace, with its eastern terminus at Byzantium.

Byzantium continued to maintain good relations with Rome, and in 53 BC the Senate remitted the annual tribute that had been imposed on the Byzantines. Early in the reign of Augustus (27 BC–AD 14) Byzantium was stripped of its possessions in Bithynia, though it retained its lands in Thrace, where it had long since absorbed the territory of its neighbour Selymbria. Byzantium was formally incorporated into the Roman Empire in AD 73 by Vespasian, and during the reign of Trajan (98–117) it was made part of the province of Bithynia. Nevertheless Byzantium still retained the status of a free city under the aegis of Rome. The Romans built an aqueduct to bring water into the city during the reign of Hadrian (117–38), who may have visited Byzantium in 123.

Byzantium remained a free city up until the last years of the second century. But then the city's privileged status was compromised when it became embroiled in a war of succession following the assassination of the emperor Pertinax in 193. The two contenders for the throne were Septimius Severus and Pescennius Niger. The Byzantines surrendered voluntarily to the forces of Niger, as a result of which Severus sent an army to attack the city. After suffering a defeat in Bithynia, Niger's forces withdrew from Byzantium and retreated across Asia Minor, leaving the city to face the army of Severus, which put the city under siege. The siege dragged on for nearly three years, during which time Severus defeated and killed Niger, establishing himself as sole emperor. The people of Byzantium were now in a desperate condition, with all of their supplies exhausted and no hope of relief; nevertheless they continued to resist the Romans. The historian Dio Cassius, in his graphic account of the siege, writes that the Byzantines hurled down stones from their theatre upon the heads of the besieging Romans, along with bronze statues, and that they built ships from the boards of their demolished houses and braided ropes from the hair of their women. Then many of them made a desperate attempt to escape by ship, while those who remained behind resorted to cannibalism to survive. The Romans easily caught up with the heavily overloaded ships of the refugees during a storm and sank them, while those who had remained in the city looked on in horror from the walls – a scene described by Dio Cassius:

The people in Byzantium, as they watched this scene, for a time kept calling on the gods for help . . . But when they saw their friends perishing all together, the united throng sent up a chorus of groans and lamentations, and after that they mourned for the rest of the day and the whole night. The total number of the wrecks proved so great that some drifted on the islands and the Asiatic coast, and the defeat became known by these relics before it had been heard of. The next day the horror was increased still more for the townspeople, for when the water had subsided, the whole sea in the vicinity of Byzantium was covered with corpses and wrecks and blood, and many of the remains were cast up on shore.

The survivors had no choice but to surrender to the Romans. Severus then took his revenge, putting to death all of the surviving soldiers and magistrates of Byzantium and depriving the city of its independence, making it tributary to Perinthus. He also demolished the walls of Byzantium, which had withstood his army for three years, thinking thus to destroy the city by leaving it defenceless. Dio Cassius visited the site not long afterwards, and he was so shocked by the desolation that he could only describe the walls of the city as they had been before its fall, when the towers of Byzantium were still standing

Septimius Severus (193–211); from a coin of his reign.

to echo his voice when he hailed them, as he writes in a haunting passage:

I myself saw the walls after they had fallen, looking as if they had been captured by some other people rather than by the Romans. I had also seen them standing and had even heard them 'talk'. I should explain that there were seven towers extending from the Thracian Gates to the sea, and if a person approached any of these but the first, it was silent, but if he shouted anything at that one or threw a stone against it, it not only echoed and 'spoke' itself, but also caused the second to do the same; and thus the sound continued from one to the other through the whole seven, and they did not interrupt one another, but all in their proper turn, as each received the sound from the one before it, took up the echo and the voice and sent it on.

Such were the walls of Byzantium.

And such was the ancient Byzantium itself, its history as an autonomous Greek city coming to an end when it fell to Septimius Severus in AD 196, though it was to rise from its ashes and begin life anew as a Roman town.

CHAPTER 3

Roman Byzantium
196–330

Byzantium remained in ruins for several years after it was sacked by Septimius Severus. But then the emperor was persuaded to pardon the Byzantines by his son Caracalla, who pointed out that the strategic importance of the city was too great for it to be abandoned. And so, early in the second century, Severus rebuilt Byzantium on a larger scale, surrounding it with a new circuit of defence walls.

The original walls of Byzantium had enclosed only the First Hill, extending around the acropolis from the Golden Horn to the Sea of Marmara. The new walls of Septimius Severus began about 500 metres further up the Golden Horn than the original fortifications, their northern end being just downstream from the present Galata Bridge. The walls extended uphill from there to the summit of the Second Hill, from where they stretched down around the Hippodrome before curving back eastward along the lower slopes of the First Hill above the Marmara. The area thus enclosed was more than twice as great as that of the archaic city of Byzantium. The new circuit also included two ports on the Golden Horn, both of them filled in during the late nineteenth century. Going westward from Saray Burnu, the first of these was known as the Prosphorion and the second as the Neorion. The Prosphorion, the larger of the two ports, occupied the area of the original harbour of archaic Byzantium.

The Hippodrome was one of the new edifices erected by Septimius Severus, its site now occupied by the At Meydanı, or Square of Horses, the park in front of the Blue Mosque. At the same time he built large *thermae*, or public baths, beside the north-eastern corner of the Hippodrome. These were known as the Baths of Zeuxippus, designed to serve the crowds that thronged the Hippodrome to see the chariot races and other entertainments. Petrus Gyllius quotes the Byzantine chronicler Cedrinus concerning the many statues with which the baths were adorned:

Cedrinus relates that in this bath there was a pleasant variety of views of surprising art, both in marble and stonework, in statues of brass and figures of persons of antiquity who seemed to want nothing but a soul to animate and enliven them ... This place was also beautified with the bronze statues of all those renowned personages who have been famous for wisdom, oratory or courage throughout the world.

Seve rus also erected a colonnaded way along the ridge between the summits of the First and Second Hills. Known as the Portico of Severus, this splendid avenue followed the route of the present Divan Yolu, which begins in Aya Sofya Meydanı, the great square outside Haghia Sophia. The square itself was a forum known as the Tetrastoon, which from its name ('four stoas') would have had porticoes on all four sides. This seems to have been one of the archaic city's agoras, or market-squares, with the surrounding porticoes added later. The Portico of Severus formed the main avenue of Byzantium, known as the Mese, or Middle Way, extending from the Tetrastoon to the summit of the Second Hill, subsequently to be extended as the city's limits were increased. The beginning of the Mese in the Tetrastoon marked the site of the Thracian Gate, the original main entryway to Byzantium on its landward side. At the point where the Mese left the Tetrastoon there was a monumental gateway called the Miliarium Aureum, or Golden Milestone, known more simply as the Milion.[1] The Milion marked the reference point from which distances from Byzantium were measured along the Via Egnatia. A marble stela that formed part of the Milion was excavated in 1952 and now stands on the northern side of Divan Yolu at the beginning of the avenue.

The Mese is mentioned in a building code enacted towards the end of the fifth century, in which reference is made to a portico identifiable as that of Septimius Severus: 'We ordain that none shall be allowed to obstruct with buildings the numerous rows of columns which are erected in the public porticoes, such as those leading from the Milion to the Capitol'; all shops and booths set in between the columns 'must be ornamented on the outside at least with marble, that they may beautify the city and give pleasure to the passers-by'.

There was a military training-ground known as the Strategion just inside the walls above the two ports, laid out on the level ground at the foot of the First and Second Hills. The site of the Strategion would have been the area around the present Sirkeci Station; in its vicinity were the state prison, a shrine of Achilles and Ajax, and the Baths of Achilles. The Strategion had been in existence since the earliest days of Byzantium, when it was outside the walls; the new fortifications of Septimius Severus enclosed it within the bounds of the enlarged city. North of the Strategion there was a city gate known in later times as the Arch of Urbicus, or more simply as the Urbicon.

The edifices erected and restored by Severus are recorded in an early Byzantine source known as the *Chronicon Paschale*, which also refers to earlier monuments in the city. After mentioning the Baths of Zeuxippus the *Chronicon* records other works of Severus:

Opposite to it in the acropolis he built the temple of Apollo, which also faced the two other temples, one to Artemis with the olive and the other to Phedalian Aphrodite. Opposite the temple of Artemis he built the Kynegion, a large menagerie for wild animals, and a theatre opposite the temple of Aphrodite.

The temple of Aphrodite mentioned in the *Chronicon* was one of the oldest in Byzantium, and it did not entirely disappear until the reign of Theodosius I (379–95), who converted it into a carriage-house. The Kynegion, an amphitheatre for gladiatorial combats and wild-animal shows, was apparently on the Marmara shore of the First Hill, while the theatre seems to have been set into the northern slope of the acropolis.

A number of the buildings of the pre-Constantinian city are mentioned by the early Byzantine source known as Dionysius Byzantius. As he writes, after noting that the citadel of Byzantium was on the acropolis above the Promentorium Bosphorium:

At a little distance over the height is the altar of Athena Ecbasia – of the landing – where the colonists [Byzas and his company] fought as for their own land. There is too a temple of Poseidon, an ancient one and hence quite plain, which stands over the sea ... Below the temple of Poseidon, but within the walls, are stadia and gymnasia, and courses for the young.

Dionysius goes on to write of a temple of Gé Onesidora – the Fruitful Earth – which consisted of 'an unroofed space surrounded by a wall of polished stone'. Nearby were 'temples of Demeter and the Maiden [Persephone], with many pictures in them, relics of their former wealth'. Dionysius was also shown the sites of temples dedicated to Hera and to Pluto, 'the former having been destroyed by Darius and the latter by Philip of Macedon'.

The territory outside the walls of Septimius Severus was not entirely unoccupied. Statements by Dionysius Byzantius, as well as references by later Byzantine sources, make it evident that there were a number of hamlets and public buildings along the shores of the Golden Horn, the Marmara and the Bosphorus, as well as others among the hills and valleys beyond the city limits. The town of Sycae, named for its figs, had already developed across the Golden Horn on the present site of Galata; the quarter known as Blachernae was situated on the northern slope of the Sixth Hill; on the west bank of the Golden Horn there was a locality that later came to be called Cosmidion and later still, in Turkish times, Eyüp; on the southern peak of the Seventh Hill, known as Xerolophos, or the Dry Hill, there was a temple of Zeus within a sacred enclosure; and on the Marmara shore below the Seventh Hill there was a village called Psamathion, the Turkish Samatya, a name that is still used for that venerable quarter of the old city. There were also settlements along the Asian coast of the Marmara beyond Chalcedon as well as on the little offshore archipelago known as the Princes' Isles.

After its rebuilding by Septimius Severus, Byzantium lived at peace for over half a century. But then around 257, during the joint reign of Valerian and his son Gallienus, the barbarian Goths moved down along the west coast of the Black Sea and invaded Thrace and Bithynia. Chalcedon fell to the invaders, but Byzantium was once again protected by its strong defence walls. The Goths invaded Thrace again in 268, soon after Gallienus had been assassinated and succeeded by Claudius II. The barbarians set out in a huge fleet across the Black Sea and sailed down the Bosphorus, making a futile attempt to take Byzantium before they went on through the straits to attack Greece. The Goths were finally defeated by Claudius, leaving 50,000 dead upon the field before they gave up their invasion and returned to their homeland. The emperor then assumed the title of Claudius Gothicus, striking coins in commemoration of his victory, but shortly afterwards he contracted the plague and died in January 270.

During the next fourteen years seven emperors succeeded to the throne, all but one of them being assassinated; the exception was Carinus, defeated and killed in battle by his successor, Diocletian, who thus began his long and illustrious reign in 284. Nine years later Diocletian instituted his famous Tetrarchy, the 'Rule of Four', for he felt that the Roman Empire was too vast for one man to rule efficiently by himself. Diocletian ruled as Augustus of the East, taking Galerius as his Caesar, while he made Maximian Augustus of the West, assigning him Constantius Chlorus as Caesar, with the four of them forming a collegium, or board of rulers. In each case the Augustus was the senior emperor, while the Caesar associated with him was junior emperor. Porphyry statues of the tetrarchs were then set up in all of the major cities of the empire, including Byzantium, where the monument stood at the crossroads that would later be called the Philadelphaeum; this was at the western end of the Mese, which by then had been extended as far as the summit of the Third Hill.

Age and poor health caused Diocletian to abdicate in 303, whereupon he forced Maximian to take a solemn oath that he too would resign in the spring of 305. Constantius then succeeded as Augustus in the West, with Severus as his Caesar, while Galerius became Augustus in the East, with Maximinus Daia as his Caesar. During the next six years a struggle for power took place between these four tetrarchs and those who succeeded them. By the spring of 311 the Roman world was split between four emperors: Maximinus, Licinius, Maxentius and Constantine, son of Constantius Chlorus – a tetrarchy that soon would be reduced to three, two and then one.

Constantine defeated Maxentius on 28 October 312 north of Rome at the Ponte Milvio, and on the following day he entered Rome in triumph, his rival's severed head carried aloft on a lance before him. Afterwards it was said that at the battle of the Milvian Bridge

Constantine had seen a sign in the sky by which he knew that he would be victorious. Constantine thus described the sign to his biographer Eusebius of Caesarea: 'He said that about midday, when the sun was beginning to decline, he saw with his own eyes the trophy of a cross of light in the heavens, above the sun, and bearing the inscription Conquer by This (*hoc Vince*). At this sight he himself was struck with amazement, and his whole army also.'

The day after his victory the Senate formally conferred upon Constantine the title of senior Augustus. By that time Constantine was in some sense converted to Christianity, though tradition holds that he was not baptized until he was on his deathbed. During the winter of 312–13 he wrote three letters in which he makes clear his new attitude towards Christianity, no longer just tolerating the Church but actively favouring it with subsidies and other measures.

The other half of the tetrarchy was reduced to one in 313, when Licinius eliminated Maximinus and made his triumphal entry into Nicomedia, the ancient capital of Bithynia. Licinius then made Nicomedia his own capital, ruling from there as emperor of the East, while Constantine reigned in Rome as emperor of the West, setting the stage for the ultimate struggle between the two Augusti for sole control of the Roman Empire.

The last act of this struggle began on 3 July 324 at Adrianople, where Constantine routed Licinius and forced him to retreat to Byzantium. The final battle was fought in the hills above Chrysopolis on 18 September 324, when Constantine once again defeated Licinius. Byzantium and Chalcedon immediately opened their gates to Constantine, while Licinius fled to his capital at Nicomedia, where shortly afterwards he accepted the surrender terms offered to him by Constantine. Licinius was then sent off into exile in Thessalonica, where he was subsequently executed, leaving Constantine the Great, as he is known to history, sole ruler of the Roman Empire.

Within a few months of his victory Constantine decided to rebuild Byzantium on a much larger scale, for he had decided that it was a better site for his capital than Rome, which had long since ceased to be the administrative centre of the empire. Also Rome, with its pagan traditions, was not a suitable capital for the Christian empire that he seems to have had in mind since his vision of the Cross at the battle of the Milvian Bridge. But Constantine left no record of his motives in founding the new capital, other than a remark in one of his edicts concerning the reconstruction of Byzantium, where he declares that he acted 'on the command of God'.

While the reconstruction of Byzantium was under way Constantine lived in Nicomedia, where Diocletian had erected a palace, and where Galerius and Licinius in turn had resided when reigning as emperor of the East. There one of his first acts was to issue a constitution to his new subjects, in which he promised to make restitution to all of the Christians who had suffered in earlier persecutions. He then took steps to bring harmony to the Christian Church, which had become involved in a widespread controversy concerning the rival theological doctrines of Alexander, bishop of Alexandria, and Arius, one of his priests, who maintained that Christ was not the immortal son of God, nor of the same substance – a doctrine that came to be known as Arianism. Constantine sought to settle the dispute by convening the First Ecumenical Council of the Church, which met in the Bithynian city of Nicaea between 20 May and 19 June 325. The council, chaired by Constantine himself, condemned Arianism as well as settling other matters, including an agreement on the date of Easter.

The reconstruction of Byzantium was completed early in 330, when Constantine took up residence in the city in preparation for its dedication. The imperial edict of foundation was engraved on a stela and publicly set up in the Strategion, recording that thenceforth Byzantium was to be named NOVA ROMA CONSTANTINOPOLITANA, 'New Rome, the City of Constantine'.

What remains of the ancient city of Byzantium is for the most part buried under the ruins and monuments of Byzantine Constantinople, which is in turn overlaid with the edifices of Ottoman and modern Istanbul. Archaeological excavations on the First Hill have unearthed architectural and sculptural fragments from Byzantium that are now exhibited in the Archaeological Museum,[2] which stands on the south-western side of the acropolis, overlooking Gülhane Parkı. Among the other exhibits in the museum the most evocative are funerary monuments found in the ancient necropolis outside the archaic walls of Byzantium, the oldest of them dating back to the fourth century BC. The reliefs on the funerary stelae are particularly interesting because

left: *Constantine the Great (sole emperor 324–37);
colossal marble head.*
right: *Tombstone from the ancient city of Byzantium.*

they represent the deceased surrounded by the objects that they used
in their daily life. The stela of the sailor Heris represents his weapons
and the prow of a trireme; the scholar son of Hecatadorus is shown
with his book, pen and inkpot; the physician Musa with her surgical
instruments and her medical text; the astronomer Theodotus with his
globe and sundial. One particularly poignant relief represents a nude
youth carrying a bird in his right hand as he looks down sadly at the
pet dog lying at his feet. Another shows the lady Lollia Salbia lying
on a couch attended by her maids, who are holding her mirror, her
perfumes and her cosmetics, for she must look her best even in the
Underworld. The stela of the comic actor Kefalo shows him in what
were probably two of his most popular roles: on one face of the tombstone he is wearing a wolf's head and on the other that of a bear; his

The Goth's Column.

head is cocked comically to one side and he is standing in the loose-jointed posture of a slapstick vaudeville performer in a burlesque show, his pendent testicles dangling between his bow legs.

Gülhane Parkı occupies part of the site of ancient Byzantium, whose original line of fortifications followed much the same course as the outer defence walls of Topkapı Sarayı, built c. 1465. The walls are studded with twenty-seven massive towers, the same number as the original walls of ancient Byzantium, and one wonders if they ever 'talk' to one another as Dio Cassius described them doing some eighteen centuries ago. Above the inner side of the park are the high walls that retain the inner courtyards of Topkapı Sarayı, which occupies the site of the acropolis of ancient Byzantium. Near the northern end of the park a path leads uphill to a little-known monument called the Goth's Column,3 almost hidden away among a grove of trees. The column is believed to have been erected in honour of Claudius II Gothicus, commemorating his great victory over the Goths in AD 269. If so, this is the only surviving monument of the pre-Constantinian city other than the stela of the Milion and those parts of the Hippodrome that date back to its original construction by Septimius Severus. According to the Byzantine historian Nicephorus Gregoras, writing in the first half of the fourteenth century, the Goth's Column was once surmounted by a statue of Byzas the Megarian, the eponymous founder of Byzantium. This monument would have had a most appropriate site, standing above the promontory at the confluence of the Bosphorus and the Golden Horn, where the Greek city of Byzantium was founded nearly a thousand years before Constantinople became the capital of the Roman Empire.

PART II

CONSTANTINOPLE

CHAPTER 4

The City of Constantine

330–337

Although the newly rebuilt city was officially called Nova Roma, in popular speech it was from the beginning known in Greek as Constantinopolis, the city of Constantine, or in English Constantinople. Nevertheless, the native-born people of the city continued to call themselves Byzantini, for 'they were of Byzantium'.

The dedication ceremonies began on 2 April 330 and lasted for forty days, celebrated with a combination of pagan and Christian ceremonies, including a high mass in Haghia Eirene, the church of the Divine Peace, which had been the cathedral of Byzantium. The final day of the ceremonies, 11 May, began with the entire populace of the city congregating in the Hippodrome, which had been rebuilt and enlarged by Constantine. After the completion of inaugural rites there, they all walked in procession to the new forum that Constantine had built on the summit of the Second Hill, where there had been erected an enormous porphyry column surmounted by a colossal statue of the emperor in the guise of Apollo. There Constantine himself presided over the dedication of his new city, which thenceforth was the capital of the Roman Empire, supplanting Old Rome.

The line of defence walls with which Constantine enclosed the city probably began on the Golden Horn somewhat above the present Atatürk Bridge, extending from there to the summit of the Fifth Hill, then across the valley of the Lycus river to the Seventh Hill, from where it descended to the shore of the Marmara. The city of Constantine was about four to five times larger than Byzantium had been after its rebuilding by Septimius Severus. The population of the new capital can be estimated from the fact that Constantine supplied daily rations of free bread for 80,000 people, the loaves being distributed at places throughout the city called 'steps'. The population of Constantine's city would have been at least four times as great as that of Byzantium in late Roman times.

The earliest description of the new city is by Zosimus in his *Historia Nova*, written at the end of the fifth century. After defining the extent of the new city, Zosimus goes on to describe some of the edifices with which Constantine adorned his capital. Among these were a forum, a hippodrome, a palace, several temples, and 'houses for certain senators who had followed him from home'.

The first of these constructions was the Forum of Constantine, on the Second Hill, centred on the porphyry column bearing his statue. Around the Forum of Constantine, which was adorned with statues both pagan and Christian, stood the usual public buildings: a senate (there was another senate house near Haghia Sophia), the Praetorium (headquarters of the praetorian prefect of the East), the Nymphaeum (a building used for the celebration of weddings), and several temples and churches. The relics of all this grandeur are now buried some three metres below the present level of Divan Yolu, and all that remains visible is the Column of Constantine.[1]

The Portico of Severus remained standing in the Constantinian city, flanking the Mese between the Forum of Constantine and the Augustaeum, a large square that had been carved out of the ancient Tetrastoon by Constantine, its boundaries much the same as those of the present Aya Sofya Meydanı. According to Zosimus, Constantine erected two pagan temples in the square, one of them dedicated to Rhea, mother of the gods, and the other to Fortuna Romana, the Greek Tyche, goddess of Fortune. On its northern side the Augustaeum gave access to Haghia Sophia; at its east end were the second senate house and the Chalke, or Brazen House, the monumental vestibule of the Great Palace, the imperial residence built by Constantine. The Chalke was located off the south-east corner of the Augustaeum, approached from the west by the Portico of Achilles, an extension of the Mese that began at the Milion, one of the structures that had survived from old Byzantium. The Milion was surmounted by a sculptural group showing Constantine and his mother, Helena, holding between them the True Cross, which she had discovered on her

Column of Constantine.

pilgrimage to Jerusalem. North-west of the Milion there was another square, known as the Stoa Basilica, or Royal Portico.

South of the Augustaeum were the Baths of Zeuxippus, and to the south-west of the baths was the Hippodrome.[2] The Hippodrome was enlarged by Constantine, with a seating capacity estimated at 80,000. Constantine adorned it with a number of monuments and works of art, of which two still stand on its spina, or central axis, namely the so-called Colossus[3] and the Serpent Column,[4] as also does the Egyptian Obelisk,[5] erected sixty years later by Theodosius I.

The inaugural rites of New Rome were the first of many moment-ous occasions celebrated in the Hippodrome. When an emperor succeeded to the throne it was traditional for him to appear in the Kathisma, or royal enclosure, where he received the acclamation of the populace. The victories of many emperors and generals were celebrated here, triumphs traditionally celebrated in ancient Roman fashion. A number of emperors were executed in the arena of the Hippodrome after being deposed, as were several patriarchs. But the Hippodrome functioned primarily as a sports centre, where the chariot races and circuses served as a diversion for the common people of Constantinople.

From late Roman times onward the circus mobs of the Hippodrome were organized into four factions, each with its own distinctive colour: the Greens, Blues, Whites and Reds. These factions were intimately associated with the various craft and market guilds, and each had its own traditional part to play in the civic and religious life of the city. During the early centuries of Constantinople the Blue and Green factions began to achieve dominance, and eventually the Whites and Reds were absorbed by the other two groups. Traditionally, the Blues were recruited from the middle and upper classes and were orthodox in religion and conservative in politics, while the Greens were from the working class and were radical in both their religious and their political beliefs. This polarization between the two dominant factions was a constant source of bitter dissension and troubled the life of the city for centuries, leading to several insurrections.

The races in the Hippodrome usually involved four quadrigas, two-wheeled chariots each pulled by a team of four horses, with the charioteers garbed in the colours of their supporting factions. A normal race required seven laps around the track, for a total distance of about two and a half kilometres. Successful charioteers became national heroes. The most famous was Porphyrius, for whom the emperor Anastasius I erected a monument in the Hippodrome that is now preserved in the Archaeological Museum. This is an indication of the great popularity of the chariot races, which led to excesses thus noted in a chronicle:

Racing seems to lead to anger rather than joy, and it has already led to the ruin of several important towns. It leads to the squandering of money, to crime and death. Men put the interests of their team higher than those of family, home or country. Both men and women are seized by a kind of madness and, indeed, racing is a very widespread sickness of the spirit.

During the intervals between the races the crowd was entertained by exhibitions of wild animals, clowns, dwarfs, jugglers, acrobats and musicians. Sigurd, king of Norway, visited the Hippodrome in 1111 and saw displays of fireworks and a spectacle in which performers appeared levitated in mid-air. Later in that century Benjamin of Tudela reported that in the intermissions he saw astonishing feats of juggling as well as a wild-animal show with lions, tigers, bears and leopards.

Chariot races and games were held throughout the year. The state calendars of the fourth and fifth centuries reveal as many as sixty-six annual holidays celebrated in the Hippodrome, each with up to twenty-four races daily. But by the tenth century there were fewer than a dozen such holidays, each with only eight races daily. The most important dates were originally the beginning of January, when the newly appointed consul would celebrate the beginning of his term with lavish entertainments, and 11 May, when the anniversary of Constantine's foundation of the city was commemorated. On such major occasions the chariot races went on all day, interspersed with circus performances, the festivals ending with the emperor and his retainers walking in procession from the Hippodrome to Haghia Sophia and the Great Palace, as described by the chronicler Attaliates:

The imperial procession having been prepared, the heads of the guilds of the agora strewed the ground with luxuriously woven silk carpets from the very palace to the gates of the revered and most holy Haghia Sophia. They had

View of the Hippodrome; fifteenth century.

prepared these so that the emperor might pass through in honour with his armed retinue.

These processions, as well as every other formal event of any kind involving the emperor and his court, are described in the *Book of Ceremonies*, compiled by Constantine VII Porphyrogenitus in the tenth century, but undoubtedly recording protocol and procedures that had been established early in the history of the empire, probably in the days of Constantine the Great. This detailed but laconic work also lays down the route to be followed by all imperial processions, both within the confines of the Great Palace and on excursions to many other places in Constantinople, principally the churches and monasteries of the city. Thus the *Book of Ceremonies* is one of the most important sources for a study of the topography of the city. It is also a record of all of the rituals that were associated with every day of the emperor's life, from the time of his birth until his death and burial. On the last of these occasions the emperor's body was carried through the Chalke for burial in the church of the Holy Apostles, and as the procession passed through the vestibule the attendants cried out, 'Go out, Sire, for it is the King of Kings who calls thee now, and the Lord of Lords!'

The church of the Holy Apostles stood on the summit of the Fourth Hill, some 400 metres inside the Constantinian walls. Processions from the Great Palace to the Holy Apostles went along the Mese, passing first through the Forum of Constantine, then through the Forum Tauri at the summit of the Third Hill, and then, on the ridge between the Third and Fourth Hills, through another square known as the Forum Amastrianum. There another branch of the Mese headed off to the south-western part of the city along the Marmara slope of the Third Hill, passing first through the Forum Bovis and then through the Forum of Arcadius. Between the Forum Tauri and the Forum Amastrianum the Mese passed the crossroads known as the Philadelphaeum, so called in honour of the 'brotherly love' that supposedly existed between Constantine's three sons, Constantius,

The Church of the Holy Apostles; early twelfth-century miniature painting from the Homilies of James of Kokkinobaphos.

Constantine and Constans, who succeeded as co-emperors on their father's death and whose statues stood there along with those of the tetrarchs. Later, after the Theodosian Walls were built, the Philadelphaeum came to be known as Mesomphalos, the Navel of the Town, since it marked the geographic centre of Constantinople.

The Mese was one of three streets extending along the whole length of the city of Constantine, forming the main arteries of communication. One started from the south-eastern end of the enclosure of the Great Palace, proceeding from there along the Marmara shore to the southern extremity of the Constantinopolitan walls. Another street began at the south-eastern end of the palace grounds by the Tzycanisterion, or polo grounds, running from there to the Promentorium Bosphorium, passing on its way the Mangana, an arsenal built by Constantine. After passing the promontory it ran westward along the Golden Horn, passing the two main harbours there, and extending as far as the northern extremity of the land walls. There were also several transverse streets running north–south across the peninsula. The most important of these began on the Marmara shore at the harbour called the Kontoskalion, now known as Kumkapı, which is still the main port for the fishing fleet of the city. From there the street extended north across the peninsula to the Golden Horn, with a tetrapylon standing at its intersection with the Mese. The section from the Mese to the Golden Horn was lined on both sides with stoas, so that it came to be called Makro Embolos, the Street of the Long Colonnade. This followed the course of the present Uzun Çarşı Caddesi, the Avenue of the Long Market, which is still the main shopping street between the Covered Bazaar and the Golden Horn.

Byzantine sources credit Constantine with founding or rebuilding a number of churches in his new capital, most notably Haghia Sophia, Haghia Eirene and the Holy Apostles. But the most reliable of these sources, the fifth-century historian Socrates, credits Constantine only with the building of the Holy Apostles and the restoration of Haghia Eirene, writing that the first church of Haghia Sophia was completed by Constantius after he succeeded his father as emperor. Constantine founded the church of the Holy Apostles as his mausoleum, and he was buried there after his death in 337. Apparently the first church of the Holy Apostles was a circular mausoleum, to which Constantius added a cruciform basilica, depositing in it the relics of SS. Timothy, Luke and Andrew. Justinian rebuilt the church in 550 and added a second mausoleum. The two mausolea served as the principal burial-place of the Byzantine emperors until 1028, after which they were laid to rest in other churches.

The circumstances of Constantine's final days are narrated by Eusebius of Caesarea in his *Vita Constantini*, where he writes that the emperor's last illness came upon him in 336. Constantine sought to cure his illness in the hot baths of Constantinople, but when this failed he went to his mother's native village near Nicomedia, where there were thermal springs renowned for their therapeutic powers. But when he found no relief there Constantine moved to Diocletian's palace in Nicomedia, where he summoned the local bishops and made a confession of his faith. Bishop Eusebius of Nicomedia then baptized Constantine and received him into the Christian fold. When the sacrament had been administered to him, Constantine exclaimed, according to Eusebius of Caesarea, 'Now I know in very truth that I am blessed; now I have confidence that I am a partaker of divine light.'

Constantine had waited until the last possible moment to be baptized, for he died a few days later, on Whit Sunday, 22 May 337. His motives for this delay have been long debated, one possible reason being that he believed that his deathbed confession and baptism would enable him to die in a state of grace and thus be certain of everlasting life.

Constantine's body, placed in a golden coffin shrouded with a purple pall, was carried from Nicomedia to Constantinople, where it lay in state in the main hall of the Great Palace for three and a half months. The long delay in burying Constantine was due to the question of his succession, for in 335 he had made plans for dividing up the empire between his surviving sons, Constantine, Constantius and Constans, all three of whom had been raised to the rank of Caesar. In addition, Constantine had allotted smaller shares of the empire to his two nephews, Dalmatius and Hannibalianus, whom he also elevated to the position of Caesar. All five of the young Caesars were abroad at the time of Constantine's death, but Constantius hurried back to Constantinople to preside over the funeral of his father. Constantine's coffin was then carried in procession from the palace along the Mese to his mausoleum in the church of the Holy Apostles, where it was placed in a huge porphyry sarcophagus, surrounded by twelve other sarcophagi. According to Eusebius, Constantine had planned this funerary arrangement as being appropriate for his self-assumed title of Isapostolos, 'Equal of the Apostles'.

Modern scholarship has cast doubt on Eusebius's statement that twelve sarcophagi representing the tombs of the Apostles surrounded that of Constantine – an arrangement that Philip Grierson says 'sounds like a stage direction for Mozart's *Magic Flute*'. Grierson's study indicates that eventually twenty sarcophagi accumulated within Constantine's mausoleum, with twenty-three more in the mortuary chamber added by Justinian, all of them containing the remains of emperors and members of their families.

Aside from the Hippodrome and the Column of Constantine, there are no monuments in the city remaining from Constantine's time, the walls with which he enclosed Constantinople having been torn down when the Theodosian Walls were erected a century after his death. But one trace of the Constantinian wall still survives in a minor monument on the Marmara slope of the Seventh Hill. This is an abandoned mosque known as Isa Kapı Mescidi,[6] built on and from the ruins of a late Byzantine church. Isa Kapı, which means the Gate of Christ, is also the name displayed on the bus-stop outside the Cerrahpaşa Hospital. It has been suggested that Isa Kapı preserves the memory of one of the gates in the Constantinian walls, which would have come down to the shore of the Marmara here below the Seventh Hill. This would have been the gate through which the southern branch of the Mese passed, to join the Via Egnatia just outside the village of Psamathion, the present Samatya.

The quarter around Isa Kapı Mescidi was known in Byzantine times as Helenianae, named for St Helena, Constantine's mother, who is supposed to have founded a monastery there. This was the Monastery of Gastria, where Helena is said to have planted the flowers that she brought back from Calvary after her discovery of the True Cross. Tradition associates the Monastery of Gastria with a monument known as Sancaktar Mescidi,[7] a Byzantine church converted to a mosque after the Turkish Conquest. But the French scholar Raymond Janin has shown that there is no mention of the Monastery of Gastria earlier than the ninth century, and so it appears that this romantic tradition may be apocryphal.

There is another monument in Samatya that has also been associated with St Helena's monastery, though here again the evidence is uncertain. This is the Martyrion of SS. Karpos and Papylos,[8] dated to the early fifth century, making it the oldest Christian building in the city.

Constantine and his mother are revered in a Greek Orthodox church dedicated to them in Samatya. The present structure of the church of SS. Constantine and Helena dates from the mid nineteenth century, but its parish probably goes back to the time when Psamathion was a seaside village outside the Constantinian walls. An old relief on the wall of the church shows Constantine and Helena flanking the Cross, the same pose in which they were represented in the statue that stood atop the Milion. Constantine and his mother are remembered in the liturgy celebrated here on their feast-day, 21 May, more than sixteen and a half centuries after he made this city the first Christian capital in the world.

CHAPTER 5

The Imperial Capital

337–395

During the three and a half months between the death of Constantine and his burial the government was in a state of crisis over the question of his successor, and in the interim affairs of state were actually carried on in the name of the dead emperor.

The hiatus ended on 9 September 337, when Constantine's three sons gave themselves the title of Augustus and then had their action confirmed by the Senate in Rome. The three Augusti then disposed of possible rivals in the imperial family, instigating an uprising among the garrison at Constantinople that led to the slaughter of two of their uncles and seven cousins. The only male survivors in the imperial family were two young sons of Julius Constantius, a half-brother of Constantine the Great; these were Gallus, who was then eleven years old, and Julian, who was five, the two of them spared because of their youth. The two princes were thereafter kept under close surveillance, first in Constantinople and later in a remote castle in Asia Minor.

The three Augusti met in the early summer of 338 to divide up the empire, retaining essentially the same regions over which they had ruled as Caesars. Constantius reigned over the eastern part of the empire, with his capital in Constantinople, while the western provinces were ruled by Constantine and Constans. This division of the empire inevitably led to a protracted three-sided struggle, in which both Constantine and Constans were killed, and in 353 Constantius emerged as sole ruler of the Roman Empire, with his capital in Constantinople.

The reigns of Constantius and his immediate successors are chronicled in the *Res Gestae* of Ammianus Marcellinus, a Greek born in Antioch *c.* 330. Ammianus evaluates the personal character of Constantius in Book XXI of the *Res Gestae*, listing first his virtues and then his faults. Among the virtues are his 'dignity of imperial majesty', the fairness of his civil administration, his exceedingly careful maintenance of the army, the prudence, temperance and chastity of his private life, and finally his good manners and athletic ability – the latter being due to the emperor's peculiar physique, as Ammianus notes, pointing out that 'his legs were very short and bowed, for which reason he was good at running and leaping'.

Among the emperor's faults Ammianus dwells particularly on his almost pathological suspicion of plots to usurp his throne, which led him to execute a number of members of the imperial family as well as other imagined rivals and internal enemies. Ammianus attributed this to the fact that Constantius 'was to an excessive degree under the influence of his wives, and the shrill-voiced eunuchs, and certain of the court officials, who applauded his every word, and listened for his "yes" or "no", in order to agree with him'.

Eunuchs played an important role in Byzantium, and many of them rose to leading positions in the civil, military and religious hierarchies, several becoming patriarch and one becoming *magister militum*, the commander-in-chief of the army. One post that was almost invariably held by a eunuch was that of *praepositus sacri cubiculi*, or grand chamberlain. During the reign of Constantius this post was held by the eunuch Eusebius, who exerted great influence on the emperor, poisoning his mind against the young captive princes Gallus and Julian.

Constantius had released Gallus from his long captivity in 351, raising him to the rank of Caesar and giving him the command of the army on the Persian front. Three years later Eusebius convinced Constantius that Gallus was plotting to usurp the throne. Constantine then had Gallus arrested and, soon after, beheaded – a sentence that was carried out under the direction of Eusebius.

The following year Constantius raised Julian to the rank of Caesar, sending him to command the army in Gaul, despite the fact that he had absolutely no military experience, having spent his life up to that point in scholarship. Though he had been a devout Christian in his youth, Julian's studies in classical Greek literature and philosophy led him to reject Christianity when he was twenty, turning instead to the gods of the ancient Graeco-Roman world, though for obvious reasons he kept his apostasy secret. When Julian arrived in Gaul, according to Libanius of Antioch, the young Caesar 'had authority to do nothing save to wear the uniform', but within five years he won four notable victories over the Franks and established himself as an outstanding general.

Another fault of Constantius noted by Ammianus was his insistence on interfering in Church affairs, as a result of which the empire was convulsed with religious struggles throughout his reign and for years afterwards, with the central figures usually being the emperor and the patriarch of Constantinople.

At that time the cathedral of Constantinople was the church of Haghia Eirene, dedicated to the Divine Peace (in Greek, 'Eirene'), just as Haghia Sophia was devoted to the Divine Wisdom (in Greek, 'Sophia'). While Haghia Sophia was called the Great Church, Haghia Eirene was always known as the Old Church, with tradition holding that it had been the cathedral of Byzantium before the founding of Constantinople.

The religious controversy surrounding Arianism emerged again early in the reign of Constantius. Constantius was himself a moderate follower of the Arian doctrine, and after the death of Bishop Alexander of Constantinople he appointed a follower of Arius to the see, but the orthodox party rejected this and appointed their own bishop. This led to a battle in which the emperor's troops attacked the partisans of orthodoxy in the church of Haghia Eirene and slaughtered more than 3,000 of them. The bitter memories of this massacre poisoned relations between Constantius and the people of Constantinople for the rest of his reign.

Constantius died on 3 November 361 while on campaign against the Persians. Julian had already been proclaimed emperor by his troops and was *en route* to Constantinople, which he reached on 11 December of that same year. He was greeted enthusiastically by the populace as the first emperor to have been born in their city, as Zosimus writes:

When he had approached Byzantium all welcomed him with songs of praise, hailing him as their fellow citizen and foster child inasmuch as he had been born and reared in this city. In other respects as well they made their obeisances as though he would be the author of the greatest blessings for mankind. Thereat he took charge of the city and the armies simultaneously.

One of Julian's first acts as emperor was to put on trial and execute the eunuch Eusebius, who had poisoned his uncle's mind against him. Julian also dismissed all of the other eunuchs in the imperial service as well as the superfluous servants who had been hired by Constantius. As Libanius writes of those who were purged by Julian, 'There were a thousand cooks, as many barbers, and even more butlers. There were swarms of lackeys, the eunuchs were more in number than flies around the flocks in spring, and a multitude of drones of every sort and kind.'

Julian then reorganized the imperial government and commissioned several public works in Constantinople, building a senate house, two harbours, and a library. The senate house, which stood on the eastern side of the Augustaeum, was subsequently rebuilt by Justinian. The two harbours, both of which were on the Marmara coast of the city, were the Port of Julian, now called Kadırga Limanı,[1] and Kontoskalion,[2] known in Turkish as Kumkapı. The library, built in the Stoa Basilica, contained Julian's own collection of books, and by the end of the fifth century it was estimated to comprise 600,000 volumes. Petrus Gyllius, quoting early Byzantine sources, writes of Julian's library that 'Among other curiosities of this place was the gut of a dragon thirty-seven metres long, on which was inscribed in golden characters the *Iliad* and *Odyssey* of Homer.'

Julian openly professed his paganism as soon as he became emperor. A few days after his arrival in Constantinople he issued several decrees that permitted the public performances of all religious ceremonies, pagan as well as Christian and Jewish, compensating the owners of all temple properties that had been confiscated since the time of Constantine and withdrawing the subsidies that the government had been giving to the orthodox clergy. He issued a further decree ordering the recall of all Christian clergy exiled for heresy or schism. When Julian was reorganizing the government he excluded Christians in his appointments, thus encouraging many who were ambitious in their careers and lukewarm in their beliefs to apostatize and become pagans. Thus did Julian attempt to restore paganism in the empire –

a reform which led his bitter enemies in the Christian Church to call him the Apostate, the name by which he is known in history.

Julian spent only five months in Constantinople, leaving the capital in June 362 for Antioch and the Persian front. He never returned, for he was mortally wounded in a battle against the Persians and died on 26 June 363, after which he was buried in Tarsus. The army chose Jovian as his successor, after which they began the long march back to Constantinople. But Jovian never reached the capital, for on the last stage of the march he became ill and he died on 17 February 364.

After Jovian's death the army marched on to Nicaea, where the commanders paused to choose a successor. They eventually agreed on Valentinian, a regimental commander of the imperial guard, who on 26 February 364 was acclaimed Augustus. The army demanded that Valentinian appoint a co-emperor, so as to ensure a successor, and a month later, after he had led the army back to Constantinople, he nominated his younger brother Valens. Valens was acclaimed Augustus on 28 March 364 in the Hebdomon, a suburb of Constantinople, now known as Bakırköy, at the seventh milestone from the Milion. The arrangement that they agreed upon made Valentinian emperor of the West, with his capital in Milan, while Valens was to rule the East from Constantinople. Both of the brothers were devout Christians; nevertheless they kept an open mind on religious matters, continuing Julian's policy of toleration to pagans and to all sects of Christianity.

Early in the spring of 365 Valens left Constantinople to deal with a new Persian incursion in Armenia. As soon as he left the capital a *coup d'état* was staged by Procopius, Julian's cousin, who had been hiding in Chalcedon. Procopius gained the support of the army in Thrace and seized Constantinople, eventually extending his control over Chalcedon and other cities in Bithynia. Valens headed back to deal with the pretender, and by the end of May he seemed to have put down the revolt. Procopius himself was captured in Phrygia and was brought before Valens, who had him beheaded. But the revolt flared up again when Chalcedon was seized by an officer of the imperial guard named Marcellus, a relative of Procopius, who held out for a few days before he was captured and executed. Valens then took savage revenge on the people of Constantinople and Chalcedon, executing anyone thought to have taken part in the revolution. He also pulled down the walls of Chalcedon to punish the populace there for having given shelter to Procopius.

Soon afterwards Valens used the stones of Chalcedon's walls to build an aqueduct in Constantinople. A large part of the Valens Aqueduct[3] still stands, spanning the valley between the Third and Fourth Hills. Valens also erected a number of monuments in the Hebdomon, the scene of his acclamation as Augustus. According to the *Book of Ceremonies*, thenceforth it became customary for emperors to receive their acclamation there on being raised to the throne. The plain of the Hebdomon was used for military exercises, so that it came to be called the Campus Martius, taking its name from the ancient Field of Mars on the Tiber. The Hebdomon became an imperial country retreat, adorned by emperors from Valens onwards with a palace, porticoes, forums, baths, fountains, churches and monasteries.

Valentinian died on 17 November 375 and was succeeded by his sixteen-year-old son Gratian. Gratian's younger brother Valentinian was made co-emperor, though Valens continued to rule in the East.

Valens was in Antioch early in 378 when he received news that a

The Valens Aqueduct.

great horde of Goths had crossed the Danube under pressure from the Huns and had migrated south into Thrace. Valens marched his army back to Constantinople, and then after a brief pause he mounted an expedition against the Goths in Thrace. After an initial victory over the Goths the Romans were totally defeated in a second battle on 9 August 378 near Adrianople, in which Valens was killed along with two-thirds of his army. The Goths, after failing to capture Adrianople, then marched rapidly against Constantinople, hoping to take and sack the unprotected capital. But the city was saved by a detachment of Saracen troops who had recently been enlisted in the imperial service.

After Gratian received word that Valens had been killed he found it necessary to appoint another co-emperor. He chose the Spanish general Theodosius, who was proclaimed Augustus on 19 January 379, his rule extending over the eastern provinces of the empire. Theodosius made his formal entry into Constantinople on 24 November 380, leading a procession that began at the Hebdomon. Zosimus writes that 'the emperor Theodosius entered Constantinople in splendour, as if in celebration of a great victory'.

Triumph of Theodosius I (379–95), shown passing through the Golden Gate; from the Anonymous of Anselmo Banduri of Ragusa, compiler of the Imperium Orientale.

Theodosius was determined to stamp out heresies, and during his reign he issued a total of eighteen edicts directed against schismatic sects. He was on the other hand tolerant towards Jews, and on several occasions he issued orders for the rebuilding of synagogues that had been destroyed by Christians, punishing those who had demolished them. He was totally opposed to paganism, enacting several laws banning sacrifices for divination and allowing a number of temples to be destroyed or converted into churches. The most drastic laws against paganism were issued in 391–2, in which all sacrifices were prohibited and the temples throughout the empire were closed to the public, with even private worship of the old pagan gods forbidden under the pain of severe penalties.

Gratian was assassinated in 383 and Valentinian II suffered the same fate in 392. Theodosius avenged both of their deaths, putting down and killing those who had overthrown them, his efforts culminating with his triumph over the usurper Maximus. He then marched on to Milan, where he began to make plans concerning the question of his successor. He decided to divide the empire between his two sons, with the East to be ruled by Arcadius and the West by Honorius, whom he proclaimed Augustus later in 393. Both sons were at that time in Constantinople, and so Theodosius summoned Honorius to Milan, where he arrived only in mid-January 395. By that time Theodosius had become seriously ill, and within a day of the arrival of Honorius he died. The remains of Theodosius were then returned to Constantinople, to be buried in the church of the Holy Apostles. He is known to history as Theodosius the Great, principally because he was the last emperor before Justinian to rule the entire Roman Empire from the western Mediterranean to the Persian frontier.

Theodosius was responsible for four monuments that can still be seen in Istanbul, although two are in ruins. One of these is the Harbour of Theodosius,[4] the largest of the Byzantine ports on the Marmara, where its impressive fortification walls are presently being rebuilt. The remains of another work of his can be seen in Beyazit Meydanı, on the summit of the Third Hill, where the ruins of the Forum of Theodosius[5] were unearthed in 1958, along with the colossal fragments of a triumphal gateway and a commemorative column. The most prominent monument of Theodosius I is the Egyptian

Obelisk, which he erected on its present site in the Hippodrome in 390. The reliefs on its base were in later times, both during the Dark Ages and in the Ottoman period, believed to represent prophecies concerning the future of the city. Evliya Çelebi, the seventeenth-century Turkish chronicler, numbered the Egyptian Obelisk among the talismans that had since antiquity protected Istanbul from its enemies, and he writes that 'The figures on its sides foretell the different fortunes of the city.'

The other extant monument of Theodosius is the Porta Aurea, the famous Golden Gate,[6] which is built into the ancient city walls some 600 metres north of the Marmara shore. This is a triumphal archway, erected by Theodosius in the latter years of his reign. At that time, before the building of the walls of Theodosius II, the Golden Gate stood by itself astride the Via Egnatia some 1,500 metres outside the Constantinian wall. According to the *Book of Ceremonies*, when a new ruler was acclaimed Augustus at the Hebdomon his procession entered the city at the Golden Gate, where the city authorities waited to welcome him, and when an emperor returned to the capital after a

The Golden Gate, triumphal entryway in the Theodosian Walls.

victorious campaign his triumphal parade followed the same route. One of these triumphal entries is described by Robert de Clari, a chronicler of the Fourth Crusade in 1204:

Elsewhere in the city there is another gate which is called the Golden Gate. On this gate there are two elephants made of copper which were so large that it was a fair marvel. This gate was never opened except when an emperor was returning from battle after conquering territory. Then the clergy of the city would come out in procession to meet him, and the gate would be opened, and they would bring out a chariot of gold which was made like a cart with four wheels, such as we call a curre. Now in the middle of this chariot there was a throne and around the throne there were four columns which bore a canopy to shade the throne, which seemed as if it were all of gold. Then the emperor, wearing his crown, would take his seat on the throne, and he would enter through this gate and be borne in this chariot, with great joy and rejoicing, to his palace.

These and other works of Theodosius the Great were part of the tremendous growth of the city that took place during his reign and those of his two immediate successors, namely his son Arcadius and his grandson Theodosius II. This civic expansion is described in an encomium by Themistius, court orator of Theodosius I, who mentions other foundations of the emperor:

No longer is the vacant ground more extensive than that occupied by buildings; nor are we cultivating more territory within our walls than we inhabit; the beauty of the city is not, as heretofore, scattered over it in patches, but covers its whole area like a robe woven to the very fringe. The city gleams with gold and porphyry. It has a new Forum named after the emperor; it owns Baths, Porticoes, Gymnasia; and its former extremity is now its centre. Were Constantine to see the capital he founded he would behold a glorious and splendid scene, not a bare and empty void ... the suburbs have expanded; the place is full of carpenters, builders, decorators and artisans of every description, and might fitly be called a workshop of magnificence. Should the zeal of the emperor to adorn the city continue, a wider circuit will be demanded, and the question will arise whether the city added to Constantinople by Theodosius is not more splendid than the city that Constantine added to Byzantium.

CHAPTER 6

The Theodosian Walls

395–450

The death of Theodosius I left the Roman Empire divided once again, with the East ruled by his older son, Arcadius, who was then not quite eighteen, and the West by his younger son, Honorius, who was only ten.

Theodosius had made provisions for the succession by appointing advisers for his two young sons. He entrusted Arcadius to the care of Rufinus, the praetorian prefect of the East, while Honorius was put in the charge of the *magister militum* in Italy, Stilicho, the son of a Vandal chieftain. Both advisers took advantage of their positions to enrich themselves and to increase their power, to the detriment of the empire.

Stilicho strengthened his hold over Honorius by arranging to have his daughter Maria marry the emperor in 398. Then, when Maria died a decade later, he persuaded Honorius to marry Thermantia, Maria's younger sister. Rufinus also had dynastic ambitions, and made plans to marry off his daughter to Arcadius. But his scheme was thwarted by the grand chamberlain Eutropius, a eunuch, who did not want to lose his own control over the weak young emperor. Taking advantage of the absence of Rufinus in Antioch, he showed Arcadius the portrait of a beautiful young girl named Eudoxia, daughter of a Frankish general and a Roman mother, who had been brought up in the house-hold of a patrician in Constantinople. Arcadius fell in love with Eudoxia, choosing her as his bride, and the preparations for the imperial wedding were completed before Rufinus returned.

Eudoxia married Arcadius on 27 April 395, just three months after he became emperor of the East. During the remaining nine years of her short life Eudoxia bore him four daughters and a son, the future Theodosius II, who was born in Constantinople on 10 April 401.

*Arcadius (395–408), son and successor of Theodosius I and
emperor of the East; marble head.*

Theodosius was made co-emperor on 10 January of the following year,
and his baptism soon afterwards was an occasion of general rejoicing,
as noted by Bishop Procopius of Gaza: 'And the child Theodosius was
born in the purple, whereupon he was proclaimed emperor at his
birth. And there was great joy in the city, and men were sent to the
cities of the empire, bearing the good news, with gifts and bounties.'

At that time the patriarch of Constantinople was John Chrysostom,
the Golden-Mouthed, so named because of his eloquent sermons.
Many of his sermons criticized the extravagance of the imperial court,
as contrasted with the poverty of the ordinary people of the city, who
were his devoted followers. He also condemned the immoral performances put on in the theatre. As he writes in one of his *Homilies*:

When you seat yourself in a theatre and feast your eyes on the naked limbs
of women, you are pleased for a time, but then what a violent fever have you
generated! Once your head is filled with such sights and the songs that go

with them, you think about them even in your dreams ... You would not choose to see a naked woman in the marketplace, yet you eagerly attend the theatre. What difference does it make if the stripper is a whore? She has the same body as a free woman. Why are such things permitted when we are gathered together and shameful when we are by ourselves? Indeed, it would be better to smear our faces with mud than to behold such spectacles.

The army of the East had been placed under the command of Gainas, a Goth who had risen to the rank of general in the imperial service. As soon as he took command Gainas marched his troops directly to Constantinople, arriving at the Hebdomon on 27 November 395. He was met there by Arcadius and Rufinus, who seems to have hoped that the troops would acclaim him as co-emperor. But instead the soldiers killed Rufinus, a murder that Zosimus says was planned by Stilicho and carried out by Gainas.

Gainas seized power in Constantinople early in 400, occupying the capital with his Gothic troops. But the people of the city rose in revolt and killed 7,000 of the Goths, according to Zosimus, and Gainas was forced to retreat northward into Thrace. He eventually fell into the hands of Uldin, king of the Huns, who killed him on 23 December 400, sending back his severed head as a present to Arcadius.

After the downfall of Eutropius, who was condemned and executed in 399, the empress Eudoxia became the power behind the throne, and on 9 January 400 Arcadius crowned her as Augusta, an imperial title granted only infrequently in the first two centuries after the establishment of Constantinople. Eudoxia appears to have had little regard for Arcadius, and she was believed to have had several lovers, most notably the emperor's chief adviser, John, who was rumoured to be the real father of her son, Theodosius. Eudoxia's behaviour eventually brought her into conflict with John Chrysostom, whose sermons also condemned the immorality of the imperial court.

The conflict came to a climax on 20 June 404, when Arcadius banished Chrysostom and sent him off to exile in the Pontus, where he died three years later. When the populace learned that their beloved patriarch had been banished they rioted at the gates of the Great Palace, starting a fire that destroyed both Haghia Sophia and the senate house at the east end of the Augustaeum.

Eudoxia did not long survive Chrysostom's departure, for she died in childbirth on 6 October 404, after which she was buried in the Holy Apostles. Eudoxia's premature death was interpreted by the people of Constantinople as divine punishment for her cruel treatment of John Chrysostom, who is revered as one of the great saints of Byzantine Constantinople. Arcadius survived Eudoxia by three and a half years, dying on 1 May 408, when he was only in his thirty-first year, after which he was laid to rest beside his wife in the Holy Apostles.

The only monument in the city surviving from the reign of Arcadius is a very obscure one indeed, almost hidden away on a back street on the Marmara slope of the Seventh Hill, in a quarter known in Ottoman times as Avret Pazarı, the Female Slave Market. This is the badly battered base of a commemorative column[1] that Arcadius erected in the centre of the forum that he constructed in 402. The column remained standing for more than thirteen centuries, and in later times, when even the name of the monument had been forgotten, it was considered to be one of the talismans that protected the city.

Arcadius was succeeded by his son, Theodosius, who was then seven years old. During the first six years of his reign Theodosius II was placed under the guidance of his late father's most trusted adviser, Anthemius, the praetorian prefect of the East, who governed the empire as regent until his death in 414. During his regency a new basilica of Haghia Sophia was erected to replace the one that had been destroyed by fire in 404 – an edifice now referred to as the Theodosian church.

After the death of Anthemius the role of regent passed to the princess Pulcheria, the eldest of the emperor's three surviving sisters, who was then fifteen – only two years older than her brother. Pulcheria, who thereupon received the title of Augusta, acted as regent until 416, when Theodosius attained his majority. Nevertheless, she continued to be the power behind the throne for the next decade.

Pulcheria had taken a public vow of chastity at the age of sixteen, and no male was allowed to enter her apartments in the Great Palace, so during her regency the court was said to have resembled a convent. It was there that she supervised her brother's education, and under her he developed a lifelong interest in science as well as theology, becoming more interested in scholarship than in affairs of state. He spent much of his spare time illuminating his manuscripts, and his superb script led historians to call him Theodosius the Calligrapher. Because of his slight stature he was known even in his mature years as 'Little Theodosius'; the chronicler Joannes Antiochenus reports that 'He grew up to no great size, because he was shut up in the palace.'

When Theodosius came of age he asked Pulcheria to find him a suitable wife. She soon found the perfect candidate: the beautiful and learned Athenais, daughter of the Athenian philosopher Leontius. At the time of her marriage Athenais took the more Christian name of Eudocia; she then bore Theodosius two children, a son named Arcadius, who died in infancy, and a daughter, Licinia Eudoxia, who at the age of fifteen was espoused to Valentinian III, emperor of the West. Valentinian had become emperor at the age of six, in 425, two years after the death of Honorius. He ruled until 455, and for most of that time the power behind the throne was his mother, the Augusta Galla Placidia, a daughter of Theodosius I. Though she moved to Ravenna when her son became emperor, Placidia continued to maintain her palace in Constantinople, where it is listed as being in Region I of the city in the *Notitia urbis Constantinopolitanae*, a description of the capital written *c*. 447–50.

By the time that the *Notitia* was written the enclosed area of Constantinople had reached its permanent limit with the construction of the Theodosian Walls.[2] The new walls were about one and a half kilometres further out into Thrace than the Constantinian walls, stretching for more than six kilometres between the Marmara and the Golden Horn. The first phase of the fortifications, a single line of walls studded with towers, was completed in 413 under the direction of the prefect Anthemius. Then in 447 a series of severe earthquakes destroyed much of the walls, throwing down fifty-seven defence towers. This happened at a very critical time, for Attila the Hun was then advancing on Constantinople with his Golden Horde. Reconstruction of the wall began immediately under the direction of the new prefect of the East, Constantine. The circus factions of the Hippodrome all worked together on the construction, and within two months the walls had been rebuilt and were far stronger than before, leading Attila to redirect his invasion towards the western regions of the empire.

The Theodosian Walls enclosed seven hills – three more than in the

The Byzantine city walls descending to the Golden Horn.

Constantinian city. Thus Constantinople now had the same number of hills as Old Rome, a matter of great symbolic importance in establishing it as the new capital of the empire. The *Notitia* records that the city of Theodosius II was divided into fourteen regions, again the same number as in Old Rome. Twelve of these regions were within the area that had been bounded by the Constantinian walls; the thirteenth was across the Golden Horn in Sycae, the present Galata, corresponding to the region beyond the Tiber in Rome; while the fourteenth comprised Blachernae, where the Theodosian Walls slope down from the summit of the Sixth Hill to the Golden Horn.

Most of the area between the bounds of the old Constantinian city and the Theodosian Walls was sparsely inhabited at first, with the newly added territory being used initially for the construction of monasteries and reservoirs. The first of these reservoirs was the open Cistern of Aetius,[3] a huge structure built *c.* 421 on the Sixth Hill. Later in the century two other reservoirs were built in this outlying area: the Cistern of Aspar[4] on the Fifth Hill and the Cistern of St Mocius[5] on the Seventh Hill. The latter cistern is today known as Altımermer, the Six Marbles, named for half a dozen statues that were apparently still standing there in Ottoman times. Evliya Çelebi considered all of these statues to be talismans, as he writes in describing the magical powers of one of them:

On top of another of the six marble columns Socrates the Sage placed a brazen cock, which clapped its wings and crowed once in every twenty-four hours, and on hearing it all the cocks of Istanbul began to crow. And it is a fact that all the cocks there crow earlier than those of other places, setting up their *ku-kiri-kud* at midnight, and thus warning the sleepy and forgetful of the approach of dawn and the hour of prayer.

The *Notitia* lists the principal monuments in each of the regions, as well as the numbers of private dwellings of various types, which beside palaces included substantial masonry houses called *domi*. Most of the major monuments were in the first four regions, including the Great Palace, the churches of Haghia Sophia and Haghia Eirene, the Hippodrome, the Senate, the theatre, the amphitheatre, the stadium, the Milion, the Augustaeum, the Stoa Basilica, the Baths of Zeuxippus, the Tribunal, or law courts, and the Tzycanisterion. Besides these, the fourteen regions are listed as having 4 harbours, 4 forums, 5 palaces, 12 churches, 8 public and 153 private baths, 20 state bakeries for those who were entitled to free bread, 120 private bakeries, 52 colonnaded avenues, 322 other streets, and 4,388 *domi*. Although not listed in the *Notitia*, there were also a considerable number of the multi-storey tenement houses known as *insulae*, where the lower classes lived. The existence of these *insulae* is evidenced by regulations concerning their height, which was limited to thirty metres for there were laws protecting the rights of house-owners to a view of the sea, as well as rules governing the distance between houses, the minimum height above the street of balconies and bay windows, and the width of streets.

All of the proper houses had running water piped in from the reservoirs, as well as lavatories, which drained into the sea, and most also had private baths. The streets were lit at night, and each region had five night-watchmen, along with a fire-brigade of twenty-five to thirty-five men selected from the various craft guilds, so that in the first century after its foundation Constantinople was a model city, well-ordered, safe and sanitary. But as Constantinople's population increased, with many of the new residents being paupers drawn to the capital in hopes of eking out a living there, abysmal slums developed in the heart of the city, some of the worst being in the shadow of the Great Palace itself, their hovels violating all of the housing regulations, making them breeding-grounds for crime and popular uprisings.

Aside from the Great Palace, the *Notitia* lists a number of other palaces, including that of Galla Placidia. It also mentions the palace of Pulcheria, which was in Region III, probably near the Hippodrome. No trace has been found of either of these two edifices, but excavations in the early 1950s unearthed the remains of a pair of contiguous palaces immediately to the west of the Hippodrome, where their foundations can still be seen today. These were the palaces of Antiochus and Lausus,[6] two prominent court officials in the reign of Theodosius II. The second of these two palaces was renowned for its many famous classical statues, which, according to Petrus Gyllius, included works by Phidias, Praxiteles and Lysippus. Gyllius was of the opinion that the Palace of Lausus was near the Cistern of Philoxenus,[7] and the excavation of the palaces of Antiochus and Lausus proved that he was right, for the cistern is a short distance to their west.

Pulcheria erected a church a short way to the west of Haghia Sophia in the Chalkoprateia, or Copper Market, where artisans who worked in copper and bronze had apparently plied their trade since the time of Constantine the Great. This was the church of the Virgin Theotokos (Mother of God), which was also known from its location as the Chalkoprateia.[8] The church may have been erected on the site of a synagogue built by the Jewish copper-workers in the Chalkoprateia, who had been given permission to build by Theodosius I. After the enraged Christians burned it down, Theodosius fined them and gave the Jews permission to build another synagogue there. But St Ambrose, bishop of Milan, castigated the emperor for 'allowing the Jews to build a synagogue in the very centre of the Queen of Cities', forcing Theodosius to revoke his permission, so that the building remained in ruins.

Aside from the erection of the second church of Haghia Sophia and the Theodosian Walls, the two most important accomplishments of Theodosius II were his founding of the University of Constantinople and the compilation of the legal code that bears his name, the *Codex*

*The Cistern of Philoxenus, known in Turkish as Binbirdirek
Sarnıçı, the Cistern of a Thousand and One Columns.*

Theodosianus. The new university, which was erected in the Stoa
Basilica, was founded on 27 February 425, with lectures in both Latin
and Greek. The university was endowed with ten chairs of Greek and
ten of Latin grammar, five for Greek and three for Latin rhetoric, as
well as two for law and one for philosophy.

The *Codex Theodosianus* was promulgated in 438, embodying all
of the laws that had been enacted since the reign of Constantine the
Great. The *Codex* was put in force throughout the empire under the
names of both Theodosius II and Valentinian III. The bonds between
the empire in the East and West were never stronger than at that time,
for just the year before Valentinian had come to Constantinople to
wed the princess Licinia Eudoxia, daughter of Theodosius and
Eudocia, the groom being eighteen and the bride fifteen. The following year Eudocia went off on a pilgrimage to Jerusalem, for after the
birth of Licinia Eudoxia she had vowed that she would do so if her
daughter became an empress.

Theological disputes continued to trouble the empire during the reign of Theodosius II, just as they had during the controversy over Arianism in the previous century. As St Gregory of Nyssa wrote at the time, having had his fill of theological disputation:

Everything is full of those who are speaking of unintelligible things – streets, markets, squares, crossroads. I ask how many oboli I have to pay; in answering they are philosophizing on the born or unborn; I wish to know the price of bread; one answers, 'The Father is greater than the Son'; I ask whether my bath is ready; one says, 'The Son has been made out of nothing.'

A new religious controversy concerned the nature of Christ and the question of his human and divine natures. The followers of Nestorius, the patriarch of Constantinople, held that the two separate natures coexisted in Christ, and they also believed that the Virgin Mary was not the Mother of God but simply the Mother of Christ. The Third Ecumenical Council, convened at Ephesus on 7 June 431, condemned Nestorianism as heretical, whereupon Theodosius deposed Nestorius and exiled him to Egypt, where he died c. 452.

Sometime not long after her return from Jerusalem in 439 the empress Eudocia was repudiated by Theodosius, who was led to believe that she had committed adultery with his close friend Paulinus, the master of offices. The details of the story are obscure, but it is known that Theodosius had Paulinus executed in 443 and that the following year Eudocia went off into voluntary exile in Jerusalem, never to return.

The last years of his reign were troubled ones for Theodosius, who was also estranged from his sister Pulcheria, so that she had left the Great Palace to take up her residence in the Hebdomon. Chroniclers of the time attribute both of these alienations to the eunuch Chrysaphus, who had apparently gained complete control over Theodosius during the latter years of his reign. Then in 447 the city was struck by the series of earthquakes that destroyed the first phase of the Theodosian Walls, leading many to think that the end of the world had come. This brought about a reconciliation between Theodosius and Pulcheria, who joined with the patriarch Proclus in leading the people of Constantinople in prayers to stop the tremors. Then when the earth finally became calm they all sang psalms in thanksgiving, including a new song of praise to Christ that had been composed for the occasion, and which is still part of the liturgy of the Greek Orthodox Church.

The army of Theodosius II was dominated by foreign mercenaries of the Arian faith, particularly the Goths and the other Germanic people known as the Alans. During the last three decades of his reign the highest-ranking general in his army was Aspar the Alan, the *magister militum*, who put down a rebellion in Italy by the usurper Johannes in 423, commanded a fleet against the Vandals in 431, and led a campaign against Attila the Hun in 441. Despite his power, Aspar did not present a threat to Theodosius, for as a barbarian of the Arian faith he could never become Augustus. This made Aspar a natural ally for Pulcheria, and during the last years of Theodosius they combined to hold the balance of power in the court at Constantinople.

The council at Ephesus was the last episode of note in the reign of Theodosius, who died on 28 July 450, after falling from his horse while riding outside the city along the banks of the Lycus. He was buried in the Holy Apostles, while Eudocia was laid to rest ten years later in the church of St Stephen in Jerusalem, which she had founded during her years of exile, separated from her husband even in death.

Theodosius is remembered today principally for the great walls that bear his name, the bulwark of Constantinople for more than a thousand years. The Theodosian Walls are still magnificent even in their ruins, the long line of towers and battlements one of the enduring symbols of Byzantium.

CHAPTER 7

The Late Roman City
450–527

The third quarter of the fifth century was a chaotic period in the history of the Roman Empire. During that time ten rulers followed one another in turn as emperor of the West, the last being Romulus Augustulus, who was overthrown in 476. He was to be the last Augustus in the West, and thenceforth the emperor in Constantinople was sole ruler of what remained of the Roman Empire.

Theodosius II was succeeded by Marcian, a retired military officer who had been Aspar's *domesticus*, or aide-de-camp. Pulcheria added legitimacy to the succession by agreeing to wed Marcian, but only as his nominal wife, for she renewed her vow of chastity.

Marcian began his reign by executing the eunuch Chrysaphus, Pulcheria's arch-enemy. He also stopped paying tribute money to Attila the Hun, a practice that had begun under Theodosius II. Marcian was then able to reduce the heavy taxes that had been imposed by his predecessor, thereby gaining great popularity.

The following year Marcian convened the Fourth Ecumenical Council, which met at the church of St Euphemia in Chalcedon in October 451. Euphemia was Constantinople's first saint, martyred in the Kynegion in 303 when she refused to renounce her Christian faith. The council set forth the orthodox doctrine in what came to be known as the Definition of Chalcedon, which held that the two natures of Christ, the human and the divine, were amalgamated in one person. Those who opposed this doctrine were known as the Monophysites, from their belief that Christ had but a single nature, which was divine. The chronicler Theophylact tells us that the orthodox *tomos*, or written statement, was chosen over that of the Monophysites in a miraculous manner by Euphemia, whose casket lay open during the meeting of the council. He writes that the bishops supporting the orthodox doctrine 'took the wise decision to lay the *tomos* on the wonder-working and flesh-clothed relic of the martyr Euphemia. And God breathed life into the dead and lifeless hand, and she stretched out to take the paper and kiss it, returning it to those who were in the service of orthodoxy.' The relics of St Euphemia remained at her church in Chalcedon until the first quarter of the seventh century, when they were moved to Constantinople because of a Persian invasion; they were then enshrined in a martyrion dedicated to her memory beside the Hippodrome. Her relics are preserved today in the church of St George in the Greek Orthodox Patriarchate, which is located in the Fener quarter of Stamboul beside the Golden Horn.

Pulcheria died in July 453, and was then buried in the Holy Apostles. She was the last of her line, ending the dynasty that had begun with her grandfather Theodosius the Great. Pulcheria is revered as a saint in the Greek Orthodox Church, her feast-days being celebrated on 11 July and 10 September.

During the last years of her life Pulcheria founded a church dedicated to the Virgin at Blachernae.[1] The church was built around an ayazma, a sacred well whose waters were endowed with healing powers by the Blachernitissa, the Virgin of Blachernae. Within a decade after Pulcheria's death the church at Blachernae was used to enshrine the sacred robe and mantle of the Virgin, which had been obtained from Jerusalem by the empress Verina, wife of Leo I, Marcian's successor.

Marcian outlived Pulcheria by four years, dying on 27 January 457 at the age of about sixty-five. He had ruled for seven years, a reign that the chronicler Theophanes would three centuries later look back upon as a golden age of civil and religious peace and good government.

One monument survives in the city to commemorate Marcian's reign, an honorific column[2] standing on the Fourth Hill. The statue of Marcian that once surmounted the column has long vanished, but his name can still be seen in a Latin inscription on the base. The monument is known in Turkish as Kız Taşı, or the Maiden's Column, because of the figures of two Nikes on its base. This column was also looked upon as a talisman in later times, and its Turkish name misled European travellers to confuse it with the famous Column of Venus nearby, which reputedly possessed the power of distinguishing true virgins from false ones.

Marcian was succeeded by a Dacian officer named Leo, who at the time was serving as Aspar's *domesticus*. Leo was crowned at the Hebdomon on 7 February 457 by the patriarch Anatolicus. This was the first time that a patriarch of Constantinople had crowned an emperor – a practice that would thenceforth be customary.

During the third year of Leo's reign a young monk ascended a column in Anaplous on the European shore of the Bosphorus, announcing his intention of spending the rest of his life there in penitential prayer. Crowds came out from Constantinople to see the monk, known to history as St Daniel the Stylite, or Pillar-Sitter. Among them was Leo, who was so taken by Daniel's action that he built him a pair of lofty pillars much higher and of greater diameter than the one upon which he had been living, with a beam between them so that the stylite could stroll from one to the other to stretch his legs occasionally. Soon afterwards Constantinople was ravaged by a great fire, which began on 2 September 465 and lasted for a week, destroying a large part of the city. Those of the populace who did not flee the city congregated around the pillars in Anaplous and implored Daniel to ask God to have mercy on them, and when the fire finally ceased the emperor Leo led his people in paying reverence to the saint for his intercession.

Two years later Constantinople was struck by a winter hurricane in which Daniel nearly froze to death. As a result of this Leo persuaded Daniel to allow an enclosure to be built atop the pillars so that he could find shelter from the elements. Thenceforth the emperor brought all distinguished foreign visitors to Anaplous to show off the famous stylite safely ensconced in his lofty perch, as is noted in the *Life* of St Daniel:

The emperor Leo with difficulty persuaded the holy man to accept his offer; and then the shelter was made. And from that time on the holy man remained untouched by storms. All the visitors who came from different nations, were they kings or emperors or ambassadors, the emperor in person would either take them to the saint or send them up, and he never ceased boasting of the saint and showing him to all and proclaiming his feats of endurance.

Daniel remained atop his pillars for more than thirty-three years, until death finally brought him to earth on 11 December 493, having outlived Leo and his two successors, as well as eight emperors of the western empire, which had by then fallen to the barbarians.

Another popular saint arose in Constantinople during Leo's reign. This was St Elisabeth the Thaumaturge, or Miracle-Worker, who was born to a 'noble and rich' couple after a long period of sterility. When Elisabeth was orphaned at fifteen she divided her inheritance among the poor, emancipated her slaves, and became a nun at the convent of St George, where she succeeded her aunt as abbess two years later. Leo gave the convent an imperial estate at the Hebdomon, which had been abandoned because a dragon dwelt there in a cave. Elisabeth 'sealed' the dragon in its cave with her crucifix, spat upon it in contempt, and then trampled it to death. After Elisabeth's death numerous miracles of healing were attributed to her and she was canonized as a saint, her feast day being celebrated on 24 April, the day after that of St George. It has been suggested that St Elisabeth the Thaumaturge is a female version of St George and other dragon-slaying saints.

Leo remained subservient to Aspar for the first six or seven years of his reign, during which time the Germans and other foreign mercenaries continued to predominate in the imperial army. Leo sought to counteract Aspar's power by enlisting the services of the Isaurians, a wild tribal people who lived in the Taurus Mountains, ruled at that time by a chieftain named Tarasicodissa. Leo brought a force of Isaurians to Constantinople and enrolled them as a new contingent in the imperial army known as the Excubitors, under the command of Tarasicodissa, who then changed his name to Zeno. Around 466 Zeno married the princess Ariadne, eldest daughter of Leo and Verina. Leo had no sons, so the marriage to Ariadne put Zeno in line for the throne. Five years after his marriage Zeno put down an insurrection by the Isaurian troops in the capital, in the course of which he killed Aspar and his son Ardaburius, thus eliminating his principal rivals.

top: *Column of Marcian.*
left: *Marcian (450–57); head of a colossal bronze statue in Barletta, Italy.*
right: *Leo I (457–74); marble head.*

Leo died on 30 January 474, aged about seventy-four, and was buried in the Holy Apostles. He is often referred to as Leo the Great, not for his eminence, but only to distinguish him from his grandson and successor, Leo II, who is known as 'Little Leo'.

The only monument in the city that has survived from the reign of Leo I is the church of St John the Baptist of Studius,³ whose noble ruins still stand in the old quarter of Samatya. The church was completed in 463 and its associated monastery, the Studion, was erected shortly thereafter. The church and monastery were founded by the Roman patrician Studius, who served as consul in 454, during the reign of Marcian, and apparently retired to the Studion after Leo came to the throne. The Studion was one of the most important monasteries in Constantinople, and for nearly a thousand years it played a leading role in the religious and intellectual life of the city. The church of St John was one of the most famous in the city, the scene of a number of momentous events, and it is mentioned frequently in the *Book of Ceremonies* in connection with the religious processions of the Byzantine court. One of these ceremonies took place on the feast-day of the Decapitation of St John, when the emperor always paid a visit to the Studion, coming by barge from the Great Palace and landing on the Marmara shore at the portal now known as Narlı Kapı, the Pomegranate Gate, where the abbot of the Studion was waiting to meet him. One can still follow the route of their procession from the ruins of the Pomegranate Gate to the Studion, for the old streets in this part of Samatya have not changed their course since the Byzantine era.

Leo II, son of Zeno and Ariadne, was seven years old when he succeeded his grandfather Leo I. A few days after his accession 'Little Leo' designated his father, Zeno, as co-emperor, acting on the advice of the Senate. Leo crowned Zeno in the Hippodrome, the first time that the coronation had been performed there rather than at the Hebdomon. Nine months later Leo died suddenly, the suspicion being that he had been murdered by his father, according to Latin sources.

Zeno began his reign by coming to terms with King Gaiseric of the Vandals, concluding a peace that was to last for nearly sixty years. But after this auspicious beginning Zeno soon found himself isolated and surrounded by enemies in Constantinople, where his mother-in-law, the Augusta Verina, had woven a conspiratorial web with the intention of overthrowing him. During the first decade of his reign he endured three attempted coups masterminded by Verina, who was finally forced to flee to a fortress in Isauria, where she died in 484.

Zeno died of an attack of epilepsy on 9 April 491, and a few days later he was laid to rest in the Holy Apostles. Legends had it that Zeno was buried alive, and that for three days after his interment a voice was heard crying 'Have pity on me!', but because he was so hated by everyone no effort was made to open his tomb. The chroniclers have nothing good to say about Zeno other than that he was a very fast runner; one reports that he was 'a repository of every kind of vice', and another that he was such a coward that he could not even look at a painting of a battle. Leo Grammaticus describes him thus: 'Bushy-haired and ill-formed, Zeno was in aspect just as the Greeks depicted Pan, goat-footed and hairy-legged, black-skinned, absurd in stature.'

Zeno was succeeded by Anastasius, a sixty-year-old court official who held the post of silentiary, one of the gentleman ushers in the imperial council. He had been nominated by the empress Ariadne – a surprising choice that she justified by saying that he was 'endowed with every virtue, as perfect as a man may be'. Anastasius was crowned as emperor on 11 April, and six weeks later he married Ariadne.

Two years after the accession of Anastasius the empire was invaded by the Bulgars, who defeated an imperial army in Thrace, attacking again twice in the following decade. These invasions devastated Thrace right up to the suburbs of Constantinople, interrupting the capital's supplies of food as well as ruining the aqueducts that brought water into the city. Anastasius set out to establish an outer line of fortifications in Thrace to prevent invaders from approaching the environs of the capital. This, the so-called Long Walls, was a line of walls sixty kilometres outside the city, beginning westward of Selymbria, and stretching from there for some seventy kilometres from the Marmara to the Black Sea. As long as they were adequately manned, the Long Walls provided an effective outer defence for the capital, stemming a number of invasions before they could reach the city itself.

Anastasius had no sooner secured his Balkan frontier than war erupted in the east, where the Persians ended a long peace by invading

Armenia in August 502. The imperial armies eventually halted the invasion, and in 505 Anastasius came to terms with the Persians, beginning a peace that was to last for more than twenty years.

Anastasius was less successful in maintaining peace in Constantinople, which was frequently troubled by riots during his reign. A serious disturbance occurred in the Hippodrome in 501 during the observance of the pagan festival known as the Brytae, which was celebrated with dancing and singing in the arena. During the festivities the Blues and Greens began fighting one another, and several of them were killed, including a bastard son of Anastasius. This provoked Anastasius into imposing a permanent ban on the celebration of the Brytae throughout the empire, leading a chronicler to complain that the emperor was thus 'depriving the city of the most beautiful dancing'.

Twelve years later a revolt broke out under the leadership of Count Vitalian, a Gothic general, who marched on Constantinople with a huge host estimated to number 50,000. Two years of skirmishes and negotiations followed, with Anastasius stalling for time while he strengthened the city's defences and re-equipped the imperial fleet. Meanwhile Vitalian had readied his own fleet, and in the autumn of 515 he sent it into the Bosphorus while his army occupied Sycae. Anastasius entrusted the command of the imperial navy to Marinus, the praetorian prefect of the East, who decisively defeated the rebel fleet in a battle at the confluence of the Bosphorus and the Golden Horn. According to the chronicler John Malalas, this victory was achieved through the use of a chemical compound that engulfed the rebel ships in flames – probably the first use of the terrible 'Greek fire' that the Byzantines were later to employ with devastating effect against the Arabs and other invaders.

Ariadne died in 515 and was buried in the Holy Apostles. Anastasius outlived her by three years, dying on 8 July 518 at the age of eighty-eight – older than any other emperor in Byzantine history. John Malalas says that Anastasius died of fright during a thunderstorm, while later sources write that the emperor was struck by lightning, which they interpreted as divine wrath for his Monophysite beliefs. He was nicknamed Diokoros, meaning 'with two pupils', because his eyes were of different colours, as Malalas writes in his description of Anastasius: 'He was very large in stature, short-haired, gracious in manner, round-faced; the hair of his head and beard were turning grey. His right eye was a light blue, the left was black, nevertheless his eyes were most attractive. He frequently shaved his beard.'

The principal monument in the city dating from the reign of Anastasius is the Palace of Blachernae,[4] whose impressive remains can still be seen on the slope of the Sixth Hill leading down to the Golden Horn. The palace, built for Anastasius himself, was probably designed as a *pied-à-terre* for use during his visits to the shrine of the Virgin at Blachernae. Later emperors added other edifices at Blachernae, which in the late Byzantine era became the principal imperial residence.

Anastasius had left no heir to the throne other than his three nephews, Probus, Pompeius and Hypatius. But the army rejected them in favour of the general Justin, who was then about sixty-six. Justin's succession was due largely to the astuteness of his nephew Justinian, a young officer in the élite imperial guards known as the Candidati. Justinian had been the first choice of the army, but he refused so that his uncle could succeed to the throne.

Justin had been born to an Illyrian peasant family near the present Skopje in Macedonia, where as a boy he had worked as a swineherd. He served in the Isaurian and Persian wars during the reigns of Leo I and Anastasius, and although unable to read or write he rose to the rank of count of the excubitors. His wife, Lupacina, was a captive whom he had purchased as a concubine and later married; when she was crowned as Augusta she changed her name to Euphemia. Justinian was her sister's son, whom she and Justin had adopted and brought to Constantinople, giving him the best education available in the capital. He was enrolled in the Candidati when he came of age, and immediately after Justin's accession Justinian was appointed count of the domestics, after which he was made a patrician. Justinian was thenceforth the power behind the throne, and when Justin made him Caesar in 525 he became the heir presumptive, succeeding his uncle two years later.

Justin's reign was for the most part peaceful both in religion and in foreign affairs. By that time the character of the empire was very different from what it had been when Constantine established his capital at Byzantium. The western regions of the empire had been overrun by barbarians, and what remained was principally the Balkans and Asia Minor, the majority of the inhabitants by then being Christians, with Greek the dominant language in the capital. Although Latin remained the official language of the court up until the mid sixth century, the empire was becoming more and more Greek and Christian in character, severing its connections with the classical traditions of Athens and Rome. Historians consider the first half of the sixth century to be the watershed in the history of the empire, which thenceforth they tend to call Byzantine rather than Roman. As the great churchman Gennadius was to write more than nine centuries later, in the twilight of the Byzantine Empire, 'Though I am a Hellene by speech yet I would never say that I was a Hellene, for I do not believe as Hellenes believe. I should like to take my name from my faith, and if anyone asks me what I am I answer, "A Christian". Though my father dwelt in Thessaly I do not call myself a Thessalian, but a Byzantine, for I am of Byzantium.'

CHAPTER 8

The Age of Justinian
527–565

Justin became seriously ill early in 527, which led him to name Justinian as his successor. Justinian was made co-emperor on 4 April 527, crowned in a chapel of the Great Palace along with his wife, Theodora, whom he had wed three years before. Justin died on 1 August 527, whereupon Justinian succeeded as emperor, with Theodora named as Augusta.

The principal source for the history of Justinian's reign is Procopius of Caesarea. Procopius is first heard of in Constantinople in 527, when he was appointed to the staff of Justinian's young general Belisarius. He accompanied Belisarius on his Persian, African, and Italian campaigns, and then in 542 he returned to Constantinople, where twenty years later he was appointed prefect of the city. He then began to write his *History of the Wars*, published c. 551, and then in the next four years he composed the *Edifices*, a laudatory work describing all of the buildings that Justinian had erected up to that time. The first of these was the church of SS. Sergius and Bacchus,[1] which Justinian erected on the Marmara shore of the First Hill, below the Hippodrome.

But at the same time Procopius also published privately a book called *Anecdota* – better known as the *Secret History* – a spiteful, scurrilous and sometimes unbelievable attack on Justinian and Theodora, whom he blamed for all that was wrong with the Roman Empire, often contradicting the praise that he lavished on the emperor in his other two books. Procopius also writes of Belisarius and his notorious wife, Antonina, in the *Secret History*. According to the *Secret History*, both women were of low origin, Theodora being the daughter of a bear-keeper in the Hippodrome, while Antonina's father and grandfather had been charioteers. Both women had been courtesans and had lived depraved lives before they married, but by then Theodora had reformed, whereas Antonina continued her wanton ways for the rest of her life, according to Procopius.

The eastern frontiers had been quiet throughout almost the whole of Justin's reign, but in the last year of his life the Persians invaded Armenia. Justinian inherited the responsibility for this conflict, the first of a series of wars on both the eastern and western frontiers that were to occupy his attention for most of his long reign. During the First Persian War (527–32) Belisarius won a great victory in 530, but the following year he was severely defeated and was recalled to Constantinople. He was still in the city early in 532, when Justinian was faced with the greatest crisis of his reign.

The crisis began as a riot in the Hippodrome on 10 January 532. Three days later this erupted into a full-scale insurrection, with the Blue and Green circus factions bursting forth together from the Hippodrome to attack the Great Palace, shouting '*Nika!*' ('Victory!'), the slogan that would give its name to the revolt. On Sunday 18 January the partisans carried Hypatius to the Kathisma and crowned him with a golden necklace, whereupon the mob in the Hippodrome hailed him as emperor.

Meanwhile Justinian and his council were meeting in the palace in a mood of despair. The council advised Justinian to flee to Heraclea on the Propontis, where he might reorganize his forces and eventually recapture the city, but a stirring speech by Theodora convinced him that he should stay and fight for his throne. Belisarius then led forth his barbarian troops and trapped the mob in the arena, killing 30,000 of them there, according to Procopius. Hypatius and his brother Pompeius were captured and executed, their bodies thrown into the sea, while the remains of the slaughtered partisans seemed to have been buried in a common grave in the Hippodrome.

The Nika Revolt left much of the imperial quarter on the First Hill in ruins, with the church of Haghia Sophia utterly destroyed, along with Haghia Eirene. The great task of restoration began on 23 February 532, forty days after the end of the revolt, when Justinian began building a new cathedral dedicated to Haghia Sophia,[2] erecting

View of Haghia Sophia from the fountain court.

it on the ruins of the Theodosian church. According to Procopius, 'the emperor, disregarding all questions of expense, eagerly pressed on to begin the work of construction, gathering all the artisans from the whole world'. Justinian's chief architect was Anthemius of Tralles, the most distinguished mathematical physicist of the age, who was assisted by Isidorus of Miletus, a renowned mathematician who had been head of the Platonic Academy in Athens. The church was completed within six years, and on 26 December 537 the patriarch Menas rededicated it to the Divine Wisdom. Theodora shared in the foundation of the church with Justinian, and her imperial monogram is linked with his on the magnificent capitals of the arcades in the nave and galleries.

Justinian also erected a commemorative monument to himself in the Augustaeum. This was a colossal column bearing a huge bronze equestrian statue of Justinian, 'habited like Achilles', according to Procopius. The monument stood for more than a thousand years; a German engraving of 1493 shows Justinian's statue still perched on top, rising as high as the dome of Haghia Sophia, the enduring monument of his reign.

During the years 532–7 Justinian also built a new church dedicated to Haghia Eirene,[3] erected on the site of the Old Church destroyed in the Nika Revolt. As Procopius writes, 'The church called after Eirene, which was next to the Great Church [Haghia Sophia] and had been burned down together with it, the emperor Justinian rebuilt on a larger scale, so that it was scarcely second to any of the churches of Byzantium, save that of Sophia.'

One of Theodora's charitable foundations was a hospice for fallen women that she founded on the Asian shore of the Bosphorus, calling it Metanoia, or Repentance. Procopius mentions it in his *Secret History*:

Theodora also devoted considerable attention to the punishment of women caught in carnal sin. She picked up more than five hundred harlots in the Forum, who earned a miserable living by selling themselves there for three obols, and sent them to the opposite mainland, where they were locked up in a monastery called Repentance to reform their way of life. Some of them, however, threw themselves from the parapets at night and thus freed themselves of an undesired salvation.

A recent study credits Justinian with the foundation of forty churches in Constantinople and its suburbs, of which thirty are mentioned by Procopius in his *Edifices*. The only ones that remain standing are Haghia Sophia, Haghia Eirene and SS. Sergius and Bacchus. The most notable of the Justinianic churches that have disappeared is that of the Holy Apostles, a great basilica that he erected on the site of the original edifice built by Constantius. Another important church dating from his reign is that of St Polycuktos,[4] whose excavated remnants can be seen on the ridge between the Third and Fourth Hills. The church was founded by the princess Anicia Juliana, daughter of Olybrius, one of the last emperors of the West. St Polyeuktos was one of the largest and grandest churches in Constantinople, surpassed in size only by Haghia Sophia. It was completed in 527, the first year of Justinian's reign.

A few of Justinian's foundations survive as sacred shrines, although the original churches that he built there have disappeared, replaced by much more modest structures erected in recent times. One of these is the famous shrine of the Virgin at Zoodochos Pege,[5] the Life-Giving

*The Virgin and Child flanked by Constantine (right) and Justinian
(left); mosaic in the lunette over the door at the southern end of
the narthex of Haghia Sophia.*

Spring, which is outside the Theodosian Walls near the Silivri Gate.
Tradition has it that Justinian, while hunting one day on the Thracian
downs, came upon a crowd of women making a pilgrimage to the
Pege, the sacred spring, and he was told by them that its waters had
great curative powers. Soon afterwards he built a large church around
the spring, using surplus materials from Haghia Sophia. A palace was
built there by one of his successors, and thenceforth the shrine of the
Zoodochos Pege became a favourite imperial retreat. Procopius, in
enumerating Justinian's foundations in his *Edifices*, gives a lyrical
description of the shrine, which is still a place of pilgrimage today:

He dedicated to the Virgin another shrine in the place called Pege. In that
place is a dense grove of cypresses and a meadow abounding in flowers in the
midst of soft glebe, a park abounding in beautiful shrubs, and a spring
bubbling silently forth with a gentle stream of sweet water – all especially
suitable to a sanctuary.

Justinian's public works included the vast subterranean reservoir on the First Hill known as the Basilica Cistern.[6] The cistern takes its name from the fact that it was built under the Stoa Basilica, which was badly damaged in the Nika Revolt and subsequently repaired by Justinian.

The Basilica Cistern, known in Turkish as Yerebatansaray, the Underground Palace.

Justinian's restorations also included those parts of the Great Palace that had been destroyed in the Nika Revolt. Remnants of the Great Palace[7] have been unearthed on the Marmara shore of the First Hill, with some mosaics and architectural members exhibited in the Mosaic Museum[8] below the Blue Mosque. The only part of the Great Palace that remains standing is the Palace of Bucoleon,[9] whose ruined shell is part of the sea walls on the Marmara shore, the imperial monogram of Justinian still legible on the capital of its single surviving column.

Procopius interrupts his account of the Second Persian War to describe the terrible bubonic plague that began in 542, striking first in Egypt and reaching Constantinople the following year. A modern historian has estimated that some 300,000 people died of this plague in Constantinople, whose population at that time was about half a million.

After Procopius completes his account of the Second Persian War he goes on to describe the reconquest of North Africa and Italy. This began early in the summer of 533, when Belisarius set off from Constantinople in command of an expedition to reconquer Africa from the Vandals. As always, Antonina accompanied Belisarius on campaign, taking along her young lover, Theodosius. Belisarius went on to defeat King Gelimer of the Vandals, sixteen kilometres outside Carthage, after which he captured the city on 15 September 533. The following year he was recalled by Justinian, bringing back some 3,000 captive Vandals, including the fallen Gelimer himself. Belisarius was then awarded a triumph in the Hippodrome, with Gelimer and other captives marching behind him in the procession.

Two years later Justinian sent Belisarius off on an expedition to reconquer Italy from the Ostrogoths, with Antonina once again accompanying her husband. Belisarius eventually found that his forces were not strong enough to achieve a decisive victory. Frustrated, he sent Antonina back to Constantinople in the spring of 548 to plead his case with Theodora. But her long journey was in vain, as Procopius writes in his account of the war in Italy: 'At about this time Antonina, the wife of Belisarius, set off for Byzantium, intending to make larger provisions for carrying on the war. But the empress Theodora had fallen sick and passed from the world, having lived as queen for twenty-one years and three months.' Thus Antonina returned to a city in mourning, with Justinian so overcome with grief that he could not receive her. But Antonina did manage to arrange for Belisarius to be recalled to Constantinople, for the imperial campaign in Italy was doomed to failure and she did not want him to bear the blame.

Justinian's efforts on behalf of religious unity included stamping out the remaining traces of paganism in the empire. His most notable action in this regard came in 529, when he closed the Platonic Academy in Athens, the last stronghold of pagan philosophy. Despite his closing of the academy, Justinian's reign produced the final renaissance of classical culture, which flourished in Constantinople after Athens and the other centres of ancient Greek learning had been destroyed by the barbarians. And it was a Greek revival, though

Christian rather than pagan, for Latin was by then little used in the capital other than for administrative and legal matters. Justinian's reign produced the historian Procopius, the jurist Tribonian, the scientists Anthemius of Tralles and Isidorus of Miletus, and the poets Agathias Scholasticus and Paul the Silentiary. Some of the works of the two poets are preserved in the *Greek Anthology*, including these three amorous epigrams, the first by Agathias and the other two by Paul, whose sentiments are quite pagan in the ambidexterity of his passion:

If you love me, do not wholly let your spirit bend the knee and cringe full of oily supplication, but be a little proof against approaches, so far at least to draw up your eyebrows and look at her with a scanting air. For it is more or less the business of women to slight the proud, and to make fun of those who are too exceedingly pitiful. He is the best lover who mixes the two, tempering piteousness with a little manly pride.

Galatea's kisses are long and smack. Demo's are soft and Doris bites one. Which excites most? My heart, thou wert strong; thou knowest already Demo's soft kiss and the sweet honey of her fresh mouth. Cleave to that; she wins without a bribe; if any take pleasure from another, he will not tear me away from Demo.

Kissing Hippomenes, my heart was fixed on Leander; clinging to Leander's lips I bear the image of Xanthus in my mind, and embracing Xanthus my heart goes back to Hippomenes. Thus ever I refuse him I have in my grasp, and receiving one after another in my ever-shifting arms, I court wealth of love. Let whosoever blames me remain in single poverty.

Another epigram by Agathias is a mock obituary for a couple caught *in flagrante* by death:

A certain man secretly took his pleasure in unholy intercourse, stealing the embraces of another man's wife; but of a sudden the roof fell in and buried the sinners still coupled. One trap holds both, and together they lie in an embrace that will never cease.

Many of the Byzantine poems in the *Greek Anthology* are about the public baths of Constantinople, which seem to have been the social centres of the city. The *Notitia* lists eight *thermae* in the city, the largest and most famous being the Baths of Zeuxippus, which were rebuilt by Justinian. The Baths of Zeuxippus are mentioned by the poet Leontius Scholasticus, in an epigram addressed to a friend:

On one side I have close to me Zeuxippus, a pleasant bath, and on another the Hippodrome. After seeing the races at the latter and taking a bath at the former, come and rest at my comfortable table. Then in the afternoon you will have plenty of time for the other races, reaching the course from your room quite close at hand.

Some of the poems about the baths of Constantinople refer to them as places of assignation, as in an anonymous epigram about a certain bathing establishment of dubious reputation:

Such women as have desire to please (and ye all have) come here, and ye shall win brighter charms. She who wants a husband will stir many to offer her marriage. And she who makes a living by her body, if she bathe here, will have swarms of lovers at her door.

A number of epigrams by Agathias and Paul describe the beauties of Constantinople, and from their poems it appears that both of them lived in houses with views of the sea. As Agathias writes, 'From three sides I view the pleasant expanse of the sea, struck by sunlight from all quarters.' And Paul, in an epigram 'On a house set on a high hill in Constantinople', observes that 'A room with a good view is a surer possession than virtue.' One of the laws enacted by Justinian again sought to protect the sea view of householders from being blocked by illegal structures, as it decrees:

In this our royal city one of the most pleasant amenities is the view of the sea; and to preserve it we enacted that no building should be erected within thirty metres of the sea front. This law has been circumvented by certain individuals. They first put up buildings conforming with this law; then put up in front of them awnings which cut off the sea view without breaking the law; next put up a building inside the awning; and finally remove the awning. Anyone who offends in this way must be made to demolish the building he has put up and further pays a fine of four and a half kilograms of gold.

Justinian was never the same after Theodora's death, staying aloof from those around him, neglecting affairs of state and postponing decisions, spending all of his time in abstruse matters of theology. His great imperial dream had by then been realized, for his empire now extended from the Persian frontiers through Asia Minor, the Balkans and Italy, as well as the south-western coast of Spain, stretching along the North African coast through Egypt, the Holy Land, Syria and Mesopotamia. Procopius, in his *Edifices*, enumerates the many hundreds of fortresses that Justinian erected to defend the frontiers of his vast realm, adding to the colossal cost of the endless wars that were fought to reconquer the lost dominions of Rome, not to mention the enormous expenditures that the emperor had made in founding churches and other buildings in Constantinople and elsewhere in the empire. All of this left the empire virtually bankrupt by the end of his reign, with the Treasury so empty that not even the Long Walls of Anastasius could be kept in repair. This led a tribe of Huns named the Kotrigurs to invade Thrace under their chieftain Zabergan, who in 559 put Constantinople under siege, at a time when all of the imperial forces were off on the frontiers. Justinian had no recourse but to call once again on Belisarius, who was living in obscure retirement. Belisarius mustered as many men as he could from the populace of Constantinople, stiffening them with a cadre of 300 veterans of his Italian campaigns, and with these he marched out to defend the city. His small force routed the huge horde of barbarians, who turned and ran for their lives, never again to threaten Constantinople.

But there was no rest for Belisarius even then, and no just reward, for three years later he was wrongly accused of involvement in a plot to assassinate Justinian. As a result he was placed under house arrest until July 563, when Justinian was persuaded to exonerate him. Belisarius died in Constantinople in March 565, just a few months before Justinian. His wife, Antonina, survived him by a few years, living in penniless retirement in a convent, for when Belisarius died the state seized all of his assets, leaving her destitute. The sad end of Belisarius gave rise to an apocryphal legend widely believed through-out Europe in later times, a tale which had him living out his last years as a blind beggar in the streets of Constantinople, those who tossed him a copper coin unaware that this was the great general who had won victories on three continents and been awarded a triumph in the Hippodrome.

The age of Justinian was coming to a close in an atmosphere of deep gloom, the sense of impending doom heightened by a series of earthquakes that struck Constantinople between 553 and 557. These tremors had weakened the structure of Haghia Sophia, and when another earthquake occurred on 7 May 558 it severely damaged the Great Church, causing the collapse of the eastern part of the main dome. Justinian roused himself to begin the repairs immediately, putting the project under the direction of Isidorus the Younger, a nephew of Isidorus of Miletus. The restored church was rededicated on Christmas Eve in 563, with Justinian heading the procession to the Great Church in a chariot along with the patriarch Eutychius.

Justinian continued to carry out his imperial duties until the last day of his life, 14 November 565, when he dropped dead of a stroke or heart attack. Two days later he was carried to the new mausoleum that he had erected in the church of the Holy Apostles, where he was buried in a porphyry sarcophagus next to that of Theodora.

Justinian was eighty-three years old when he died, having ruled for more than thirty-eight years – the most illustrious reign in the history of the Byzantine Empire. Yet the chronicler Evagrius wrote, concluding his account of Justinian's reign, 'Thus died this prince, after having filled the whole world with noise and troubles: and having since the end of his life received the wages of his misdeeds, he has gone to seek the justice which was his due before the judgement-seat of hell.' Modern historians take a loftier view, looking upon the reign of Justinian as a golden age in the history of Byzantium, as exemplified by his great church of Haghia Sophia and his imperial vision in re-conquering the lost dominions of the Roman Empire.

Such was the impression that Justinian's edifice created a thousand years ago, when the envoys sent by Prince Vladimir of Kiev reported back to their lord what they had seen in the imperial city, speaking in awe of the Great Church:

We knew not whether we were on heaven or earth. For on earth there is no such splendour or such beauty, and we are at a loss how to describe it. We only know that God dwells there among men, and their service is fairer than the ceremonies of other nations. For we cannot forget that beauty.

CHAPTER 9

The Struggle for Survival
565–717

Within a few years of Justinian's death the Byzantine frontiers were breached on all sides by invaders, and for the next century and a half the empire endured a desperate struggle for survival.

Justinian was succeeded by his nephew Justin II, whose wife, Sophia, was Theodora's niece. During Justin's reign the empire was invaded on the east by the Persians and on the north by the Avars, a central-Asian people who had moved into the Balkans. The onslaught of the invaders caused the unstable Justin to have a complete mental breakdown, from which he never recovered. The chronicler John of Ephesus reports that in his calmer moments Justin's only amusement was to be pulled around the palace in a toy cart while being serenaded by musicians. But then he would explode in violent rages and attempt to bite his attendants, after which he would try to hurl himself from the palace windows, which had to be fitted with bars for his protection.

After Justin's death in 578 Tiberius II came to the throne. He ruled until his death in 582 and was succeeded by Maurice, a Cappadocian who had commanded the imperial army in Asia Minor. During the two decades of his reign Maurice kept both the Persians and the Avars at bay. Meanwhile he established the exarchates of Ravenna and Carthage under imperial viceroys, so that by the end of the sixth century the future of the empire seemed secure.

Maurice was sceptical by nature, and this led him to investigate the supposed miracle that occurred each year at the shrine of St Euphemia in Chalcedon on the anniversary of her martyrdom. The incident was recorded thus by the chronicler Theophylact:

The miracle was most incredible to those who have not witnessed it. For although the body has lain in the tomb for four hundred years or so already, on the aforesaid day [the anniversary of her martyrdom] the leader of the priestly church of those parts draws up with sponges founts of blood from the dead body ... and distributes it to the throngs in little vessels made out of glass. Then there rashly occurred to the emperor Maurice, in the twelfth year of his imperial power, a certain notion concerning the divinity of the soul, and attributed the miracle to man's crafty devices. Accordingly the grave was stripped of its silver ornament, and the tomb guarded by seals, for such was the counsel of bold disbelief. But when the appointed day had arrived, the seal was tested, the mystery examined, the miracles investigated, and through the miracles she became an indisputable witness to her own power: once again rivers of aromatic blood sprang from the tomb, the mystery gushed with the discharges, sponges were enriched with sacred blood, and the martyrdom multiplied the effluences. And so in this way the martyr educated the emperor's disbelief. But the emperor sent, in return for the gushing forth of blood, an inundation of tears, and repaid the effluences and aromatics with a shower from his eyes, saying 'God is wonderful in his saints.'

Early in the autumn of 602 the imperial army on the Danube revolted under a centurion named Phocas, who usurped the throne and beheaded Maurice and his five sons. The chronicler Theophanes, who begins his account with this event, writes that 'Phocas ordered their heads placed in the Hebdomon for a number of days. The inhabitants of the city went out to look at them until they began to stink.'

During the next six years the Persians under King Chosroes II overran Armenia, Mesopotamia, Syria and Palestine, after which they invaded Asia Minor and penetrated all the way to Chalcedon, leaving death and total destruction in their wake. By that time Constantinople was being torn apart by a series of riots and insurrections, all put down savagely by Phocas. Meanwhile the Avars were set to invade in the Balkans, for they and all others now believed that the empire was doomed.

When all seemed lost, the empire was saved by Heraclius, the exarch of Carthage, who sent a fleet to Constantinople under the command of his son, also named Heraclius. The fleet reached Constantinople on 3 October 610, whereupon an insurrection broke out in the city and overthrew Phocas. Phocas was brought before Heraclius the

*Phocas (602–10), reputed to be the worst emperor
in the history of Byzantium.*

Younger and then beheaded, after which his remains were publicly
burned in the Forum Bovis. Later that same day the young Heraclius
was crowned as emperor.

Heraclius spent his long reign in almost continuous battle against
the Persians and the Avars, who at first continued their advances
despite his efforts. A Persian army swept across Asia Minor in 615,
once again advancing as far as Chalcedon. This led Heraclius to transfer the body of St Euphemia to Constantinople, where it was enshrined
in a martyrion that had been dedicated to her by the Hippodrome.
The Avars raided the suburbs of the city in June 617, but the great
Theodosian Walls were too much for them and so they turned back,
carrying away more than a quarter of a million captives from Thrace.

The situation now seemed hopeless, and Heraclius considered the
possibility of leaving Constantinople to establish his capital at
Carthage. This caused panic among the people of Constantinople,
and they forced the patriarch Sergius to have Heraclius swear that he
would not abandon their city to the barbarians.

Before Heraclius departed to campaign against the Persians he brought to Constantinople the remains of St Theodore of Sykeon, whom he believed would protect the city. This is recorded in the *Life* of St Theodore, who was born late in Justinian's reign. The *Life* begins with an account of the birth of Theodore to a 'very beautiful girl' named Mary, who with her mother and sister kept an inn on the highway between the capital and Ancyra, where they 'followed the profession of courtesans'. One night Mary entertained a guest from Constantinople, 'a certain well-known man, Cosmas by name, who had become popular in the Hippodrome performing acrobatic feats on camels'.

Triumph of Heraclius after his victory over the Persians in 627; from the Anonymous of Anselmo Banduri.

On this man's journey to the East he stayed for some time in the inn, and seeing Mary and how fair she was, he desired her and took her to his bed. From this union she conceived and saw in a dream a very brilliant star descending from heaven into her womb. She awoke all trembling with fear and related the vision she had seen in the night to Cosmas ... and he said to her, 'Take good care of yourself dear, for perchance God will watch over you and give you a son who will be deemed worthy to become a bishop.' With these words he left her in the morning and went on his way rejoicing.

Theodore did in fact become a bishop, early in Maurice's reign, by which time he was renowned as a worker of miracles. Maurice invited him to Constantinople and 'accorded him much honour', and 'during the short time Theodore stayed in the capital God through him performed great miracles in the city'. Theodore returned to the city after Maurice was overthrown by Phocas, whom he cured of the gout. But at the same time Theodore admonished Phocas, saying that 'he must cease his killing of men and shedding of blood, and at these words the emperor became very incensed against him'.

Theodore was also critical of the notables in Constantinople, as his biographer writes:

Many in Constantinople, especially those in high places, were accustomed to go to the baths after communion. Theodore condemns the practice. A number of the cathedral clergy come to Theodore and ask him whether this condemnation has support in scripture or is based on a special revelation. Theodore replies that God had revealed to him that those who take a bath after receiving the Eucharist through wantonness and for bodily enjoyment commit a sin, 'For no one who has anointed himself with myrrh and perfumes washes off the pleasant scent thereof, and no one who has lunched with the emperor straightaway runs to the baths.'

Many of Theodore's miracles involved exorcism, as in an incident when he was crossing the strait from the Bithynian port of Pylae:

Theodore drives out the demon from a fellow-traveller in the boat when crossing from Pylae to Constantinople; the demon had been secretly active in the man for many years and during the crossing violently abused the saint. The other passengers, not knowing that the man was possessed, told him to hold the peace and not malign the saint in this scandalous and drunken fashion. Theodore beat upon the man's chest and making the sign of the Cross compelled the hidden demon to go out. The demon was seen by those in the boat to leave the man's mouth in the form of a mouse.

A number of incidents in the *Life* of St Theodore reveal his power of clairvoyance, as in one that occurred early in his career, after he became abbot of a monastery in Galatia. Theodore had decided that his old communion vessel of marble was no longer adequate, and so he ordered one of his monks to buy a new silver chalice in

Constantinople. The chalice bore an imperial stamp attesting that it was made of pure silver, but Theodore had reason to believe that the precious metal had in some way been profaned, and so he sent it back to the shop. When he did so the silversmith admitted that the chalice had indeed been profaned, for the silver from which it had been made came from the melted-down chamberpot of a common courtesan.

Theodore was also a great healer, of physical and mental ailments along with those of the spirit, serving as physician and psychiatrist as well as priest, as his biographer writes towards the end of the *Life*:

Again if any required medical treatment for certain illnesses or surgery or a purging draught or hot-springs, this God-inspired man would prescribe the best thing for each, for even in technical matters he had become an experienced doctor ... And to those who exposed to him the doubts and the hidden diseases of their heart he gave appropriate and healing counsel; and to those who had transgressed in various ways he ordained a certain period for repentance, and cleansed them by fastings, prayers and acts of charity.

Heraclius led his army in two successful campaigns against the Persians, in the second of which he was wounded in a closely fought battle. Before the beginning of the second campaign the threat of an Avar invasion in Thrace had led Heraclius to send part of his army back to defend Constantinople. Then in 626 the Avar khagan invaded Thrace with a great horde that also included Bulgars, Slavs, Huns, Scythians and Gepids. At the same time a huge Persian army swept across Asia Minor and encamped in Chalcedon, waiting to coordinate their attack on Constantinople with the Avars. At one point the Avars almost broke through the walls at their weakest point, where the fortifications sloped down to the Golden Horn at Blachernae, but the Virgin Blachernitissa suddenly appeared and dispersed the barbarians – or so said the Greek defenders there. Then in mid-August news arrived of a great Roman victory in Mesopotamia, and at that both the Persians and Avars broke off their siege and headed back to their homelands. Thus the 'god-guarded' city of Constantinople was saved, and the populace gave particular thanks to the Virgin at her shrine in Blachernae, singing a hymn composed by the patriarch Sergius – the 'Akathistos' – which is still part of the liturgy of the Greek Orthodox Church.

Soon afterwards Heraclius ordered new fortifications to be built at the northern end of the land walls by the Golden Horn. These fortifications, known as the Wall of Heraclius,[1] were meant to protect the shrine at Blachernae, where the Avars had almost broken into the city.

Heraclius then concentrated all of his forces on the eastern frontiers, and on 12 December 627 he won a great victory over the Persian king Chosroes, who was killed soon afterwards and succeeded by his son Kavadh-Siroes. The new king sued for peace and Heraclius accepted his terms, which included the return to the empire of all disputed territory.

Meanwhile a new and far more formidable power had emerged in Arabia, where the Islamic era began with the flight of the Prophet Muhammad from Mecca in 622. The armed might of Islam became evident in 636, when a Roman army commanded by the emperor's brother Theodorus was virtually annihilated by the Arabs at the battle of the Yarmuk in Jordan. This opened up all of Syria and Jordan to the Arabs, who captured Jerusalem in 638 and Caesarea two years later, at which time their forces also overran Egypt.

By this time Heraclius was a dying man, his spirit broken by the loss of all that he had fought so hard to win. He finally passed away on 11 February 641 and was buried in the Holy Apostles. The chronicler Nicephorus notes that by the emperor's dying wish his tomb was left open for three days after his interment, for he seems to have feared that he might share the same fate as was rumoured to have befallen Zeno and be buried alive.

Heraclius began a dynasty that lasted for seventy years after his death. Two of his sons, Constantine II and Heraclonas, ruled as co-emperors for a few months in 641. Constantine died of tuberculosis on 24 May of that year, and towards the end of September Heraclonas was deposed by the Senate and exiled along with his mother, Martina. The Senate ordered that Heraclonas have his nose cut off to prevent his return to power – the first instance in Byzantine history of the mutilation known as *rhinometia* – while Martina had her tongue slit.

Heraclonas was succeeded by his eleven-year-old nephew Constantine, son of Constantine II. The reign of Constantine III was an almost continual struggle against the Arabs, who first invaded Asia Minor in 641, with their fleets ravaging the coasts and islands of the eastern Mediterranean. The Arab invasions so depressed Constantine that in 660 he decided to abandon Constantinople and re-establish his capital in the West. He eventually made his way to Sicily, and in 663 he settled in Syracuse, which he made his headquarters. Two years later he sent for his wife and sons to join him there, but the people of Constantinople refused to let them go, fearing that their city would lose its imperial status and be abandoned to the barbarians. This sealed Constantine's fate, and on 15 July 668 he was assassinated in Syracuse.

He was succeeded by his eldest son, also called Constantine, who was sixteen when he came to the throne. Constantine IV spent much of his reign defending the empire against Arab invasions launched by the caliph Muawiya. The first of these occurred in 668, when an Arab force under Muawiya's son Yazid reached Chalcedon. The following spring the Arabs crossed the strait and attacked Constantinople by land, but they were unable to breach the Theodosian Walls and were forced to withdraw.

The next assault began in 674, when an Arab army occupied Cyzicus, which Muawiya's fleet then used as a base to attack Constantinople. The Byzantines used their 'Greek fire' with devastating effect, employing siphons to spray the fiery fluid on the Arab warships and engulf them in flames. The Arab fleet was forced to withdraw to Cyzicus, from where new assaults were mounted against Constantinople annually for the next four years, each attack defeated by the terrible 'Greek fire'. The Arabs finally gave up after their fifth attack on Constantinople, in the summer of 678, and sailed back to the Mediterranean, where their fleet was wrecked in a storm. Muawiya was then forced to come to terms with Constantine, agreeing to a thirty-year peace treaty.

Constantine also had to contend with a theological controversy over the doctrine of Monotheletism, which held that though Christ had two natures, human and divine, he had but a single will. Constantine sought to end the controversy by convening the Sixth Ecumenical Council, which met in Constantinople from 7 November 680 to 16 September 681. He took an active part in the conclave, which finally condemned Monotheletism and excommunicated its supporters.

While the council was still in session, a Monothelete monk named

*Scene from a siege of Constantinople; from a French
manuscript of 1499.*

Polychronius appeared and claimed that he could bring back the dead
to life by placing over them his profession of faith. The assembled
bishops arranged to have Polychronius give a demonstration of his
powers in public, holding it 'in the courtyard of the public bath which
is called Zeuxippus'. A man who had just died was brought for the
demonstration, whereupon Polychronius placed his profession of faith
on the corpse and prayed over it for several hours, but to no avail.

Constantine died in late July 685 and was succeeded by his son
Justinian, who was then sixteen. Two years later Justinian II led a
successful campaign against the Slavs, who had so completely overrun Greece that the country was known as Sclavinia. Justinian then
resettled the Slavs in Asia Minor, continuing a policy that had been
initiated by his father, but on a larger scale.

During the sixth year of Justinian's reign he presided over a council
known as the Quinisextum, since it supplemented the decrees of the
Fifth and Sixth Ecumenical Councils. Some of the 102 canons forbade the continued observance of pagan festivals and customs, such

as that of the Brumelia, when the people of Constantinople disguised themselves with masques and danced in the streets – a celebration that is nevertheless perpetuated today in the Greek Apokreas, or Carnival. Canon 21 banned the mime, the pantomime and spectacles involving wild animals; Canon 24 prohibited priests from attending theatrical performances and the games in the Hippodrome; Canon 62 forbade the dancing of women in public, the wearing of female dress by men and vice versa, invoking the name of Dionysus at vintage time, and celebrating the summer solstice with young men leaping over bonfires, though the latter practice still survives on the feast of St John Kynegos, the Hunter.

Towards the end of 695 Justinian was deposed and replaced as emperor by the patrician Leontius. Leontius persuaded his supporters to spare Justinian's life, so instead they slit his tongue and cut off his nose. Justinian – who was thenceforth known as Rhinometos, or 'the man with the cut-off nose' – was then confined in the monastery of Dalmatou in Psamathion. He was subsequently exiled in the Crimea, after which, according to George the Monk, 'there was peace on all sides'.

But there was to be no peace in Byzantium, which now entered one of the most chaotic eras in its history. Three years after his accession Leontius was himself overthrown and replaced by the admiral Apsimar, who succeeded as Tiberius III. Leontius then had his nose cut off, after which he himself was imprisoned in the monastery of Dalmatou.

Meanwhile Justinian had begun a new life. He had fled from the Crimea in 704 and taken refuge with the khagan of the Khazars. The khagan treated him with great honour and gave him the hand of his sister, who took the name of Theodora when she married Justinian. Justinian then made his way to the court of Terval, khan of the Bulgars, who agreed to supply him with an army to regain his throne. Justinian and his Bulgar allies then marched on Constantinople, which they captured with little bloodshed in the spring of 705, with Tiberius fleeing for his life. Justinian was then acclaimed as emperor, regaining the throne that he had lost ten years before. And *rhinokopia* was no impediment, for the chronicler Agnellus of Ravenna says that Justinian wore an artificial nose of 'pure gold' to hide his mutilation.

Justinian's men captured Tiberius and brought him back to Constantinople, where on 15 February 706 he and Leontius were taken to the Hippodrome to face Justinian. Then Justinian took his sweet revenge, as he sat enthroned in the Kathisma with his two deposed emperors bound beneath him, placing his feet on their necks while he watched the races. At the conclusion of the races Leontius and Tiberius were beheaded, after which their remains were thrown into the sea.

Justinian's second reign lasted until 711, when he was overthrown and killed in a revolt led by an Armenian general named Philippicus Vardan. Immediately after his accession Philippicus ordered the execution of Justinian's young son, Tiberius, who was 'slaughtered like a sheep', according to one of the chronicles. The imperial Heraclian dynasty thus ended in the sixth generation, 101 years after Heraclius had ascended the throne.

Philippicus was the first of three ephemeral emperors who ruled in turn during the next six years, his successors being Anastasius II and Theodosius III, all three of them being deposed and confined to monasteries. Before his accession Theodosius had been a tax-collector in Adramyttion. He was working in his office one day in the summer of 715 when the rebel soldiers who were about to overthrow Anastasius II passed through Adramyttion on their way to Constantinople. One of the rebel commanders asked what his name was, and when he replied 'Theodosius' he was told that this was good enough to qualify him as emperor. Theodosius protested vigorously, but the rebels took him away and brought him to Constantinople, where he was proclaimed as emperor after Anastasius II was deposed. Theodosius ruled for only two years before he was forced to abdicate in favour of a new and far more qualified candidate, who came to the throne as Leo III. Theodosius was then allowed to retire to a monastery in Ephesus, where he lived in peace and sanctity for the rest of his days. His tomb in Ephesus soon became a sacred shrine, and miracles of healing were attributed to him so that he was eventually canonized as a saint. He is known to Byzantine historians as Theodosius the Reluctant.

Meanwhile a new dynasty was beginning in Constantinople, where the long night of the Dark Ages had begun – a time in which the light of classical Graeco-Roman culture would almost be extinguished there, as it had already been in Rome and Athens.

CHAPTER 10

The Iconoclastic Crisis
717–845

Leo III was thirty-two when he usurped the throne, using his power as commander of the army in Asia Minor to gain control of the capital. He led his troops through the Golden Gate on 25 March 717, and later that day he was crowned emperor in Haghia Sophia.

The Arabs besieged Constantinople in 717–18, but without success, as Leo led his forces in beating back attacks by both land and sea, destroying the Saracen fleet with 'Greek fire'. The populace attributed the deliverance of their city to the Virgin Hodegetria, the Conductress, whose sacred icon, supposedly painted by St Luke, had been carried in procession along the Theodosian Walls during the siege.

Leo's reign saw the beginning of the greatest religious controversy in the history of Byzantium, the Iconoclastic Crisis. The crisis began in 726 when Leo sent his imperial guards to remove the large painting of Christ that hung over the gateway of the Chalke. This was the most prominent religious painting in the city, and Leo thought that its removal would be an appropriate beginning for his campaign to destroy all of the icons in the empire, for he believed that veneration of these was a form of idolatry. The iconodules, those who venerated icons, tried to prevent the removal of the picture, and in the struggle the commander of the guards was killed. The guards then turned on the iconodules and killed their leader, the lady Theodosia. Theodosia was subsequently canonized and became the patron saint of the iconodules, who dedicated a church[1] to her, the edifice known today as Gül Camii.

Leo also set out to destroy cults associated with the veneration of saints, of whom St Euphemia of Chalcedon was perhaps the most popular in the city. The chronicler Constantine of Teos, writing in the tenth century, describes how Leo broke into the martyrion of St Euphemia, by the Hippodrome, where her body still remained uncorrupted in a larnax, or sarcophagus.

That unholy emperor came, one dark night, with others of his impious religion, and opening the larnax, took the relic [Euphemia's body] with the coffin in which it was enclosed, substituting some dry bones he had brought with him, and departed. He began by placing the relic in one of the chapels of the palace, where his sisters and daughters were able to come secretly and honour it with perfumes and incense. Hearing of this that abomination [Leo] threw it into the sea ... and the next day held an unholy *selention* [synod], wagging his tongue against the saint, and saying 'Go and see yourself the error of those who say the relic of Euphemia is preserved whole, and that myrrh flows from it.' So they went and found no flesh on the dry bones – the bones he had thrown into the larnax – and cried out in their folly that the cures were all deceptions and frauds, and they destroyed the larnax and the altar with it, and made of the church a dwelling for unbaptized and uneducated men, unloading here prisoners of war given as booty to the capital. And others, armour-makers and coarse workmen, set up their forges here. So they turned the church into a worldly building, and as the bema [the elevated area containing the altar and the seats of the clergy] was a sacred place, they put the lavatory there.

Leo's actions led to revolts in both the army and the navy, but he put these down easily. He then formalized his iconoclastic policy in 730 with an imperial edict banning images in the churches and monasteries of the empire. He died on 18 June 741, leaving behind him an empire riven by internal turmoil because of his campaign against icons.

Leo's policy of iconoclasm was carried on relentlessly by his son and successor, Constantine V – known to Byzantine chroniclers as Copronymous, or 'called from dung', because he had supposedly defecated while being baptized in Haghia Sophia.

Six years after Constantine's succession Constantinople was stricken by a terrible outbreak of the plague, which left the city 'almost uninhabited', according to the chronicler Nicephorus. The populace believed that the plague was due to the wrath of God, incurred by the emperor's iconoclasm. Constantine was forced to repopulate the city with people from Greece and the Aegean islands. But the population of Constantinople never again in Byzantine times regained the level of Justinian's reign.

The *Lives* of the saints are rich sources concerning life in the city during the Dark Ages. Among these saints are the holy madmen such as St Andrew the Fool. Andrew was a former Scythian slave who, after seeing the light, began a new life wandering the streets of the city, sleeping at night in the Forum of Constantine. His *Life* tells us that Andrew's epiphany took place in a church in the Makelloi, the butchers' quarter, and that afterwards his favourite haunt was the Artopoleia, the quarter of the bakers. One day Andrew wandered into a square where the street merchants were accustomed to selling expensive ornaments, and when he contemptuously cried 'Chaff!' a passer-by replied, 'If you want to sell straw go to the Anemodoulion.'

This is one of the rare references to the Anemodoulion, a monument between the Artopoleia and the Forum Tauri. Erected by Theodosius II, it was a pyramidal structure surmounted by a female figure that served as a weather-vane, its base adorned with sculptures symbolizing the four seasons and their characteristic winds.

Andrew was devoted to the poor in Constantinople, of whom there were many in his time. But he was sensitive to the pride of even the lowliest beggar, and so, as related in an incident in his *Life*, he contrived to give them money without their being aware that it was charity.

Some lovers of Christ gave Andrew money voluntarily, though he did not seek this. But Christ was looking out for him. As much as they gave he accepted. During the whole day he received twenty to thirty copper coins and more. He knew an out-of-the-way place where the poor gathered and he went there, holding the coins in his hand as if he were playing with them so that they would not know what he was up to, and, sitting in the midst of these poor people, he played with the coins. When one of the poor tried to grab some of the coins he struck him. Then the other beggars, running to the aid of their comrade, hit Andrew with their staves. He, taking this as a pretext for flight, then scattered all the coins and each grabbed some for himself and kept them.

St Andrew was an exorcist, and his aid was sought by a woman who thought she was possessed by a demon. The woman's husband was an alcoholic, and she tried to cure him by hiring a magician. Her husband was cured by the magician, but then she herself began to have alarming dreams, in which she was pursued by Ethiopians and enormous black dogs, and in another nightmare she saw herself in the Hippodrome embracing the nude male statues there, 'urged by an impure desire of having intercourse with them'. St Andrew exorcized her demon of desire, and she and her sober husband lived happily ever after.

Some of the biographies of the medieval Byzantine saints are in the form of 'miracle collections', as in the *Life* of St Artemius. One of the miracles attributed to St Artemius is his curing of a man suffering from a disease of the testicles. He sent the man to a Cilician bronze-worker in the Chalkoprateia. A comical argument ensued, in which the Cilician struck the poor man in the testicles with his hammer and thereby cured him of his disease.

The miracles of St Artemius involved many of the craft guilds of Constantinople, his patients including an arrowsmith, a tanner, a maker of candles, a jeweller and a silversmith, whose story reveals that the members of his guild also acted as bankers and moneylenders. The silversmiths are also mentioned in the *Life* of St Theodore Tyro, whose miracles are concerned with the return of missing possessions to those who had been the victim of robberies or other misfortunes. The final episode in his *Life* refers to the building of a church[2] in Constantinople dedicated to St Theodore Tyro, an edifice known today as Kilise Cami.

The guilds of the city are listed in the *Book of the Prefect*, a collection of regulations governing the activity of the guilds in Constantinople, which came under the supervision of the prefect of the city. This is another rich source of information about life in Constantinople during the medieval era. As an example, the *Book of the Prefect* notes that the guild of meat-sellers was divided into two corporations, the butchers proper and the swine-merchants, with another guild for those who slaughtered animals and then sold their meat. Members of all three of these guilds had to operate in two authorized market areas, the Strategion and the Forum Tauri. They had to set prices under the supervision of the prefect, although they

Church of St Theodore Tyro, known in Turkish as Kilise Cami.

could charge whatever the traffic would bear for the heads, feet and entrails of the slaughtered animals. Their operations were regulated by an official known as the bothros, who supervised the cattle market in the Forum Amastrianum, which was also the site of the horse market.

The *Book of the Prefect* notes that many of the candlemakers had their shops in the vicinity of Haghia Sophia, where they could supply tapers for the great religious processions that formed there. The fishmongers had their shops around all of the city's ports, where the fishermen sold their catch just as they do today, as well as in the Forum Tauri, as noted in the *Life* of St Andrew. The slave-dealers had their establishments near the Forum of Constantine, where many of the brothels were located. Furriers also had their shops in the Forum of Constantine, many of their owners being Jews, particularly from Venice in later Byzantine times. Jews also worked as tanners, most of them in the quarter known as Vlanga on the shore of the Marmara by the Harbour of Theodosius. The historian Nicetas Choniates listed the tanners along with harness-makers, cobblers and sausage-makers among the 'stupid and ignorant' members of the populace of

Constantinople, and it was generally agreed that being a swine-merchant was a bar to social advancement. The most socially accepted of the guilds were those of the goldsmiths and silversmiths, who took precedence over the members of other trades in imperial processions. Many of them had their shops around Haghia Sophia, as did the makers of perfumes, whose place is thus specified in the *Book of the Prefect*: 'They shall place their display tables with their containers in a line extending from the sacred image of Christ our Lord which is by the Chalke up to the Milion, and make pleasant the porches of the palace.'

A number of the guilds were open to members of the clergy, and the *Life* of St Theodore the Studite describes the monks of his monastery working as carpenters, tanners, shoemakers, and tailors. Members of the clergy were not allowed to operate taverns, although they were permitted to own one if they rented it out to someone else. The *Book of the Prefect* notes that there were two types of tavern: those in which wine was also sold for consumption off the premises, and those that served as inns. Some of the latter had notorious reputations, being frequented by prostitutes, and in the *Life* of St Andrew they are referred to as 'inns of fornication'. The tavern-owners were frequently accused of watering their wine, although not that of the highest quality, for which they charged much more. This is noted in the *Life* of St Andrew, where in one incident he is dragged into a tavern by a group of young ruffians, who begin pummelling him. The saint orders and drinks a mug of high-quality wine and then breaks the cup over the head of one of his attackers, allowing him to escape momentarily. But he is soon caught and dragged back into the tavern and abused further, while the young men drink themselves senseless on the cheap, rot-gut wine served up to them by the tavern-keeper.

Constantine V renewed the campaign against idolatry in 754, when he convened a synod of the church that condemned icon worship anew. He thereupon carried out his iconoclastic policy with even greater vigour than before, directing it particularly against the monks in the city, forcing many of them to flee to Greece or to the wilds of Cappadocia. Those who did not escape were subject to imprisonment, sometimes after torture and mutilation, and many were executed in what became a reign of terror. The *Life* of St Stephen the Younger describes how he and 432 other monks were imprisoned and tortured in Constantinople during Constantine's reign, after which they were all executed.

The *Life* of St Andrew of Crete tells of how he travelled to Constantinople to denounce Constantine for his iconoclasm. As soon as Andrew spoke in public he was arrested and dragged through the streets of the city in derision, whereupon a demented fisherman stabbed him to death. Andrew's body was then flung in the place where the corpses of convicted murderers were consigned, but eventually some of his followers came and gave him a proper burial 'in a sacred place which was named Krisis'. Subsequently a church[3] was built there and dedicated to his memory; it still stands on the Marmara slope of the Seventh Hill, in Samatya.

Constantine died on 14 September 775 while on campaign against the Bulgars. He was succeeded by his son Leo, who carried on his father's policy of iconoclasm. Leo's wife, Eirene, an Athenian, was a dedicated iconodule, but she kept this secret from her husband. Leo IV renewed the persecution of iconodules in 780, when he confiscated the treasures of churches and monasteries, imprisoning and torturing many monks and nuns. That same year he went off on campaign against the Bulgars, but *en route* he fell ill and then died on 8 September 780.

Leo was succeeded by his son Constantine. The new emperor was not yet ten, and so his mother, Eirene, was appointed regent. Eirene immediately set out to restore icons, dismissing iconoclasts

Eirene (797–802), the first empress to rule Byzantium in her own right; from a coin of her reign.

in the government and army and replacing them with iconodules. Her policy led to two insurrections on the eastern frontiers, allowing the Arabs to invade Asia Minor, while the Slavs in Greece rose up in revolt.

The climax of Eirene's efforts to restore icons came with the Seventh Ecumenical Council, which began at Nicaea on 24 September 787. After a month of meetings the council issued a decree restoring icons, with the provision that holy pictures should be venerated and not adored. Eirene also restored the martyrion of St Euphemia, defiled by Leo III, returning to the shrine those fragments of the saint's remains that had been recovered by the devotees of her cult. Constantine of Teos writes of Euphemia's remains that 'a few fragments of the head were restored to the larnax, with some other relics ... and are kept there to this day'.

Constantine VI had now come of age, but Eirene continued to keep all power to herself as regent. But military affairs were going badly, and in 790 the troops in Asia Minor revolted and demanded that the regency be ended. Eirene was thus forced to abdicate in December of that year, leaving Constantine to rule on his own.

Constantine VI (780–97) presiding over the Seventh Ecumenical Council; miniature from a Byzantine manuscript.

But Constantine was eventually persuaded to restore his mother as co-emperor. Eirene then decided to take power into her own hands, and on 15 August 797 she had her bodyguards seize Constantine and imprison him in the Great Palace, where later that same day she had her son blinded. She then sent him and his two daughters to a convent that she had founded on Prinkipo, the largest of the Princes' Isles, where he died soon afterwards. Thus Eirene became sole ruler of the empire, although her unnatural crime profoundly shocked Byzantium, as noted by the chronicler Theophanes: 'And the sun was darkened during seventeen days, and gave not his light, so that the ships ran off course, and all men said and confess that because the emperor was blinded, the sun had put away his rays. And in this way power came into the hands of Eirene, his mother.'

Charlemagne, who had been crowned as emperor of the West by Pope Leo III in 800, sent envoys to Constantinople with an offer of marriage to Eirene, a dynastic union that would have united the empires of East and West. But shortly after their arrival a palace coup overthrew Eirene, and on 31 October 802 she was replaced by the former minister of finance, who took the throne as Nicephorus I. Eirene was then exiled from Constantinople, never to return.

Nicephorus spent most of the nine years of his reign at war with the Arabs, the Slavs and the Bulgars. On his last campaign he and his son, Stauracius, took the field against Krum, the khan of the Bulgars, whose capital, Pliska, they captured in the early summer of 811. But on 26 July of that year the Byzantines fell into a trap near Adrianople and the Bulgars slaughtered them almost to a man, with only a few cavalry escaping. Nicephorus himself was killed – the first Byzantine emperor to die in battle since Valens. The Bulgars cut off the emperor's head and fashioned it into a silver-lined beer-mug, which Krum used as a trophy for the rest of his days. Stauracius was badly wounded, but he was rescued and carried back to Constantinople, where he was acclaimed as emperor. He died on 11 January 812, having abdicated three months before in favour of his brother-in-law, Michael Rhangabe.

Michael I began his reign by trying to restore religious peace to the empire, bringing back the many monks who had been forced to flee into exile. This outraged the zealots of the iconoclastic party, who maintained that God had brought the barbarian Bulgars down upon the city to punish them for their idolatry. While the populace was praying in the church of the Holy Apostles for the salvation of the city from the Bulgars, a mob of iconoclasts broke into the imperial mausoleum there and opened up the tomb of Constantine V, whom they venerated because of his efforts to stamp out icon worship. Theophanes tells the bizarre tale, referring to the iconoclasts as heretics:

While the city was praying with its chief prelate in the church of the Holy Apostles, some impious followers of the heresy of Constantine [V] (who was abominable to God) pried open the door to the imperial tombs. While no one was paying attention to them because of the crowd's anguish, they suddenly opened the door with a crash, as if by a divine miracle. Rushing inside, they fell at the feet of the heretic's remains and called on him, not on God, saying, 'Arise and help the state, which is being destroyed.' They put it about that Constantine, who dwells in Tartaros with the demons, rose up on horseback and went off to attack the Bulgars.

Michael ruled for only twenty months. On 21 June 813 he was defeated by Krum near Adrianople, he and his general Leo the Armenian barely managing to escape back to Constantinople. Michael then abdicated in favour of Leo and retired to a monastery on the Princes' Isles, where he remained until his death seven years later.

The new emperor was crowned in Haghia Sophia as Leo V on 22 July 813. Five days before that Krum had put Constantinople under siege, but he eventually withdrew, ravaging Thrace in his retreat. A new line of defences known as the Wall of Leo[4] was then built in front of the Wall of Heraclius. This strengthened the defences in the Blachernae quarter, which had always been a weak spot when the city was besieged.

Leo was an iconoclast, and as soon as peace was restored he set out to renew the ban on images. He convened a synod in Haghia Sophia in April 815; this revoked the decrees of the Seventh Ecumenical Council of 787 and confirmed those of the iconoclastic synod of 754. His policy brought him into conflict with the clergy, and as a result he closed many of the monasteries in Constantinople, most notably the Studion, whose abbot, Theodore the Studite, was sent into exile – the third banishment he had suffered at the hands of the iconoclastic emperors.

Late in 820 rumours reached Leo that an old comrade-in-arms, Michael the Amorian, was plotting against him. Leo had Michael arrested and dragged to the Great Palace, where on Christmas Eve he was put in irons and sentenced to death. But on Christmas Day Leo was beheaded in the palace chapel by Michael's friends, who had been disguised as monks of the choir. The assassins freed Michael from the palace dungeon and carried him to the throne, where he was seated and dressed in the emperor's robes with his hands still manacled. A blacksmith was called in to cut away his handcuffs, and when this was done he was escorted to Haghia Sophia, where the patriarch Theodotus crowned him as Michael II. That same day Leo's remains were exposed in the Hippodrome for public derision, after which they were carried away by his widow, Theodosia, to be buried on one of the Princes' Isles.

One of Michael's first acts as emperor was to release all the monks who had been imprisoned and to bring back to the city those who had been exiled, most notably Theodore the Studite. Theodore returned to serve as abbot of the Studion for the last five years of his life, when the monastery established the reputation that has led modern historians to refer to it as 'the Cluny of the East'. The monks of the Studion were renowned as poets and composers of hymns, as scholars and transcribers of ancient manuscripts, as illuminators of books and painters of icons. Theodore kept the monks busy at their various tasks, and when their assigned work was done they were expected to improve their minds by reading in the library. 'Is it work time?' said Theodore, 'then to your labours; is it leisure time? then to your studies.'

Michael died on 2 October 829 and was succeeded by his son Theophilus. Theophilus was already married to Theodora, whom he had chosen as his bride in a 'contest of beauty' soon after he was made co-emperor in 821. Theodora presented Michael with five daughters in succession before the birth of their first son, Constantine, who died in infancy. Then on 19 January 840 she gave birth to a healthy son, the future Michael III, who was made co-emperor soon after his baptism.

Theophilus spent most of his reign in warfare against the Arabs, beginning with his expeditions against them in 829 and 830. The latter campaign, which penetrated into the Arab domains in Cilicia, was so successful that Theophilus awarded himself a triumph when he returned to Constantinople. The chroniclers report that the city was 'decked like a bridal chamber' for the occasion, with the path of the emperor's procession strewn with flowers. Theophilus then repaired the land walls of the city and greatly strengthened the sea walls[5] along the Marmara and the Golden Horn, as evidenced by the many inscriptions that bear his name on the defence towers there.

Theophilus was an iconoclast, but like his father he was reasonably tolerant. Theodora, on the other hand, was a devoted iconodule, though she had to keep her icons hidden from her husband.

Theophilus erected a number of new edifices within the Great Palace, most notably the Palace of Magnaura, where he had his technicians build a fantastic mechanical tree above his throne to dazzle foreign ambassadors. The tree and other marvels were described by Liutprand of Cremona, who came to Constantinople in the tenth century. His account seems to have inspired Yeats to write 'Sailing to Byzantium': 'I have read somewhere', Yeats wrote in a note on this poem, 'that in the Emperor's palace at Byzantium was a tree made of gold and silver, and artificial birds that sang.'

Theophilus died of dysentery on 20 January 842, in his thirty-ninth year. He was the last of the iconoclastic emperors, and as such he was reviled by later chroniclers, most notably Theophanes, who called him Theophilus the Unfortunate. But even Theophanes had to admit that Theophilus was a just emperor, and he records many anecdotes to illustrate the emperor's concern for the welfare of his subjects.

Theophilus was succeeded by his son Michael III, who was just two years old. Michael's mother, Theodora, was appointed as regent, assisted by her brother, the Caesar Bardas. Both Theodora and Bardas were devoted iconodules who felt that the time had come to restore icons, and so in early March 845 they convened a council packed with their supporters. The council repealed the decrees of the iconoclastic synod of 754, confirming instead those of the Seventh Ecumenical Council of 787. A ceremony of thanksgiving was held in Haghia Sophia on 11 March 845, a Sunday, celebrating the return of sacred images to the churches and monasteries of Byzantium; this ceremony is perpetuated today as the Feast of Orthodoxy in the Greek Orthodox Church.

Thus ended the Iconoclastic Crisis, which tore Byzantium ѣ while the barbarians were threatening its existence on all sides. During that time the teeming metropolis of the late Roman period had diminished considerably in population, the populace huddling for protection within the circuit of its great walls. But the light of culture was kept burning throughout the Dark Ages by scholars and artists in monasteries such as the Studion, which continued to flourish until the early sixteenth century, outliving the Byzantine Empire by half a century. As one of the misogynous monks of the Studion wrote in the twilight of Byzantium, apparently in a moment of transcendent happiness:

No barbarian looks upon my face, no woman hears my voice. For a thousand years no useless man has entered the monastery of the Studion, none of the female sex has trodden its court. I dwell in a cell that is like a palace; a garden, an olive grove and a vineyard surround me. Before me there are graceful and luxuriant cypress trees. On one hand is the great city with its market place and on the other the mother of churches and the empire of the world.

CHAPTER II

Born in the Purple
845–1056

Michael III is known as 'the Sot', for from his youth he spent his time carousing with his favourites, while his mother, Theodora, directed affairs of state as regent. Theodora's regency lasted until March 856, when Michael reached the age of sixteen, after which he confined his mother to a convent and ruled on his own, with his uncle the Caesar Bardas acting as first minister and commander-in-chief of the army.

Although Michael was now sole emperor, Bardas completely controlled the empire for the next decade, mounting several successful campaigns against the Arabs while he kept the Bulgars and Slavs at bay. He initiated a cultural renaissance in Byzantium by refounding the University of Constantinople, which had been closed during the Dark Ages. The leading figures of this renaissance were the mathematician Leo, whose influence spread to the West and to Islam; the linguist Cyril (né Constantine), whose creation of the Slavonic script led to the conversion of the Slavs to Christianity through the missionary work of Cyril and Methodius; and the theologian Photius, who became patriarch in 858.

The final triumph of the iconodules was celebrated in Haghia Sophia on Easter Sunday 867, when Photius unveiled a huge mosaic in the apse of the church depicting the Virgin and Child. He marked the occasion with an eloquent homily, in which he reminded the congregation of how the Virgin had saved them from 'the Rus', the fierce Vikings of Kiev, who had made a surprise attack on the city in 860.

Do you recall that unbearable and bitter hour when the barbarians' boats came sailing down at you, wafting a breath of cruelty, savagery and murder?

When the sea spread out its serene and unruffled surface, granting them gentle and agreeable sailing, while, waxing wild, it stirred against us waves of war? When the boats came past the city showing their crews with swords raised, as if threatening the city with death by the sword? When all hope ebbed away from men, and the city was moored only with recourse to the divine?

The mosaic still survives, along with part of its dedicatory inscription, an iambic distich that once read thus in full: 'These icons the deceivers once put down the pious emperors have again restored.' The pious emperors referred to in the inscription are Michael III and Basil I, the Macedonian, whom Michael had crowned as his co-emperor.

Basil was actually of Armenian descent, at least on his father's side. The chronicler Simeon Magister tells the story of how Basil came to Constantinople as a poor peasant youth. He entered the city at dusk one Sunday, and since he had no place to stay he lay down to sleep outside the monastery of St Diomede near the Golden Gate. The abbot noticed him there and gave him supper and a bed for the night. The next day Basil found work in the palace stables, where his strength and

Basil I (867–86), founder of the Macedonian dynasty, shown dispensing justice; miniature from the Chronicle of Skylitzes.

good looks brought him to the attention of the emperor Michael. Michael appointed Basil as his grand chamberlain, and then on 26 May 866 he crowned him as co-emperor. Basil bided his time until the night of 23–24 September 867, when he murdered Michael and usurped the throne.

Basil thus became sole emperor, beginning the illustrious Macedonian dynasty which was to rule Byzantium for nearly two centuries. The lives of the last two generations of this dynasty are described in the *Chronographia* of Michael Psellus, who writes thus of their beginning:

I doubt whether any other family has been so much favoured by God as theirs has been: which is strange when one considers the criminal manner of its coming to power, and how it was born of murder and bloodshed. And yet the plant took root, and sent out such mighty shoots, each bearing imperial fruit, that no other can be compared with it for beauty and splendour.

The continuity of the Macedonian dynasty was threatened during the reign of Basil's son and successor Leo VI, who came to the throne in 886. Leo was widowed three times before he was thirty-five, with none of his wives having produced a son. Since fourth marriages were forbidden in the Orthodox Church, Leo had to content himself with his mistress, Zoë Carbonopsina ('Coal-Black Eyes'). A year or so later Zoë bore him a daughter and then in September 905 a son, who was sickly at first but then recovered. The patriarch Nicholas agreed to baptize the child, the future Constantine VII, on the condition that Zoë leave the Great Palace. But three days after the baptism Leo brought her back, whereupon they were married privately in the royal chapel.

Thus began the affair known as the Tetragamy, or the Fourth Marriage, a scandal that troubled Byzantium for eighteen months before a compromise was agreed upon between Leo and the new patriarch, Euthemius I. Thereupon the Fourth Marriage was recognized as valid and the infant Constantine was legitimized as 'the Porphyrogenitus', or 'Born in the Purple'. When Leo died, on 11 May 912, Constantine was only six, and though he had been crowned as co-emperor four years before he did not inherit his father's throne. Instead Leo was succeeded by his brother Alexander, who had been co-emperor since 879.

*Leo VI (886–912) kneeling before Christ; mosaic over the
Imperial Gate in Haghia Sophia.*

Alexander ruled for only thirteen months. His short reign was a dis-
grace to the empire, beginning when he received the Bulgar ambassadors while drunk, dismissing them with insults, leading Tsar Symeon
to make immediate preparations for war. Alexander staggered from
one alcoholic orgy to another, putting on pagan processions in
public in mockery of the divine liturgy, until he finally collapsed
during a drunken polo match, dying two days later, on 4 June 913.

Zoë's son now succeeded to the throne as Constantine VII. Zoë herself ruled as his regent until 25 March 919, when the general Romanus
Lecapenus took control of Constantinople, establishing himself as
Constantine's protector. Romanus betrothed his daughter Helena to
Constantine, and they were wed in Haghia Sophia on 4 May 919,
three weeks before the emperor's fourteenth birthday. Constantine
appointed his father-in-law as Caesar on 24 September 920, and then
on 17 December 920 Romanus was crowned as co-emperor.

Soon afterwards Romanus built a church and monastery near the

Philadelphaeum, and when these were completed he also erected a palace there. The monastery was known as the Myrelaion, the Place of Myrrh-Oil, a name of ancient but unknown origin. The monastery has long since vanished, but the church of the Myrelaion[1] still stands.

Romanus planned to establish his own dynasty to replace the Macedonian line, crowning his sons Christopher, Stephen and Constantine as co-emperors. But fate intervened to frustrate his plans, beginning with the premature death of Christopher in 932. Romanus was overthrown in a palace revolt on 17 December 944 by his sons Stephen and Constantine. He was then sent off into exile in a monastery on Proti, one of the Princes' Isles, while Stephen and Constantine set themselves up as emperors. But a second palace revolution overthrew them in turn on 27 September 945, after which they were sent off to join their father in his monastery. Stephen and Constantine were subsequently sent off to more distant exile in the Aegean, while their father remained on Proti, where he died on 15 June 948.

Death of Romanus I Lecapenus (919–44); miniature from the Chronicle of Skylitzes.

Thus Constantine VII finally became sole emperor in 945, reigning until his death on 19 November 959. His forces won several notable victories against the Arabs under the leadership of two brilliant generals, Nicephorus Phocas and John Tzimisces, both of whom would also subsequently succeed to the throne of Byzantium.

Constantine devoted much of his time to scholarship, writing several works that are among the most important sources for the history of medieval Byzantium, the best-known being the *Book of Ceremonies*.

We catch a glimpse of the world of Constantine Porphyrogenitus in the writings of Liutprand of Cremona, who first came to Constantinople in 949 as ambassador of King Berengar of Italy. Liutprand describes the incredible scene that he witnessed when he came to the Palace of Magnaura to present his credentials to the emperor:

Next to the imperial residence at Constantinople there is a palace of remarkable size and beauty, which the Greeks call Magnaura, the name signifying 'fresh breeze' . . . Before the throne of the emperor there stood a tree of gilded bronze, its branches full of birds fashioned of the same material, all singing different songs according to their kind. The throne itself was so contrived that at one moment it stood low on the ground and the next moment it would suddenly be raised high in the air. It was of immense size, made of either wood or bronze (for I cannot be sure), and guarded by gilded lions who beat the ground with their tails and emitted dreadful roars, their mouths open and their tongues quivering. Leaning on the shoulders of two eunuchs, I was led into the emperor's presence. Immediately the lions began to roar and the birds began to sing, but I myself displayed no terror or surprise at these marvels, having received prior warnings from others who were already well acquainted with them. After I had three times made my obeisance I raised my head and lo! he whom I had seen only a moment before on a throne scarcely elevated from the ground was now clad in different robes and sitting on a level with the roof. How this was achieved I cannot tell, unless it was by a device similar to those we employ for lifting the timbers of a wine press. He did not address me on this occasion – in view of the distance between us any conversation would have been unseemly – but inquired through his logothete [chief minister] as to the life and health of Berengar. I made an appropriate reply, and then at a signal from the interpreter left the chamber and returned to my lodging.

Constantine was succeeded by his son Romanus, who three years before had scandalized Byzantium by marrying a beautiful courtesan named Theophano, the daughter of a tavern-keeper. Theophano bore Romanus two sons, Basil and Constantine, both of whom were crowned as co-emperor when they were infants.

At the beginning of his reign Romanus II appointed Nicephorus

Phocas as commander-in-chief of the imperial armed forces. Nicephorus mounted an expedition against the Saracens on Crete, and on 7 March 961 he captured their capital at Candia (Heraclion), ending 134 years of Arab rule on the island. Early the following year he led a lightning offensive across the Cilician plain, capturing fifty-five walled towns in twenty-two days. He was about to embark on a renewed offensive the following spring, but it was cancelled when news arrived that Romanus had been killed in a riding accident on 15 March 963.

Theophano had given birth to their daughter Anna just two days before Romanus died. His death left her completely vulnerable, for she had no one to look after her and her three young children. This led her to send a secret message of appeal to Nicephorus Phocas, who assured her that he would be her protector. His soldiers proclaimed him emperor, and on 16 August 963 he entered Constantinople in triumph, riding in procession to Haghia Sophia. There the patriarch Polyeuktos crowned him as Nicephorus II, with the two boy co-emperors Basil and Constantine seated on thrones flanking his own. Then on 20 September Nicephorus was married to Theophano.

Nicephorus mounted a new campaign against the Saracens in 965, when he took Tarsus, using that as a base to reconquer Cyprus. Then in 969 he recaptured Antioch, which had been in Arab hands for 332 years, whereupon he was hailed as 'the Pale Death of the Saracens'.

Theophano had by then become the mistress of the general John Tzimisces, a cousin of Nicephorus. He and Theophano plotted to do away with Nicephorus, and on the night of 10–11 December 969 John and his supporters killed the emperor while he slept in the Bucoleon Palace, after which they took control of the city.

Theophano fully expected that John would now marry her. The patriarch Polyeuktos refused to give his permission, but he agreed that he would crown John if Theophano was exiled. John agreed and sent Theophano to the convent on Proti, after which Polyeuktos crowned him as emperor on Christmas Day 969. John sought to gain legitimacy by wedding the princess Theodora, sister of the late Romanus II, who had been forced into a convent by Theophano. They were duly married in Haghia Sophia in November 971 by the new patriarch, Basil.

John spent the last five years of his reign in a series of brilliant campaigns, beginning with his defeat of Prince Svyatoslav of Kiev in 972. Then in 975 he set off on campaign in the East, conquering Palestine, Syria and the Lebanon – the first Byzantine emperor since Heraclius to set foot in this region. But later that year John became seriously ill and was forced to return to Constantinople, where he died on 11 January 976.

The throne then passed to Basil, eldest son of the late Romanus II, who was seventeen. He was crowned as senior Augustus, while his fourteen-year-old brother Constantine was named as co-emperor. Basil II is one of the very few Byzantine emperors who never married, devoting all of his long and illustrious reign to the affairs of his empire.

Basil's reign was troubled by two revolts led by Bardas Sclerus, brother-in-law of the late emperor John I Tzimisces, the first in 979 and the second in 986–9, both of which were put down. Basil was aided in the second of these struggles by Prince Vladimir of Kiev, to whom he gave his sister Anna in marriage, thus establishing the first dynastic links between Byzantium and Russia. Vladimir sent a fleet to Constantinople early in 989 with a force of 8,000 Varangarians, Russianized Norsemen who afterwards formed the emperor's bodyguard. The Varangarian guard continued in existence until the late Byzantine period, when it was made up largely of mercenary soldiers from England.

In 986 Basil led an army against the Bulgars, who had overrun Greece under Tsar Samuel. Samuel ambushed the imperial army and almost wiped it out, though Basil escaped to fight another day, vowing to take revenge. Basil spent the next quarter of a century campaigning against the Bulgars. The turning-point of this long struggle came in 1014, when his army decisively defeated the Bulgars, capturing some 15,000 of them, although Samuel himself escaped. Basil blinded all of his captives except for one in each hundred, whom he left with one eye each so that they could lead their comrades home. The long line of mutilated Bulgars finally reached the camp of Samuel, who was so shocked by the sight that he dropped dead of apoplexy. Nevertheless the Bulgars fought on for another four years before they surrendered. Thenceforth Basil was known as Bulgaroctonus, the Bulgar-Slayer.

Basil campaigned in north-western Asia in 1021, annexing Georgia and the Armenian kingdom of Ani that same year, thus extending the frontier of the empire to the Araxes river. This was to be his last campaign, and after a short illness he died on 15 December 1025.

Basil was succeeded by his brother, Constantine VIII, who was sixty-five when he came to the throne. Although he had been co-emperor for half a century he had played virtually no part in the governing of the empire, devoting his life exclusively to pleasure. Michael Psellus writes of Constantine's enjoyment of his favourite pastimes – the theatre, horse-racing, gladiatorial combats, hunting, wild-animal combats, and gambling – for which he neglected even the most important affairs of state, including the choice of a successor as his end approached.

Constantine passed over his eldest child, Eudocia, for she had become a nun, and so he chose his second daughter, Zoë, to continue the imperial line. As Psellus describes Zoë, 'The second daughter, whom I saw in her extreme old age, was very regal in her ways, a woman of great beauty, most imposing in her manner and commanding respect.' As her consort the dying Constantine finally selected his distant relative Romanus Argyrus, who was sixty-one. Romanus had been happily married for forty years, but Constantine threatened him with blinding if he did not consent to wed Zoë, forcing his wife to enter a convent so that he would be free to remarry. Thereupon Romanus was married to Zoë, who was then in her fiftieth year. Constantine died three days later, on 10 November 1028. He was laid to rest in the church of the Holy Apostles – the last emperor to be buried there.

The new emperor ascended the throne as Romanus III. Although past his prime, he was still a splendid figure, albeit shallow and lacking the imperial qualities of his great predecessor Basil II. He set off on campaign against the Arabs in 1030, determined to establish himself as a warrior king like his predecessor. But the campaign was a fiasco, as the Byzantines were ambushed by the Saracens and then turned and fled without fighting, with the emperor leading the headlong retreat.

Romanus soon lost interest in Zoë and took a mistress. Zoë herself thereupon took a lover, a youth named Michael the Paphlagonian, to whom she had been introduced by one of his brothers, the eunuch John the Orphanotrophus ('Guardian of the Orphans'). Soon afterwards Romanus became ill, and when taking a therapeutic swim in the palace baths he drowned, on the night of 11–12 April 1034. Psellus tells us that everyone was convinced that Romanus had been killed by the empress and her lover. In any event, Zoë and Michael were married in the Great Palace the next morning by the patriarch Alexis, while the body of Romanus still lay uncovered beside the pool in which he had drowned. The patriarch crowned Zoë's new husband as Michael IV, and later that same day Romanus was buried in the church of the Peribleptos.

Michael's health was poor, and from the symptoms reported by Psellus it would appear that the emperor suffered from oedema and epilepsy. His brother John the Orphanotrophus, who served as prime minister, made plans to keep his family in control of the throne, and so he introduced Zoë to his nephew Michael. This young man was

The empress Zoë (1042) – she and her sister Theodora were the last of the Macedonian dynasty, ruling in their own right; detail of mosaic in the gallery of Haghia Sophia.

generally known as Michael Calaphates, the Caulker, after his father's original profession. Zoë formally adopted him as her son, whereupon the emperor Michael raised him to the rank of Caesar.

Michael IV died on 10 December 1041 and was buried in the monastery of SS. Cosmas and Damian. Immediately after the funeral John the Orphanotrophus asked Zoë to name Michael Calaphates as the successor. Zoë readily agreed, and so on 13 December 1041 her adopted son was crowned as Michael V.

The new emperor was at first subservient to Zoë, behaving deferentially to her whenever they appeared in public. By then he had found an ally in his uncle Constantine, whom he appointed to the post of grand domestic. Constantine had always been jealous of his brother John, and he now used his influence with the emperor to have the Orphanotrophus exiled. Michael decided to get rid of Zoë too, so that he could rule as sole emperor. And so on 18 April 1042 Zoë was forced into a convent on the island of Prinkipo, accepting her fate without protest. The populace were outraged when they heard the news, and they stormed the Great Palace, demanding the restoration of their beloved empress. The fighting continued through the next day, when some 3,000 insurgents were killed by the imperial troops, but the people were now so fired up that they overwhelmed the defenders and captured the building. Michael and Constantine fled and took sanctuary in the church St John of Studius. The mob found them there and dragged them to the square outside, where the two fugitives had their eyes gouged out before being sent into exile, never to return.

Then on 21 April 1042 Zoë was raised to the throne along with her younger sister Theodora, who fifteen years before had been forced into a convent by Constantine VIII. Zoë was then about sixty-four, Theodora a year or two younger, but neither of them looked or acted her age, according to what Psellus writes of the imperial sisters:

The elder was naturally more plump, although she was not strikingly tall. Her eyes were large, set wide apart with imposing eyebrows. Her nose was inclined to be aquiline, without being altogether so. She had golden hair, and her whole body was radiant with the whiteness of her skin. There were few signs of age; in fact, if you marked well the perfect harmony of her limbs, not knowing who she was, you would have said that here is a young woman,

for no part of her skin was wrinkled, but all smooth and taut, and no fur-
rows anywhere. Theodora, on the other hand, was taller and more taper of
form. Her head was small, and out of proportion with the rest of her body.
She was more ready with her tongue than Zoë ... and quicker in her movements. There was nothing stern in her glance: on the contrary, she was cheerful and smiling, eager to find any opportunity to talk.

The joint reign of Zoë and Theodora lasted for less than three
months. During that time it was agreed that a vigorous man was
needed to rule the empire. Theodora absolutely refused to marry, while
Zoë was anxious to wed again, and so the search began to find a suitable candidate. The final choice was Constantine Monomachus, a
wealthy aristocrat who had been exiled seven years before. The patriarch Alexis refused to sanction the wedding, since both Constantine
and Zoë had been wed twice, and so they were married by a palace
chaplain. Alexis then relented, and on the following day, 12 June 1042,
he officiated in Haghia Sophia as Zoë crowned her husband as
Constantine IX.

Constantine was a splendid figure of a man, according to Psellus,
but he was totally ineffectual as a ruler. His spirit of generosity led
him to confer honours and high positions on everyone he liked, regardless of social class, as Psellus writes in Book VI of the *Chronographia*:

At the start of his reign Constantine ruled neither with vigour nor with dis-
cretion ... the doors of the Senate were thrown open to nearly all the rascally
vagabonds of the market, and the honour was bestowed not on two or three,
nor a mere handful, but the whole gang was elevated to the highest offices of
state by single decree, immediately after he became emperor. Inevitably this
provided occasion for rites and solemn ceremonies, with all the city overjoyed
at the thought that their new sovereign was a person of such generosity.

Some of the working class took advantage of the emperor's liber-
ality by pursuing careers in the Church. This is recorded by the chronicler Christopher of Mitylene, who notes that 'Gatekeepers, vineyard
workers, cattle merchants, greengrocers, bakers, blacksmiths, gar-
deners, cobblers, pedlars, all want to become priests.' He complains
that these people are so ignorant, most of them scarcely literate, that
they cannot conduct Church services properly and keep introducing

into the liturgy words used in their trades. He also mocks the super-stitions of the uneducated clergy, noting that a monk named Andrew had a relic collection that had ten hands of St Procopius and eight feet of St Nestor, along with many parts of other saints. Psellus similarly mocked the superstitious clergy, but he was fascinated by a saint-fool named Elias, who, according to Michael Angold, 'seems to have had an encyclopaedic knowledge of Constantinople's low life. He was just as much at home in a brothel as he was in a monastery, by day giving himself to God and by night sharing himself with Satan. He was quite original, worshipping God and Mammon equally.'

By the time Constantine married Zoë he already had a mistress, a beautiful patrician named Sclerina. Soon after he became emperor Constantine brought her to the palace and introduced her to Zoë, after which he set up his mistress in the Palace of Magnaura. Constantine carried on his affair with Sclerina quite openly, often appearing in public together with her and Zoë, who apparently had no objection to his living with his mistress. According to Psellus, Zoë spent all of her time making perfumes and unguents in her apartment, which he says took on the appearance of an alchemist's laboratory, with her servants working away in an inferno of blazing braziers. 'Zoë was apparently unaffected by the heat,' Psellus notes. 'In fact, both she and her sister seemed naturally perverse. They despised fresh air, fine houses, meadows, gardens; the charm of such things meant nothing to them. On the other hand, once they were inside their own private rooms . . . then they really enjoyed themselves.'

Constantine's affair with Sclerina became common knowledge in Constantinople, where the populace highly disapproved of his behaviour. This led to a revolt on 9 March 1044, with the rioters laying down their arms only after an appeal by Zoë and Theodora. Constantine took strong measures to punish those who had taken part in the revolt, and a chronicler writes of 'Jews, Mussulmans, and Armenians' being driven from Constantinople. Sclerina died soon afterwards, and the grief-stricken Constantine buried her at St George of the Mangana.

Zoë died in 1050, though the chronicles do not give the exact date of her death. Psellus reports that Constantine was 'completely heart-broken' at the death of Zoë, but he consoled himself with his new mistress, a young Alan princess who was being held hostage by the

Byzantines. He spent all of his time with her and his court jester, a dwarf who shared the emperor's bed at night.

During the last year of Constantine's reign a serious dispute arose between Pope Leo IX and the patriarch Michael Cerularius. The dispute reached its climax in Haghia Sophia during an afternoon service on Saturday 16 July 1054, when Cardinal Humbert, one of three papal legates, strode down the main aisle and placed a scroll on the high altar, a formal bull of excommunication against Cerularius and his supporters. Soon afterwards Cerularius convened a synod which excommunicated the three papal legates, causing a schism between the Greek Orthodox and Roman Catholic churches that continues to the present day.

By then Constantine Monomachus was a dying man. He lingered on into the new year, finally passing away on 11 January 1055, after which he was buried in the church of St George beside his beloved Sclerina.

Since Constantine died without a legal heir, 'supreme power passed into the hands of Theodora', as Psellus writes. Theodora was about seventy-five when she began her last reign, which lasted for only eighteen months. Despite her advanced years she showed few signs of her age, taking full charge of the government. Nevertheless there was unanimous agreement that she should appoint a man as her successor; but as long as she remained in good health she refused to do so. Towards the end of August 1056 Theodora was suddenly stricken by an abdominal illness that caused her severe pain, and it was apparent to all that her end was near. Her councillors then put forward their candidate for emperor, an aged civil servant named Michael Bringas, whom Theodora accepted as her successor. She died that same day, 31 August 1056, whereupon Bringas succeeded as Michael VI.

Theodora was the last of the Macedonian house, the dynasty that had ruled Byzantium for 189 years, beginning with her great-great-great-grandfather Basil I. It was the end of an age in which Byzantium had been re-established as the empire beyond compare, its boundaries stretching from Persia to the Adriatic and from the Danube to the Aegean isles, the capital at Constantinople emerging from the darkness of the Middle Ages in a renaissance that made it a centre of classical culture in a world that had nearly descended to barbarism. But the great dynasty that had reigned through this revival died with Theodora, the Porphyrogenita, Born in the Purple.

CHAPTER 12

The Dynasty of the Comneni
1056–1185

The reign of Michael VI lasted less than a year. During the spring of 1057 the general staff of the army decided that they would overthrow him in favour of one of their own number. The commander-in-chief Isaac Comnenus was the obvious choice, and the army in Asia Minor proclaimed him as emperor on 8 June 1057. When news of this reached the capital the Senate forced Michael VI to abdicate, whereupon he fled to Haghia Sophia for sanctuary. He was then allowed to retire to a monastery, where he died soon afterwards.

Isaac Comnenus entered Constantinople at the head of his army on 1 September 1057 and received an enthusiastic welcome, as Michael Psellus writes:

All the populace of the city poured out to honour him. Some brought lighted torches, as though he were God himself. Others sprinkled sweet perfumes over him. Everyone in his own peculiar way tried to please him. Without exception the people treated the occasion as a festal day. There was dancing and rejoicing everywhere ... in all my life I have not seen such splendour. It was not merely the people of the city, nor the Senate, nor the host of farmers and merchants that made up that happy throng; there were students of the theological colleges there, and dwellers on the mountain-tops, and hermits who had left their communal homes in the carved rock-tombs; the stylites too, who lived in mid-air, joined in the crowds. All of them, whether they had slipped out from their rocks, or come down from their aerial perches, or exchanged the mountain heights for the level plains, all made the emperor's procession into the City a most memorable sight.

Isaac immediately began a complete reform of the government, restoring the neglected armed forces of the empire. He successfully defended the empire's frontiers in both Asia and Europe, holding the Magyars at bay and leading a successful expedition against the Patzinaks, a nomadic people from the plains of southern Russia, when they crossed the Danube in 1059. But that was to be his last campaign, for late in that year he caught cold while out hunting and came down with pneumonia, from which he never recovered.

During his last days Isaac considered the question of his succession, the likeliest candidate being his brother John. But the landowning military aristocracy persuaded him to pass over John and choose one of their own, Constantine Doucas. Doucas was thereupon crowned as Constantine X on 23 November 1059. Isaac then retired to the monastery of the Studion, where he died the following year.

After Isaac's death his brother John Comnenus retired into obscurity, along with his wife, Anna Dalassena, and their eight children. After John died, c. 1067, Anna used every effort to have her family regain the throne from the Doucas clan, with her three sons – Manuel, Isaac and Alexius – becoming generals.

When Constantine came to the throne he was married to his second wife, Eudocia Macrembolitissa, described by Psellus as 'a woman of great spirit and exceptional beauty', who bore him seven children. Constantine proved to be completely ineffective as an emperor. He neglected the armed forces, hiring unreliable foreign mercenaries, and he allowed the bureaucracy to become as bloated and corrupt as it had been before Isaac's reforms. Thus the government and the military were seriously weakened, and at a time when the empire was facing great danger from new and powerful enemies. The Normans under Robert Guiscard had overrun southern Italy, and the Selcuk (or Seljuk) Turks had conquered Persia, penetrating deep into Asia Minor and setting the stage for their subsequent conquest of the subcontinent.

The year 1066 was marked by the appearance of a fiery celestial phenomenon now recognized to be Halley's comet, which in Constantinople was believed to be an omen of impending doom. Constantine became seriously ill, and on his deathbed he declared that his wife, Eudocia, should succeed him with the rank of autocrator, with their sixteen-year-old son Michael as co-emperor. Constantine also named his brother, the Caesar John, as guardian of Michael and his other children, after which he died in May 1067.

Thus Eudocia succeeded to the throne, though as autocrator rather than Augusta, with her son Michael the nominal co-emperor. Eudocia ruled only until the end of the year, by which time she had arranged to marry the general Romanus Diogenes, who had been exiled by Constantine. After his return to Constantinople they were married on 1 January 1068, and that same day he was crowned as Romanus IV.

Romanus immediately reorganized the armed forces of the empire to take action against the Selcuks, leading expeditions against them in 1068 and 1069. Then in the summer of 1071 he set out on what he hoped would be a decisive campaign; but on 26 August his army was virtually annihilated by the Selcuk sultan Alp Arslan at Manzikert in eastern Anatolia. Romanus was captured by Alp Arslan and then released after agreeing to the sultan's terms, which were that the empire would cede its south-eastern provinces to the Selcuks and pay a large annual indemnity. That same year the Normans took the last remaining Byzantine possessions in Italy.

When news of the catastrophe at Manzikert arrived in Constantinople the Caesar John Doucas took control of the government before Romanus could return to the capital. He then had his nephew Michael Doucas proclaimed as sole emperor, while he sent the empress Eudocia into exile, along with the late Isaac's sister-in-law, Anna Dalassena. The patriarch John Xiphilinus crowned the new emperor as Michael VII in Haghia Sophia on 24 October 1071.

Meanwhile Romanus had gathered a force to regain his throne, but he was eventually captured and blinded. He was then exiled to a monastery on the isle of Proti, where he died on 4 August 1072.

Soon after Michael came to the throne he married the princess Martha, daughter of King Bagrat IV of Georgia, who then changed her name to Maria. She was known popularly as Maria of Alania, on the mistaken notion that she was an Alan princess. Their marriage produced only one child, a son named Constantine. Michael reigned until the spring of 1078, when he was overthrown by the general Nicephorus Botaneiates. Michael was allowed to retire as a monk in the Studion, where he lived on for another twelve years, while his wife had her marriage annulled and took refuge in the Petrion monastery with her son, Constantine. Botaneiates led his troops into Constantinople on 24 March 1078, and on that same day he was crowned in Haghia Sophia as Nicephorus III.

Nicephorus was in his late seventies when he became emperor. Since he was a childless widower, he sought to strengthen his hold on the throne by proposing marriage to Maria of Alania. Maria agreed, hoping thus to give her son an opportunity to succeed to the throne. But after their marriage Nicephorus refused to recognize Constantine as his heir, and so Maria began to conspire with Alexius Comnenus, son of Anna Dalassena. Alexius was appointed commander-in-chief of the army in the West, and then in 1078 he married Eirene Doucina,

Nicephorus III Botaneiates (1078–81) between
St John Chrysostom and an angel; miniature from a
Byzantine manuscript.

granddaughter of the Caesar John Doucas, thus forming a powerful alliance between the Comnenus and Doucas families.

John Doucas gave his backing to Alexius Comnenus when he made a move to seize the throne in 1081. On 1 April of that year the Caesar bribed the German mercenaries guarding the gates of Constantinople to permit the entry of Alexius and his troops, who quickly seized control of the city. Nicephorus abdicated and was forced to retire to the Peribleptos monastery, where he died soon afterwards.

The new emperor was crowned as Alexius I on 4 April 1081. Alexius was about twenty-four when he came to the throne, while his wife, Eirene, was not yet fifteen. They eventually had four sons and five daughters, the first born being Anna, who would later write the history of her father's reign in the *Alexiad*. Their first son was the future John II, who was born in 1088 and four years later crowned as co-emperor.

At the outset of his reign Alexius raised his mother, Anna Dalassena, to the rank of Augusta. She remained the power behind the throne until 1100. She then retired to the convent of the church of St Saviour Pantepoptes,[1] Christ the All-Seeing, which she had founded on the summit of the Fourth Hill, above the Golden Horn, where she died five years later.

Alexius began his reign faced with powerful enemies on all of the empire's frontiers. By then the Selcuks had overrun most of Asia Minor, establishing a state known as the Sultanate of Rum, with its capital at Iconium (Konya). At the same time the Normans had invaded Greece, though Robert Guiscard's dream of capturing Constantinople ended with his sudden death in 1085. No sooner had the Norman threat ended than new crises arose in the Balkans, and Alexius had to fight off invasions by the Patzinaks and another Turkic tribe called the Cumans. The Patzinaks besieged Constantinople in 1090, while at the same time the city was attacked from the sea by the fleet of Tzachas, the Turkish emir of Smyrna. But the Byzantine navy destroyed the Turkish fleet in a blaze of 'Greek fire', while Alexius annihilated the Patzinak army.

Alexius then faced a new challenge with the onset of the First Crusade. The great feudal lords of western Europe began arriving in Constantinople towards the end of 1096, most notably Counts

Godfrey of Bouillon and Bohemund of Taranto, son of the late Robert Guiscard. After a battle with the crusaders outside the Theodosian Walls, Alexius persuaded Godfrey and Bohemund to swear an oath of allegiance to him, in which they pledged that they would return to the empire any of its former possessions that they might recapture.

Early in the twelfth century Alexius began a campaign to suppress the Bogomils, a heretical sect that had developed in the Balkans. He arrested their leader, a monk named Basil, who was brought to Constantinople for trial along with his followers. The Bogomils who refused to renounce their heresy were at first threatened with being burned at the stake, but Alexius relented and instead had them imprisoned for life. But Basil was so contemptuous of all threats that Alexius condemned him to be burned at the stake in the Hippodrome, a scene described by Anna Comnena in Book XV of the *Alexiad*:

So there stood the abominable Basil, unmoved by any threat or fear, and gaped now at the fire and now at the bystanders. And all thought him quite mad for he did not rush to the pyre nor did he draw back, but stood fixed and immobile on the spot he had first taken up ... Then they ... took him and pushed him, clothes, shoes and all, into the middle of the pyre. And the flames, as if deeply enraged against him, ate the impious man up, without any odour arising or even a fresh appearance of smoke, only one thin smoky line could be seen in the midst of the flames ... Then the people looking on clamoured loudly that the rest who belonged to Basil's pernicious sect should be thrown into the fire as well, but the emperor did not allow it but ordered them to be confined to the porches and verandahs of the largest palace.

Alexius spent the last two decades of his reign campaigning against the Turks in Asia Minor. He died on 15 August 1118, after which he was succeeded by his son John. John had already married the princess Priska, daughter of King Ladislaus of Hungary, who changed her name to Eirene. Eirene eventually bore John four sons and four daughters, including a set of twins. She died in 1126, and John buried her in the monastery of the church of St Saviour Pantocrator,[2] Christ the All-Powerful, which he and Eirene had built on the Fourth Hill.

John II's first campaign was in 1119, when he cleared the Turks from Ionia, Lydia and Pamphylia. Then in the years 1121-2 he defeated the Patzinaks, who thenceforth furnished troops to the imperial forces. This victory was long remembered in Constantinople, commemorated with an annual holiday known as Patzinak Day.

John fought a war against Venice in the years 1122–5, and then in 1129 he defeated King Stephen II of Hungary. During 1137–43 he led a series of campaigns to recapture Antioch from the Latins. On the last of these campaigns he accidentally wounded himself with a poisoned arrow while hunting, dying on 8 April 1143. His remains were brought back to Constantinople, where he was laid to rest in the church of the Pantocrator beside his wife. The emperor was known in his time as Kalo Ioannis, or John the Good; the chronicler Nicetas Choniates writes that 'He was the best of all the emperors, from the family of the Comneni, who ever sat upon the Roman throne.'

John was succeeded by his son Manuel, who was crowned in Haghia Sophia on 28 November 1143. Manuel's first wife, Eirene, died in 1160 without producing a son. The following year Manuel married Maria of Antioch, described by a chronicler as 'the most beautiful princess of her time'. Eight years later Maria gave birth to a boy, Alexius, and Manuel finally had a legitimate heir to the throne, having already sired a bastard son by his mistress Theodora, his niece.

During the first three years of his reign Manuel strengthened the defences of Constantinople, replacing part of the Theodosian Walls on the Sixth Hill with a new fortification known as the Wall of Manuel Comnenus.[3] He also fortified an islet off the Asian shore at the mouth of the Bosphorus, a place now known as Kız Kulesi,[4] the Maiden's Tower.

Manuel's first campaign was against the Latins of Antioch, whom he defeated in 1144, forcing them to surrender several fortresses in Cilicia that they had taken when his father died. The Latins were now so weak that the Turks easily conquered the county of Edessa, leading Pope Eugenius III to call for the Second Crusade in 1146.

One contingent of crusaders set out from Germany under the leadership of King Conrad and a second one left from France led by Louis VII, both of them planning to pass through Constantinople *en route* to the Holy Land. The Germans were the first to arrive in Constantinople, and the Byzantines fought a pitched battle with them before they were ferried across the strait to Nicomedia.

Manuel had no trouble with the French, and he entertained King

The Wall of Manuel Comnenus.

Kız Kulesi, the Maiden's Tower, known in English
as Leander's Tower.

Louis at a banquet in the Blachernae Palace. Odo of Deuil, in his chronicle of the Second Crusade, writes of Blachernae and other places that Louis and his knights were shown in their tour of 'Constantinople, rich in renown and richer still in possessions'. But although he lavishes praise on Blachernae and Haghia Sophia, Odo was appalled at the conditions in which the poorer people of the city lived, as he writes:

The city itself is squalid and fetid and in many places harmed by permanent darkness, for the wealthy overshadow the streets with buildings and leave these dirty, dark places to the poor and travellers; there murders and robberies and other crimes which love the darkness are committed. Moreover, since people live lawlessly in this city, which has as many lords as rich men and almost as many thieves as poor men, a criminal knows neither fear nor shame, because crime is not punished by law and never entirely comes to light. In every respect she exceeds moderation; for, just as she surpasses other cities in wealth, so, too, does she surpass them in vice.

Benjamin of Tudela, a Sephardic Jew from Spain, describes some of the sights he saw in Constantinople during Manuel's reign:

Great stir and bustle prevails at Constantinople in consequence of the conflux of many merchants, who resort thither, both by land and sea, from all parts of the world for purposes of trade, including merchants from Babylon and from Mesopotamia, from Media and Persia, from Egypt and Palestine, as well as from Russia, Hungary, Patzinakia, Budia, Lombardy and Spain ...

At Constantinople is the place of worship called St Sophia and the metropolitan seat of the pope of the Greeks, who are at variance with the pope of Rome ... The Hippodrome is a public place near the wall of the palace, set aside for the king's sports. Every year the birthday of Jesus the Nazarene is celebrated there with public rejoicings. On these occasions you may see there representations of all the nations who inhabit the different parts of the world, with surprising feats of jugglery. Lions, bears, leopards, and wild asses, as well as birds, which have been trained to fight each other, are also exhibited. All this sport, the equal of which is nowhere to be met with, is carried on in the presence of the king and queen.

King Manuel has built a large palace for his residence on the sea-shore, near the palace built by his predecessors; and to this edifice is given the name Blachernes. The pillars and walls are covered with pure gold, and all the wars of the ancients, as well as his own, are represented in pictures.

Benjamin also reports on the oppressive life of the Jews in Constantinople, who included schismatic Karaites as well as those of the Orthodox community.

The number of Jews at Constantinople amounts to two thousand Rabbanites and five hundred Caraites, who live on one spot, but divided by a wall ... Many of them are manufacturers of silk cloth, many others are merchants, some being extremely rich, but no Jew is allowed to ride upon a horse, except Solomon Hamitsri, who is the king's physician, and by whose influence the Jews enjoy many advantages even in their state of oppression, which is very severely felt by them; and the hatred against them is increased by the practice of the tanners, who pour their filthy water in the streets and even before the very doors of the Jews, who, being thus defiled, become objects of contempt to the Greeks.

Their yoke is severely felt by the Jews, both good and bad; for they are exposed to being beaten in the streets, and must submit to all kinds of bad treatment. Still the Jews are rich, good, benevolent and religious men, who bear the misfortunes of their exile with humility.

A Greek chronicler writes of how even the main avenues of twelfth-century Constantinople were quagmires of mud during the winter rains, becoming 'infernal lakes' in which men and beasts of burden were bemired and sometimes drowned, the unlighted streets infested with thieves and other criminals, along with packs of stray dogs.

We catch another glimpse of life in twelfth-century Constantinople in the letters of John Tzetzes, a poet who had been hired as a tutor by the emperor Manuel. He remarks in one letter that the Byzantine capital had become a polyglot Babel: 'those dwelling in Constantinople are not of one language or one race, but use a mixture of strange tongues. There are Cretans and Turks, Alans, Rhodians, and Chiots, notorious thieves.' Another of his letters describes the saint-fools who continued to be popular in Constantinople. The letter is addressed to a runaway slave, Demetrius Gobinos, who had started life as a sausage-maker; Tzetzes asks why he does not return to

Constantinople, when hordes of holy lunatics and mendicant monks are living well on charity there:

For now, every disgusting and thrice-accursed wretch like you only has to put on a monastic habit, or hang bells from his penis or wrap fetters or chains round his feet, or a rope or chain around his neck – in short to dress himself up to look self-effacing in an ostentatious and highly calculated air of artless simplicity. Immediately the city of Constantinople showers him with honours, and the rogue is publicly feted as a saint above the apostles, above the martyrs.

Twelfth-century Constantinople was a violent city, its people always ready to riot or revolt, according to the historian Nicetas Choniates:

The throngs of other cities rejoice in disorder and are with great difficulty kept in hand. But the populace of the market-place in Constantinople is the most disorderly of all, rejoicing in rashness and walking in crooked ways. As it is governed by different peoples and because of the variety of the trades, one may say that its mind is easily altered. But since the worst always wins out, and one scarcely finds among the sour grapes a ripe one, the populace of the market-place upon whatever undertaking it embarks, does not do so reasonably, nor with good will, nor suitably. But at a mere word it disposes itself to rebellion and becomes more destructive than fire … accordingly, it suffers from an inconstancy of character and is untrustworthy. Nor are these people ever detected doing those things which are most advantageous to themselves, nor were they ever persuaded by others who counselled them for their own good. But they always do those things which are detrimental … Their indifference to the rulers is preserved in them as if it were inborn. Him whom today they raise as local magistrate, this same one next year they will tear to pieces. They do not perform these things with any logic, but through simple-mindedness and ignorance.

The civil bureaucracy proliferated during Manuel's reign. This new class of petty bourgeoisie is described in a satirical poem attributed to one Theodorus Ptochoprodromos, who contrasts its affluence with the impoverishment of clergymen like himself. The poem is in the form of a letter to Theodorus by his father, who advises him to get a good education so that he can prosper as a civil servant:

My child, learn your letters as soon as you are able. See that man over there, my child, he used to walk on foot, and now he has a fat mule with a fine harness. This one, when he was a student, used to go barefoot, and see him now in his pointed boots! The other one, when he was a student, never combed his hair, and now he is well-combed and proud of his locks. That one in his student days never saw a bath door from afar, and now he bathes three times a week. That one was full of lice as big as almonds, and now his purse is full of gold pieces with the emperor Manuel's effigy.

Manuel had dreams of recreating the empire as it had been in the days of Justinian, and this involved him in a series of campaigns and negotiations that occupied him for most of his long reign. He fought the Normans, Venetians, Serbs and Hungarians in the West, and in the East he battled against the Selcuk Turks and the Armenians.

The empire's conflict with Venice began on 12 March 1171, when Manuel evicted the Venetian merchants from Constantinople, where for nearly a century they had occupied a quarter on the Golden Horn adjacent to those of the Genoese and the Pisans. The Venetians retaliated by sending their fleet to attack Byzantine ports on the coasts and islands of Greece, and in addition they formed alliances with the Germans and Normans against Byzantium. An armed truce followed, but for the remainder of Manuel's reign all diplomatic and commercial relations between Byzantium and Venice were broken off. The alienation between Greek East and Latin West grew apace, with all of Roman Catholic Europe aligned against the schismatic Byzantines, who on their part were contemptuous of the only recently civilized westerners and their upstart rulers. Hugh Eteriano, a Pisan who had settled in Constantinople during Manuel's reign, notes that Latins (who included Italians, French, Normans and Spaniards) were then 'pointed out in the streets of the capital as objects of hate and detestation'. Nicetas Choniates writes that 'The accursed Latins ... lust after our possessions and would like to destroy our race ... between them and us there is a wide gulf of hatred, our outlooks are completely different, and our paths go in opposite directions.'

Despite this mutual antipathy Manuel himself was held in high esteem in the West. He admired the prowess of the western knights with whom he came in contact, striving to outdo the Latins in the jousting tournaments that he held in the Hippodrome. He also gave preferment to Latins over Greeks in his court, leading the populace to despise the foreigners even more intensely. The Byzantine contempt for the Latin West led the Greeks of Constantinople to look back to their roots in ancient Hellas, proudly referring to themselves as Hellenes.

Manuel's last diplomatic effort in the West was to arrange the betrothal of his son Alexius to Princess Agnes of France, daughter of Louis VII. The little princess, who was barely eight years old when she left France, took the name of Anna when she was married to the twelve-year-old Alexius in Haghia Sophia on 2 March 1180.

Manuel was at that time suffering through his last illness and had retired as a monk to the monastery of the Pantocrator, where he died on 24 September 1180. Beside his tomb was one of the most sacred of the relics that had been brought back from Jerusalem after it had been liberated in the First Crusade, a porphyry slab on which Christ's body is supposed to have been laid after his deposition from the Cross, and on which the stains of Mary's tears could still be seen, it was said.

Manuel was succeeded by his son Alexius. Since Alexius was only twelve at the time, his mother, Maria of Antioch, was appointed to serve as regent. Maria gave all of the most prestigious positions in her court to Latins, and this made her extremely unpopular among both the common people and the Greek aristocracy of Constantinople, who referred to her contemptuously as 'the foreign woman'. This led them to give their support to Andronicus Comnenus, a nephew of John II.

Andronicus was a dashing and handsome adventurer who had won renown for his courage in battle, though his intrigues had led Manuel to exile him. At the time of Manuel's death Andronicus was about sixty-five, living in retirement at his estate in Paphlagonia. But despite his age, according to Nicetas Choniates, Andronicus was still vigorous and in rude health: 'The condition of his body was excellent, of venerable aspect, of heroic stature, and even in his old age, he had a youthful face. His body was outstandingly healthy because he was neither voluptuous nor gluttonous, nor a drunkard, but like the Homeric heroes lived simply and moderately.' Andronicus mustered his supporters and marched on Constantinople in the early spring of

1182, pausing when he reached the Bosphorus. He sent his troops into Constantinople, where they were joined by the townspeople in a general massacre of the Latins, after which he himself finally entered the city and took control. The empress Maria was tried and convicted of treason, whereupon she was at first confined to a convent and soon afterwards secretly drowned. Andronicus thereupon declared himself regent for Alexius II, and in September 1182 he was crowned as co-emperor. Shortly afterwards Andronicus had Alexius strangled, leaving the empress Anna a widow at the age of thirteen. Towards the end of the year Andronicus married Anna, though they differed in age by half a century, scandalizing both Byzantium and western Europe.

Andronicus soon began a reign of terror, executing anyone he thought might be a threat to the throne. At the same time the empire came under attack by the Selcuks, the Hungarians and the Normans, who invaded Greece. The Normans took Thessalonica in the summer of 1185 and then advanced upon Constantinople. The populace panicked at the approach of the Latins and castigated Andronicus for not making adequate preparations for defending the city. Andronicus responded by arresting all of his opponents and condemning them to death. Among them was a distant relative of the Comneni named Isaac Angelus, who escaped from his captors and took refuge in Haghia Sophia, where he called on the populace for support. They responded to his call, and on 12 September 1185 he was raised to the throne as Isaac II.

Andronicus fled, but was captured and imprisoned in a tower of the Blachernae Palace. Soon afterwards he was dragged from his prison and paraded through the streets of the city riding backwards on a camel, which brought him to the Hippodrome. There he was mutilated and then hacked to death, his body left to rot near the arena for days afterwards, until his remains were finally flung into the sea.

The death of Andronicus brought to an end the dynasty of the Comneni, who had ruled over Byzantium for more than a century. But the lineage survived through Alexius and David Comnenus, grandsons of Andronicus, who began another Byzantine dynasty in Trebizond – one that would outlast Byzantium itself, though only by a few years.

CHAPTER 13

The Latin Conquest
1185–1261

When Isaac II Angelus came to the throne the Normans were marching on Constantinople. But within a year he defeated the invaders and
forced them to return to Italy, where they had established a kingdom
in the southern end of the peninsula, as well as in Sicily.

Isaac was thirty years old when he became emperor, a widower with
two daughters and a son, the future Alexius IV. His daughter Eirene
was married in 1192 to King Roger of Sicily, who died eighteen
months after their wedding. Then in 1197 Eirene was married to
Philip of Swabia, brother of the German emperor Henry VI.

Since Isaac was a widower he sought a suitable wife among the royal
families of western Europe, and when an embassy came from Bela III
of Hungary he began negotiations for the hand of the king's daughter
Margaret. The negotiations were successful, and in 1186 the princess,
who was then not quite ten years old, came to Constantinople and was
married to Isaac, changing her name to Maria.

Two years after Isaac came to the throne he had to deal with the
onset of the Third Crusade. The Germans under Frederick I
Barbarossa passed through Constantinople without incident, while
the other crusaders travelled by sea to the southern shore of Asia
Minor. Barbarossa never reached the Holy Land, for on 10 June 1190
he drowned while fording a river in southern Asia Minor.

Meanwhile Isaac had dealt with the Selcuks in Asia Minor,
successfully keeping them at bay while he fought against the Vlachs,
Bulgars, Serbs and Cumans in the Balkans. The Vlachs and Bulgars
defeated imperial armies in 1190 and again in 1194, after which Isaac
himself took the field against them. But while he was on campaign in

the summer of 1195 his older brother Alexius staged a coup in the camp and took him prisoner, after which he was blinded. Isaac was then imprisoned in a tower of the Blachernae Palace along with his son, Alexius. The new emperor was crowned in Haghia Sophia as Alexius III, with his wife, Euphrosyne, enthroned as empress.

During the first five years of his reign Alexius personally led several campaigns, fighting against the Selcuks in Asia Minor and the Vlachs in the Balkans. While on campaign against the Vlachs in 1201 the emperor was accompanied by his young nephew Alexius, whom he had released from prison. Alexius took the opportunity to escape from his uncle and fled to take refuge with his sister Eirene and her husband, Philip of Swabia, after which he began making appeals in the West to have his father restored to the throne of Byzantium.

left to right: *Isaac II Angelus (1185–95, 1203–4), Alexius III Angelus (1195–1203) and Alexius IV Angelus (1203–4); pen-and-wash drawings from the* Zonaras Chronicle.

Pope Innocent III succeeded to the papal throne in January 1198, and in August he issued an encyclical calling for a Fourth Crusade. The nucleus of an expeditionary force came into being in November 1199, when a number of French nobles took the Cross, most notably Count Baldwin of Flanders. Envoys of the French counts went to Venice to arrange with Doge Enrico Dandolo and his council for ships to transport the crusaders overseas. The Venetians set a price for the transports that they would supply, also contributing fifty of their own warships fully manned, on the condition that Venice should share fully with the crusaders in any conquests made on the campaign. After the return of the envoys a council was held at Soissons, where the marquis Boniface of Montferrat was chosen to lead the Crusade.

When the crusader leaders finally mustered their forces in Italy they had only some 11,000 fighting men – about a third of the number that they had expected. They were thus unable to pay the Venetians the sum that they had agreed upon, and at first it looked as if the expedition would be aborted. But Doge Dandolo struck a deal with them, in which Venice would defer payment of the remaining passage money if the crusaders helped them recapture the Dalmatian city of Zara, which had defected to the Hungarians. The knights agreed, whereupon they embarked at Venice on 8 September 1202, bound for Zara in a Venetian fleet of 480 ships led by the galley of the doge.

The fleet reached Zara on 10 November and attacked the city, which surrendered after a two-week siege. The garrison and populace were unharmed, but the Latins stripped the city of all of its movable possessions, dividing the loot between them. It was then too late in the season to sail on to the Aegean, so the expedition wintered in Zara.

Boniface joined the crusaders at Zara in mid-December. Two weeks later envoys arrived bearing a message from Alexius Angelus, who promised that if the expedition restored his father, Isaac, to the Byzantine throne he would agree to a union of the Greek and Roman Churches under the papacy. Moreover he would give a huge sum of money to the Latins, as well as paying all of their expenses for an additional year. The crusader leaders accepted the offer, and Doge Dandolo agreed to divert the expedition to Constantinople.

The Latin fleet finally reached Chalcedon on 24 June 1203 and disembarked on the Asian side of the strait. The crusaders then crossed the Bosphorus and stormed the Castle of Galata, a fortress at the mouth of the Golden Horn, breaking the chain that closed the entrance to the port. They constructed a bridge of boats to cross over the Golden Horn, after which they set up their encampment outside the walls at Blachernae. The Venetian fleet then sailed into the port, bombarding the sea walls along the Golden Horn.

After ten days of preparations the crusaders launched their attack on 17 July, making an all-out assault on the sea walls along the Golden Horn. Doge Dandolo stood on the bow of his flagship with the banner of St Mark unfurled before him, and his men put him ashore as they made their initial attack on the walls of the Petrion. The assault captured twenty-five towers of the sea walls, with the crusaders throwing down burning brands to set fire to the houses inside the fortifications, destroying the whole neighbourhood below the Fifth Hill.

As soon as night fell Alexius III escaped from the city with his daughter Eirene, taking with him 10,000 gold pieces and the crown jewels. That same night the abandoned Byzantine officials released Isaac II from his prison tower and restored him to the throne. Shortly before dawn they sent messengers to inform the Latins of their action, with Isaac pledging to honour all of the commitments that his son, Alexius, had made to the crusaders. The Byzantines then opened the gates of the city and the Latins marched into Constantinople, bringing Isaac's son with them. The following day the Latins withdrew their troops from the city in order to avoid a riot with the populace. Isaac's son was then raised to the throne as Alexius IV, crowned as co-emperor with his father in Haghia Sophia on 1 August 1203.

Alexius soon became very unpopular among the people of Constantinople, for he spent all of his time carousing with the Latins who had placed him on the throne. At the same time the Latins were growing increasingly impatient with him, for he was unable to make good the promises he had made, so they began seizing gold and silver objects from the churches of the city. A riot broke out on 19 August, when a mob stormed the Latin quarter, starting a fire that spread as far as the summit of the First Hill and damaged the porch of Haghia Sophia, adding to the frustrated rage of the populace.

The aristocracy in Constantinople was as unhappy with Alexius IV as were the populace and the Latins. The leader of the opposition was Alexius Ducas, known as Mourtzouphlos, or Black-Browed. Mourtzouphlos was a great-great-grandson of Alexius I Comnenus, and his supporters held that he had a far more valid claim to the throne than the upstart Angeli. Late in January 1204, after the populace had held a mass meeting in Haghia Sophia demanding the overthrow of the emperor, Mourtzouphlos came to tell the terrified Alexius IV that he had come to help him escape from a mob that was marching on the palace to kill him. Alexius let himself be smuggled from Blachernae by Mourtzouphlos, who had him imprisoned in a hiding-place outside the city. Then, on 5 February 1204, Mourtzouphlos had himself raised to the throne as Alexius V. Isaac II died of natural causes at about this time, reducing the number of rivals that Mourtzouphlos now set out to eliminate. Twice he tried to poison the imprisoned Alexius IV, but when both attempts failed Mourtzouphlos had him strangled.

As soon as he was in full control Mourtzouphlos sent a message to the crusaders telling them to clear out of his territory within a week. Then, after one last futile meeting with Dandolo, he began making preparations to defend the city against a renewed Latin assault.

The Latins began their assault on 9 April 1204, making their first attack on the land walls outside the Blachernae Palace. The attack was repelled, as was the assault that the Latin fleet made against the sea walls along the Golden Horn, their efforts frustrated by a south wind that drove the galleys away from the shore. The Latins attacked again three days later, when the prevailing north wind once again began to blow, and this time they succeeded in gaining a foothold. They then broke through the gates in the sea walls, allowing the mounted knights to disembark from the Venetian ships and enter the city, assembling a large force at the foot of the Fifth Hill. The German count Berthold set several fires to keep off the Byzantines while he looted the houses on the Fifth Hill, and the blaze spread to destroy most of the buildings along the Golden Horn. This was the third great conflagration to burn Constantinople within the year, the three fires together destroying about half of all the buildings in the city.

Mourtzouphlos spent the night trying to rally his supporters, but all of them either had fled or had barricaded themselves in their homes. So he gathered his family and retainers and fled from the city before dawn, eventually making his way to where Alexius III and his supporters were hiding at Mosynopolis in Thrace. Soon after he arrived Mourtzouphlos was blinded and imprisoned by Alexius, who thus eliminated him as a rival. Mourtzouphlos was captured by the Latins later that year and brought back to Constantinople, where he was hurled to his death from the top of the Column of Theodosius.

Meanwhile the Latins took control of Constantinople and then sacked it for three days, killing some 2,000 Greeks. Nicetas Choniates writes of how the Latins looted and profaned Haghia Sophia, leaving the city in utter desolation.

> They destroyed the high altar, a work of art admired by the entire world, and shared out the pieces among themselves ... And they brought horses and mules into the church, the better to carry off the holy vessels and the engraved silver and gold they had torn from the throne, and the pulpit ... A common harlot was enthroned in the patriarch's chair, to hurl insults at Jesus Christ; and she sang bawdy songs and profaned the holy place ... nor was there any mercy shown to virtuous maidens, innocent maids or even virgins consecrated to God ... In the streets, houses and churches there could be heard only cries and lamentations ... Here there were fights and quarrels over loot, there prisoners were being led away, and everywhere among the raped and wounded lay the dead.

The Latins met to choose an emperor on the evening of 9 May 1204, forming a committee of twelve, half of them Venetians. The first ballot was nine votes for Baldwin of Flanders and three for Boniface of Montferrat. Boniface's supporters thereupon threw in their hand and gave their support to Baldwin, who was thus unanimously elected in the next ballot. The following day Baldwin was crowned as emperor in Haghia Sophia, after which he moved into the Palace of Bucoleon.

The Latins then divided up the Byzantine Empire in an agreement known as the Partitio Romanum, the final details of which were set forth in October 1204. This treaty divided the empire into three major shares: a quarter for the Latin emperor, and three-eighths each for the Venetians and the other crusaders, with the portion of each beneficiary further subdivided into a share near Constantinople and a share more remote. Thus began the Latin empire that came to be known as Romania, the 'kingdom of the Romans', with its capital in Constantinople. Doge Dandolo, who styled himself 'Lord and Despot of a quarter and half of a quarter of the Roman Empire', ruled only briefly over his fractional principality, for he died in May 1205 and was buried in Haghia Sophia, where his name can still be seen engraved on the lid of his sarcophagus in the floor of the south gallery.

During the Latin occupation Haghia Sophia and a number of other churches in Constantinople were converted to the Roman Catholic

rite. One church that is known to have been used by the Latins during
their occupation of the city is that of the Theotokos Kyriotissa,[1] which
still stands on the Fourth Hill, beside the Valens Aqueduct.

The Church of the Kyriotissa.

The emperor Baldwin's rule was also brief, for on 14 April 1205
he was defeated in Thrace by the Bulgar tsar Kalojan, dying not
long afterwards in a Bulgarian prison. Baldwin's brother, Henry of
Hainault, served as regent until 20 August 1206, when he was
crowned emperor in Haghia Sophia. The coronation was performed
by the new Latin patriarch of Constantinople, the Venetian Thomas
Morosini. Most of the Greek Orthodox bishops in Constantinople
either refused to obey Morosini or else fled from the city to Nicaea,
where a fragment of the Byzantine Empire was now developing in
exile. This was one of three Byzantine states that emerged after the
fall of Constantinople in 1204, the others being the Empire of
Trebizond and the Despotate of Epirus.

The Empire of Nicaea was founded by Theodore I Lascaris, a son-
in-law of Alexius III. Theodore had fled from Constantinople in 1204
and established himself in Nicaea. Two years later he appointed
a patriarch, Michael Autoreanus, who then crowned Theodore as

emperor in the local cathedral of Haghia Sophia. Thenceforth the Greeks in western Asia Minor came to regard Nicaea as the capital of the Byzantine Empire in exile.

The most immediate threat to the new empire was the Selcuk Sultanate of Rum, whose sultan, Giyaseddin Keyhüsrev I, was harbouring Theodore's father-in-law, Alexius III. The sultan marched on Nicaea in 1211, bringing Alexius with him. But in the battle that followed Theodore defeated and killed the sultan, capturing Alexius III, who was then confined to a monastery in Nicaea for the rest of his days.

During the next half century the Lascarid dynasty ruled brilliantly in Nicaea, beginning a renaissance of Byzantine culture, while a series of half a dozen ineffective rulers succeeded one another on the Latin throne in Constantinople. The fourth and last of the Lascarids was John IV, who was only seven and a half when his father, Theodore II, died on 16 August 1258. Just before he died Theodore appointed George Muzalon as regent for his son. But nine days later the nobles of Nicaea assassinated Muzalon and replaced him as regent by their acknowledged leader, Michael Palaeologus, who was given the title of grand duke. Three months later Palaeologus was named despot, and then in December he was proclaimed co-emperor. Early the following year the patriarch performed the double coronation of Michael VIII Palaeologus and John IV Lascaris. Palaeologus was crowned first, for there was no doubt in anyone's mind that he was the emperor, and the young John IV soon disappeared from sight as a virtual prisoner of his co-ruler.

The following year Michael won a great victory over a coalition of Latin forces at the battle of Pelagonia. This victory eliminated all but one of the obstacles in the way of the Greek recovery of Constantinople, and that was the Republic of Venice. Michael thus sought the aid of Genoa, which had long been the principal rival of Venice. He signed a treaty of alliance with the Genoese at Nymphaeum on 13 March 1261, giving them extensive commercial privileges in return for their support.

The recapture of Constantinople in the end occurred quite by chance, coming almost as an anticlimax. A one-year truce had been agreed between the Greeks and Latins in August 1260, and towards the end of that period Michael Palaeologus sent a small force to

Michael VIII Palaeologus (1259–82), founder of the Palaeologian dynasty; miniature from Codex Monacensis.

Thrace under the command of Alexius Strategopoulos, who had orders to reconnoitre the environs of Constantinople. When Strategopoulos reached Selymbria he was told that Constantinople was virtually unprotected, since the Venetian fleet had left with most of the Latin garrison on a raid in the Black Sea. Strategopoulos approached the city under the cover of night, and some of his men made their way through a secret passageway under the walls by the Gate of the Pege. They surprised the guards inside the gate, which they forced open to allow their comrades in before the alarm was raised. Early the following day, 25 July 1261, Strategopoulos gained control of the city after some street-fighting with the remnants of the Latin garrison. The noise awakened the emperor Baldwin II, who had been sleeping in the Blachernae Palace, whereupon he rushed aboard a

Venetian ship in the port and ordered it to sail away at once, leaving his crown and sceptre behind him in his apartment. Strategopoulos, acting on the advice of the Greek populace, then set fire to the buildings in the Venetian quarter on the Golden Horn. When the Latin fleet returned, the Venetians found their homes and warehouses in flames and their families milling about on the shore of the Golden Horn 'like smoked-out bees', according to one chronicler. All that the Venetians could do was load their families aboard the galleys, after which they sailed away, ending the Latin occupation of Constantinople.

The emperor Michael was 300 kilometres away in Greece when the news arrived, whereupon he immediately struck camp and headed for Constantinople. He arrived at the walls of the city on 14 August, setting up his tents in the monastery of the Cosmidion, delaying his formal entry through the Golden Gate until the following day, the Feast of the Assumption. Early the next morning the metropolitan of Cyzicus, George Kelidas, mounted one of the towers of the Golden Gate and held up the sacred icon of the Virgin Hodegetria. He then recited prayers while the emperor and his entourage fell to their knees, along with the great crowd of local Greeks who had come to welcome him to the city he was now about to see for the first time. Then, when the prayers were over, the emperor entered the city in procession, going first to the church of St John of Studius and then to Haghia Sophia, where he escorted the patriarch Arsenius to the patriarchal throne once occupied by St John Chrysostom, a scene described by the historian George Acropolites:

... the emperor entered the holy building, the temple of Divine Wisdom, in order that he might hand over the cathedra to the prelate. And finally there assembled with the emperor all the notables of the archons and the entire multitude. Then the emperor, taking the arm of the patriarch, said, 'Take your throne now, O lord, and enjoy it, that of which you were so long deprived.'

The Byzantine Empire was thus restored to its ancient capital on the Bosphorus, beginning the last two centuries of its long history.

CHAPTER 14

Renaissance and Civil War
1261–1354

After his triumphal return to Constantinople, on 15 August 1261, Michael VIII Palaeologus was crowned once again in Haghia Sophia, with his wife, Theodora, enthroned as empress. At the same time their two-year-old son Andronicus was crowned as co-emperor and proclaimed as heir presumptive to the throne.

The legitimate emperor, the ten-year-old John IV Lascaris, was not present at the coronation in Haghia Sophia, for Michael Palaeologus had left him behind in Nicaea. A few months later Michael had John blinded and confined to the fortress of Dakibyze on the Marmara. When the patriarch Arsenius learned of this he excommunicated Michael. Michael deposed Arsenius, but his successor, Germanus III, refused to allow the emperor to return to the church and so he was replaced by a new patriarch, Joseph II. The new patriarch finally received the emperor back into the fold on 2 February 1267, at a mass in Haghia Sophia.

Constantinople was a ruined and half-abandoned city when it was re-established as the capital of the Byzantine Empire. Besides the destruction caused in the sack of 1204, the city had been seared by four major fires during the Latin occupation. Also the Latin emperors had left the imperial palaces of Blachernae and Bucoleon in appalling condition, while many of the city's churches had been allowed to fall into ruins. The condition of Constantinople after its recapture is described by Nicephorus Gregoras (1295–1359), writing in his *Romaiki Historia*:

Constantinople was then an enormous desolate city, full of ruins and stones, razed to the ground ... Enslaved, it had received no care from the Latins except destruction of every kind day and night. The first and foremost task facing the emperor was as much as possible to cleanse the city and transfer its great disorder into good order; to strengthen all the churches which had completely collapsed, and to fill the emptied houses with people.

Among the churches restored during Michael's reign was that of the Theotokos Panachrantos,[1] the Immaculate Mother of God. This was refounded by Michael's wife, who was buried there in 1304. Another church dating from his reign is that of the Mouchliotissa, St Mary of the Mongols,[2] founded by Michael's illegitimate daughter Maria. The Mouchliotissa is still in the hands of the Greeks, the only functioning church in the city dating from Byzantine times.

The enormous effort of rebuilding and repopulating Constantinople brought the empire to near-bankruptcy. This eventually led Michael to reduce the Byzantine armed forces and merchant navy

Church of St Mary of the Mongols, the only Byzantine church in the city still used by the Greeks.

as an economy measure, relying on the Genoese to carry on the empire's maritime commerce. The Genoese were allotted land across the Golden Horn from Constantinople in Galata, where they established an autonomous city-state governed by a podestà sent out each year by the mother-city of Genoa. They also took over the Byzantine fortress of Hieron on the Asian shore of the upper Bosphorus, where its impressive ruins are still referred to today as the Genoese Castle.[3]

Other Italian merchants were allotted land along the Golden Horn in Constantinople, with the Pisans and Venetians regaining the concessions they had had before the Latin conquest. Amalfi and Ancona were awarded new concessions, which like the earlier ones were narrow strips of land extending inward from the Golden Horn in the port.

The restored Byzantine Empire was only a small fraction of what it had been in the days of its greatness, and was surrounded by enemies on all sides. The principal threat came from the Sicilian monarch Charles I of Anjou, who in 1267 signed an agreement with Pope Clement IV at Viterbo, in which he committed himself to the 'sacred task' of reconquering Constantinople from the schismatic Greeks. Michael's efforts to stave off the threatened invasion of the empire by Charles and his allies took all of his considerable energies for most of the rest of his reign. The climax of this struggle came in the spring of 1282, when Charles assembled an armada in Messina to embark his army on his long-awaited crusade to take Constantinople. But on 30 March of that year the citizens of Palermo suddenly erupted in a rebellion that began when they assembled for vespers in the church of the Holy Spirit, massacring all of the French in the city. The revolt, which took the name of the Sicilian Vespers, spread rapidly throughout the island, with the people of Messina completely destroying the Angevin fleet and driving the French army from the island, so that Charles was forced to abandon his designs on Constantinople.

Michael Palaeologus died on 11 December 1282 while on campaign in Thrace. His son, Andronicus, was present at his bedside, and Michael's last words were to confirm him as his successor. After burying his father the new emperor returned to Constantinople, where he was crowned in Haghia Sophia as Andronicus II.

Andronicus was twenty-three when he came to the throne, after having been co-emperor for twenty years. He had been married in 1272 to Anna of Hungary, who bore him two sons, Michael and Constantine. Andronicus had his son Michael crowned as co-emperor on 21 May 1294. The following year Michael IX married the princess Rita of Armenia, who then changed her name to Maria. Maria bore Michael two daughters and two sons, the eldest being the future Andronicus III.

Andronicus II Palaeologus (1282–1328), from the Codex Monacensis; *and his grandson Andronicus III Palaeologus (1328–41), from a Byzantine manuscript.*

A series of earthquakes in the summer of 1296 caused considerable damage in Constantinople and north-western Asia Minor. Within a week after the last tremor, on 21 July, a Venetian fleet attacked the Genoese colony in Galata, setting their warehouses on fire and burning down the Greek houses outside the sea walls on the Golden Horn. Andronicus responded by arresting all of the Venetians in the city and confiscating their property. The local Genoese took the law into their own hands, and in December 1296 they massacred the leading

Venetians in Constantinople. The Venetians retaliated the following summer and their fleet bombarded the city, leaving only after exacting compensation for the losses they had suffered. The Greeks were powerless to stop the Venetian attacks because the Byzantine navy had been effectively disbanded by the economies of Michael VIII.

The Venetian fleet attacked Constantinople again in July 1302, and Andronicus was forced to pay a large indemnity to the doge in order to obtain a peace agreement. But at the very moment when the peace treaty was being signed in Venice news arrived that the Byzantines had suffered a serious defeat at the hands of the Turks near Nicomedia. These Turks were led by the chieftain Osman, who was known as Gazi, or Warrior for the Faith, and his followers came to be called Osmanlı – known in the West as Ottomans. By the time that Osman died, in 1324, the Ottomans controlled all of Bithynia except the fortified towns, which were fated to fall to his son and successor Orhan Gazi.

The Genoese took advantage of the situation to build a defence wall around Galata in 1304. The stronghold of this defence system was the great Tower of Christ, now known as the Galata Tower,[4] erected in 1348 on the hill above the port. They also built a number of churches in Galata, including one dedicated to SS. Domenic and Paul,[5] which survives today as Arap Camii, the Mosque of the Arabs.

Andronicus was desperate for help, and in 1303 he hired an army of Catalans under the leadership of Roger de Flor. The Catalan Grand Company, numbering about 6,500 fighting men, arrived in Constantinople that September, along with their wives and children. The Catalans achieved some temporary successes, but the Turks soon recaptured all of the places they had lost to them. Then in 1305 Roger de Flor was assassinated by one of the Alan mercenaries of Andronicus, whereupon the Catalans elected a new commander and established themselves as an independent power in Gallipoli on the Dardanelles.

Andronicus sought to secure the dynastic succession for two generations to come in 1316, when he made his grandson Andronicus co-emperor and second in line for the throne. The young Andronicus III, who was then nineteen, was wed the following year to the princess Adelaide of Brunswick, who then changed her name to Eirene. But Andronicus neglected his wife and took a mistress, who aroused his jealousy by carrying on with another lover. He hired assassins to do

The Galata Tower.

away with his rival, but by mistake they killed Prince Manuel, his own younger brother. The shock proved too much for their father, Michael IX, who went into a decline from which he never recovered, dying in Thessalonica on 12 October 1320. The emperor Andronicus was so furious at all of this that he disinherited his grandson. This inevitably led to a civil war, the first in a series of internal conflicts that would bring the Byzantine Empire to the brink of ruin during the remainder of the fourteenth century.

The first conflict began at Easter in 1321, when Andronicus III made his way to Adrianople and declared war on his grandfather. His principal supporter was his childhood friend John Cantacuzenus, who became his chief minister in the civil war, which lasted for seven years, interrupted by two armed truces. Andronicus III finally gained the upper hand, and on 23 May 1328 he and John Cantacuzenus led their troops into Constantinople and took control of the city. The young Andronicus then forced his grandfather to abdicate, and he himself then became sole emperor. Andronicus II was treated kindly and allowed to remain in the Palace of Blachernae, though two years later he was forced to retire to a monastery, where he died on 13 February 1332.

The empire had declined greatly during the long reign of Andronicus II, but through his patronage of scholarship and art Byzantium had flowered culturally, the culmination of the renaissance that had begun under the Lascarids in Nicaea. The art of the Palaeologan revival produced masterpieces such as the Deesis panel in Haghia Sophia and the mosaics and frescos in the churches of St Saviour in Chora[6] and the Theotokos Pammakaristos.[7] The art works in St Saviour in Chora were commissioned by Theodore Metochites, who is buried there with his friend Nicephorus Gregoras, the historian. Metochites was grand logothete, or prime minister, during the reign of Andronicus II, and he was also one of the leading scholars of the age, writing works in theology, philosophy, astronomy and poetry. As Nicephorus Gregoras wrote of him: 'From morning to evening he was most wholly and eagerly devoted to public affairs as if scholarship was absolutely indifferent to him; but later in the evening, having left the palace, he became absorbed in science to such a degree as if he were a scholar with absolutely no connection with any other affairs.'

Andronicus III was thirty-one when he became undisputed emperor. His first wife, Eirene, had died in 1324, and their only child had died in infancy. His second wife, Anna of Savoy, finally gave birth to a son on 18 June 1332. Nicephoras Gregoras writes of how the emperor celebrated the birth of his son, the future John V, with a joust and tournament in the western fashion introduced to the court by his Latin wife.

Meanwhile the Ottoman Turks had conquered Prusa, which fell to Orhan Gazi in 1326. The Turks then made Prusa their first capital, under the name of Bursa, whereupon Orhan took the title of sultan – the first of the Ottoman imperial line that was to continue without interruption for nearly six centuries. Andronicus mounted a campaign against the Turks in the spring of 1329, when he and John Cantacuzenus led an army across the strait into Bithynia, where they attacked Orhan's forces at Pelekanon. The Greeks were defeated and Andronicus was wounded in the leg by an arrow, but Cantacuzenus managed to rally the survivors and march them back to Chrysopolis.

The Greek defeat at Pelekanon doomed the remaining Byzantine possessions in Bithynia, with Nicaea falling to Orhan on 2 March 1331. The loss of Nicaea persuaded Andronicus to come to terms with the Turks, and in September 1333 he signed a treaty with the sultan.

Andronicus died on 15 June 1341 after a brief illness, aged forty-three. His unexpected death created a crisis in the succession, for his eldest son, John, who was barely nine, had not been made co-emperor. And so John Cantacuzenus was appointed as regent by the empress Anna and the patriarch John XIV Kalekas, the agreement being that John V would succeed to his father's throne when he came of age.

Both the Turks and the Bulgarians took advantage of the emperor's death to raid the territory of the empire. Cantacuzenus was forced to leave Constantinople on 23 September 1341 to campaign in Thrace, appointing Alexius Apocaucus as commander of the Byzantine fleet to guard the Bosphorus. Apocaucus began plotting against him, convincing both the patriarch and Anna of Savoy that Cantacuzenus was planning to seize the throne for himself. The empress Anna signed an order for Cantacuzenus to be arrested, whereupon all of his property in Constantinople was confiscated. About forty supporters of Cantacuzenus fled from Constantinople and joined him at his camp at Didymoteichon, where on 26 October they proclaimed him emperor. Historians generally number him on the list of Byzantine emperors as John VI, after the young John V Palaeologus, whose name was mentioned in the ceremony of investiture at Didymoteichon ahead of that of Cantacuzenus.

The internal conflict that began in 1341 differed from any of the many civil wars in the previous history of the Byzantine Empire, because it almost immediately developed into a struggle between social classes, with the landowning aristocracy supporting Cantacuzenus and the ordinary people of the cities and the serfs in the countryside taking the law into their own hands under the banner of John V. John Cantacuzenus, writing in his *Historia*, told of the horrors of the civil war:

It spread like a malignant and horrible disease, producing the same forms of excess even in those who before had been moderate and sensible men . . . All the cities joined in this rebellion against the aristocracy, and those that were late in doing so made up for their lost time by excelling the example set them by others. They perpetuated all manner of inhumanity and even massacres. Senseless impulse was glorified with the name of valour and lack of feeling or human sympathy was called loyalty to the emperor.

This civil war dragged on for six years, by which time Cantacuzenus had established an alliance with the Ottoman Turks, giving his daughter Theodora in marriage to Sultan Orhan. Meanwhile conspirators in Constantinople were working in the interests of Cantacuzenus, and on the night of 2–3 February 1347 they admitted him and his men through a breach in the Theodosian Walls. By sunrise he had drawn up his troops around the Blachernae Palace, as word spread throughout the city and the populace rushed to support him. Anna of Savoy was thus forced to come to terms with Cantacuzenus, and a week later it was agreed that he and John V would rule as co-emperors.

John Cantacuzenus was crowned on 13 May 1347 by the new patriarch of Constantinople, Isidore I. Cantacuzenus then arranged for his daughter Helena to be married to John V, who was barely fifteen. The marriage took place in the church of the Virgin Blachernitissa, since Haghia Sophia was in ruins, the eastern half of its great dome having collapsed the previous year. The wedding was lacking in customary Byzantine splendour, for the city and its people were still suffering from the horrors of the long civil war, the treasury completely empty, even the crown jewels gone, pawned in Venice by the empress Anna to raise money for her son. Funds for the repair of Haghia Sophia were eventually contributed by Symeon, the grand duke of Moscow, who saw himself as the protector of Orthodoxy. But Cantacuzenus was forced to use the money for the hire of Turkish mercenaries, and the restoration of the Great Church was delayed until 1355, when additional funds became available.

Cantacuzenus had barely begun his reign when Constantinople was struck by the terrible Black Plague, which first appeared in the city in 1347 in Genoese ships from the Crimea. By the time the plague was over, in the following year, a third of the population of Constantinople had died.

Byzantium then became involved in the maritime wars between

Venice and Genoa, with battles taking place in the Golden Horn on a number of occasions between 1348 and 1352. The Byzantines equipped a fleet, but when they set out to do battle with the Genoese on 13 February 1351 all of their ships were destroyed in a sudden storm. Constantinople was thus left to the mercy of the Italians, though Cantacuzenus managed to negotiate favourable treaties with both the Genoese and the Venetians to keep them at bay.

Meanwhile Cantacuzenus had sent out his two sons to rule provinces of the empire. Matthew, the elder, governed western Thrace from Didymoteichon, while Manuel ruled in the Peloponnesus from Mistra. The latter principality came to be known as the Despotate of the Morea, which was fated to be one of the last outposts of the Byzantine Empire.

Cantacuzenus sent John V to rule as emperor in Thessalonica after the city was recaptured by the Byzantines in 1350. This led to another civil war, which lasted for another four years, giving the Turks the opportunity to cross the Hellespont and take possession of the Gallipoli peninsula. The war finally ended when John V made his way back into Constantinople under cover of night on 29 November 1354. The news of his arrival spread rapidly through the city, and the populace flocked to join him as he set up his headquarters in the imperial residence on the Sixth Hill known as the Palace of the Porphyrogenitus, the Turkish Tekfursarayı.[8] Two days later John V and John Cantacuzenus met and agreed on a truce. Cantacuzenus formally abdicated in a ceremony at the Blachernae Palace on 10 December 1354, after which he became a monk and retired to the monastery of St George of the Mangana.

John Cantacuzenus lived for more than a quarter of a century after his abdication, dying in Mistra in 1383 at the age of eighty-eight. During the first three years of his retirement he wrote a chronicle of his times, the *Historia*, one of the most important sources for the history of Byzantium during the first half of the fourteenth century, when the empire flowered in a last renaissance before its final decline and fall. Writing in his *Historia*, Cantacuzenus looked back upon the ceremony of his investiture at Didymoteichon as being the beginning of the end for Byzantium. For, as he wrote, it brought on 'the worst civil war that the Romans had ever experienced, a conflict that destroyed almost everything, reducing the Roman Empire to a feeble shadow of its former self'. He wrote these words in St George of the Mangana on the Marmara slope of the First Hill, where the fragmentary ruins of the monastery can still be seen among the half-buried remnants of the Great Palace of Byzantium.

CHAPTER 15

The Fall of Byzantium
1354–1453

John V Palaeologus was twenty-two when he became sole emperor in December 1354, beginning what was to be Byzantium's last century. He knew that his only hope was to obtain help from the Christian powers in Europe, so he set out to form alliances with them against the rapidly advancing Ottoman Turks.

Early in 1355 John gave his sister Maria in marriage to the Genoese adventurer Francesco Gattilusio, whom he made lord of Mitylene, the capital of Lesbos. Later that same year John gave the Genoese the island of Chios, which thenceforth was governed by a company of merchant adventurers of the Giustiniani family.

Orhan Gazi died in 1362, to be succeeded as sultan by his son Murat. The following year Murat captured Didymoteichon, cutting off Byzantium from the West. Nine years later he captured Adrianople, which the Turks called Edirne, making it their new capital.

Meanwhile John had gone to Italy to seek help from the pope. He left Constantinople in charge of his eldest son, who had been crowned co-emperor as Andronicus IV, while his second son, Manuel, was appointed governor of Thessalonica. John met with Pope Urban V in Rome on 21 October 1367, agreeing to a union of the Greek and Roman Churches under the papacy. The pope then sent an encyclical to the princes of western Europe saying that John was now a Roman Catholic and fully deserving of assistance. After leaving Rome John went to Venice, where he was detained because of his inability to pay off the huge debt that Byzantium owed the Venetians. He was saved by his son Manuel, who came to Venice and arranged for a loan that enabled his father to return home, while he himself remained as a hostage until the first payment was made on the borrowed money.

John finally reached Constantinople in October 1371. A year after his return he signed a treaty with Murat acknowledging his suzerainty to the sultan. Early in 1373 John was in Murat's camp in Asia Minor fighting in a campaign as the sultan's vassal, leading the pope to remark that the emperor, though now a Catholic prince, had been reduced to making 'an impious alliance' with the infidel.

While John was off on campaign with Murat he once again left Andronicus to rule in Constantinople as his regent. Andronicus took the opportunity to revolt against his father in May 1373, but John quickly quelled the revolt. This was the first in a series of civil wars that lasted until the death of John V on 16 February 1391, by which time Andronicus had also died. John VII, son and successor of Andronicus IV, held Constantinople for six months before he was forced out by Manuel II, son and heir of John V, who became sole emperor in 1391.

Manuel was crowned in Haghia Sophia on 11 February 1392, the day after his marriage to the Serbian princess Helena Dragas. The coronation was witnessed by the Russian pilgrim Ignatius of Smolensk, who wrote that he arrived in Haghia Sophia before dawn, to find the church packed with worshippers who had been at an all-night vigil:

A multitude of people were there, the men inside the church, the women in the galleries. The arrangement was very artful; all who were of the female sex stood behind silken drapes, so that none of the male congregation could see the adornment of their faces, while they could see everything that was to be seen. The singers stood robed in marvellous vestments . . . some of brocade, others of silk, with gold and braid on the shoulders, and on their heads they wore pointed hats with braid ... Present were Franks [Europeans] from Galata, and others from Constantinople, Genoese and Venetian. Their order was wondrous to see, for they stood in two groups, some wearing purple velvet robes, the others cerise velvet.

Ignatius then describes the imperial procession, which began at dawn when the emperor descended from the galleries and entered the nave through the Imperial Gate, 'while the singers chanted indescribable, unusual music':

*Manuel II Palaeologus (1391–1425); miniature from
a Byzantine manuscript.*

Twelve men-at-arms walked on either side of the emperor, all in mail from
head to foot, and in front of them walked two black-haired standard-
bearers with red staffs, clothing and hats. Heralds with silver-covered staffs
walked before the two standard-bearers. When the emperor had entered the
chamber he donned the purple and the diadem, and placed on his brow
the crown of the Caesars. Then leaving the chamber, he went up to escort
the empress to the throne. After they had sat down on their thrones the liturgy
began, with both the emperor and empress seated.

Meanwhile the Turks were becoming stronger by the day, attracting numerous recruits, both Christian and Muslim, through the
opportunities for plunder offered by Murat's victorious campaigns.
Early in 1389 Murat mounted a campaign against Serbia, where an
anti-Turkish coalition had been formed by Prince Lazar. The two
armies met on the plain of Kossova on 15 June 1389, where the
Ottomans defeated the Christian allies with great slaughter. Murat
was killed at the very moment of victory, whereupon his son Beyazit

took command and massacred Lazar and all the other surviving Serbian nobles.

The new sultan came to be known as Yıldırım, or Lightning, from the speed with which he marched his armies back and forth between his European and Asian frontiers. Beyazit's Asian campaigns conquered the beyliks, or principalities, ruled by the emirs of Aydın, Saruhan and Menteşe, while in Europe he consolidated his father's conquests.

By that time the Ottomans had conquered all of the remaining Byzantine possessions in Asia Minor, and Manuel was reduced to the status of the sultan's vassal, paying him an annual indemnity. Beyazit allowed Manuel to rule only within the city, insisting that all territory outside the walls belonged to the sultan. Beyazit also made Manuel establish a Turkish quarter in Constantinople, where the Muslims would have their own kadı, or judge. By that time the Byzantine Empire had been reduced to little more than the city itself, which Beyazıt put under siege early in 1394.

The rapid Ottoman advance alarmed the Christian powers of Europe, and King Sigismund of Hungary led the call for a crusade against the Turks. A Christian army of nearly 100,000 mustered at Buda in July 1396 under the leadership of Sigismund, with contingents from Hungary, Wallachia, France, Germany, Poland, Italy, Spain and England, while an allied fleet with ships from Genoa, Venice and the knights of Rhodes patrolled the straits and the Black Sea coast. The Christian army headed down along the Danube valley to Nicopolis, where they put the Turkish-occupied fortress under siege. Beyazit caught up with them there, and on 25 September 1396 he totally routed the crusaders.

After his victory Beyazit renewed the siege of Constantinople. The following year he built the fortress of Anadolu Hisarı[1] on the Asian side of the Bosphorus at the Narrows, thus putting himself in position to cut off Constantinople from its grain supplies on the Black Sea.

Manuel appealed to the Christian princes of Europe to send aid to his beleaguered city. Charles VI of France equipped an expedition under Marshal Boucicaut, who in the summer of 1399 brought 1,200 troops to Constantinople. The marshal soon saw that a far greater force was needed to deliver the city from the Turks, and so he advised

Anadolu Hisarı: as reconstructed by Albert Gabriel.

Manuel to accompany him back to France so that he could present his case in person to King Charles. Manuel made a royal tour of the capitals of western Europe, meeting with Charles VI in Paris, then going on to see Henry IV in London, where he was welcomed as 'a great Christian prince from the East'. But, despite his initial high hopes, Manuel eventually realized that no real help would be forthcoming, for the Christian princes of western Europe were too involved in their own problems to embark on a crusade.

By that time the population of Constantinople was less than a fifth of what it had been in the days of Justinian, and many of its buildings had been abandoned and were in ruins. The Spanish traveller Ruy Gonzalez de Clavijo, who visited Constantinople in 1400 *en route* on an embassy to the court of Tamerlane in Samarkand, wrote, 'Everywhere throughout the city there are many great palaces, churches and monasteries, but most of them are now in ruins. It is however plain that in former times when Constantinople was in its pristine state it was one of the noblest capitals of the world.'

The siege of Constantinople was lifted in the spring of 1402, when Beyazit was forced to march all of his forces to Asia Minor to meet an invasion by the Mongols under Tamerlane. The two armies met near

Ankara on 28 July 1402, when the Mongols crushed the Ottomans and their Christian vassals. Beyazit was captured by Tamerlane and died soon afterwards. This led to an eleven-year war of succession between Beyazit's four surviving sons: Süleyman, Musa, Isa and Mehmet, giving Byzantium an unexpected respite. The struggle was finally won by Mehmet, who with Byzantine help established himself as sultan in 1413, his three brothers having been killed in the interim.

Mehmet I died in 1421 and was succeeded by his son Murat II, who was then seventeen. The next year Murat mounted campaigns against both Thessalonica and Constantinople, taking command of the latter siege himself. But the Theodosian Walls proved too strong for him, and he abandoned his siege on 6 September 1422.

Manuel suffered a crippling stroke on 1 October 1422, whereupon his son John was made regent and assumed control of the government. Manuel died on 21 July 1425, aged seventy-five, having reigned for thirty-four years. That same day he was buried in the church of the Pantocrator, where his funeral oration was delivered by Bessarion of Trebizond, the future archbishop of Nicaea and later still a cardinal in the Roman Catholic Church. The historian George Sphrantzes wrote of Manuel's funeral that it was attended 'with such mournings and such assemblages as there had never been for any of the other emperors'.

John VIII was thirty-two when he succeeded his father as emperor. His first wife, Sophia, daughter of Basil I of Moscow, had died of the plague in 1418. Then in 1421 he married Sophia of Monteferrat, but he took such an aversion to her that she fled from Constantinople and returned to Italy in 1426. John then married the beautiful Maria Comnena, daughter of the emperor Alexius IV of Trebizond. But all three of these marriages were childless, so there was a crisis of succession even in the last days of Byzantium.

Thessalonica finally fell to the Turks on 29 March 1430, after which some 7,000 of its inhabitants were carried off into slavery. This led John VIII to seek help from the West, and he proposed to Pope Martin V that a council might be called to reconcile the Greek and Latin Churches. This eventually gave rise to a council that was convened by Pope Eugenius IV at Ferrara in 1438, after which it moved on to Florence the following year, with the Byzantine delegation

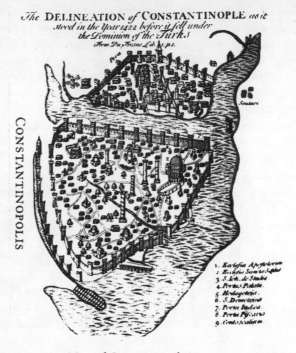

The DELINEATION of CONSTANTINOPLE as it stood in the year 1422 before it fell under the Dominion of the Turks

From Du Fresne Lib. 1. p. 1.

CONSTANTINOPOLIS

1. Ecclesia Apostolorum
2. Ecclesia Sanctae Sophiae
3. S. Joh. de Studio
4. Porta Palatii
5. Hodogetria
6. S. Demetrius
7. Porta Iudaa
8. Porta Piscaria
9. Contoscalium

Map of Constantinople in 1422.

headed by John VIII and the patriarch of Constantinople, Joseph II. The Union was finally agreed upon on Sunday 5 July 1439, uniting the Greek and Latin Churches under the aegis of the pope. Pope Eugenius then prepared to call for a crusade to save Constantinople from the Turks.

John did not return to Constantinople until February 1440, when he received news that his beloved Maria had died of the plague the previous year. The following year some of the clerics who had signed the decree of Union publicly repudiated their action in a manifesto. The emperor's brother Demetrius, who was ruling as despot in Selymbria, took advantage of the situation, and tried to usurp the throne by posing as the champion of Orthodoxy. He mounted an expedition with the aid of the Turks and attacked Constantinople in the summer of 1442, but John was saved when his brother Constantine, despot of the Morea, arrived with reinforcements and put down the rebellion.

Meanwhile the Pope's call for a crusade had brought together an army under the leadership of Ladislas III, king of Poland and Hungary, and his general John Hunyadi, with naval contingents provided by the pope, the duke of Burgundy, and the doge of Venice. Murat was in Asia Minor when the allies set off in June 1444, but he quickly moved his forces and met the crusaders five months later at Varna on the Black Sea coast of Bulgaria. Murat's forces virtually annihilated the crusaders there on 10 November 1444, John Hunyadi being one of the few to escape.

Shortly after the battle of Varna Murat retired in favour of his son Mehmet, who was then not yet thirteen. But Mehmet's extreme youth and inexperience led Murat to resume his reign in September 1446, whereupon Mehmet was made provincial governor in Manisa.

Meanwhile John Hunyadi had mustered an army and tried to join forces with the Albanian rebel leader Skanderberg to fight against the Turks. Murat caught up with Hunyadi's army at Kossova, where the Serbs had gone down fighting against the Turks in 1389. The outcome of the second battle of Kossova, fought from 17 to 20 October 1448, was the same as that of the first, with the Turks routing the Christians.

John VIII died on 31 October 1448 and was buried in the church of the Pantocrator next to his wife Maria and his father, Manuel II. John was survived by three of his brothers – Constantine, Demetrius and Thomas – as well as by his mother, Helena Dragas. Constantine, the oldest, used the surname Dragases, the Greek form of his mother's maiden name. At the time of John's death Constantine and his brother Thomas were in Mistra, the capital of the Despotate of the Morea, while Demetrius was in Selymbria. As soon as he received news of John's death Demetrius rushed back to Constantinople to make a claim for the throne. But Helena was determined that Constantine should succeed, and so she stopped Demetrius from taking control and asserted her right to serve as regent in the interim. She then dispatched couriers to Mistra to inform Constantine that he had succeeded his brother John. When the news arrived at Mistra Constantine was acclaimed as emperor. It was decided that the coronation should be carried out there rather than in Constantinople, and so on 6 January 1449 he was crowned as Constantine XI in the church of St Demetrius in Mistra.

Constantine XI Dragases (1449–53), the last emperor of Byzantium; from a seal in a work by Joseph Eckhel.

Constantine was forty-four when he became emperor. He had been married twice: first to Magdalena Tocco, who died in 1429, and then to Dorino Gattilusio, who died in 1442. Neither wife had borne him a child, and so after he came to the throne efforts were made to negotiate a dynastic marriage, but without success.

After his coronation Constantine divided the Despotate of the Morea between his two brothers, with Thomas ruling in Achaia and Demetrius in Mistra. He then left Mistra for Constantinople, where he arrived on 12 March 1449. Shortly afterwards he sent a courier to Murat to convey his greetings and to ask for a peace agreement.

Constantine began his reign in a divided city, for most of the clergy and people were totally opposed to the decree of Union. Constantine was determined to uphold the Union, for he believed that it offered the only hope of obtaining aid from the West, without which the empire was doomed. The principal opponent to this policy was George Scholarius, who in 1450 left the emperor's service and retired to the monastery of the Pantocrator as a monk, taking the name Gennadius. The patriarch, Gregory III Mammes, tried to support the emperor and at the same time keep peace within the Church. But Gennadius and other opponents of Union wrote and spoke against the policy with such force that Gregory eventually found his position untenable, and in August 1451 he abandoned Constantinople and went to Rome, never to return.

Murat II died at Edirne on 3 February 1451. His death was kept secret by the grand vezir Halil Çandarlı so that Prince Mehmet could make his way to Edirne to take control. He arrived on 18 February 1451, and that day he was acclaimed by the army as Sultan Mehmet II.

Soon after Mehmet came to the throne he began making plans for the conquest of Constantinople. His first step was to order the construction of the fortress of Rumeli Hisarı[2] on the European shore of the Bosphorus directly across from Anadolu Hisarı. The fortress was completed in August 1452, cutting off Constantinople from the Black Sea.

Constantine made desperate efforts to obtain help from the West. Pope Nicholas V appointed Cardinal Isidore of Kiev as papal legate to Constantinople. He also sent 200 Neapolitan archers, who arrived with Isidore on 26 October 1452. Isidore pressed Constantine to agree to a formal declaration of Union, which was read out in Haghia Sophia on 12 December of that year. But most of the populace refused to accept the Union, and thenceforth they stayed away from the Great Church.

Throughout that winter Constantine feverishly prepared for the coming siege, stocking food and munitions and mobilizing the populace to repair the city's defences. He assigned Sphrantzes the task of taking a census of the able-bodied men in the city, and the number amounted to only about 7,000, including the Venetians and Genoese who had volunteered to help the Greeks. The small number of fighting men is a measure of how much the population of Constantinople had declined in the first half of the fifteenth century, as people fled the doomed city to seek refuge in the West. The only other reinforcements came from the Genoese, a contingent of 700 troops under Giovanni Giustiniani Longo, who was given command of the city's defences, while the local Venetians put their fleet at the disposal of the emperor.

Mehmet set his entire army under march towards Constantinople early in the spring of 1453, with his advance guard pitching their camp in view of the Theodosian Walls on 2 April, Easter Monday. Three days later Mehmet arrived with the rest of his army, a force estimated at about 80,000, establishing his headquarters within sight of the Gate of St Romanus, midway along the Theodosian Walls. Then the sultan set up his artillery park, the pride of which was a colossal cannon called Urban, which could fire a 500-kilogram stone cannon-ball a kilometre and a half. The first bombardment began on 6 April, with Urban's huge cannon-balls smashing against the land walls with devastating effect. But each night the entire populace worked to repair the damage done to the walls, as the emperor offered advice and encouragement.

The Turkish fleet was repelled when it made an attempt to break through the chain at the mouth of the Golden Horn. Then on 18 April the Turkish infantry launched a surprise attack on the section of walls that had suffered the most damage. This was the Mesoteichion, literally 'the middle of the wall', where it descends into the valley of the Lycus. But despite the ferocity of the offensive and the ruinous condition of the wall the attack was beaten back. Two days later four ships arrived with supplies from Genoa and Sicily, eluding the Turkish warships that tried to prevent them from entering the Golden Horn. But this was the last relief to reach the city, for on 22 April Mehmet had his fleet dragged over the heights of Pera into the Golden Horn, bypassing the great chain and giving the Turks control of the harbour.

The Turkish bombardment continued until Sunday 27 May, when Mehmet sent a message demanding unconditional surrender, though he offered to let Constantine leave unharmed to establish a fief else-where under Ottoman suzerainty. The sultan also indicated that he would be 'merciful' to the people of the city if they surrendered; otherwise they would face the full fury of his wrath. Constantine rejected the sultan's offer, whereupon Mehmet commanded his vezirs to begin preparations for an all-out attack on the city, promising his troops three days of plunder when they conquered Constantinople.

Constantine spent the following day making final preparations to defend against the attack. He ordered all of the sacred relics to be brought forth from the city's churches and carried in procession behind the icons of the Virgin Hodegetria and the Virgin Blachernitissa, which had for so many centuries protected Constantinople from its enemies.

That evening everyone who was not on duty along the walls began congregating in Haghia Sophia, praying for the city's salvation. Constantine appeared in the Great Church shortly before midnight, accompanied by his Greek and Italian knights, and he prostrated himself before the high altar, lying there for some time in absolute silence. He then went to the Blachernae Palace, accompanied by his friend George Sphrantzes. According to Sphrantzes, Constantine assembled the members of his household and said goodbye to each of them in turn, asking their forgiveness for any unkindness he might ever have shown them. 'Who could describe the tears and groans in the palace?' Sphrantzes writes. 'Even a man of wood or stone could not help weeping.' After leaving the palace, Constantine and Sphrantzes rode to the Gate of the Kaligaria. They dismounted there and Sphrantzes waited while Constantine ascended one of the towers nearby, listening to the ominous sounds of the Turkish army preparing for the final assault, after which he returned and mounted his horse once again. Sphrantzes then said goodbye to Constantine for the last time, watching as the emperor rode off towards his command post on the Murus Bacchatureus, the section of the Mesoteichion by the Gate of St Romanus.

The Turkish engineering battalions had been working throughout the night filling in the fosse in front of the Theodosian Walls along the Mesoteichion, where the main attack was to be made. About two o'clock in the morning of Tuesday 29 May, seeing that preparations were complete, Mehmet gave the signal for the attack to begin. The first assault was made by the Başıbozuks, irregular shock troops who charged with wild battle-cries to the sound of drums and bagpipes. The watchmen on the towers within Constantinople heard the noise and began ringing all of the church bells of the city to alert the populace. Meanwhile the Başıbozuks had made their way across the fosse and set up scaling-ladders against the walls, some of them ascending to the battlements before they were cut down by the defenders. After two hours of intense fighting the Başıbozuks were withdrawn, having worn down the defenders with their unrelenting attack.

Mehmet then launched the second wave, the regular Anatolian infantry under the command of Ishak Pasha, their charge accompanied by a heavy bombardment from the Turkish artillery. An hour before dawn Urban scored a direct hit on the Mesoteichion, creating a breach through which some 300 of the Turkish infantry began to make their way into the city. But they were quickly surrounded and slaughtered by the defenders, led by the emperor himself. This broke the brunt of the assault and led Ishak Pasha to withdraw his infantry.

The sultan then brought on the Janissaries, the élite corps of the Ottoman army. Their charge carried them to the ramparts of the inner wall, where they fought hand-to-hand with the defenders. A group of them made their way through a sally-port called the Kerkoporta, capturing a tower beside the gate, from which they flew the Turkish star and crescent. At that moment Giustiniani was gravely wounded, whereupon Constantine hurried to his side and pleaded with him to remain at his post. But Giustiniani was unable to remain, and his men carried him away to a Genoese ship in the Golden Horn.

The sultan then ordered another assault on the walls, the spearhead being a company led by a giant Janissary named Ulubatlı Hasan. Hasan made his way up on to the ramparts of the inner wall before he was struck down, his men fighting their way through into the city. Then, seeing the star and crescent flying from the tower beside the Kerkoporta, the cry went out that the city was taken, and as the defenders faltered the Turks began pouring through the walls. Constantine tried to stem the flood, and when last seen he was at his command post on the Murus Bacchatureus, fighting valiantly alongside his faithful comrade John Dalmata. The emperor's body was never identified, though legend has it that he was secretly buried by the local Greeks at a church in the quarter now known as Vefa.

The last pockets of resistance were mopped up before the morning was over, with many of the surviving Italians escaping aboard Venetian ships, leaving the Greeks to face their fate. Mehmet then turned loose his soldiers to loot Constantinople for three days, on the proviso that they did not destroy the city's buildings, which now belonged to him. But from contemporary accounts it would appear that the Turkish troops destroyed much of the city during the orgy of looting, enslavement, rape and massacre. A number of contemporary chroniclers write of the horrors of the Turkish sack of Constantinople, the most reliable account being perhaps that of Kritovoulos of Imbros, who estimated that some 4,000 of the civilian population were killed when the city fell. Kritovoulos describes Sultan Mehmet's entry into the great city he had just conquered, shocked at the destruction he saw on all sides:

After this the sultan entered the City and looked about to see its great size, its situation, its grandeur and beauty, its teeming population, its loveliness, and the costliness of its churches and public buildings ... When he saw that a large number had been killed, and ... the wholesale ruin of the City, he was filled with compassion and repented not a little at the destruction and plundering. Tears fell from his eyes as he groaned deeply and passionately, 'What a city have we given over to plunder and destruction!'

That same day the sultan inspected the ruins of the Great Palace on the First Hill, long abandoned by the emperors of Byzantium in favour of the Blachernae Palace. When the Conqueror walked through the ruined halls of the palace he was deeply saddened, and a Turkish chronicler reports that Mehmet was moved to recite a melancholy distich by the Persian poet Saadi:

The spider is the curtain-holder in the Palace of the Caesars.
The owl hoots its night call on the Towers of Afrasiab

The news of the fall of Constantinople first reached the West when a Cretan ship docked at Candia on 9 June 1453. A monk from the mountains of central Crete brought the news back to his brethren at the monastery of Angarathos, where one of them recorded it in their archives. 'There has never been and there will never be a more dreadful happening,' he wrote. This feeling of desolation still echoes in the folk-songs of Greece, where the fall of the City is lamented in threnodies such as 'The Last Mass in Haghia Sophia', collected by C. A. Trypanis and translated thus by Richard Stoneham:

God rings the bells, earth rings the bells, the sky itself is ringing,
The Holy Wisdom, the Great Church, is ringing out the message,
Four hundred sounding boards sound out, and two and sixty bells.
For every bell there is a priest, and for every priest a deacon.
To the left the emperor is singing, to the right the patriarch,
And all the columns tremble with the thunder of the chant.
And as the emperor began the hymn to the Cherubim,
A voice came down to them from the sky, from the archangel's mouth:
Cease the Cherubic hymn and let the sacred objects bow;
Priests take the holy things away, extinguish all the candles;
God's will has made our city now a Turkish city.
But send a message to the West, and let them send three ships:
The first to take the cross, the second to remove the Gospel,
The third, the finest, shall rescue for us our holy altar . . .
The Holy Virgin was distressed, the very icons wept.
Be calm, beloved Lady, be calm and do not weep for them;
Though years, though centuries shall pass, they shall be yours again.

Thus the City began another life as Istanbul, while the Judas-trees blossomed on the shattered walls of Byzantium, just as they do today, when the ruins of another empire have been added to the layered history of this ancient place.

PART III

ISTANBUL

CHAPTER 16

Istanbul, Capital of the Ottoman Empire

1453–1520

Sultan Mehmet II made his triumphal entry into the city late in the afternoon of Tuesday 29 May 1453, passing through the Adrianople Gate, now known as Edirne Kapı. The Turks acclaimed him as Fatih, or the Conqueror, the name by which he would thenceforth be known. He was just twenty-one years old, having been sultan for little more than two years, but now he had captured the most famous city in the world, known to the Turks as Istanbul. A plaque on the gate records Fatih's triumphal entry, a scene described by the seventeenth-century Turkish chronicler Evliya Çelebi in his *Seyahatname*, or *Narrative of Travels*:

The sultan then having the pontifical turban on his head and sky-blue boots on his feet, mounted on a mule and bearing the sword of Muhammad in his hand, marched in at the head of seventy or eighty thousand Muslim heroes, crying out, 'Halt not conquerors! God be praised! Ye are the conquerors of Constantinople!'

The Conqueror rode directly to Haghia Sophia, the Great Church that was as renowned in Islam as it was in Christianity, and when he arrived there he dismounted and fell to his knees, sprinkling a handful of earth over his turban as a sign of humility. Fatih then surveyed the church and ordered that it be immediately converted to Islamic worship under the name of Aya Sofya Camii Kabir, the Great Mosque of Haghia Sophia. This required the erection of a minaret for the müezzin to give the call to prayer, and also some internal constructions, including the mimber, or pulpit, and the mihrab, the niche that indicates the kible, the direction of Mecca. This done, Fatih attended

Mehmet II (Fatih) and an unidentified youth, c. 1480;
drawing attributed to Gentile Bellini.

the noon prayer in the mosque that Friday, 1 June 1453, accompanied
by his two chief clerics, Akşemsettin and Karaşemsettin. Evliya Çelebi
describes the scene:

On the following Friday, the faithful were summoned to prayer by the müezzins,
who proclaimed with a loud voice this text of the Koran: 'Verily, God and his
angels bless the Prophet.' Akşemsettin and Karaşemsettin then arose, and,
placing themselves on each side of the sultan, supported him under his arms;
the former placed his own turban on the head of the Conqueror, fixing in it
the black and white feather of a crane, and putting into his hand a naked
sword. Thus conducted to the mimber he ascended it, and cried out with a
voice as loud as David's, 'Praise be to God, the Lord of all the world,' on
which the victorious Muslims lifted up their hands and uttered a shout of joy.

Muslim rulers traditionally allowed their troops to sack a captured
city for three days, but Fatih seems to have called a halt to the looting
on 30 May 1453, the day after the Conquest. He then made an inspection of the city, after which he announced that Istanbul would be
his new capital as soon as it was restored and repopulated. Fatih
encouraged the return of those Greeks who had fled from Constantinople before the Conquest. He also resettled in the city all of the
prisoners who had been part of his share of the spoils; a chronicler

writes that he gave them land and houses 'along the shores of the city harbour', and 'freed them from taxes for a specified time'. Aside from these, most of the new population resulted from an imperial decree calling for a resettlement. The new settlers, who included Muslims, Christians and Jews, came from all over the empire, many of them taken in Fatih's numerous campaigns following the conquest of Constantinople.

The Muslims among the new settlers built mosques or converted Byzantine churches to the services of Islam, as Fatih had done to Haghia Sophia. A number of the first mosques founded after the Conquest are still to be seen in the market quarter along the Golden Horn between the Galata and Atatürk Bridges, although all of them have been rebuilt to at least some extent in the intervening centuries. The oldest of these is probably Yavuz Ersinan Camii.[1] This was built in 1455 by Yavuz Ersinan, who was standard-bearer in Fatih's army at the time of the Conquest and an ancestor of Evliya Çelebi, who was born in a house beside the mosque. The founder himself is buried in a little graveyard there. Beside him is his old comrade-in-arms Horoz Dede, or Grandfather Rooster, one of the famous Muslim folk-saints of Istanbul. Horoz Dede received his name during the siege of Constantinople, when he made his rounds each morning and woke the troops of Fatih's army with his loud rooster call. He was killed in the final assault on the city, and then after the Conquest he was reburied by Yavuz Ersinan beside his mosque.

The non-Muslims among the new settlers were grouped into *millets*, or 'nations', according to their religion, each headed by its own religious leader. Thus the Greek *millet* was headed by the Orthodox patriarch, the Armenian by the Gregorian patriarch, and the Jewish by the chief rabbi. The authority granted by Fatih extended not only to religious matters but also to most legal questions other than criminal cases, which were always tried before the sultan's judges. Thus the *millet* system, which was continued by Fatih's successors right down to the end of the Ottoman Empire, became an instrument of government policy – one that fitted in well with the multi-ethnic character of the Ottoman state.

There was no patriarch of Constantinople at the time of the Conquest, and so after peace was restored the Greek clergy in the city were allowed to elect a new prelate, who was approved by Fatih. The new patriarch was the monk Gennadius, formerly known as George Scholarius, who was undoubtedly chosen because of his opposition to the policy of Union with Rome in the latter years of the Byzantine era. Gennadius took office on 1 January 1454, when he was consecrated by the archbishop of Heraclea. Fatih presented Gennadius with a sceptre and personally escorted him at the beginning of the procession to the church of the Holy Apostles, which had been assigned to the new patriarch as his headquarters. Fatih issued a firman, or imperial decree, which guaranteed to Gennadius 'that no one should vex or disturb him; that unmolested, untaxed, and unoppressed by an adversary, he should, with all the bishops under him, be exempted from all taxation for all time'. The Greek Orthodox Patriarchate[2] was subsequently moved to the church of the Pammakaristos, and later still to several other places before it settled in its present quarters at the church of St George in Fener, the Greek quarter of the city. The first Armenian patriarch after the Conquest was Bishop Hovakim, whose patriarchate was the church of the Peribleptos in Samatya. The first chief rabbi was Moshe Capsali, whose headquarters were in Balat, which had been the principal Jewish quarter since Byzantine times.

Fatih had accepted the surrender of Galata just two days after the fall of Byzantium. He forced the Genoese to pull down sections of their fortifications, sparing the Galata Tower. Galata lost its independence, but as long as the Genoese obeyed the law and paid their taxes Fatih allowed them some local autonomy as well as the right to trade, travel and own property. He also gave them the right to worship as they pleased and to retain their Roman Catholic churches.

Soon after the Conquest Fatih built inside the Golden Gate a fortress known as Yedikule,[3] the Castle of the Seven Towers. Towards the end of 1453 he finally moved his court from Edirne to Istanbul, which thenceforth became the capital of the Ottoman Empire. At that time he built a palace on the Third Hill, which Kritovoulos described as 'the finest location in the City'. It came to be known as Eski Saray, the Old Palace, because six years later Fatih decided to build a new palace on the First Hill, the famous Topkapı Sarayı,[4] of which the oldest surviving building is Çinili Köşk,[5] the Tiled Kiosk, erected in 1472.

Ten years after the Conquest Fatih decided to build a huge mosque complex on the Fourth Hill, and to make way for it he demolished the church of the Holy Apostles. The mosque itself, known as Fatih Camii,[6] was the centre of a vast külliye, or complex of religious and philanthropic institutions of one kind or another, which together constituted a vakıf, or pious foundation. Besides the great mosque, which was totally rebuilt after an earthquake in 1766, the külliye of Fatih Camii consisted of eight medreses (theological schools) and their annexes, with a hospice (tabhane), public kitchen (imaret), hospital (darüşşifa), caravansarai, primary school (mektep), library (kütüphane), public bath (hamam), çarşı (market), and a graveyard with two türbes (tombs), one of which was to be Fatih's last resting-place.

At Fatih's urging several of his vezirs also built mosque complexes in the city, of which three are still functioning. The first of these was Mahmut Pasha Camii[7] on the Second Hill, founded by a Greek of noble ancestry who converted to Islam and became grand vezir.

The new Turkish city of Istanbul developed around the mosque complexes built by the sultan and his vezirs – a development that continued under Fatih's successors. Fatih Camii and the other great külliyes became the civic centres of the Muslim city, which was divided into thirteen nahiye, or districts, each of which was subdivided into a number of mahalle, or neighbourhoods. Each of the nahiye, with one exception, was named after the mosque complex that formed its centre and focus, such as Aya Sofya Camii, Mahmut Pasha Camii and Fatih Camii, the latter being the largest district in the city, with forty-one mahalle. Fatih Camii had all of the facilities for a civic centre, for in addition to the mosque and its medreses and other religious and philanthropic institutions it also had a large market with 280 shops, 32 workrooms, and four storehouses, the income from which went to support the rest of the külliye. The Fatih külliye also included another çarşı known as Saraçhane, or the Saddlers' Market, with 142 saddlers employed, many of them Janissaries. The Saddlers' Market has disappeared, but its name survives as that of a mahalle near Şehzade Camii. Another part of it was the At Pazarı, or Horse Market, whose name also survives as that of a quarter in the nahiye of Fatih, although horses have not been bought or sold there since late Ottoman times.

Fatih also founded the famous Kapalı Çarşı,[8] or Covered Bazaar, a huge enclosed market on the Third Hill by Beyazit Meydanı. Arrayed around the Kapalı Çarşı are the huge hans, or inner-city caravanserais, where the Ottoman merchants brought their goods to be sold in the vaulted shops that still line the covered arcade of this vast labyrinth. This was the heart of commercial Istanbul in Fatih's time, and it is still today. The main artery of the quarter is Uzun Çarşı Caddesi, the Avenue of the Long Market; this was the ancient Makro Embolos, the Long Arcade, which had been the principal shopping street in Byzantine Constantinople.

left: *The Covered Bazaar.*
right: *The mosque courtyard at Eyüp.*

Fatih also founded another mosque complex at Eyüp,[9] the ancient Cosmidion, outside the land walls of the city on the upper reaches of the Golden Horn. Turks rank Eyüp as the third most sacred place in the Islamic world after Mecca and Jerusalem. This is because it is the reputed burial-place of Eyüp (Job) Ensari, the friend and standard-bearer of the Prophet Muhammad. Eyüp is said to have been among the leaders of the first Arab siege of Constantinople from 674 to 678 and to have been killed and buried somewhere outside the walls. The tomb of Eyüp was miraculously discovered during the Turkish siege of Constantinople, and after the Conquest Fatih built a külliye there. Thenceforth when a sultan came to the throne he was girded with the sword of Osman Gazi at Eyüp's tomb – a ceremony equivalent to coronation, which continued down to the end of the Ottoman Empire.

The first diplomatic treaty between the Ottoman Empire and the Christian powers of the West dates to 18 April 1454, when Fatih signed an agreement with the Venetians giving them the right to trade freely in Istanbul on the condition that they pay a customs duty of 2 per cent. The agreement also gave the Venetians the right to maintain a commercial colony in the city, with a bailo appointed by the doge to direct their affairs and represent them with the sultan. The residence of the bailo, the Palazzo di Venezia, was eventually built in Pera, in the hills above Galata. The representatives of other European powers later built their embassies there as well, along with the houses and churches of their communities, all of them erected on the high-road that came to be known as the Grande Rue de Pera, the modern Istiklal Caddesi.

During the eighteen years after his conquest of Constantinople Fatih launched annual campaigns, leading many of them himself, extending the boundaries of the empire in both Europe and Asia. He mounted a major campaign in 1458 into the Peloponnesus, where Thomas and Demetrius Palaeologus were still ruling as despots of the Morea. The Ottoman army conquered virtually all of the Peloponnesus in two years, with Mistra surrendering on 29 May 1460, seven years to the day after the fall of Constantinople. Thomas Palaeologus fled to Corfu and then went on to Italy, where he died in May 1465. His brother Demetrius surrendered to Fatih and accompanied the sultan back to Edirne, after which he was allowed to live in Didymoteichon until his death in 1470. By that time the only other surviving fragment of Byzantium had come to an end with the fall of Trebizond to Fatih in August 1461. The last emperor of Trebizond, David Comnenus, was imprisoned in Edirne along with his family. Then on 1 November

1463 Fatih ordered the execution of David and his sons, bringing their dynasty to an end.

The first census of Ottoman Istanbul, including Galata, was ordered by Fatih in 1477. The census, which counted only the civilian households and did not include the military class or those residing in the imperial palace, numbered the families in the various religious and ethnic categories. It recorded 9,486 Muslim Turkish, 4,127 Greek, 1,687 Jewish, 434 Armenian, 267 Genoese, and 332 European families from places other than Genoa, with all of the latter two groups living in Galata. The total population of Istanbul is estimated from the census as being between 80,000 and 100,000 – about double what it had been just before the Conquest. The population within the old walled city of Istanbul comprised 88 per cent of the total, with the rest in Galata, not counting the Bosphorus villages nor the environs of the capital on both sides of the strait. Seventy per cent of those living in the walled city of Istanbul were Muslim Turks and the rest non-Muslims, with just the reverse being true in Galata. The census of 1477 also recorded that there were 31 Gypsy families in Istanbul. These all lived in the mahalle known as Sulukule, just inside the Theodosian Walls on the Sixth Hill, where their encampment is noted as early as the fourteenth century, and where their descendants still live to the present day, despite repeated attempts to evict them and their dancing bears.

Fatih spent all of 1479 in his new palace of Topkapı Sarayı, which had been completed in January of that year. That summer he sent a message to the doge of Venice, Giovanni Mocenigo, inviting him to Istanbul for the circumcision feast of one of the sultan's grandsons – an invitation that was politely declined. Fatih also asked the doge to send him a 'good painter', and the Venetian Senate chose Gentile Bellini, who arrived in Istanbul in September 1479 and remained until mid-January 1481. While there Bellini painted the famous portrait of Fatih now exhibited in the National Gallery in London (though the gallery's catalogue states that there is insufficient evidence for deciding whether this picture is a very damaged original or a copy).

Fatih's health was failing, but despite this he launched two major campaigns in 1480. The first of these was an attempted invasion of Rhodes, where the knights of St John withstood a five-month siege before the Turkish commander, Mesih Pasha, finally sailed his fleet back to Istanbul. That same year Gedik Ahmet Pasha captured Otranto on the heel of Italy, which the Turks held for only a few months.

Fatih began making preparations for a new campaign early in 1481, possibly to invade Egypt. No one ever learned the sultan's plans, for on the first day's march into Anatolia, 3 May 1481, his illness finally laid him low and he died on the following day 'at the twenty-second hour', according to an Italian chronicler.

Fatih's death was kept secret for seventeen days, giving his eldest son Beyazit time to return to Istanbul and be acclaimed as sultan. Beyazit II was girded with the sword of Osman at Eyüp, and immediately afterwards he buried Fatih in the türbe of his mosque. Thenceforth it became customary for a new sultan to visit Fatih's türbe after the ceremony at Eyüp – a practice that continued down to the end of the empire. Fatih's türbe soon became a religious shrine, and to this day it is a popular place of pilgrimage.

Beside Fatih's türbe stands the tomb of his wife, Gülbahar, mother of Beyazit II. An apocryphal legend has it that Gülbahar was a daughter of 'the king of France', sent by him as a bride for the emperor Constantine Dragases and captured by the Turks when they were besieging the city. The legend goes on to say that Gülbahar, although she was the wife of Fatih and the mother of Beyazit, never embraced Islam and died a Christian. Evliya Çelebi recounts a version of this legend and comments thus on Gülbahar's türbe:

I myself have often observed, at morning prayer, that the readers appointed to chant lessons from the Koran all turned their backs upon the coffin of this lady, of whom it was so doubtful whether she departed in the faith of Islam. I have often seen Franks come by stealth and give a few aspers to the tomb-keeper to open her türbe for them, as the gate is always kept locked.

This story is also repeated by the Italian traveller Cornelio Magni, who was led by the tomb-keeper to believe that Gülbahar was a Christian princess who had died in her faith. 'The türbe', he says, 'remains always shut, even the windows. I asked the reason for this and was told: "The sepulchre of her who lives among the shades deserves not a ray of light!"' After much entreaty and the intervention of an emir who passed by, the tomb-keeper let him in. 'I entered with veneration and awe ... and silently recited a *de profundis* for the soul of this unfortunate princess.'

Beyazit II was thirty-three when he became sultan, having served as military governor in Amasya for fourteen years. He began his reign in a war of succession with his brother Cem, who was defeated and forced to spend the rest of his life in exile, dying in Rome in 1495.

At the beginning of the sixteenth century Beyazit decided to build a mosque complex called the Beyazidiye[10] on the Third Hill, demolishing the Forum of Theodosius to make way for it. The Beyazidiye marks the beginning of the classical period of Ottoman architecture, which continued for more than 200 years. Beyazit's külliye became the focal point of the commercial life of the city, with the Covered Bazaar and other markets clustering around it – a scene described by Evliya Çelebi: 'As this mosque was entirely built with lawful money, it has great spiritual advantage, and being situated in the centre of the markets of Istanbul, is crowded day and night by thousands of devout Muslims, who are offering up their prayers there without ceasing.'

Another foundation dating from Beyazit's reign is the Galata Mevlevihane,[11] the oldest of Istanbul's extant tekkes, or dervish

Mevlevi dervishes whirling in their tekke in Pera;
nineteenth-century drawing.

monasteries, of which there were some 300 in the city. All of the earlier large mosques also had hostels for mendicant dervishes, who were as numerous in Ottoman Istanbul as the monks had been in Byzantine Constantinople. There were more than a score of different dervish orders with tekkes in Istanbul. Each of the orders sought to attain communion with the divine in one way or another, some through contemplation and mysticism, others through the renunciation of worldly goods, and a few – particularly the Mevlevi, the famous 'Whirling Dervishes' – through the divine harmonies of music and dance. Evliya Çelebi describes the scene in one of the Mevlevi dervish tekkes of his time:

The Mevlevi tekke in Beşiktaş is only one storey high. The room for the dancing and singing of the dervishes looks out towards the sea ... The cells of the fakirs [dervishes] on the west side of the dancing-floor are of nut-tree wood and three sides are enclosed with windows. Their sheikh, Hasan Dede, who was more than a hundred and ten years old at the time of his death, used to mount the chair on assembly days and, falling into ecstasy, would many times interpret the verses of the Mesnevi [the poem of Mevlana, the thirteenth-century mystic] according to the author's original meaning. His successor, Nizen Dervish Yusuf Çelebi, would at times hurl himself down from his chair among the performing fakirs. When he sang, his voice was so inspired that his audience would remain spellbound. All the lovers of the deity would gather around him and listen to the divine chanting until they were completely out of their wits. He was a very prince of the speculative way of contemplation.

During the last decade of the fifteenth century Beyazit welcomed large numbers of Sephardic Jewish refugees, who had been expelled from Spain and Portugal beginning in 1492. Beyazit resettled the Jews principally in Thessalonica, Edirne, Izmir and Istanbul, where they were concentrated mostly in Balat.

On 24 April 1512 Beyazit was forced to abdicate by his son Selim, who had gained the support of the Janissaries. Selim was girded as sultan that same day, after which the deposed Beyazit set off to his place of retirement in Didymoteichon. But Beyazit never reached his destination, for he died *en route* on 26 May, the suspicion being that he was poisoned by Selim. Selim brought Beyazit's body back to Istanbul for burial in the türbe of the Beyazidiye. His tomb became a place of pilgrimage, according to Evliya Çelebi, who writes that 'It is now generally visited by the sick, who here find relief in their diseases, because Sultan Beyazit was a saintly monarch.' Evliya then goes on to tell a bizarre tale about Beyazit and his tomb:

The last seven years of his life he ate nothing which had blood and life in it. One day, longing much to eat calves or sheep's feet, he struggled long in this glorious contest with his soul; and as at last a well-seasoned dish of the feet was put before him, he said unto his soul, 'See my soul, the feet are before thee; if thou wishest to enjoy them, leave the body and feed on them.' At the same moment a living creature was seen to come out of his mouth, which drank of the juice in the dish; and after having satisfied his appetite endeavoured to return from whence it came. But Beyazit having prevented it with his hand from re-entering his mouth, it fell on the ground, and the sultan ordered it to be beaten. The pages kicked it to death on the ground. The mufti of that time decided that, as the soul was an essential part of a man, this dead soul should be buried; prayers were performed over it, and the dead soul was interred in a small tomb near Beyazit's türbe. This is the truth of the famous story of Beyazit II having died twice and twice been buried.

Selim's two major campaigns won him victories over the Safavids in Persia and the Mamluks in Egypt. The latter campaign was climaxed by his capture of Cairo on 25 January 1517. Legend has it that at this time the caliph al-Mutawakkil transferred the rights of the caliphate, the leadership of Islam, to Selim and his successors in the Osmanlı line. This legend was later revived to establish the right of the Ottoman sultans to the title of caliph, which they retained down to the end of the empire.

After his return from Cairo, Selim spent some time in Istanbul re-organizing his government and army in preparation for his first campaign into Europe. He made Topkapı Sarayı the centre of his government as well as his imperial residence – a practice that was continued by his successors. His supreme council, the Divan, met four days a week in its headquarters in the second courtyard of Topkapı Sarayı, the grand vezir presiding and then afterwards reporting to the sultan. The name of the council is preserved in that of Divan Yolu, the avenue that follows the course of the ancient Mese between the First and Second Hills, so called because of the colourful processions that passed along it on days when the sultan's ministers were in session.

Selim set out from Istanbul at the head of his army on 18 July 1520, beginning a campaign against Hungary. But an infected boil or abscess on his back forced him to call a halt halfway to Edirne near Çorlu, the ancient Cenopurio. His illness grew steadily worse, leading some to believe that he was suffering from cancer or even the plague, and he finally died there on 21 September 1520. He was fifty years old and had reigned eight and a half years, nearly all of which he had spent on campaign. Because of his ruthlessness he is known in Turkey as Selim the Grim, the most notable victims of his wrath being the seven grand vezirs whom he executed during his reign – almost one a year. When news of his death reached the West there was a great relief, and one chronicler there noted that 'Selim died of an infected boil, and thereby Hungary was spared.'

Selim was succeeded by his son Süleyman, who soon afterwards erected a mosque – the Selim I Camii[17] – on the Fourth Hill in honour of his father, who was reburied there in a splendid türbe. The huge catafalque of Selim the Grim stands alone in the centre of the domed tomb, with the sultan's enormous turban at its head – a scene described by Evliya Çelebi: 'There is no royal sepulchre that fills the visitor with so much awe as Selim's. There he lies with the turban called Selimiye on his coffin like a seven-headed dragon. I, the humble Evliya, was for three years the reader of hymns at his tomb.'

CHAPTER 17

The Age of Süleyman the Magnificent

1520–1566

Süleyman was not yet twenty-six when he became sultan. He had been educated at the palace school in Topkapı Sarayı, after which he served as provincial governor in Manisa throughout his father's reign.

The earliest extant description of Süleyman is that of the Venetian envoy Bartolomeo Contarini, who saw the young sultan shortly after his accession, and wrote:

He is twenty-five years of age, tall, but wiry, and of a delicate complexion. His neck is a little too long, his face thin, and his nose aquiline. He has a shadow of a moustache and a small beard; nevertheless he has a pleasant mien, though his skin tends to pallor. He is said to be a wise lord, fond of study, and all men hope for good from his rule.

When Süleyman came to the throne he already had several children, the heir apparent being his son Mustafa, born in 1515 to Gülbahar, who had previously been his favourite concubine. By then, however, Süleyman's favourite was Haseki Hürrem, known in the west as Roxelana, or the Russian, because of her supposed origin. During the first five years of his reign Roxelana bore Süleyman five children: a son, Mehmet, in 1521; a daughter, Mihrimah, in 1522; and then three sons, Abdullah, Selim and Beyazit. Abdullah died in 1526, succumbing to one of the many plagues that ravaged the Harem. Then in 1530 Roxelana bore Süleyman another son, Cihangir, a hunchback who came to be known as Eğri, or Crooked. As soon as Roxelana's son Mehmet was born her influence over Süleyman became even greater than before, and she eventually persuaded him to put aside his other women and make her his legal wife – the first time in Ottoman

*Süleyman the Magnificent (1520–66) and an elephant from his
menagerie, with Süleymaniye Camii in the background; drawing
by Melchior Lorichs, 1559.*

history that this had happened. Süleyman's enthralment by Roxelana
became common gossip in the bazaars of Istanbul, as noted by the
Italian page Bassano: 'He bears her such love and keeps such faith in
her that all his subjects marvel, and they say that she has bewitched him.'

Each wife of the sultan was known as a kadın, which means simply
'woman', and the two who were the first to bear sons ordinarily took
precedence as first (birinci) and second (ikinci) kadın. When a new
sultan succeeded to the throne his mother became the valide sultan,
or queen mother, who ruled supreme in the Harem. Süleyman's
mother, the valide sultan Hafise, died in 1534, after which Roxelana
became the highest-ranking woman in the Harem. But Roxelana could

not rest easy, for her eldest son, Mehmet, was second in the line of succession, after Mustafa, and she was waiting for the opportunity to have Mustafa eliminated as heir apparent in favour of her own son.

At the very outset of his reign Süleyman began the programme of judicial reform from which he takes his Turkish nickname of Kanuni, or the Law-Maker. This reform ended the arbitrary warrior code of his predecessors and created a new system of laws that protected the lives, property and civil rights of his subjects.

Süleyman's first campaign took him to Belgrade, which he captured on 29 August 1521. He then attacked Rhodes, where the knights of St John surrendered on 20 December 1522, following a siege of 145 days, after which they went on to establish their new headquarters on Malta.

Early in 1523 Süleyman appointed a new grand vezir, Ibrahim Pasha, a Greek captive who had been raised with him in the palace and became his most intimate friend. The following year Süleyman gave his sister Hadice in marriage to Ibrahim, marking the occasion with a gala festival in the Hippodrome that lasted for eight days. Ibrahim had already amassed vast wealth through his association with the sultan, and that same year he completed a great palace[1] on the west side of the Hippodrome, which was partly demolished to make way for it, leaving the arena as a place of public muster.

Süleyman then mounted an expedition into Hungary, with Ibrahim Pasha in command of the army. This campaign climaxed on 29 August 1526 at the battle of Mohács, where the Ottomans utterly defeated the Hungarians in a battle that lasted less than two hours. Most of the Hungarian nobility died in the battle or were executed by Süleyman, who ordered that no prisoners be taken. As Süleyman noted in his diary for 31 August: 'The sultan, seated on a golden throne, receives the homage of the vezirs and the beys; massacre of 2,000 prisoners; the rain falls in torrents.' Then on 2 September he recorded his postscript on the battle: 'Rest at Mohács; 20,000 Hungarian infantry and 4,000 of their cavalry are buried.'

Süleyman's next campaign into Europe got under way on 10 May 1529, with Ibrahim Pasha once again in command. The goal of the expedition was Vienna, before which Süleyman drew up his forces on 27 September, putting the city under siege. But though the Turks outnumbered the defenders by at least three to one, they were unable to take the city, and Süleyman was forced to raise the siege on 15 October so as to march his army back to Istanbul before winter began.

This was the first reverse suffered by Süleyman, and he tried to save face by pretending that he had invaded Austria only to protect his vassal John Zapolya against the archduke Ferdinand of Habsburg, brother of the emperor Charles V. Süleyman also tried to distract the attention of his subjects from the failure of his campaign, and on 27 June 1530 he celebrated the circumcision of his four sons with a festival in the Hippodrome that lasted for three weeks.

Two years later Süleyman mounted another expedition against Vienna, but his army penetrated only as far as the Austrian frontier. When the Ottoman army returned to Istanbul, Süleyman once again held a celebration to mark the conclusion of what his subjects were told was another successful Ottoman campaign. As Süleyman wrote in his diary at the time: 'Five days of feasts and illuminations ... The bazaars remain open all night, and Süleyman goes to visit them incognito.'

A peace treaty was signed between the Habsburgs and the Ottomans on 22 June 1533. This left Süleyman free to turn to his eastern frontier. Three months after the treaty Ibrahim Pasha took an army into north-eastern Anatolia in preparation for an attack on Azerbaijan, and later Süleyman led another army in an invasion of Iran and Iraq, with Tabriz surrendering to him on 13 July 1534 and Baghdad soon afterwards.

Süleyman spent the winter in Baghdad, and while there he received a letter from Roxelana complaining about her plight in the Harem:

My Lord, your absence has kindled in me a fire that does not abate. Take pity on this suffering soul and speed your letter, so that I may find in it at least a little consolation ... When I read your letter, your son Mehmet and your daughter Mihrimah were by my side, and tears streamed from their eyes. Their tears drove me from my mind ... You ask me why I am angry with Ibrahim Pasha. When – God willing – we are together again, I shall explain, and you will learn the cause.

Ibrahim by that time had reached the peak of his power, and this was undoubtedly the source of Roxelana's unhappiness. Just a year or so before Ibrahim had boasted to a foreign ambassador of the great power that he wielded – unsurpassed even by that of Süleyman. The Venetian envoy heard much the same story from the grand vezir at a later interview, which led him to remark that if Süleyman 'should send one of his cooks to kill Ibrahim Pasha, there would be nothing to prevent the killing'. Ibrahim met his end on 15 March 1536, when he was invited by Süleyman to have dinner with him in the imperial apartments at Topkapı Sarayı. What happened that night is a mystery, but the following morning Ibrahim's body was found outside the Imperial Gate of the saray, the condition of his corpse indicating that he had been strangled after fighting for his life. All of Ibrahim's vast wealth was confiscated by the state immediately after his death, including his great palace on the Hippodrome.

Early in Süleyman's reign he renewed an alliance that his father, Selim, had made with a corsair from Mitylene named Barbarossa – known to the Turks as Hayrettin Pasha – who had gained control of Algiers. Süleyman appointed him as high admiral of the Ottoman fleet in 1534, and two years later Barbarossa recaptured several places that had been taken from the Turks by Charles V, the Habsburg emperor.

In 1536 Süleyman and François I of France entered into a formal alliance against Charles. This treaty included a trade agreement called the Capitulations, which gave French merchants freedom to trade without restriction in the Ottoman Empire. This led to the formation of a Frankish *millet* that would be the prototype for other European 'nations' in Turkey. These European communities were established in the heights above Galata, with their embassies and churches being erected along the Grande Rue de Pera.

Barbarossa unsuccessfully besieged Corfu in 1536, after which he sailed back into the Aegean, attacking many of the Venetian-held islands and carrying off thousands of their inhabitants to be sold as slaves in Istanbul. As a result the Ottoman Empire established its control over most of the Aegean islands except Cyprus and Crete, which the Venetians still held. Barbarossa returned to the Adriatic the following year, defeating an allied fleet at Preveza on 28 September 1538. He continued to ravage the coasts and islands of the Mediterranean for another five years before retiring in Istanbul, where he died in 1546. He was buried at Beşiktaş on the European shore of the Bosphorus, in a splendid türbe[2] that had been built for him by the architect Sinan, then at the beginning of his remarkable career.

Sinan, who was born c. 1497, had started out as a recruit in the devşirme, the annual levy in which Christian youths were taken into the Janissaries and became Muslims, and he served as a military engineer in four of Süleyman's campaigns. Süleyman appointed him as chief of the imperial architects in 1538, by which time Sinan had already built a number of structures for the sultan. Soon afterwards Süleyman commissioned Sinan to build a mosque complex for Roxelana – Haseki Hürrem Camii[3] – which the sultan presented to his wife as a surprise gift on her birthday. This was the first külliye built in the city by Sinan, who in a career of half a century erected a total of 321 structures all over the Ottoman Empire, of which 85 still remain standing in Istanbul alone, including 22 mosques.

Late in the autumn of 1539 Süleyman and Roxelana marked the circumcision of their two sons Beyazit and Cihangir with a celebration in the Hippodrome that lasted for fifteen days. At the same time they also celebrated the wedding of their daughter, Mihrimah, with Rüstem Pasha, who would go on to serve two terms as Süleyman's grand vezir. Rüstem was known as Kehle-i-Ikbal, the Louse of Fortune, a nickname that he had acquired when he married the princess Mihrimah. It seems that Rüstem's enemies had tried to prevent him from marrying the princess by spreading the rumour that he had leprosy. But when the palace doctors examined Rüstem they discovered that he was infested with lice, whereupon they declared that he was not leprous, for accepted medical belief had it that lice never inhabit lepers. Thus Rüstem was allowed to marry Mihrimah, acquiring his nickname from the old Turkish proverb that 'When a man has his luck in place even a louse can bring him good fortune.'

An epidemic of smallpox in 1543 took the life of the şehzade (prince) Mehmet, eldest son of Süleyman and Roxelana, who was only twenty-one when he died. Süleyman was heartbroken at the death of his beloved son and sat beside Mehmet's body for three days before he would permit the burial to take place. Süleyman then decided to commemorate Mehmet by the erection of a great mosque complex on the Third Hill, to be named Şehzade Camii,[4] the Mosque of the Prince. Sinan was given the commission and began work early the following

Şehzade Camii.

year, completing the külliye in 1548. Sinan himself later called Şehzade Camii his 'apprentice work', but if so it is the work of an apprentice of genius, his first imperial mosque complex on a truly imperial scale.

The same year that he finished Şehzade Camii, Sinan also completed a mosque for the princess Mihrimah. This was built in Üsküdar above the iskele, or landing-place, and hence it was called Iskele Camii.[5] The princess later commissioned Sinan to build another mosque in Istanbul, Mihrimah Camii,[6] the principal landmark on the Sixth Hill of the old city.

Süleyman mounted a campaign into north-eastern Anatolia in 1548, capturing Van on 25 August of that year. The following summer he extended his conquests into Georgia, after which he returned to Istanbul triumphantly on 12 December 1549.

Among those who were in Süleyman's entourage when he returned to Istanbul was the French scholar Pierre Gilles, better known as Petrus Gyllius. Gyllius had first come to Istanbul in 1544 along with the embassy of François I. He spent the next four years there, studying ancient sources as well as the topography of the city and its Byzantine monuments. He then went off with Süleyman on a campaign to Iran, and after his return to Istanbul he spent a few more months in the city before leaving for Rome, where he died on 5 January 1555. The results of his researches were published at Lyon in 1561 by his nephew Antonie Gilles, namely the *Three Books on the Thracian Bosphorus* and the *Four Books on the Topography of Constantinople and its Antiquities*, which have endured as classics in the study of the imperial city.

The most remarkable accomplishment that Gyllius made during his stay in Istanbul was his discovery of the Basilica Cistern, the huge underground reservoir that Justinian had built under the Stoa Basilica. He describes how he came upon the cistern while searching in vain for the stoa, which he calls the Imperial Portico:

The Imperial Portico is not to be seen, though the Cistern remains. Through the inhabitants' carelessness and contempt for everything that is curious it was never discovered except by me, who is a stranger among them, after a long and diligent search. The whole area was built over, which made it less suspect that there was a cistern there. The people had not the least suspicion of it, although they daily drew their water out of the wells that were sunk into it. By chance I went into a little house where there was a way down to it and went aboard a little skiff. I discovered it after the master of the house lit some torches and rowed me here and there across the pillars, which lay very deep in the water. He was very intent upon catching his fish, with which the Cistern abounds, and speared some of them by the light of the torches.

Gyllius saw a number of other monuments that have since vanished, including the colossal equestrian statue of Justinian that stood in front of Haghia Sophia. Gyllius reports on the fate of the monument:

About thirty years ago the whole shaft was taken down to the pedestal, and that was demolished down to the base about a year ago [*c.* 1545] ... I recently saw the equestrian statue of Justinian erected on the pillar that stood here and which had been preserved a long time in the imperial precinct, carried into the melting-pot where they cast their ordnance. Among the fragments were the leg of Justinian, which exceeded my height, and his nose, which was over twenty-three centimetres long. I dared not measure the horse's legs as they lay on the ground but privately measured one of the hoofs and found it to be twenty-three centimetres in height.

Gyllius found that a number of ancient monuments had been partly or wholly demolished by Süleyman, who used them to provide building materials for edifices that he had founded. He notes that the arcade on the uppermost level of the Hippodrome had recently been taken down, with the columns and their bases 'removed by order of Emperor Süleyman to build a hospital'. This hospital was part of the Süleymaniye,[7] a great mosque complex on the Third Hill that Sinan began building for Süleyman while Gyllius was in Istanbul.

The Süleymaniye was the second largest mosque complex ever built in Istanbul, surpassed in size only by that of Fatih Camii. But Süleyman's külliye surpasses that of Fatih in its splendour, particularly the magnificent Süleymaniye Camii, the grandest and most beautiful of all the imperial mosques in the city. Sinan completed the mosque in 1557, but it took several more years to finish the rest of the külliye.

During the decade or so that Sinan was working on the Süleymaniye he erected a number of other edifices in Istanbul, including a beautiful public bath for Roxelana, known as Haseki Hürrem Hamamı.[8] Five years after his completion of the Süleymaniye, Sinan built one of the finest of all his grand-vezirial mosques, Rüstem Pasha Camii.[9] By then, in addition to the edifices already mentioned, he had adorned Istanbul with eight other mosques, along with four medreses, four türbes, a hamam, a han, and six aqueducts in the environs of the city. All of this building activity was part of the great expansion of the Ottoman Empire during Süleyman's reign, when wealth from the sultan's vast realm was pouring into Istanbul.

The population of Istanbul during Süleyman's reign may have reached half a million – about what it had been in the time of Justinian. The census of 1535, which numbered 80,000 households in Istanbul and Galata, recorded that 58 per cent of these were Muslim, 32 per cent Christian, and 10 per cent Jewish, while a French traveller in 1550 estimated that there were 120,000 households in the city – an increase of 50 per cent in 15 years. These figures do not include those living in the palace and the sultan's household troops, the kapıkulu, who together probably amounted to about 25,000 during Süleyman's reign. During the early Ottoman period Istanbul was hit by periodic epidemics of plague, cholera and smallpox, the first one in 1466, when 600 people a day were dying within the walls and the survivors fleeing for their lives, according to Kritovoulos. During Süleyman's reign there were two serious epidemics in Istanbul, the first in 1526 and the second in 1561. Nevertheless, the population soon increased to its previous number or more after each of these epidemics, because of the constant immigration of poorer people from the provinces.

Süleyman mounted a campaign into Transylvania in 1551 under the command of Sokollu Mehmet Pasha, a devşirme recruit from Bosnia who had been trained in the palace school in Istanbul. Mehmet Pasha captured Temesvar on 26 July 1552, after which most of Transylvania was placed under Ottoman suzerainty.

Süleyman mounted another campaign against the Safavids in Iran in 1553. While the Ottoman army was still in central Anatolia, the grand vezir Rüstem Pasha convinced Süleyman that his eldest son, Prince Mustafa, was conspiring with the Safavids to usurp the Ottoman throne. Rüstem was undoubtedly in league with his mother-in-law, Roxelana, who for some time seems to have been plotting to remove Mustafa so that her eldest surviving son, Selim, would be first in line as successor to the throne. Mustafa, who was described by a contemporary source as 'marvellously well-educated and prudent and of the age to reign', was idolized by the Janissaries, and so it is easy to see how Rüstem Pasha was able to persuade Süleyman that his son was planning to overthrow him. On 6 November 1553 Süleyman summoned Mustafa to his headquarters at Ereğli in Karaman, and when the prince appeared in his tent he had him strangled, leaving his dead body exposed in the camp for all to see. When the news reached Prince Cihangir, who was serving as provincial governor in Aleppo, he was so overcome with grief that he took sick and died on 27 December of that same year.

The Janissaries were outraged by Mustafa's execution and were on the point of revolting, but Süleyman appeased them by dismissing Rüstem Pasha, replacing him with Kara Ahmet Pasha. Two years later Ahmet Pasha was executed by Süleyman, who then reappointed Rüstem Pasha as grand vezir, undoubtedly through the influence of Roxelana.

Roxelana was now on the verge of achieving her great ambition, for Süleyman's only two surviving sons – Selim and Beyazit – were her children, and whichever of them succeeded to the throne she would be the valide sultan. She favoured Selim, who being the older of the two was the heir apparent, though he was so dissolute that he was known as Sarhoş, or the Sot. He won the support of the Janissaries and eventually defeated and eliminated Beyazit, leaving himself as the heir apparent.

Roxelana did not live to see her favourite son's ascendancy, for she died on 16 March 1558. Süleyman was desolate with grief as she was laid to rest that same day in her türbe at the Süleymaniye.

Süleyman mounted a great expedition against Malta in 1564, with Mustafa Pasha commanding the army and Piyale Pasha the fleet, while Turgut Reis sailed with another flotilla from Tripoli. But the expedition was a failure, for the knights of St John held out in their fortress in Malta through a memorable siege that began on 20 May 1565. The siege ended on 11 September of that year, when the arrival of a Christian fleet from Sicily persuaded Mustafa Pasha to end the expedition and sail back to Istanbul.

The following spring Süleyman decided to mount a campaign into Europe under his new grand vezir, Sokollu Mehmet Pasha. The expedition set off from Istanbul on 1 May 1566, Süleyman's objective being the fortress of Sziget (Szigetvár), the last important Habsburg stronghold in Hungary. By the time they reached the Danube Süleyman was so ill that he could no longer ride his horse and had to be carried in a litter. The army reached Sziget on 5 August and put it under siege, meeting stiff resistance from the garrison under the valiant count Nicholas Zrinyi, who held out for another month in the citadel. Zrinyi's last act was to set a fuse that ignited the powder magazine of the citadel, blowing it to bits and killing some 3,000 Turks.

Süleyman did not live to see the capture of Sziget, for he died the evening before the citadel fell, on 7 September 1566. Mehmet Pasha withheld news of Süleyman's death from the army, sending a courier to inform Prince Selim, who was serving as governor in Kütahya, advising him to proceed to Istanbul to secure the throne before any opposition to his succession could arise. Meanwhile Süleyman's body

left: *Mihrab and mimber in Süleymaniye Camii*
right: *Interior of Süleyman's tomb.*

was secretly embalmed, after which he was dressed in his imperial robes and set up in the grand vezir's tent as if still alive. Mehmet Pasha forged the imperial signature on the documents that continued to be issued in Süleyman's name – a pretence that continued until Selim sent word that he had in fact been proclaimed sultan in Istanbul. Süleyman's remains were then brought back to Istanbul for burial in his türbe behind the Süleymaniye, next to the tomb of Roxelana.

Such was the life of Süleyman the Magnificent, who ruled over his empire for forty-six years, the longest reign in Ottoman history. Süleyman's enduring memorial in Istanbul is the Süleymaniye, just as that of Justinian is Haghia Sophia, two magnificent edifices erected a thousand years apart in time, both visible in the same view of the city's majestic skyline above the Golden Horn.

CHAPTER 18

The House of Felicity
1566–1623

The Ottoman Empire began its decline with the death of Süleyman, whose immediate successors, beginning with Selim II, were ineffective rulers who spent most of their time in the Inner Palace of Topkapı Sarayı, the pleasure dome known as Dar-üs Saadet, the House of Felicity. This was closed off from the outer part of the saray by the closely guarded portal known as Bab-üs Saadet, the Gate of Felicity, which is thus described by an anonymous European traveller at the time:

When you go to the Seraglio you have to enter by a gate which is very richly gilded, and is called the 'Gate of Felicity'. Sometimes you see over it, stuck upon the point of a pike, the head of a grand vezir, or some other personage, who has been decapitated in the morning, at the caprice of the Grand Signor.

Selim II was forty-two years old when he came to the throne. By then he was a completely dissolute alcoholic, neglecting affairs of state and spending all of his time with his favourite pages and his concubines in the Inner Palace. As Evliya Çelebi writes of him, 'He was a sweet-natured sovereign, but given to pleasure and wine.'

During Selim's reign all affairs of state were under the control of Sokollu Mehmet Pasha. He had married Selim's daughter Esmahan in 1562, and three years later he had been appointed grand vezir by Süleyman. He continued in office throughout the reign of Selim, leaving the sultan free to enjoy his pleasures undisturbed in the House of Felicity.

Selim's favourite wife was Nurubanu, mother of the future Murat III. She may have been of Venetian origin, and was the power behind the throne throughout Selim's reign, corresponding with the Venetian doge and other heads of state. Thus began a period in Ottoman history known in Turkish as Kadınlar Sultanatı, the Sultanate of Women, in which a series of concubines in the Harem exercised considerable influence over affairs of state.

Mehmet Pasha arranged a peace treaty with the Habsburg emperor Ferdinand in 1568. The following year he mounted an expedition into southern Russia, at the same time increasing Ottoman influence over the vassal princes of Moldavia and Wallachia. This first war between the Ottomans and Russians ended with a peace treaty signed in 1570 by Selim and Tsar Ivan IV, the Terrible.

By that time Selim had fallen under the influence of Joseph Nasi, a Portuguese Jew who had taken refuge in the Ottoman Empire and become the sultan's most trusted adviser. Nasi persuaded Selim to attack Cyprus, which was then held by the Venetians. Selim sent a fleet under the command of Piyale Pasha, who in 1570 landed an army on Cyprus under Lala Mustafa Pasha. Mustafa besieged the Venetian fortress at Famagusta, which surrendered to him on 1 August 1571, with the other fortified cities on the island capitulating soon afterwards.

The Turkish invasion of Cyprus led to the formation of a Holy League against the Ottomans – an alliance that included Spain, Venice, the knights of Malta, the papacy, and several other Italian states. The League outfitted an armada under the command of Don Juan of Austria, bastard son of Charles V. The Turkish fleet had taken up winter quarters in the port of Lepanto, near the western end of the Gulf of Corinth, where it was joined by a contingent from Algiers under Uluç Ali. The two armadas met off Lepanto on 7 October 1571, and in the last great battle between galleys the Christians were victorious, sinking most of the Ottoman fleet. Miguel Cervantes, who was wounded in the battle, writes in *Don Quixote* of 'that day so fortunate to Christendom when all nations were undeceived of their error in believing that the Turks were invincible'.

The only Ottoman ships to escape were part of the Algerian contingent under Uluç Ali, who made his way back to Istanbul with forty galleys. He was given a hero's welcome, and thenceforth he was known as Kılıç, or the Sword, from the way he had cut his way through the

Christian fleet to escape. Kılıç Ali Pasha was then given command of the Ottoman fleet, which was completely rebuilt within two years. The revival of the Turkish navy forced Venice to sign a peace treaty with the Ottomans on 7 March 1573, and the following summer a Turkish fleet captured Tripoli, re-establishing Ottoman control over the western Mediterranean.

Meanwhile Selim had hardly stirred from the Harem, most of his excursions having been to Edirne to inspect the mosque complex that he was building there. This magnificent külliye – the Selimiye – was erected by Sinan, who had continued as chief of the imperial architects under Selim II. Sinan also erected a great many buildings for Sokollu Mehmet Pasha throughout the empire, including two mosques in Istanbul. The most notable of the latter is Sokollu Mehmet Pasha Camii,[1] which he erected on the Marmara slope of the First Hill.

Selim died on 15 December 1574, having collapsed in a drunken stupor while bathing in the Harem. News of his death was kept secret so that his eldest son, Murat, could return to Istanbul from Manisa, where he had been serving as provincial governor. The prince arrived in Istanbul on 21 December 1574, whereupon he was immediately girded with the sword of Osman at Eyüp and raised to the throne as Murat III. That same day Murat ordered the execution of his five younger brothers, to prevent them from contesting his throne. The murdered princes were buried together with their father in the garden of Haghia Sophia, where Murat commissioned Sinan to build a splendid türbe[2] for them.

Murat III was twenty-eight when he came to the throne. At that time his favourite wife was Safiye, mother of the future Mehmet III, who is also believed to have been of Venetian origin. A power struggle took place in the Harem between Safiye and Nurubanu, the valide sultan. Nurubanu's principal ally was her daughter Esmahan, wife of Sokollu Mehmet Pasha, who continued as grand vezir under Murat III. Nurubanu and Esmahan sought to weaken Safiye's hold on Murat by purchasing the most beautiful girls who were offered for sale in the Istanbul slave market, introducing them into the sultan's harem. Nurubanu's scheme worked, for Murat took on a succession of concubines, though Safiye remained as his first kadın. Murat sired 103

left: *The kızlar ağası, or chief black eunuch.*
right: *A kadın of the Harem in indoor costume.*

children during his reign, when he seems to have done little else than
serve as the royal stud.

During the summer of 1582 Murat celebrated the circumcision of
his eldest son, the future Mehmet III, with an extravaganza in the
Hippodrome that lasted for fifty-two days. The festival was described
by an anonymous French traveller, whose account soon appeared in
an English translation:

The inhabitants, and Artificers of Constantinople [took part in] those fore-
noone sports with all theyre royall and brave attyre. The souldiers and men

of warr, the labourers, the minstrels, the leapers, and dauncers, the juglers, and suchlyke, did employ and busie themselves ... The midnight sports were passed away with burning of Fortresses, Holdes, Horses, Elephantes, and other creatures made by arte ...

I must now set down for the afterward, and last company, the Singers, Players of Instruments, Schollers, Monkes, Jugglers, Tumblers, and Plaiers ... there you might have seen Arabians, Mores, Persians, Grecians, and Spaniards, sounding on theyr Cornets, Trumpets, Tabors, Cyterons, and other instruments within the Parke, or Tiltyard, where they made such a confused noyse and sound, without tune, change of note, or keeping of tune and space, that all the whole Toune sounded and rong with the route of theyre voices and soundes.

Murat's large harem necessitated considerable reconstruction in Topkapı Sarayı. The rebuilding began in the first year of Murat's reign, when Sinan constructed ten huge kitchens along the eastern side of the Second Court. Four years later Sinan completely rebuilt the great hall in the Inner Palace now known as the Salon of Murat III.

During the last eight years of his life Sinan erected four more mosques in Istanbul – Kılıç Ali Pasha Camii,[3] Şemsi Ahmet Pasha Camii,[4] Atik Valide Camii,[5] and Ramazan Efendi Camii,[6] the last of these completed just two years before his death in 1588, when he was well past ninety. He was buried in the türbe he had built for himself at the north-west corner of the Süleymaniye complex, the enduring monument to his fame.

Sokollu Mehmet Pasha met his end on 12 December 1579, when he was assassinated at a meeting of the Divan by a mad soldier from Bosnia. The Venetian bailo, Maffeo Venier, commented on the passing of the great grand vezir in his report to the doge: 'With Sokollu Mehmet, Turkish virtue sank into the grave.'

After the assassination of Sokollu Mehmet Pasha, Murat changed grand vezirs ten times in sixteen years, with Siyavuş Pasha and Koca Sinan Pasha each holding the office for three terms. These frequent shifts in government were part of the general instability that followed Sokollu Mehmet Pasha's passing, evidence of a decline in the empire that he had held in check during his time in office. A debasement of the gold coinage led in 1589 to a revolt of the Janissaries, who were already dissatisfied because of the steady decline in their pay and living-conditions. They overthrew their huge bronze kazans, or cauldrons, this being their customary signal of discontent, and forced their way into the Second Court of the saray while the Divan was in session, demanding the heads of the ministers responsible for the debasement of the coinage. Murat was forced to comply with their demands, but in the next three years the Janissaries revolted twice more and forced the sultan to dismiss grand vezirs and other ministers. By that time the Janissaries had already declined as a fighting force, partly because the old devşirme system had been to a large extent abandoned and replaced by the enlistment of native-born Turks. Then in 1593 the sultan's feudal cavalry – the Sipahis – revolted, only to be put down by the Janissaries, who used this as a way of increasing their influence. This heralded the end of the Sipahis as a fief-holding military aristocracy, and many thousands of them were eventually forced off their lands in Anatolia, adding to the general anarchy.

Murat grew ill at the beginning of 1595 and felt that death was near. As his end approached he asked to be taken to Incili Köşkü, the Kiosk of the Pearl, which still survives on the Marmara shore below the First Hill. His musicians played a melancholy Persian song to which he mouthed the words, 'Come and keep watch with me tonight, O Death.' Two galleys of the fleet passed the kiosk and, knowing that the sultan was therein, fired a salute, whose blasts shattered the windows in the walls and dome of the pavilion, scattering shards of glass around the room and reducing Murat to tears. 'Once the salvoes of my fleet would not have broken those windows, but now ...' he moaned. 'Such is the kiosk of my life.' Murat was then carried back to his room in the House of Felicity, where he had begun his days and where they now ended.

Murat III died on 16 January 1595. News of his death was kept secret so that his eldest son, Mehmet, could return to Istanbul from Manisa, where he had been serving as provincial governor. The prince arrived in Istanbul and ascended to the throne as Mehmet III on 28 January 1595, being then in his thirtieth year. That same day Mehmet executed all nineteen of his younger brothers, following the same policy of fratricide as his father and grandfather before him. Murat and his nineteen sons were then buried in the garden of Haghia

Sophia, where a handsome türbe[7] was built for them by Davut Ağa, Sinan's successor as chief of the imperial architects. Immediately after the burials the women of Murat's harem were sent off to Eski Saray, the Old Palace on the Third Hill.

The English traveller Fynes Moryson, who visited Istanbul in 1597, noted that the daughters and concubines of the departed Murat III were still living in the Eski Saray, but that the most beautiful women of the imperial household were in the Harem of Topkapı Sarayı with Mehmet III, 'for the fairest and dearest to him are taken to live in his court'.

The Women's Bath in the Harem; miniature.

Moryson was one of a number of travellers who commented with wonder on the strange animals kept by the sultans in their menageries. One of these zoos was at Tekfursarayı, the Byzantine palace on the Sixth Hill. When Moryson visited Tekfursarayı it was being used to house two elephants and a giraffe. He was particularly amazed by the giraffe, which had never before been seen in Europe; he describes it as 'a beaste newly brought out of Affricke (the Mother of Monsters), which beaste is altogether unknowne in our parts, he many times put his nose in my necke, when I thought my self furthest from him, which familiarity I liked not; and however his Keeper assured me he would not hurt me, yet I avoided his familiar kisses as much as I could'.

When Mehmet III came to the throne his mother, Safiye, became the valide sultan. Soon after coming to power she commissioned Davut Ağa to build her an imperial mosque on the shore of the Golden Horn in the market quarter known as Eminönü, which had long been inhabited by a community of Karaite Jews. Safiye evicted the Karaim and resettled them some three kilometres up the Golden Horn on its opposite shore, in the quarter of Hasköy, the Royal Village, where their descendants live to this day. Davut Ağa died in 1599 and was replaced as chief of the imperial architects by Ahmet Çavuş, who continued working on Safiye's mosque, part of which was built on filled-in land. His work in filling in this land earned the architect the nickname Dalgıç, or the Diver, and thenceforth he was known as Dalgıç Ahmet Çavuş.

After Mehmet III came to the throne the Levant Company of England had to renew the capitulations agreement with the Ottoman Empire, and to facilitate this Queen Elizabeth sent along rich presents for the sultan, the grand vezir and other Ottoman officials. Among these was an extraordinary water-organ that the queen sent as a personal present to the sultan. This had been specially built by the organ-maker Thomas Dallaam, who was sent by the queen to install it in Topkapı Sarayı. Dallaam finally arrived in Istanbul in August 1599 and installed the organ in the Privy Chamber, where he played it for Mehmet and his favourite pages. While he was installing the organ, Dallaam befriended one of the pages, who led him to a place where he could catch a glimpse of the women in the Harem, as he wrote:

Crossinge throughe a little squar courte paved with marble, he poynted me to goo to a graite in a wale, but made me a sine that he myghte not goo thether him selfe. When I came to the grait the wale was verrie thicke, and graited

on both sides with iron verrie strongly; but through that graite I did see thir-
tie of the Grand Sinyor's Concobines that weare playinge with a bale in
another courte. At the firste sighte of them I thoughte they had bene yonge
men, but when I saw the hare of their heades hange doone on their backes,
platted together with a tasle of small pearle hanging in the lower end of it,
and by other plaine tokens, I did know them to be women, and verrie pret-
tie ones in deede . . . I stood so longe loukinge upon them that he which had
showed me all this kindness began to be verrie angrie with me. He made a
wrye mouthe, and stamped with his foute to make me give over looking, the
which I was verrie lothe to dow, for the sighte did please me wondrous well.

Early in June 1603 Mehmet's eldest son, Prince Mahmut, who was
then twenty-one years old, was accused by the chief black eunuch of
plotting against the sultan. (The chief black eunuch had the responsibility of guarding the sultan's women in the Harem of Topkapı Sarayı
– a position that gave him great power.) Mehmet believed the accusa-
tion, and on 7 June 1603 he had Mahmut and his mother executed. It
is possible this execution was the result of a plot by another of Mehmet's
concubines, Handan, whose son Ahmet became heir apparent after
Mahmut's execution, while she herself became the sultan's first kadın.

Mehmet III died of a heart attack on 23 December 1603. He was
succeeded by the elder of his two surviving sons, who was girded as
Ahmet I that same day, when he was thirteen and a half years old. The
late sultan's only other surviving son, the mentally retarded Mustafa,
who was then eleven, was spared the customary execution that had
been carried out in the previous three generations under the bloody
Ottoman code of fratricide. His survival was undoubtedly due to the
fact that he was a son of Handan, who became valide sultan when
Ahmet I succeeded to the throne. Ahmet sent Mustafa to live at the
Eski Saray in Beyazit along with their grandmother, Safiye, who lost
her position as valide sultan. Safiye thus had to abandon the project
of building her imperial mosque on the Golden Horn at Eminönü,
and the half-completed building was abandoned.

Handan did not enjoy her power for long, for on 26 November
1605 she was killed in the Inner Palace, probably in some Harem
intrigue, though one source has it that she was poisoned by Sultan
Ahmet. She had outlived Safiye, who had died in the Eski Saray on 10

November of that same year. Handan was buried beside her husband, Mehmet III, in a splendid tomb[8] that their son Ahmet I commissioned for them in the garden of Haghia Sophia, a work of Dalgıç Ahmet Çavuş.

When Ahmet came to the throne his first kadın was a girl named Mahfiruze, better known as Hadice, who was probably of Greek origin. The following year Hadice bore him a son, Osman. Then around 1608 Ahmet found a new favourite, a Greek girl named Anastasia, who had been captured on the island of Tinos and sold as a slave to the Harem, where she took the name of Kösem. The following year Kösem bore Ahmet a son, Murat, whereupon he made her his first kadın and put aside Hadice. Then in 1615 Kösem bore another son, Ibrahim, by which time she was the power behind the throne, leading an Italian chronicler to remark that 'One knows not in truth who is the sovereign.'

The slave-market in which Kösem had been sold, the Avret Pazarı, is described thus by William Lithgow, who visited Istanbul in 1610:

I have seen men and women as usually sold here in Markets, as Horses and other beasts are with us: The most part of which are Hungarians, Transilvanians, Carindians, Istrians, and Dalmatian Captives, and of other places besides, which they can overcome. Whom, if no compassionable Christian will buy, or relieve; then must they either turne Turke, or be addicted to perpetual slavery.

Lithgow then goes on to tell of how his French friend, a 'Maister Gunner, named Monsieur Nerack', decided that he 'would gladly for Conscience and Merit's sake, redeeme some poore Christian slave from Turkish Captivity':

To the which, I applauded his advice, and told him the next Friday following, I would assist him to so worthy an action: Friday comes, and he and I went to Constantinople, where the Market of the slaves being ready, we spent two hours in viewing, and reviewing five hundred Males and Females. At last I pointed him to have bought an old man or woman, but his minde was a contrary set, shewing me that he would buy some virgin, or young widdow, to save their bodies undefloured with Infidels. The price of a virgin was too deare for him, being a hundred Duckets, and widdows were farre under, and at an easier rate: When we did visite and search them that we were mindfull to buy, they were strip'd starke naked before our eyes, where the sweetest face, the youngest age, and whitest skin was in greatest value and request: The Jewes sold them, for they had bought them from the Turkes: At last we fell upon a Dalmatian widdow, whose pittifull lookes, and sprinkling teares, stroke my soule almost to the death for compassion: whereupon I grew earnest for her reliefe, and he yielding to my advice, she is bought and delivered unto him, the man being 60 years of age, and her price 36 Duckets. We leave the market and came over againe to Galata, where he and I tooke a Chamber for her, and leaving them there, the next morning I returned earely, suspecting greatly the dissembling devotion of the gunner to be nought but luxurious lust, and so it proved: I knocked at the Chamber doore, that he had newly locked, and taken the key with him to the ship, for he had tarried with her all that night; and she answering me with teares, told me all the manner of his usage, wishing her selfe to be againe in her former captivity: whereupon I went a shipboord to him, & in my griefe I swore, that if he abused her any more after that manner, and not returned to her distresse, her Christian liberty; I would first make it knowne to his Maister, the Captaine of the ship, and then to the French Ambassadour: for he was mindfull also, his lust being satisfied to have sold her all over againe to some other: At which threatning the old Passyard became so fearefull, that he entred in a reasonable condition with me, and the ship departing thence six dayes thereafter, he freely resigned to me her life, her liberty and freedome: which being done, and he gone, under my hand before some divers Greekes, I subscribed her libertie, and hyr'd her in the same Taverne for a yeare, taking nothing from her, for as little had she to give me, except many blessings and thankefull prayers.

During the years 1609–16 Ahmet spent all of his spare time supervising the construction of a great imperial mosque complex on the Hippodrome. Sultan Ahmet I Camii,[9] better known in English as the Blue Mosque, was designed and built by Mehmet Ağa, who had succeeded Dalgıç Ahmet Çavuş as chief of the imperial architects. When the mosque was dedicated in 1616 the sultan wore a turban shaped like the Prophet's foot in token of his humility. But Ahmet did not have long to enjoy his mosque, for he died of typhus the following year, on 22 November 1617, when he was only in his twenty-eighth year, and on that same day he was laid to rest in the türbe of his mosque complex.

Courtyard of Ahmet I Camii.

When Ahmet died the heir apparent was his eldest son, Osman, who was then barely thirteen. Kösem opposed Osman's succession, because she was afraid that if he came to the throne he would execute her sons, Murat and Ibrahim. And so she persuaded the Ulema, the Islamic religious hierarchy, to rule that the succession should go to Ahmet's brother, Mustafa, who was then twenty-five. Thus Mustafa was girded as sultan on 22 November 1617. This was the first break in the direct line of descent in the imperial Osmanlı line, which had passed from father to son for fourteen generations – a span of three centuries. Thenceforth the succession would pass not from father to son but instead to the departed sultan's oldest brother.

Mustafa was so mentally retarded that he was utterly incapable of rule, and on 26 February 1618 the Ulema deposed him in favour of his nephew, who that same day was girded as Osman II. Because of his youth the new sultan was known to his people as Genç (Young) Osman. Mustafa was then imprisoned in the Kafes, or Cage, an apartment in the Inner Palace that was subsequently used to confine the

*Osman II (1618–22), assassinated by the Janissaries when he
was only eighteen; anonymous miniature.*

younger brothers of a sultan after he came to the throne – a substitute
for the earlier practice of fratricide.

Osman's mother, Hadice, who had now become valide sultan, was
empowered by the Ulema to act as regent for her son, because of his
youth. Hadice immediately used her powers to have Kösem evicted
from the Harem and confined to the Eski Saray in Beyazit, along with
her young sons, Murat and Ibrahim. Kösem and her sons remained
there even after Hadice's death in 1622. But Kösem's power was still
great enough to save Murat and Ibrahim from being killed by Sultan
Osman.

Osman by that time was ruling in his own right, and in 1620 he had
personally led a campaign against the Polish fortress of Hotin on the

Dneister. Although Osman was unable to capture Hotin, he forced the Poles to come to terms, and on 6 October a peace agreement was reached in which the fortress was surrendered to the Ottomans. Osman then returned to Istanbul and initiated a series of internal reforms, beginning with an attempt to curb the power of the Janissaries and of the şeyhülislam, the head of the Ulema. The sultan then announced that he was going to mount a great campaign to bring order to the southern provinces of the empire in the Middle East. His attempts at reform had outraged the Janissaries, and, with the approval of the şeyhülislam, they deposed Osman on 19 May 1622 and restored his uncle Mustafa to the throne. Osman was then taken to Yedikule, where on the following day he was brutally murdered. Evliya Çelebi tells of Osman's fall in the *Seyahatname*, writing that 'he was removed by a rebellion of the Janissaries and put to death in the Castle of the Seven Towers, by the compression of his testicles, a mode of execution reserved by custom to the Ottoman emperors'. Osman was then buried beside his father, Ahmet I, in the türbe of the Blue Mosque.

As soon as Mustafa came to the throne for his second reign he executed all of those who had overthrown Osman. He also used the code of fratricide to justify the execution of two sons of Ahmet I, but Kosem managed to save her own sons, Murat and Ibrahim.

Mustafa was so mentally unstable that he was unable to rule effectively, and the grand vezir Kemankes Ali Pasha could not control the various dissident factions, particularly the Janissaries and the military governors in Anatolia. The governors refused to obey orders issued in the sultan's name or to remit taxes to Istanbul, so the central government was unable to pay the Janissaries, adding to their rebelliousness. The situation became so desperate that the grand vezir and all factions in the army agreed that Mustafa must go, and on 10 September 1623 the Janissaries and Sipahis deposed him in favour of Kösem's elder son, who was on the following day girded as Murat IV. Meanwhile Mustafa had been taken back to the Inner Palace and confined in the Kafes, where he lived for the remaining fifteen years of his life. He died there on 20 January 1639, after which he was buried in the former baptistery of Haghia Sophia.

Mustafa had lived virtually all his life within the walls of Topkapı

Sarayı. He was forty-six when he died, and had spent more than a third of his years as a prisoner in the gilded cage of the Kafes, from which he emerged only for his burial. Such was life in the House of Felicity.

CHAPTER 19

The Procession of the Guilds
1623–1638

The principal Turkish source for the reign of Murat IV is Evliya Çelebi, author of the *Seyahatname*. The first volume of the *Seyahatname*, subdivided into eighty sections, is entirely devoted to a description of Istanbul during the reigns of Murat and his two immediate successors, Ibrahim and Mehmet IV. Evliya was born just two years after Murat, and their lives were intertwined during the latter years of Murat's reign, when Evliya served as a page in the House of Felicity.

Evliya was born in Istanbul in 1611 in the quarter of Unkapanı, the Wood Store, on the shore of the Golden Horn just above the present Atatürk Bridge. The house in which he was born is no longer standing, but its site is marked by the little graveyard next to Yavuz Ersinan Camii, whose founder was an ancestor of Evliya's father, Dervish Mehmet Ağa. Dervish Mehmet had been standard-bearer for Süleyman the Magnificent, and during the reign of Selim II he became chief of the Goldsmiths, a guild to which Evliya was apprenticed in his youth. Evliya's mother, a descendant of the great sheikh Ahmet Vesov, called the Turk of the Turks, had been presented to Dervish Mehmet by Ahmet I, who kept her brother Melek ('Angel') Ahmet as his page. Melek Ahmet Pasha, as he was later called, became silahtar, or swordbearer, and during the reign of Murat IV he was appointed grand vezir.

When Evliya was six years old he was enrolled in the school of Hamit Efendi, which was in the quarter called Fil Yokuşu, the Elephant's Path. The street from which this quarter takes its name is still in existence, winding up from the shore of the Golden Horn to the heights above Unkapanı. Evliya studied in Hamit Efendi's school for seven years, during which time he was tutored by his namesake

Evliya Mehmet Efendi, chief imam in the court of Murat IV. While there he studied calligraphy, music, grammar and the Koran, in the singing and reading of which he excelled. After leaving Hamit Efendi's school Evliya continued his studies privately with Evliya Mehmet Efendi, who seems to have given him a remarkably good education. As Evliya remarked to Murat IV during his first audience with the sultan: 'I am versed in seventy-two sciences; does Your Majesty wish to hear something of Persian, Arabic, Syriac, Greek or Turkish; something of the different tunes of music, or poetry in various measures?' But then he began to neglect his studies in day-dreams of becoming a traveller, as he writes in the introduction to his *Seyahatname*:

It was during the illustrious reign of Murat IV that I first began to wander in the gardens around Istanbul and to think of extensive travels, hoping thus to escape from the power of my father, mother, and brethren. Forming a design for travelling over the whole earth, I entreated God to give me health for my body and faith for my soul. I sought the conversation of dervishes, and when I heard a description of the seven climates and of the four corners of the earth, I became still more anxious to see the world, to visit the Holy Land, Cairo, Damascus, Mecca and Medina, and to prostrate myself on the purified soil of the places where the Prophet, the glory of all creatures, was born and died.

And with that hope Evliya prayed for divine guidance – a request eventually granted to him on his twenty-first birthday, 25 February 1632. He writes of how he fell asleep that night in his father's house in Unkapanı, where he dreamt that he was in Ahi Çelebi Camii,[1] a mosque on the shore of the Golden Horn just above the present Galata Bridge. The moment that Evliya realized that he was in the mosque, at the beginning of his dream, the main door opened and a brilliant crowd entered, all chanting the morning prayer. Evliya tells us that he was lost in astonishment at the sight of this glorious assembly, whereupon he turned to the distinguished stranger next to him and said, 'May I ask, my lord, who you are and what is your illustrious name?' The stranger answered and identified himself as Sa'd Vakkas, one of the ten evangelists and the patron of archers. Evliya kissed the hand of Sa'd Vakkas and asked further, 'Who are the refulgent multitude on my right hand?' 'They are all blessed saints and pure souls,'

1. A youth feeding his donkey; mosaic from the Great Palace of Byzantium, Constantinople, early sixth century.

2 and 3. Justinian I (527–65) and his wife, the empress Theodora; mosaic portraits in the basilica of San Vitale in Ravenna, second quarter of the sixth century.

4. Orhan Gazi (1326–62), the first sultan of the Osmanlı dynasty, conqueror of Bursa (Prusa), the first Ottoman capital.
5. Murat I (1362–89), conqueror of Edirne (Adrianople), the second Ottoman capital.

6. Beyazit I (1389–1402), known in Turkish as Yıldırım, or Lightning, because of the speed with which he moved his armies between Europe and Asia.
7. Mehmet II (1451–81), known to the Turks as Fatih, or the Conqueror.

8. Beyazit I comes to the rescue of Niğbolu.

9. Beyazit II (1481–1512), son and successor of Fatih.
10. Selim I (1512–20), known in Turkish as Yavuz, or the Grim, because of the ferocity that led him to execute his grand vezirs at the rate of one a year.

11. Roxelana, wife of Süleyman the Magnificent and mother of Selim II.
12. Mihrimah Sultan, daughter of Süleyman and Roxelana.

13. Süleyman's funeral procession. Süleyman died on 7 September 1566 while he was besieging Sziget in Hungary, and after the city fell his body was brought back to Istanbul for burial in the Süleymaniye.

14. Procession with musicians at the celebration of the circumcision of an Ottoman sultan's son.

15. Selim II (1566–74), son and successor of Süleyman, known in Turkish as Sarhos, or the Sot.

16. Murat IV (1623–40), the last of the great warrior sultans, dead from drink at the age of thirty.

17. Selim III (1789–1807) receiving notables at Bab-üs Saadet, the Gate of Felicity.

18. Mustafa II (*1695–1703*).   19. Mahmut I (1730–54).

20. Foreign ambassador presenting his credentials to Koca Yusuf Pasha,
grand vezir of Selim III.

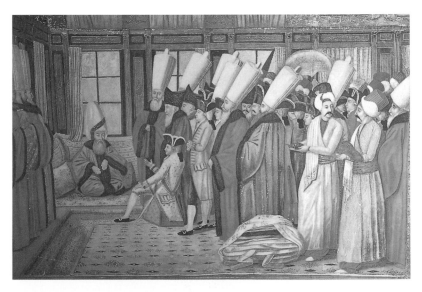

answered Sa'd Vakkas, 'the spirits of the followers of the Prophet.'
Then he told Evliya that the Prophet himself was expected in the
mosque at any moment to perform the morning service, along with
his grandsons Hasan and Hüseyin. No sooner had Sa'd Vakkas said
this, Evliya writes, than flashes of lightning burst from the doors of
the mosque and the room filled with a crowd of saints and martyrs:

It was the Prophet! overshadowed by his green banner, covered by his green
veil, carrying his staff in his right hand, his sword girded on his thigh, with
the imam Hasan on his right side and the imam Hüseyin on his left. As he
placed his right foot on the threshold he cried out 'Bismillah!' ['In the name
of God'], and throwing off his veil said, 'Health unto thee, O my people!'
The whole assembly answered, 'Unto thee be health, O Prophet of God, Lord
of the Nations!'

Evliya says that he trembled in every limb, but still he was able to give
a detailed description of the Prophet's appearance, saying that it
agreed exactly with that given in the sacred Islamic book called the
Hallyehi Khakani: 'The veil on his face was a white shawl and his
turban was formed of a white sash with twelve folds; his mantle was
of camel's hair inclining to yellow; on his neck he wore a yellow shawl.
His boots were yellow and in his turban was stuck a toothpick.'
    The Prophet advanced to the mihrab of the mosque, commanding
Evliya to take the lead in saying the morning prayers. Evliya did so,
and the Prophet followed by reciting the Fatihah, the first chapter of
the Koran, along with other verses. After more verses were chanted by
Evliya and Belal, the first müezzin of Islam, the morning prayers were
concluded. 'The service was closed with a general cry of "Allah!",
which very nearly woke me from my sleep,' Evliya writes.
    He goes on to tell of how Sa'd Vakkas took him by the hand and
escorted him into the Prophet's presence, saying, 'Thy loving and
faithful servant Evliya entreats thy intercession.' Evliya, weeping in his
excitement, kissed the Prophet's hands and received his blessings,
along with the assurance that his desire to travel would be fulfilled.
The Prophet then repeated the Fatihah, followed by all of his sainted
companions, after which Evliya went round and kissed their hands,
receiving from each his blessings.

Their hands were perfumed with musk, ambergris, spikenard, sweet-basil, violets and carnations; but that of the Prophet himself smelt of nothing but saffron and roses, felt when touched as if it had no bones, and was as soft as cotton. The hands of the other prophets had the odour of quinces, that of Abu Bekr had the fragrance of lemons, Omar's smelt like ambergris, Osman's like carnations, and Hüseyin's like white roses.

Then Evliya writes that 'The Prophet himself pronounced the parting salutation from the mihrab, after which he advanced towards the door and the whole illustrious assembly, giving me various greetings and blessings, went out of the mosque.'

The last to leave was Sa'd Vakkas, who took the quiver from his belt and gave it to Evliya, saying:

Go, be victorious with thy bow and arrow; be in God's keeping, and receive from me the good tidings that thou shalt visit the tombs of all the prophets and holy men whose hands thou hast now kissed. Thou shalt travel through the whole world, and be a marvel among men. Of the countries through which thou shalt pass, of their castles, strongholds, wonderful antiquities, products, eatables and drinkables, arts and manufactures, the extent of their provinces, and the lengths of their days there, draw up a description, which shall be a monument worthy of thee. Use my arms and never depart, my son, from the ways of God. Be free from fraud and malice, thankful for bread and salt, a faithful friend to the good, but no friend to the bad.

Then Sa'd Vakkas kissed his hand and departed from the mosque, leaving Evliya alone at the end of his dream, from which he awakened back in his father's house in Unkapanı. As he writes:

When I awoke I was in great doubt whether what I had seen were a dream or reality; and I enjoyed for some time the beatific contemplations which filled my soul. Having afterwards performed my ablutions and offered up the morning prayer, I crossed over from Constantinople to the suburb of Kasım Pasha, and consulted the interpreter of dreams, Ibrahim Efendi, about my vision. From him I received the comfortable news that I should become a great traveller, and after making my way through the world, by the inter-cession of the Prophet, should close my career by being admitted into Paradise. I next went to Abdullah Dede, sheikh of the Mevlevi dervishes in the same suburb, and having kissed his hand, related my vision to him. He interpreted it in the same satisfactory manner, and presenting to me seven historical works, and recommending me to follow the counsels of Sa'd Vakkas, dismissed me with prayers for my success. I then retired to my humble abode, applied myself to the study of history, and began a study of my birthplace, Istanbul, that envy of kings, the celestial haven, and stronghold of Macedonia.

Evliya's description of Istanbul takes up more than two-thirds of the surviving text of his *Seyahatname*. The remainder is devoted to an account of Evliya's travels in the Asian provinces of the Ottoman Empire, but his description of the European provinces is now lost, except for references that he makes to some of his adventures there in the earlier sections of his narrative. Evliya tells us that he travelled for 40 years, fought in 22 battles, passed through the countries of 18 monarchs, and heard 147 languages, but he concludes by saying that nothing that he saw in his journeys compared in beauty or interest with his beloved Istanbul.

Evliya begins his account of Murat's reign with a description of the young sultan's accession to the throne on 10 September 1623 and his girding at Eyüp the following day:

A new aspect was given to the capital, and old and young rejoiced in the auspicious event. On the following day Sultan Murat repaired to the mosque of Eyüp, where two swords were girded on him; one being that of Sultan Selim, and the other being that of the blessed Prophet (on whom be the peace of God!); no monarch was ever girt in this manner. On his return he entered the city by the Edirne gate, and in passing he saluted the people who assembled in crowds on his right and left, and received him with loud acclamations. He then proceeded to the saray, in the inner apartment of which he saluted the Hirkai-Şerif, or Cloak of the Prophet ... he then offered up a prayer of two inclinations, in which he prayed that he might be acceptable to God and the people, and be enabled to perform important services to religion and to the state. Though young in years he was remarkable for prudence and intelligence.

Murat was barely thirteen when he came to the throne, and during the early years of his reign he was dominated by his mother, the valide sultan Kösem. The political instability of the empire at that time is evidenced by the fact that there were eight grand vezirs in the first nine years of Murat's reign. Anatolia was racked by a series of three revolts led by Abaza Mehmet Pasha, and the soldiers in Istanbul were growing increasingly rebellious. The Janissaries and Sipahis in Istanbul rioted on 18 November 1631 and broke into the Inner Palace, killing the grand vezir, the şeyhülislam and fifteen other members of Murat's council and court, including his favourite page, Musa Çelebi. The rebels then forced Murat to appoint Topal Recep Pasha as grand vezir, and as soon as he was in control the Janissaries and Sipahis had free rein to run amok in Istanbul, looting and killing without restraint. Murat finally managed to strike back on 18 May 1632, when he had Recep Pasha strangled and replaced as grand vezir by Tabani Yassı ('Flatfooted') Arnavut Mehmet Pasha, who had been his trusted adviser throughout the period of chaos.

Murat thus gained full control of his empire, whereupon he purged the army of all its mutinous elements and put down the rebels in Anatolia, executing 20,000 men in the process. He then instituted a radical programme of reform in all aspects of life in the empire, banning coffee and alcohol and even boza, the unfermented beverage made from millet which was the favourite drink of the Janissaries, and killing all who transgressed in any way, beginning a reign of terror in Istanbul. Then, taking personal command of the army, he mounted a campaign against the Safavids in Iran, capturing Erivan and Tabriz in the summer of 1634. After the campaign Murat returned to Istanbul, where he was given a hero's welcome by the people of the city – a scene described by Evliya:

On the 19th of Rajab 1045 [29 December 1635] the illustrious emperor made his entry into Istanbul with a splendour and magnificence which no tongue can describe nor pen illustrate. The populace who poured out of the city to meet the emperor had been dissatisfied with the kaymakan Bayram Pasha [the governor of Istanbul], but, gratified by the sight of their emperor, they became animated by a new spirit. The windows and roofs of the houses in every direction were crowded with people, who exclaimed, 'The blessing of God be upon thee, O conqueror! Welcome, Murat! May thy victories be fortunate!' In short, they recovered their spirits, and joy was manifest in every countenance. The sultan was dressed in steel armour, and had a threefold aigrette in his turban, stuck obliquely on one side in the Persian manner: he was mounted on a Noghai steed, followed by seven led horses of the Arab breed, decked out in embroidered trappings set with jewels. Emirgüneh, the khan of Erivan, Yusuf Khan, and other Persian khans walked on foot before him, while the bands with cymbals, flutes, drums, and fifes, played the airs of Afrasiab. The emperor looked with dignity on both sides of him, like a lion who has scized his prey, and saluted the people as he went on, followed by three thousand pages clad in armour. The people shouted 'God be praised!' as he passed, and threw themselves on their faces to the ground ... During this triumphant procession to the saray all the ships at Saray Burnu, at Kızkule and at Tophane, fired salutes, so that the sea seemed in a blaze. The public criers announced that seven days and seven nights were to be devoted to festivity and rejoicing.

That same year Evliya, who was then twenty-four, first came to the attention of Murat IV. This took place on the holy evening of Kadır, the Night of Power, which commemorates the Prophet's visit to heaven. That evening Evliya was serving as müezzin in Haghia Sophia, and, in the sultan's presence, he recited the entire Koran from memory. This so impressed Murat that he sent Evliya's uncle Melek Ahmet Pasha and another aide to fetch the young müezzin and bring him to the royal loge. There, before the entire congregation, they placed a golden turban on Evliya's head and led him by the hand into the sultan's presence. As Evliya writes:

On beholding the dignified countenance of Sultan Murat, I bowed and kissed the ground. The emperor received me very graciously, and, after salutations, asked me in how many hours I could repeat the Koran. I said, if it please God, and if I proceed at a rapid pace, I could repeat it in seven hours, but if I do it moderately without much alteration of voice, I could accomplish it in eight hours. The sultan then said, 'Please God, let him be admitted into the number of my intimate associates in the room of the deceased Musa.' He then gave me two or three handfuls of gold, which altogether amounted to 623 pieces.

At the conclusion of the service Evliya was escorted to Topkapı Sarayı, where he was enrolled among the pages in the Inner Service – those who waited on the sultan himself. Melek Ahmet Pasha acted as

Evliya's patron and instructed him how he should behave in the sultan's presence. He was then dressed in the costume of a page and escorted to the Has Oda, or Throne Room, where Murat soon made his appearance, as Evliya writes:

The emperor made his appearance, like the rising sun, by the door leading to the inner Harem. He saluted the forty pages of the Inner Service and all the müsahibs [the sultan's favourite pages], who returned the salutation with prayers for his prosperity. The emperor having with great dignity seated himself on one of the thrones, I kissed the ground before him and trembled all over. The next moment, none the less, I complimented him with some verses that most fortunately came to my mind.

After he recited these verses Evliya matched wits with the sultan and his favourites, recited poetry, played upon the tambourine, and danced like a dervish before the throne, and then sang a plaintive love-song about the deceased Musa that reduced Murat to tears. When he recovered his composure the sultan immediately directed that Evliya be admitted into the company of his müsahibs. This singular interview ended when the call to prayer was heard, whereupon, as Evliya writes, 'The emperor ordering me to assist the müezzin, I flew like a peacock to the top of the staircase and began to exclaim, "Ho to good works!"'

Soon afterwards Evliya was enrolled in the Palace School, taking courses in music, writing, grammar, Persian, Arabic, and in reading the Koran. During the course of his studies he only occasionally saw Murat, usually in the gymnasium near the sultan's private bath. Murat loved to wrestle there with his favourites, and one day Evliya had a dizzying demonstration of the sultan's prowess, as he writes:

On one occasion I saw him seize his silahtars Melek Ahmet and Musa Ağa, both remarkably stout men, take them by their belts, lift them over his head, and fling one to the right and the other to the left ... The sultan frequently stripped himself and wrestled with these two men, on a spot of the saray called Çemen Sofa. It was I who on such occasions read the prayer of the wrestlers ... One day he came out from the hamam in the Has Oda, saluted those present, and said, 'Now I have had a bath.' 'May it be to your health,' was the general reply. I said, 'My emperor, you are now clean and comfortable, do not therefore oil yourself for wrestling today, especially as you have already exerted yourself with others, and your strength must be considerably reduced.' 'Have I no strength left?' said he, 'let us see'; whereupon he seized me like an eagle, by my belt, raised me over his head, and whirled me about as children do a top. I exclaimed, 'Do not let me fall, my emperor, hold me fast!' He said, 'Hold fast yourself,' and continued to swing me round, until I cried out, 'For God's sake, my emperor, cease for I am quite giddy.' He then began to laugh, released me, and gave me forty-eight pieces of gold for the amusement I had offered him.

The reign of Murat IV reached its climax, so far as Istanbul is concerned, in the great procession of the guilds that he ordered in 1638, in preparation for his campaign to capture Baghdad from the Safavids. Evliya Çelebi devotes more than a third of Volume I of his *Seyahatname* to this procession, in which he gives an account 'Of all the Guilds and Professions, Merchants and Artisans, Shops and Occupations in this vast town of Constantinople, with the Regulations handed down to them by their Sheikhs or Ancients'.

According to Evliya, Murat called for this procession at a meeting of the Divan, addressing his remarks in particular to Yahya Efendi, Istanbul's mufti, or chief judge of religious law:

Dear companions, and you, Mufti Yahya Efendi, if it pleases God we will wrest Baghdad from the hands of the Persians and deliver from their heresy the tomb of the founder of our Orthodox sect. In order to assist me in our great expedition, I desire that all the guilds of the city of Constantinople, both great and small, shall repair to my imperial camp. They shall exhibit the number of their men, shops and professions, according to their old constitutions. They shall all pass before the Alay Köşkü with their sheikhs and chiefs, on foot and on horseback, playing their eight-fold music, so that I may see how many thousand men and how many guilds there are. It will be a procession the likes of which has never been seen before.

The parade lasted for three days, beginning daily at dawn and ending at sunset, with the sultan and his court looking on from the Alay Köşkü,[2] the Kiosk of the Processions, a review pavilion in the outer defence walls of Topkapı Sarayı. Evliya says that 'They were distributed into fifty-seven sections and consist altogether of a thousand and

left: *Procession of the guilds, including the Makers of Silver Thread, Blacksmiths, Shipbuilders, Embroiderers, Saddlers and Feltmakers, with foreigners looking on at the rear; one face of a double miniature.*
right: *Procession of the guilds, with Sultan Ahmet III looking on at the rear; other face of the double miniature.*

one guilds', although the number of guilds that he actually describes is just 735. Representatives of each of these guilds paraded in their characteristic costumes or uniforms or sometimes in bizarre outfits, exhibiting on floats their various trades and enterprises, trying to outdo one another in amusing or amazing the sultan and the other spectators, as Evliya writes, describing them and their antics:

All these guilds pass in wagons or on foot, with the instruments of their handi-craft, and are busy with great noise at their work. The Carpenters prepare wooden houses, the Builders raise walls, the Woodcutters pass with loads of trees, the Sawyers pass sawing them, the Masons whiten their shops, the Chalk-Makers crunch chalk and whiten their faces, playing a thousand tricks ... The Toy-Makers of Eyüp exhibit on wagons a thousand trifles and toys for children to play with. In their train you see bearded fellows and men of thirty years of age, some dressed as children with hoods and bibs, some as nurses who care for them, while the bearded babies cry after playthings or amuse themselves with spinning tops or sounding little trumpets ... The Bakers pass working at their trade, some baking and throwing small loaves among the crowd. They also make for this occasion immense loaves the size of the cupola of a hamam, covered with sesame and fennel; these loaves are carried on wagons which are dragged along by seventy to eighty pairs of oxen. No oven being capable of holding loaves of so large a size, they bake them in pits for that purpose, where the loaf is covered from above with cinders, and from the four sides baked slowly by the fire ... These guilds pass before the Alay Köşkü with a thousand tricks and fits, which it is impossible to describe, and behind them walk their sheikhs followed by their pages playing the eight-fold Turkish music.

Evliya tells us that there were several disputes concerning precedence in the imperial procession. The first of these quarrels was between the Butchers and the Captains of the White Sea, or Mediterranean. Sultan Murat settled the dispute in favour of the Captains, issuing this imperial edict: 'Indeed, beside the fact that they supply the capital with provisions, they have also taken Noah for their protector. They are a respectable guild of men, who militate in God's ways against the Infidels, and are well-skilled in many sciences. They may also pass in great solemnity, and then be followed by the Butchers.'

Thus the Captains of the White Sea were moved up in the imperial procession, whereupon they put on one of the most elaborate and spirited displays seen during the festivities, as Evliya describes it:

The Captains of the Caravellas, Galleons and other ships, having fired from them a triple salute at Saray Point, pour all their men on shore, where they place on floats some hundred small boats and drag them along with cables, shouting 'Aya Mola!' In their boats are seen the finest cabin boys dressed in gold doing service to their masters, who make free with drinking. Music is played on all sides, the masts and oars are adorned with pearls and set with jewels, the sails are of rich stuffs and embroidered muslin, and on top of each mast are a couple of boys whistling tunes of Silistria. Arriving at the Alay Köşkü they meet five or ten ships of the infidels, with whom they engage in a battle in the presence of the emperor. Thus the show of a great sea-fight is represented with the roaring of cannons, the smoke covering the sky. At last, the Muslims becoming victors, they board the ships of the infidels, take booty and chase the fine Frank boys, carrying them off from the old bearded Christians, whom they put in chains. They upset the crosses of the Christian flags, and dragging the captured vessels astern of their own ships, they cry out the universal Muslim slogan of 'Allah! Allah!' Never before the time of Sultan Murat IV was there seen so brilliant a union of mariners.

After the Captains of the White Sea passed the Alay Köşkü the Butchers attempted to join the line of march, but their place was disputed by the guilds of the Egyptian Merchants. The adversaries assembled before the kiosk, where once again the sultan decided against the Butchers, 'to the great delight of the Egyptian Merchants, who, leaping for joy, passed immediately after the Captains of the White Sea'. The Egyptian Merchants were organized in eight separate guilds, of which the most popular among the spectators was that of the Merchants of Musk-Sherbets. As Evliya describes it, 'They pass exposing to public view in china vases and tankards every kind of sherbet made of rhubarb, ambergris, roses, lemons, tamarinds, etc., of different colours and scent, which they distribute among the spectators.'

Then finally the Butchers were allowed to take their place in the procession, marching at the head of the tenth section before the Men of the Slaughter-House and the Jewish Meat-Merchants, as Evliya writes:

The Butchers, who are almost all Janissaries, pass clad in armour on wagons, exposing to public view in their shops, adorned with rich stuffs and flowers, fat sheep of Karamania weighing from forty to fifty occas [50 to 65 kilograms]. They trace on their white flesh figures with saffron, gild their horns, cut them up with their large knives, and weighing them in yellow-coloured scales, cry, 'Take the occa for an asper, take it my soul, it is an excellent roast dish!' Thus chanting, they parade with their large knives and cutlasses, passing on foot in the procession.

Still another quarrel over precedence took place, between the Fish-Cooks and the Helvacıs, or Sugar-Bakers, as Evliya writes:

The emperor decided that the latter should go first, to the great annoyance of the Fish-Cooks, who appealed to their patron Jonah and blamed the Helvacıs, and they in turn reproached the Fish-Cooks, saying fish is a very unwholesome and infatuating food ... To this reproach the Helvacıs added the praise of Helva contained in the Koran, and quoted the Prophet, who once said: 'The faithful are sweet, the wicked sour.' Having put forth their claims in this way in the emperor's presence, they carried the votes of the whole assembly that the precedence was due to them rather than to the Fish-Cooks, and accordingly obtained the imperial diploma.

Thus the Helvacıs took their place in the procession, as Evliya writes:

fitting up their shops on litters with all kinds of sweets, which bring water into the mouths of the boys of the town, who devour them with their eyes. They exhibit on litters different kinds of confectionaries in basins, and perfume the brains of the spectators with amber scent. They produce at this public exhibition trees of sugar with sweets upon them, an admirable show! Behind them walks the Chief Confectioner of the saray, followed by the troops of the confectioners playing the eight-fold Turkish music.

So they passed before the Alay Köşkü in turn, every one of the guilds and corporations of Istanbul: tradesmen, artisans, merchants, labourers, civil servants, scholars, poets, musicians, entertainers, and functionaries of the religious, civil and military hierarchies of the empire, all making a spirited display before the sultan and his court. Evliya describes them all in the most minute detail, including even the lowliest of the guilds, such as the Gravediggers: 'Five hundred Gravediggers pass with shovels and hoes in their hands, asking the spectators where they shall dig their graves, and set up in this way a warning for many.'

Besides the reputable merchants and workmen of the city, the procession also included some of the criminal classes and other less respectable groups, all of them marching in the second section under the watchful eye of the town provost, as Evliya writes:

The Corporation of Thieves and Footpads might be here noted as a very numerous one, who have an eye to our purses; but far be they from us. We say the same of the Corporation of Pimps and Bankrupts, who are innumerable. The thieves pay tribute to the two chief officers of the police, and get their subsistence by mingling in the crowds of Constantinople and by cheating foreigners.

Also represented in the procession were the Corporation of Beggars, numbering, according to Evliya, 7,000 with their sheikh.

Relying on the text of the Koran: 'Alms for the poor and wretched', they pass in a great crowd of strange figures dressed in woollen cloth and turbans of palm leaves, some lame, some having lost a hand or foot, some naked and barefoot, and some mounted on asses. They place their sheikh in the centre, and after his prayer is performed they all cry together, 'Allah, Allah, Amen!' Their prayer is performed for the emperor's health immediately under the Alay Köşkü, where they receive alms.

Even the poor madmen of the city were given an outing in the procession, and Evliya describes them as they pass in the train of the head physician:

Three hundred keepers of the bedlams of Constantinople pass in the procession, leading several hundred madmen in gold and silver chains. Some of the keepers carry bottles in their hands from which they give medicines to the madmen, while others beat or box the fools to keep them in order. Some of them are naked, some cry, some laugh, some swear and attack their keepers, which puts the spectators to flight. If I were to describe all the fits of the madmen and fools on such a day of public procession, I should fill a book.

The penultimate section in the procession was made up of the Fools and Mimics of Constantinople. According to Evliya, 'Wherever there is a feast of imperial circumcision, nuptials, or victory, from two to three hundred singers, comics, mimics and mischievous boys of the town, who have exhausted seventy cups of the poison of life and misrule, crowd together and play, day and night.'

The last guild in the procession was that of the Tavern-Keepers. Evliya tells us that in Istanbul there were 'one thousand such places of misrule, kept by Greeks, Armenians and Jews. In the procession wine is not produced openly, and the Tavern-Keepers pass all in disguise and clad in armour. The boys of the taverns, all shameless drunkards, and all the partisans of wine pass singing songs, tumbling down and rising again.' The last of all to pass were the Jewish tavern-keepers, 'all masked and wearing the most precious dresses bedecked with jewels, carrying in their hands crystal and porcelain cups, out of which they pour sherbet instead of wine for the spectators.'

At sunset on the third day the parade came to an end as the last of the marchers passed the Alay Köşkü 'after which the guilds accompanied their officers to their lodgings and everyone returned home.' As Evliya writes of the parade's end:

The procession of the imperial camp began its march at dawn and continued the whole day until sunset. On account of this parade all work and trade in Constantinople were stopped for three days, during which time the riot and confusion filled the town to such a degree which is not to be expressed by language, and which I, the humble Evliya, only dared to describe.

Most of the guilds that Evliya describes in the *Seyahatname* are still practising their trades in the same places that they were in his time, particularly in the market quarter between the Galata Bridge and Beyazit Meydanı. This has been the principal market area of the city since Byzantine times, and most of the streets are named after the tradesmen and artisans who work there as their predecessors have done for centuries past. One ancient place-name in this quarter is Yemiş Iskelesi, the Fruit Pier, which was the landing-stage for the fruit and vegetable market which is noted as being here on the shore of the Golden Horn since the days of Justinian. Only a small fragment of this market remains today, beside the Spice Bazaar, but one can picture what it was like in Evliya's time from his description of the guild of Fruit-Sellers, who passed in the seventeenth section of the imperial procession.

They pass on wagons adorned with all kinds of fruit. They also make artificial trees of apples, apricots and other kinds of fruit, each carried on poles by eight or ten men. Others make kiosks with fountains playing, the four sides of which are festooned with fruit. Their boys, who are seated in these kiosks, bargain with the spectators and throw fruit to them. Some dress in robes made of chestnuts, reciting verses of the Koran while holding rosaries of dried raisins. They also build artificial ships, which are full of fruits, each ship being towed by a thousand men. The sails, mast, prow and stern of each of these ships are ornamented with fruit kernels. Merchants flock in crowds to enter these fruit-ships to fill their baskets. With the greatest noise and quarrelling arising from these simulated sales, they pass the Alay Köşkü. This is a faithful representation of what occurs at the port of Constantinople on the arrival of every fruit-ship, where such noise arises, and many heads are broken without the injured persons allowed to ask for legal satisfaction.

Evliya concludes his account of the parade with a tribute to Murat IV, and then with a sigh of relief he congratulates himself for having given a full account of the procession of the guilds:

Nowhere else has such a procession been seen or shall be seen; it could only be carried into effect by the imperial orders of Sultan Murat IV . . . Amen! By the Lord of all the Prophets: God be praised that I have overcome the task of describing the guilds and corporations of Constantinople!

CHAPTER 20

Decline and Gilded Decadence
1638–1730

Murat IV mounted his campaign to take Baghdad in the early summer of 1638, with the Safavids finally surrendering the city to him on 25 December of that year. The following year the Safavids signed a peace treaty with the Ottomans, establishing boundaries between Turkey and Iran that survived with little change up to modern times.

During the latter years of his reign Murat became addicted to drink, apparently under the influence of an alcoholic layabout known as Bekri ('the Drunkard') Mustafa. The story of Murat's meeting with Bekri Mustafa is told by the historian Demetrius Cantemir. According to Cantemir, Murat was wandering through the market quarter in disguise one day when he came upon Bekri Mustafa 'wallowing in the dirt dead drunk'. Murat was intrigued by the drunkard and brought him back to the palace, where Mustafa introduced the sultan to the joys of wine, showing him that the best cure for a hangover is more of the same. Bekri Mustafa soon died of drink, leaving Murat bereft, as Cantemir writes:

At his death the emperor ordered the court to go into mourning, but caused his body to be buried with great pomp in a tavern among the hogsheads. After his death the emperor declar'd that he never enjoy'd one merry day, and whenever Mustafa chanc'd to be mention'd, was often seen to burst into tears, and to sigh from the bottom of his heart.

According to Cantemir, during the last months of Murat's life his alcoholism turned him into a homicidal maniac:

Very often at midnight he stole out of the women's quarters through the private gate of the palace with his drawn sword, and running through the streets barefooted with only a loose gown around him, like a madman, killed whoever came his way. Frequently from the windows of the higher rooms, where he used to drink and divert himself, he shot with arrows such as accidentally passed by. In the day time he ran up and down in disguise, and did not return till he had killed some unfortunate wretches for little or no cause.

Murat died of cirrhosis of the liver on 9 February 1640, and on that same day he was buried in the türbe of the Blue Mosque beside his father, Ahmet I. Murat's four young sons had died of the plague earlier that year, and the only other surviving male of the imperial Osmanlı line was Murat's younger brother, Ibrahim, who had been locked up in the Kafes throughout his brother's reign, living in constant fear of his life. Just before Murat died he gave orders that his brother should be executed, but Kösem managed to save Ibrahim. When Kösem brought news of Murat's death Ibrahim refused to believe her, thinking that it was a ruse to get him to open the door of his room. Kösem finally convinced him by producing Murat's corpse, whereupon Ibrahim emerged and began dancing through the Harem, singing 'The butcher is dead, the butcher is dead!' That same day Ibrahim was girded with the sword of Osman at Eyüp, being then in his twenty-fifth year.

At the time there was serious concern about whether the imperial line would continue, for Ibrahim was thought to be impotent. Kösem sought to remedy this by dosing her son with aphrodisiacs prescribed by his tutor, a quacksalver named Cinci Hoca, while she supplied him with a succession of beautiful concubines from the slave market procured for her by a confidant called Pezevenk, or the Pimp. Finally, on 2 January 1642, Ibrahim's concubine Turhan Hadice gave birth to a son, the future Mehmet IV, whereupon she became his first kadın. Within the next fourteen months two more of Ibrahim's concubines presented him with sons, the future sultans Süleyman II and Ahmet II. By that time Ibrahim had developed a prodigious sexual appetite, as Cantemir writes:

As Murat was wholly addicted to wine, so was Ibrahim to lust. They say he spent all his time in sensual pleasure, and when nature was exhausted with the frequent repetition of venereal delights he endeavoured to restore it with potions or commanded a beautiful virgin richly habited to be brought to him by his mother ... In the palace gardens he frequently assembled all the virgins, made them strip themselves naked, and neighing like a stallion ran amongst them and as it were ravished one or the other, kicking or struggling by his order. Happening once to see the private parts of a wild heifer, he sent the shape of them in gold all over the empire with orders to make enquiry whether a woman made in just that manner could be found for his lust. At last such a one was found and received into the women's quarters. [She was an Armenian from Arnavutköy on the Bosphorus; her name was Şeker Para, or Piece of Sugar, and she weighed in at 150 kilograms.] He made a collection of great and voluminous books expressing the various ways of coition, whence he even invented some new and previously unknown postures.

The Ottoman treasury was by now empty, and Kösem and her hench-men persuaded Ibrahim that he could replenish the imperial coffers by conquering Crete from the Venetians. An invasion of Crete was launched in the spring of 1645, beginning a struggle that would last for nearly a quarter of a century.

By now the sultan was known to his people as Ibrahim the Mad, and his insane excesses had alienated every segment of the popula-tion, including the army and the Ulema. The Janissaries finally revolted on 8 August 1648, deposing Ibrahim in favour of his six-year-old son Mehmet. Ibrahim was then imprisoned in the Kafes along with Mehmet's two younger brothers, Süleyman and Ahmet. Six days later Ibrahim was strangled there by the chief executioner, Black Ali, after which he was buried in the baptistery of Haghia Sophia beside Mustafa I. According to Evliya, 'Ibrahim's tomb is frequently visited by women, because he was much addicted to them.'

Kösem continued to dominate the Harem during the first three years of the reign of her grandson Mehmet IV, ruling as regent in his stead. The sultan's mother, Turhan Hadice, was consequently deprived of her right to be valide sultan, and she bided her time until she was able to challenge Kösem. She finally made her move with the help of the chief black eunuch, Uzun Süleyman Ağa. He and his men strangled Kösem in the Harem on 2 June 1651, after which she was buried in the türbe of the Blue Mosque beside her husband, Ahmet I, and her son Murat IV.

Turhan Hadice now assumed her rightful place as valide sultan, ruling as regent for her son until he came of age. The empire remained in a state of chaos during this time, with a succession of fourteen grand vezirs during the first eight years of Mehmet's reign, when first his grandmother and then his mother were acting as regents. The debasement of the coinage, one of the many consequences of this chaos, led the Janissaries and Sipahis to join in a major revolt in Istanbul on 4 March 1656. The rebellious troops forced the populace of the city to close their shops and workplaces and stay home in a general strike – the first action of its kind in Ottoman history. The strike continued until Turhan Hadice, acting as regent, gave in to the demands of the rebels, who then hanged thirty high government and palace officials in turn before the main gateway to the Blue Mosque. Turhan Hadice then appointed a new grand vezir, Mehmet Köprülü, to whom she relinquished her role of regent.

Mehmet Pasha was eighty when he became grand vezir, climaxing a remarkable career in which he had risen from being a scullion in the saray kitchens to the highest post in the empire, though he never learned how to read or write. A few years before his appointment he had built a mansion across the road from the Alay Köşkü, and when he became grand vezir this served as his headquarters, as it did for those who succeeded him in his office. The gateway to the grand vezir's headquarters was referred to by foreigners as the Sublime Porte, and from Mehmet Pasha's time onwards the foreign affairs of the empire were centred there rather than in the Hall of the Divan. Hence it came to stand for the Ottoman government itself, and ambassadors to Turkey presented their credentials to the Sublime Porte, just as in England they are accredited to the Court of St James.

Mehmet Pasha began his term as grand vezir by hanging 3,000 rebellious Janissaries in Istanbul. His severity brought discipline to the Janissary Corps and revived its efficiency as a military force, enabling him to restore order in Istanbul and in the provinces.

Mehmet Pasha died in office in 1661. On his deathbed he gave some words of advice to Mehmet IV, then in his twentieth year: 'Never heed the advice of a woman, never allow one of your subjects to become too rich, always keep the treasury well filled, always be on horseback and keep the army constantly on the march.'

He was succeeded as grand vezir by his son Fazıl ('Learned') Ahmet Pasha. Ahmet Pasha proved to be a worthy successor to his father, serving as grand vezir for fifteen years, a tenure equalled in length and distinction only by that of Sokollu Mehmet Pasha.

The competence of the Köprülü grand vezirs allowed Turhan Hadice to retire from an active role in government. She now used her great wealth to rebuild the imperial mosque at Eminönü on the Golden Horn, which had been begun in 1597 by the valide sultan Safiye, mother of Mehmet III. Turhan Hadice completed it as part of an imperial külliye that came to be called Yeni Cami,[1] the New Mosque, which included the great market hall called Mısır Çarşısı,[2] the Egyptian Market, better known in English as the Spice Bazaar. The French scholar Grelot, writing c. 1680, remarked of Turhan Hadice that 'she was one of the greatest and most brilliant ladies who ever entered the saray', and that it was fitting 'that she should leave to posterity a jewel of Ottoman architecture to serve as an eternal monument to her generous enterprises'.

Yeni Cami, the New Mosque of the valide sultan.

As soon as Mehmet IV came of age he moved his court to Edirne, where he spent all of his spare time hunting. Mehmet was often accompanied on his hunting expeditions by his first kadın, Rabia Gülnus, a Greek girl who had been captured in the Ottoman invasion of Crete. Rabia Gülnus was the mother of Mehmet's first two sons, the future sultans Mustafa II and Ahmet III, both of whom were raised while their father's court was in Edirne, which allowed them more freedom than they would have had in Istanbul.

Fazıl Ahmet Pasha mounted a new expedition against Crete in 1665, the capital at Candia having been under siege for more than twenty years. The Venetian garrison on Candia finally surrendered to him on 5 September 1669, completing the Ottoman conquest of the island.

Ahmet Pasha died of drink in 1676 and was succeeded as grand vezir by his foster brother Kara ('Black') Mustafa Pasha of Merzifon. Early in the summer of 1683 Mustafa Pasha mounted a campaign against Vienna with an army of 200,000 putting the city under siege in mid-July. The defenders fought him off until reinforcements arrived under John Sobieski. Then on 11 September the Christian allies utterly defeated the Ottomans, who fled in disorder with Kara Mustafa leading the way. The grand vezir led the remnants of his army back to Belgrade, where on 15 December he was beheaded on the sultan's orders.

The Ottoman defeat encouraged the Christian powers of Europe to create a Holy League for another crusade against the Turks. Emissaries from Austria, Poland and Venice met in March 1684, with the support of Pope Innocent XI, and the following year they invaded the Ottoman dominions on several fronts, beginning a war that would drag on for thirty years. At the same time there was widespread starvation in Anatolia, leading to a popular uprising in Istanbul under Fazıl Mustafa Pasha, younger brother of Fazıl Ahmet Pasha. The rebels, who included the leading figures of the Ottoman civil, military and religious hierarchies, obtained from the şeyhülislam a fetva deposing Mehmet IV on the grounds that he was no longer fulfilling his duties. Mehmet was officially deposed in Edirne on 8 November 1687, after which he and his family were brought back to Istanbul. Mehmet's younger brother, Süleyman, was released from the Kafes, and on 9 November he was girded at Eyüp. Mehmet and his sons Mustafa and Ahmet were confined in the Kafes, while his wife Rabia Gülnus was relegated to the Eski Saray. Mehmet remained a prisoner in the Kafes for the rest of his days, dying there on 6 June 1693, after which he was buried in the türbe of Yeni Cami next to his mother, Turhan Hadice.

Evliya Çelebi, in Section XXXI of his *Seyahatname*, describes 'The Mausoleums of the Ottoman Sultans from the time of Mehmet II to the Present Day'. The last of the imperial Ottoman tombs described in this section is that of Ibrahim, and so it appears that Evliya died before Mehmet IV – probably in the early 1680s. Evliya's passing was the end of an age, and so before going on with the march of history one might pause for a last look at the colourful Istanbul of his day, which he brings to life in the pages of the *Seyahatname*.

Section XLII of the *Seyahatname* begins with a description of 'the Sepulchral Monuments of the Saints and Holy Men buried in Istanbul (God be propitious to them all!)', as well as those of the 'Saint-Fools, Idiots and Ecstatic Men'. Evliya's description of these Moslem folk-saints, who are usually known as Baba ('Father') or Dede ('Grand-father'), shows that they had much the same character as the Christian saint-fools of medieval Byzantium. Some of them were renowned for their ability to see into the future, such as Durmuş Dede in Rumeli Hisarı, of whom Evliya writes, 'Durmuş Dede at the castle of Rumeli; all the sailors used to give him in passing an occa of meat. He advised some captains to undertake such a voyage, and others not to sail for such a place, and his advice, if followed, turned to their advantage.' Others were revered as healers, such as Ilikçi Baba, whom Evliya records as being buried by the Silivri Gate, 'where all sufferers from palpitation of the heart would be cured by drinking water, with a little of the dust from his grave in it'.

The most famous of the saint-fools in Evliya's time was Ahmet Dede, who is described thus in the *Seyahatname*:

In the long days he used to sit upon the bridge as Kasım Pasha and greet all who passed. The wonder was that he knew men by their names whom he had never seen before and saluted them as old aquaintances, and instantly remembered those whom he had not seen for twenty or thirty years, as well as the names of all their relations. His bosom was filled with horns of goats, gazelles and sheep. Merry fellows frequently went to try him by saying, 'Ahmet, show me my horn!' If they happened to be married he would answer with some anecdote concerning their wives, and would give to some a small, to others a great horn from his collection. If the one who asked him was not married he used to answer, 'Thy horn is not yet grown.' If someone said, 'Ahmet Dede, I'll give thee a horn, dance a little,' he would get up instantly, knock with the fingers of his right hand like a stork, and begin to dance like Venus in the sky, while people brought him all kinds of horns. If you went to see him a month afterwards and asked him where your horn was, he would put his hand into his bosom and show you the very same which you had given him. In brief, he was a light-hearted fool. Since he undertook the journey into Abyssinia and the country of the negroes, we have not heard of him.

Some of the folk-saints of Evliya's time were renowned for their discovery of ayazmas, the holy wells which were as much frequented in Ottoman Istanbul as they were in Byzantine Constantinople by those seeking relief from their ailments. Evliya writes of the discovery of an ayazma by the sainted dervish sheikh Merkez Efendi:

He once said to his fakirs, 'I heard here underneath the ground a voice saying: "O sheikh! I am a spring of reddish water imprisoned in this place for seven thousand years, and am destined to come to the surface of the earth by your efforts as a remedy for fever. Endeavour then to release me from my subterranean prison."' Upon this speech all the fakirs began to dig a well with him, and forth rushed a sweet water of a reddish colour, which if drunk in the morning with coffee is a proven cure for fever, known all over the world as the Ayazma of Merkez.

Evliya also writes of an ayazma that he visited at Hasköy, on the north side of the Golden Horn, where he had a rather weird experience:

Close to the Jewish cemetery in Hasköy there is a holy well, whose water if drunk seven times cures the quartan ague. It is much frequented by the Greeks. In the days when I, poor Evliya, was in love, I went for a walk and began to cry aloud: 'Good luck to me! Good luck to me!' In answer to my cry a spectre started up, whereupon I fell, calling upon God with the words

'Ya Hafız!' [Oh Protector!], and went and hid inside the well, where I spent the night. In another place, please God, I will relate the strange things that befell me that night.

Evliya devotes a large part of the *Seyahatname* to the suburbs of Istanbul. The most interesting of these was Galata, which was virtually a town in itself, the hedonistic ways of its infidels totally different from those of the Muslims in Stamboul, as Evliya describes them:

In Galata there are eighteen wards inhabited by Muslims, seventy by Greeks, three by Franks, one by Jews, and two by Armenians. The town is full of infidels, who number 200,000 according to the census taken in the reign of Murat IV, whereas the Muslims are only 64,000. The different wards of the town are patrolled day and night by watchmen to prevent disorders among the population, who are of a rebellious disposition, on account of which they have from time to time been chastised by the sword. The inhabitants are either sailors, merchants or craftsmen such as joiners or caulkers. They dress for the most part in the Algerine fashion, for a great number of them are Arabs or Moors. The Greeks keep the taverns; most of the Armenians are merchants or money-changers; the Jews are the go-betweens in amorous intrigues and their youths are the worst of all the devotees of debauchery.

In Galata there are two hundred taverns and wine-shops where the infidels divert themselves with music and drinking. The taverns are celebrated for the wines of Ancona, Mudanya, Smyrna and Tenedos. The word *günaha* (temptation) is most particularly to be applied to the taverns of Galata because there all kinds of playing and dancing boys, mimics and fools, flock together and delight themselves, day and night. When I passed through this district I saw many bareheaded and barefooted lying drunk in the street; some confessed aloud the state they were in by singing such couplets as these: 'I drank the ruby wine, how drunk, how drunk am I!/ A prisoner of the locks, how mad, how mad, am I!' Another sang, 'My foot goes to the tavern, nowhere else./ My hand grasps tight the cup and nothing else./ Cut short your sermon for no ears have I,/ But for the bottle's murmur, nothing else.'

Evliya assures us that he was not led astray by the taverns of Galata, and that he never drank anything but sweet boza, the unfermented drink made from millet:

Celebration in a tavern; miniature.

God is my witness that not a drop did I drink at the invitation of those drunkards, but mingling amongst them I could not but become aware of their condition. I, who spent so much time in coffee-houses, boza-parlours and wine-taverns, can call God to witness that I never drank anything in my travels except the sweet boza of Constantinople. Since I was born I never tasted in my life of fermented beverages or prohibited things, neither tobacco nor coffee nor tea ... My father was of the same temper; but I being of a vagabond nature, ready to sacrifice my soul for my friends, have spoken only for their pleasure's sake of these prohibited beverages.

Süleyman II was forty-five when he came to the throne, and had spent the previous thirty-nine years as a prisoner in the Kafes. He was powerless at first, and the Janissaries took advantage of this to run amok in Istanbul, looting the city. But on 1 March 1688 Süleyman called a meeting of the notables of the city, persuading them to form a loyal defence force. The sultan took personal command of the loyal troops, whose members included Janissaries who had become merchants and artisans, and soon they put down the insurrection, slaughtering all of the rebels who did not flee beyond the walls.

The empire was still in a state of crisis, with a severe food shortage threatening famine, while the powers of the Holy League were advancing on all fronts, capturing Belgrade on 8 September 1688. Süleyman then turned to Fazıl Mustafa Pasha, whom he appointed as grand vezir on 25 October 1689. Mustafa Pasha mustered his forces in Edirne during the winter of 1689–90, and the following spring he mounted a campaign against the Habsburgs, recapturing Belgrade on 14 October 1690. But the Ottoman army was ambushed by the Austrians near Karlowitz on 20 August 1691, and when Mustafa Pasha was killed in action his troops fled in disarray.

Meanwhile Süleyman II had died in Edirne on 22 June 1691. The following day his younger brother was released from the Kafes and raised to the throne as Ahmet II. The new sultan was then forty-eight, and had spent the previous forty-three years as a prisoner in the Kafes.

The war with the European powers dragged on in a stalemate, while internal conditions in the empire degenerated into almost total anarchy, with the sultan spending all of his time in the Harem and leaving affairs of state to be directed by a series of half a dozen grand vezirs. Ahmet II died in Edirne on 6 February 1695. He was succeeded that same day by his nephew Mustafa, a son of Mehmet IV.

Mustafa II was thirty when he came to the throne, and had been a prisoner in the Kafes for the previous seven years. As soon as he became sultan his mother, Rabia Gülnus, took her place in the Harem as valide sultan. Mustafa had been given a far broader education than his two uncles, Süleyman II and Ahmet II, for during his youth he and his brother Ahmet had enjoyed considerable freedom.

The new sultan began his reign with the noblest of intentions, issuing a Hatti Şerif, or imperial rescript, in which he announced his intention of ridding the sultanate of its corrupt practices and of renouncing the pleasures of the Harem to lead his army in person. As he stated, 'Henceforth voluptuousness, idle pastime, and sloth are banished from this court ... I therefore have resolved, with the help of the Lord, to take a signal revenge upon the unbelievers, that brood of hell; and I will myself begin the holy war against them.'

Thus in the summer of 1696 Mustafa set out at the head of a

considerable army from Belgrade, capturing a number of forts *en route* to the relief of the Ottoman garrison at Temesvar, which was under siege by the Austrians. He succeeded in lifting the siege, for which he received the title of Gazi, and returned in triumph to Istanbul.

The following year Mustafa led the Ottoman army from Belgrade on another campaign against the Austrians. But this time he had the ill fortune to encounter an army led by Prince Eugene of Savoy, the most outstanding general of his time, who routed the Ottomans. Some 36,000 Turkish soldiers were killed, including the grand vezir, though the sultan escaped and eventually made his way back to Istanbul.

Six days after the battle Sultan Mustafa appointed Amcazade Hüseyin Pasha as grand vezir. He was the fourth Köprülü to serve as grand vezir, and he proved to be as able as his predecessors. Hüseyin negotiated a conference with the Christian powers at the Peace of Karlowitz, the final articles of which were signed on 26 January 1699, and served as grand vezir until September 1702, when ill health forced him to resign. He died later that year.

The empire by that time was bankrupt and in a state of chaos. The economic situation of the merchants and artisans in Istanbul had become so desperate that a social revolution was imminent. The revolution began in Istanbul on 18 July 1703, when the populace and the students in the medreses joined forces with the Janissaries and rioted. The rebels marched on Edirne, joined by many soldiers of the imperial guard, and on 22 August 1703 they deposed Mustafa II. That same day they released Mustafa's younger brother from the Kafes and raised him to the throne as Ahmet III. Mustafa was then confined to the Kafes, along with his two sons, the future sultans Mahmut I and Osman III. The deposed sultan died in the Kafes on 29 December that same year, aged thirty-nine. Demetrius Cantemir, who knew him personally, writes thus in concluding his account of Mustafa's reign:

He was a sultan of great expectations in the beginning of his reign; but fortune afterwards blasted them ... He had greater advantages from nature than both of his predecessors; for he was of a mature judgement, great application and sobriety; neither prodigal nor avaricious in collecting the public monies; just, a good archer and horseman, and very devout in his religion ... He was of a moderate size, his face round and beautified with red and white;

his beard red, thin, and not long; his nose short and a little turned up, and his eyebrows thin and yellow. In the spring he used to have spots break out on his face, which disappeared again in the winter.

Ahmet III was nearly thirty when he came to the throne, and had spent the previous sixteen years as a prisoner in the Kafes. His mother, Rabia Gülnus, continued to reign in the Harem as valide sultan. The names of fourteen of his wives are known – far more than for any other sultan – and they bore him more than forty children, including three sets of twins. Sultan Ahmet had been brought up in the more informal atmosphere of his father's court in Edirne, and he complained about the rituals that hampered his movements in Topkapı Sarayı: as he wrote to his grand vezir, 'If I go up to one of the rooms, forty pages of the Privy Chamber are lined up; if I have to put on my trousers, I do not feel the least comfort, so the sword-bearer has to dismiss them, keeping only three or four men so that I may be at ease in the small room.'

Ahmet took an active part in the government during the early part of his reign, changing grand vezirs at the rate of nearly one a year as he strove to play off the various contending factions against one another. He finally settled on a permanent first minister in 1715, when the loss of Belgrade to the Austrians led him to appoint his son-in-law Nevşehirli Damat Ibrahim Pasha as grand vezir, committed to a policy of peace with the European powers. The English and Dutch ambassadors eventually arranged a peace conference, and on 21 July 1718 the Ottoman and Austrian representatives signed the Treaty of Passarowitz. As a result, the Ottomans lost all of their remaining territory in Hungary, along with much of Serbia, Bosnia and Wallachia.

Ibrahim Pasha sought to broaden the empire's contacts with western Europe, sending ambassadors to Paris, Vienna, Moscow and Poland. The first Turkish ambassador was Yermisekiz ('Twenty-seven' – his age at the time of his appointment) Mehmet Çelebi, who was instructed by Ibrahim Pasha 'to visit the fortresses, factories and works of French civilization generally and report on those that might be applicable' in the Ottoman Empire. One result of this was the introduction of the first printing-press in Istanbul, installed in 1727 by

Ibrahim Müteferrika, a Hungarian nobleman who had joined the sultan's service.

These contacts with Europe, particularly France, brought baroque architecture to Istanbul during the reign of Ahmet III. The first major edifice to show the influence of this new style was Yeni Valide Camii[3] in Üsküdar, erected by Ahmet III for his mother, the valide sultan Rabia Gülnus.

During the remaining years of Ahmet's reign the Ottoman Empire enjoyed almost uninterrupted peace. Ibrahim Pasha personally supervised the construction of an imperial summer palace on the upper reaches of the Golden Horn at Kâğithane, known in English as the Sweet Waters of Europe. This pleasure-dome was called Sa'adabat, the Place of Happiness, modelled on the French château of Marly, whose plans had been sent by the Ottoman ambassador in Paris. Ibrahim Pasha erected a palace for himself at Kandilli on the Asian side of the Bosphorus, just below the Sweet Waters of Asia, and other members of the court built palatial residences along both sides of the strait. These palaces were all surrounded by gardens, in which the

View of the Golden Horn from the cemetery at Eyüp.

dominant flower was the tulip, known in Turkish as *lale*. The Ottoman court developed such a passion for this flower – a veritable tulipomania – that the reign of Ahmet III is known as Lale Devri, the Tulip Period, and the sultan himself is referred to as the Tulip King. During that time Ahmet and Ibrahim Pasha presided over a continual series of garden fêtes that climaxed each year with the blossoming of the tulip, celebrated at the time of the first full moon in spring in the gardens of Sa'adabat. The French ambassador Louis de Villeneuve, who came to Istanbul in 1717, writes of the Tulip King's progress from one of these festivals to another, catching the exotic splendour of the age:

Sometimes the court appears floating on the waters of the Bosphorus or the Golden Horn, in elegant caiques, covered with silken tents; sometimes it moves forward in a long cavalcade towards one or another of the pleasure palaces ... These processions are made especially attractive by the beauty of the horses and the luxury of their caparisons; they progress, with golden or silver harnesses and plumed foreheads, their coverings resplendent with precious stones.

Another foreign visitor to Istanbul during the Tulip Period was Lady Mary Wortley Montagu, who arrived in the spring of 1717, when her husband came as the new English ambassador to Ahmet III. She describes their arrival in a letter dated 29 May of that year:

We arrived the next morning at Constantinople; but I can yet tell you very little of it, all my time having been taken up with receiving visits, which are, at least, a very good entertainment to the eyes, the young women being all beauties, and their beauty highly improved by the good taste of their dress. Our palace is in Pera, which is no more a suburb of Constantinople than Westminster is a suburb of London. All the ambassadors are lodged very near to one another. One part of our house shews us the port, the city and the seraglio, and the distant hills of Asia; perhaps, all together, the most beautiful prospect in the world.

The long period of peace under Ibrahim Pasha's government led to dissatisfaction among the Janissaries, who were denied their customary spoils of war. The defeat of an Ottoman army by the Iranians in the summer of 1730 provoked a revolt by the Janissaries and other dissidents. The revolt broke out on 28 September 1730 under the leadership of an Albanian ex-Janissary named Patrona Halil, who made his living as a dealer in secondhand clothes. Patrona led the rebels on a rampage through the city, sacking the shops and houses of the wealthy and killing anyone who stood in their way. Among the buildings they destroyed was the summer palace at Sa'adabat. The sultan entered into negotiations with the rebel leaders, and he agreed to hand over to them the grand vezir and two other ministers if they would spare his life and those of his children. Ahmet was thus forced to order the chief executioner to strangle Ibrahim Pasha and the two others, after which their bodies were handed over to the rebels. Ahmet was then deposed and imprisoned in the Kafes, while his nephew Mahmut was released from the Cage and girded with the sword of Osman that same day, 1 October 1730.

Ahmet spent the remainder of his life in the Kafes, dying there on 1 July 1736, possibly after being poisoned. He was sixty-two when he died, having reigned for twenty-seven years. He was buried in the türbe of Yeni Cami beside the Flower Market – an appropriate resting-place for the Tulip King. His death marked the end of an age – one of decline and gilded decadence, when festivals marked the blossoming of tulips in Istanbul, while the Ottoman Empire was collapsing along all of its frontiers. The court poet Ahmet Nedim, a bosom friend of Ahmet III, wrote at the time, 'Let us laugh, let us play, let us enjoy the delights of the world to the full.'

CHAPTER 21

In the Days of the Janissaries
1730–1826

Mahmut I was thirty-four when he became sultan, and he had spent the previous twenty-seven years of his life as a prisoner in the Kafes. As soon as he came to the throne his mother, Saliha, was installed in the Harem as valide sultan, having been relegated to the Eski Saray in Beyazit after the fall of her husband, Mustafa II. The names of six of Mahmut's wives are known, but he fathered no children. The first description of the new sultan is that of Angelo Emo, the Venetian bailo, who saw Mahmut as he rode to Eyüp on the day that he was girded with the sword of Osman, writing that he left 'in every one an agreeable idea of his royal appearance and propitious predictions for the future'.

Mahmut's position was very precarious at the time, for the Janissaries, under Patrona Halil, controlled the city. Patrona sought no office for himself, and at first he continued to wear the ragged costume of a secondhand-clothing merchant; when he was later prevailed upon to don a proper uniform, he still wore his rags beneath with pride. He did, however, secure appointments for his friends to the highest offices of the realm, nominating a Greek butcher named Yannaki to be hospodar [prince] of Moldavia and Wallachia, for example. But the appointment was never made, for Mahmut lured Patrona Halil to the palace on the promise of appointing him as a pasha, and as soon as he entered he was set upon by the palace guards, who killed him and twenty-six of his followers. The sultan and his supporters then began a reign of terror, executing some 7,000 Janissaries who had taken part in the revolt.

Another revolt took place in Istanbul in March 1731, led by an

Albanian named Kara Ali, but this was put down more quickly. Then a palace coup was attempted by the princess Fatma, daughter of Ahmet III and widow of Damat Ibrahim Pasha, who tried to restore her father to the throne, but the plot was crushed. Another reign of terror followed, and 10,000 people were executed in the next eleven days, according to Angelo Emo. All of the coffee-shops and other gathering-places were closed to prevent public discussions, and an unnatural quiet descended upon Istanbul, leading Angelo Emo to note that 'Sad it is to see the aspect of the city.'

A treaty with Iran on 4 September 1746 was followed by the longest period of peace in Ottoman history, lasting for twenty-two years. This allowed Mahmut to revive for a time the tulip fêtes that had ceased with the fall of Ahmet III, and since the palace of Sa'adabat had been destroyed the parties were now held in the gardens of Topkapı Sarayı. Jean-Claude Flachat, French ambassador to the Porte, was permitted to observe one of these fêtes by Beşir Ağa, the kızlar ağasi, or chief black eunuch. This was a festival that the sultan gave just for the women of his Harem, and at its climax he chose a new favourite, as Flachat writes:

The mistress of the Harem finally presents to him the girl that most takes his fancy. No pains have been spared to ensure her success. She hastens to exhibit every pleasing talent she possesses. The handkerchief that he throws to her signifies his wish to be alone with her. The curtain which covers the sofa on which he is sitting is made up to fall. The kızlar ağa remains to pull it aside at the first signal, and the other women, who have scattered here and there, all occupied – some with dancing, some with singing, these with playing on their instruments, and those with partaking of refreshments – all come to the kiosk in a moment to pay their respects to the sultan and congratulate the new favourite. The fête continues some time longer, and terminates by the distribution which the kızlar ağa makes of jewels, stuffs, and trinkets, following the wishes of his master. The presents are proportional to the pleasures received. But Mahmut always sees to it that they are of sufficient value for the girls to return to the Harem with an air of gratitude and contentment.

Mahmut took advantage of the long peace to modernize the water-supply system of the city, which had been neglected for two centuries, erecting an aqueduct in the Belgrade Forest and a taksim, or water-distribution centre, that gave its name to the present Taksim Meydanı in Beyoğlu. He also built a library in Haghia Sophia, which was supported by the revenues of the Cağaloğlu Hamamı,[1] the beautiful bath that he built on the Second Hill.

Interior of the Cağaloğlu Hamamı, drawing by Thomas Allom.

Mahmut spent the last six years of his reign building an imperial mosque on the Third Hill. But he did not live to complete it, dying suddenly on 14 December 1754. He was interred in the türbe of Yeni Cami the following day, and soon afterwards a rumour spread through the city that he had been buried alive.

Mahmut was succeeded by his half-brother Osman III, whose mother, Şehsuvar, thereupon became valide sultan. Osman was nearly fifty-five at the time, and had spent the previous fifty-one years as a prisoner in the Kafes. Like the other captive princes before him, the only women permitted to him in captivity were sterilized, and so he had no children when he became sultan, nor did he sire any during his short reign. The only other living males of the Ottoman royal line were his three cousins, Beyazit, Mustafa and Abdül Hamit, whom he kept locked up in the Kafes. He executed Beyazit in 1756, but he spared his other two cousins, who would succeed him in turn as Mustafa III and

Abdül Hamit I. During the first year of his reign Osman completed work on the imperial külliye that had been begun by his brother Mahmut, calling it Nuruosmaniye Camii,[2] the Mosque of the Sacred Light ('Nur') of Osman.

Osman died on 30 October 1757 and was buried in the türbe of Yeni Cami. That same day he was succeeded by his cousin Mustafa, a son of Ahmet III, who was nearly forty-one when he came to the throne, and had spent the previous twenty-seven years as a prisoner in the Kafes. His first kadın was Mihrişah, who on Christmas Eve 1761 bore his first son, the future Selim III.

During the first four years of his reign Mustafa III built two imperial mosques: Ayazma Camii[3] in Üsküdar and Laleli Camii[4] on the Fourth Hill, both of them in the baroque style. Laleli Camii was the work of Mehmet Tahir Ağa, the greatest of the Turkish baroque architects.

The long period of peace enjoyed by the Ottoman Empire ended on 4 October 1768, when the aggressive policies of Catherine the Great forced the Porte to declare war on Russia. The Russians trapped the Ottoman fleet in the harbour of Çeşme, west of Izmir, virtually annihilating it on 6–7 July 1770. At the same time Russian armies attacked the Ottomans on several fronts, and within two years they had conquered Moldavia, Wallachia and the Crimea. The Porte was thus forced to sue for terms, which were agreed to at the Treaty of Küçük Kaynarca on 21 July 1774. One of the provisions in the treaty allowed Catherine to build a church in Istanbul, a privilege that was subsequently interpreted as establishing Russia as the protector of all Orthodox Christians in the Ottoman Empire.

Meanwhile Mustafa III had died of a heart attack on 21 January 1774, being buried in the türbe of Laleli Camii. He was succeeded by his cousin Abdül Hamit, who was then forty-eight, and had spent the previous forty-three years of his life as a prisoner in the Kafes. The only other living male in the imperial Osmanlı line was Mustafa's son, Selim, who then took Abdül Hamit's place in the Kafes.

The new sultan made up for lost time in the Harem after he came to the throne, and in the remaining fifteen years of his life he fathered twenty-six children on his seven favourite women. These included twelve sons, but only two of them survived infancy: the future sultans Mustafa IV and Mahmut II.

Abdül Hamit I began a programme of reform in the Ottoman armed forces. This reform was influenced principally by Baron François de Tott, a Hungarian nobleman who had served in the French army before joining the service of the Ottomans under Mustafa III, continuing as adviser to Abdül Hamit until 1776. At the same time the Ottoman navy was reformed under Gazi Hasan Pasha, who was appointed grand admiral in 1774. But these reforms were limited in their effect, for appointments to the officer corps continued to be made through bribery and political connections, and as a result the Ottoman armed forces were no match for those of the European powers.

The central government in Istanbul had little control over the provinces, as virtually independent war-lords ruled in the Balkans, Anatolia and Egypt. The decadence of the Ottoman state was now so evident that the western powers began to refer to it as the 'Sick Man of Europe', as they prepared to divide up its remaining provinces.

Abdül Hamit died of a stroke on 7 April 1789 and was succeeded by his nephew Selim, who was then twenty seven. Selim had been nominally confined to the Kafes since the death of his father, Mustafa III, in 1757, at which time his mother, Mihrişah, had been sent to the Eski Saray in Beyazit. But Abdül Hamit had given Selim considerable freedom, and so when he succeeded his uncle as sultan he was far better prepared to rule than were most of his predecessors who had been strictly confined in the Kafes. He had been well educated and was a talented calligrapher and composer. Calligraphic inscriptions by Selim are still displayed in a number of mosques and türbes in the city, and some of his compositions of Turkish classical music are occasionally played on Istanbul Radio.

When Selim came to the throne his place in the Kafes was taken by his two young cousins, the future sultans Mustafa IV and Mahmut II, the only other surviving males in the imperial Osmanlı line, whom he allowed as much freedom as he himself had enjoyed during his confinement. The names of seven of Selim's favourite women are recorded, but he sired no sons and so none of his wives was ever given the title of first kadın. Selim brought his mother, Mihrişah, back to the Harem of Topkapı Sarayı, where she took her honoured place as valide sultan. Five years later she built a külliye⁵ in Eyüp, which included the baroque türbe in which she was laid to rest when she died in 1805.

Mustafa III (1757–74) and the young Prince Selim,
the future Selim III; anonymous miniature.

Selim III was committed to a programme of reform in all of the
institutions of the Ottoman Empire, particularly its armed forces. One
of his reforms was the development of a new Artillery Corps along
the lines laid down by Baron de Tott, and this soon became the most
modern and efficient part of the Ottoman army. But the Janissaries
and Sipahis resisted all attempts to reform their corps, which led Selim
to develop an infantry known as the Nizamı Cedit, or New Order. The
main barracks for the Nizamı Cedit was at Kadıköy, where a huge
structure known as the Selimiye was erected. Selim also built a new
complex for his Artillery Corps at Tophane on the European shore of
the Bosphorus.

Selim's Nizamı Cedit aroused great opposition among the leaders
in the old Ottoman army. When Selim sent a force of the Nizamı Cedit
to Edirne to enrol and train recruits the local notables there rebelled

on 20 June 1806 under the leadership of Ismail Ağa, who demanded that the commanders of the Nizamı Cedit be dismissed. Selim gave in to the demands, putting the command of the Nizamı Cedit in the hands of the rebels, who after the death of Ismail Ağa were led by Alemdar Mustafa Pasha. Thus Selim lost control of the only military force that he might rely upon at a time of crisis.

The crisis occurred in late May 1807, when the Janissaries in Istanbul revolted and were joined by the religious students in the medreses. When the Janissaries stormed Topkapı Sarayı, Selim tried to appease them by surrendering seventeen officers of his Nizamı Cedit to the rebels, who killed them and displayed their severed heads outside the palace. The Janissaries then obtained a fetva from the şeyhülislam justifying the removal of Selim, and on 29 May 1807 he was deposed in favour of his cousin Mustafa, whose place he took in the Kafes.

Mustafa IV was twenty-eight when he came to the throne, and had spent the previous eighteen years of his life in the Kafes. The new sultan, who was mentally ill, was completely in the power of the rebels. The Janissaries were free to run amok in Istanbul, killing anyone wearing the uniform of the Nizamı Cedit, as they looted houses and shops and struck down anyone who tried to stop them.

The opponents of the Janissaries gave their support to Alemdar Mustafa Pasha, commander of the Nizamı Cedit, who had in the meanwhile established his headquarters at Rusçuk on the Danube. Alemdar marched his troops back to Istanbul, arriving on 1 July 1808, and within five days he took control of the city, while Sultan Mustafa and his supporters barricaded themselves in Topkapı Sarayı. Alemdar surrounded the palace on 7 July and called on the sultan to surrender. Mustafa responded by ordering the execution of both Selim and Mahmut, for that would leave him as the only surviving male of the imperial dynasty. The chief black eunuch and his men caught Selim in his mother's apartment and stabbed him to death, after which they went off in search of Prince Mahmut. But Mahmut's nurse, Cevri Khalfa, threw ashes into the faces of the pursuers and temporarily blinded them, allowing the prince time to escape on to the roof of the Harem, where he managed to hide himself from his pursuers. Meanwhile Alemdar had succeeded in making his way into the Court of the Divan, where Selim's corpse was hurled out from the Gate of

Salutations. Alemdar and his men broke through into the Inner Palace and captured Mustafa in the throne-room, whereupon Mahmut emerged from his hiding-place. Alemdar then obtained a fetva from the şeyhülislam deposing Mustafa, who was sent back to the Kafes, and Mahmut was raised to the throne.

Mahmut II was twenty-three when he became sultan, and had spent the previous nineteen years of his life nominally confined to the Kafes, though he had been allowed considerable freedom. His mother, Nakşidil, had been relegated to the Eski Saray after the death of his father, Abdül Hamit I, and Mahmut now restored her to the Harem of Topkapı Sarayı as valide sultan. Mahmut's eighteen wives of record bore him nineteen boys and seventeen girls, of whom only two sons and two daughters survived into their adult years. The two surviving sons were the future sultans Abdül Mecit I and Abdül Aziz, the first of whom was born in 1823 to Bezmialem and the second in 1830 to Pertevniyal.

Mahmut was intent on reforming the Ottoman state, but during the early years of his reign he was unable to accomplish his aims because of the vested interests of the old order, particularly the Janissaries. His first grand vezir was Alemdar Mustafa Pasha, who tried to begin Mahmut's programme of reform by organizing a new army called the Segbanı Cedit. This aroused the opposition of the Janissaries, who received widespread support from the populace of Istanbul. The Janissaries revolted on 14 November 1808 and stormed both Topkapı Sarayı and the grand vezir's headquarters at the Sublime Porte. Early the next morning the rebels broke into the Porte, forcing Alemdar and his men to take refuge in a powder magazine, which shortly afterwards exploded, killing them and several hundred Janissaries. The Janissaries then tried to break into Topkapı Sarayı, but were beaten back by the troops of the Segbanı Cedit. A full-scale civil war then ensued, as the Janissaries gained the support of the city's artisans and unemployed labourers, cutting off the water supply of Topkapı Sarayı and putting the palace under siege. The Ottoman fleet had remained loyal to the sultan, and when the captains saw that the palace was being besieged their warships in the Golden Horn began bombarding the main Janissary barracks in Beyazit. The warships also began firing at the rebels besieging Topkapı Sarayı, and in the process they started fires that ravaged both the First and Third Hills, killing thousands of townspeople.

Meanwhile Mahmut sent the chief executioner to the Kafes and had his cousin Mustafa strangled, so that he himself was now the sole surviving male in the imperial Osmanlı line. The Ulema finally persuaded both sides to come to an agreement, and a cease-fire was called on 17 November. Mahmut agreed to disband the Segbanı Cedit, provided that its soldiers who had been garrisoning Topkapı Sarayı be given safe conduct to return to their homes. But the rebels did not keep their promise, and as the loyal troops left the palace they were set upon and slaughtered by the mob, who also killed a number of the notables who had supported Mahmut's reforms. Mahmut managed to save his throne, but he now realized that before trying to create a new army he would first have to destroy the old one, particularly the Janissaries. He also knew that any programme of reform would have to encompass more than just the military, for the whole of Ottoman society and all of its institutions would have to be reshaped if the empire was to survive.

The only part of the new army that survived for Mahmut to rely upon was the Artillery Corps, which he eventually built up into a loyal and effective force of some 15,000 men. At the same time he rebuilt the Ottoman fleet, which was placed under the able direction of the grand admiral Husrev Pasha.

Robert Adair, British ambassador to the Porte, was granted an audience with Mahmut on 4 July 1810, bringing along with him two English travellers who had recently arrived in Istanbul. These were Lord Byron and his companion John Cam Hobhouse, who described the sultan in the account of his journey:

Sultan Mahmoud was placed in the middle of the throne, with his feet upon the ground ... He was dressed in a robe of yellow satin, with a broad border of the darkest sable; his dagger, and an ornament on his breast, were covered with diamonds: the front of his white and blue turban shone with a treble sprig of diamonds, which served as a buckle to a high straight plume of bird-of-paradise feathers. He for the most part kept a hand on each knee, and neither moved his body nor his head, but rolled his eyes from side to side, without fixing them for an instant upon the Ambassador or any other person present. Occasionally he stroked and turned up his beard, displaying a milk-white hand glittering with diamond rings. His eye-brows, eyes, and beard, being of a glossy jet black, did not appear natural, but added to that indescribable majesty that would be difficult for any but an Oriental sovereign to assume: his face was pale, and regularly formed, except that his nose (contrary to the usual form of that feature in the Ottoman princes) was slightly turned up and pointed: his whole physiognomy was mild and benevolent, but expressive and full of dignity. He appeared of a short and small stature, and about thirty years old, which is somewhat more than his actual age.

Byron recorded his impressions of Istanbul in his letters and journals, his favourite prospect being the view of the Theodosian Walls from the downs of Thrace, where he frequently rode. As he wrote in a letter to his mother:

The walls of the Seraglio are like the walls of Newstead gardens, only higher, and much in the same order; but the ride by the walls of the city, on the land side, is beautiful. Imagine four miles of immense, triple battlements, covered with ivy, surmounted with 218 towers, and on either side of the road, Turkish burying-grounds (the loveliest spots on earth), full of enormous cypresses. I have seen the ruins of Athens, of Ephesus, and Delphi. I have traversed great part of Turkey, and some of Asia; but I never beheld a work of nature or art which yielded an impression like the prospect on each side from the Seven Towers to the end of the Golden Horn.

Byron recorded his impressions of the Turks in a letter written to Henry Drury:

I see not much difference between ourselves & the Turks, save that we have foreskins and they none, that they have long dresses and we short, and that we talk much and they little. – In England the vices in fashion are whoring and drinking, in Turkey, Sodomy and smoking, we prefer a girl and bottle, they a pipe and pathic. They are sensible people ... I can swear in Turkish, but except for one terrible oath, and 'pimp' and 'bread' and 'water' I have got no great vocabulary in that language.

Meanwhile a movement for Greek independence had been gathering force through the activities of a secret philhellenic organization known as the Philiki Hetairia, or Society of Friends. The Greeks finally raised the banner of revolt against the Turks at the monastery of Ayia Lavra in the Peloponnesus on 25 March 1821. News of the revolt caused Mahmut to panic, for he feared that it would lead to a general uprising of the Greeks in the Ottoman Empire. He immediately sought a fetva from the Ulema declaring a cihad, or holy war (jihad), against all of the Greek Christians in the empire, but the şeyhülislam refused to grant it, having received assurance from the ecumenical patriarch Gregory V that his flock was loyal to the sultan. Nevertheless, on 2 April 1821, Easter Sunday, armed soldiers seized Gregory after he had finished saying mass at the patriarchal church of St George, whereupon they hung him from Orta Kapı, the main gate of the Patriarchate. Orta Kapı was sealed shut and painted black after Gregory's body was cut down, and it has remained closed to the present day – a symbol of Greek–Turkish intransigence.

Mahmut turned to Mehmet Ali of Egypt for help in putting down the Greek rebellion. Mehmet Ali sent his son Ibrahim Pasha to the Peloponnesus with a force of 10,000 men, along with artillery and cavalry, while the regular Turkish army marched down through Greece. Ibrahim landed at Modon in February 1825, and before the year was over he had conquered all of the Peloponnesus except for Nauplion, and then on 14 April 1826 he captured Mesolongi.

Meanwhile Mahmut had been continuing his efforts to rebuild the Ottoman military forces, particularly the Janissaries, who had proved to be completely ineffective in putting down the Greek revolt. But the Janissaries frustrated all of his efforts at reform, as they continued to perpetrate outrages in Istanbul and in the provinces.

Mahmut bided his time, and in the spring of 1826 he finally announced his intention to reorganize the armed forces of the empire, beginning with the Janissaries. The Janissary officers had agreed to cooperate in this programme, but many of them began secretly plotting an insurrection against the sultan. The uprising began on the evening of 14 June 1826, when the Janissaries mustered outside their main barracks on the Et Meydanı in Beyazit and overturned their huge bronze cauldrons as a sign of their discontent. The following day they were joined by thousands of artisans as well as unemployed labourers and drifters. The revolt began that evening when the Janissaries mustered in the Et Meydanı, after which they and their supporters sacked the palace of the grand vezir, Selim Pasha Benderli, who happened to be away at his summer palace on the Bosphorus.

When word reached the grand vezir he informed Mahmut and quickly mobilized the sultan's Artillery Corps and the other loyal troops, after which he besieged the Janissaries in their barracks on the Et Meydanı. The artillery bombarded the barracks and reduced it to a flaming ruin, while the sultan's troops shot down all of those who tried to escape; more than a thousand Janissaries died in the holocaust. The surviving Janissaries were then hunted down throughout the city, and those who were not killed outright were brought to the Hippodrome, where hundreds of them were executed and their bodies thrown on to a growing pile of corpses. Before the day was over the Janissary Corps had been completely destroyed in Istanbul, the death toll estimated at 10,000. Messengers were sent to the provinces to disband the Janissaries there, while the gates of Istanbul were closed to hunt down and kill any who might have remained alive in the city.

Meanwhile the Council of the Divan, meeting early on Friday 16 June 1826, issued a firman formally dissolving the Janissary Corps. The firman was immediately approved by Mahmut, and at the noon prayer that day it was announced to the faithful in all the mosques of Istanbul. The Janissaries were no more, and the day of their fall was thereafter known as Vakayı Hayriye, the Auspicious Event.

Every trace of the Janissaries was then obliterated in Istanbul, with all of their barracks being demolished and even their tombstones destroyed, so that not even one of their distinctive headstones, marked with their curious turbans, can now be identified in the cemeteries around the city. Thus ended the days of the Janissaries, a military corps that had been in existence for five centuries, its members renowned for both their valour and their villainy. Their passing left Istanbul safer but less colourful.

Some of the few survivors of the Auspicious Event literally went underground to escape, living in kulhans, the stoke-holes of Istanbul's hamams, surviving on food smuggled in to them by old friends or lovers, who also brought them the hashish that stoked their pipe-dreams of former glory. These last survivors of the Janissaries were known as the Kulhan Beyler, the Men of the Stoke-Hole, and some of them wrote love-songs and threnodies of astonishing beauty, which

High officers of the Janissaries.

are still sung in the subterranean dives of Istanbul – or so one is told. Some of the coffee-houses where they gathered are still pointed out in old quarters like Samatya, where of an evening one of the *habitués* who has been drinking something stronger than coffee will unburden his soul in a song of the Kulhan Beyler, evoking a vision of what life was like here in the days of the Janissaries.

CHAPTER 22

The Age of Reform
1826–1876

Mahmut II had commissioned an imperial mosque in 1822, to be erected on the European shore of the Bosphorus near his new cannon foundry at Tophane. The mosque was completed in 1826 soon after the Auspicious Event. Thus Mahmut called it Nusretiye Camii,[1] the Mosque of Victory, to commemorate his triumph over the Janissaries.

The following year Britain, France and Russia signed a treaty in London agreeing to intervene in the Greek War of Independence if the Ottomans refused mediation. When Mahmut refused to negotiate, the allied navies under Admiral Codrington sailed to Navarino in the Peloponnesus, where on 20 October 1827 they totally destroyed the Ottoman and Egyptian fleets, cutting off Ibrahim Pasha from his supplies and reinforcements in Egypt. The European powers forced Mahmut to give independence to Greece in 1830, leading to the establishment of the first Greek kingdom three years later.

Mehmet Ali of Egypt, who had dreams of founding a new dynasty, mounted an expedition under Ibrahim Pasha in the summer of 1831, and within a year he conquered all of Syria and the Lebanon, taking Damascus on 18 June 1832. Ibrahim then led his troops across the Anatolian plateau, defeating two Ottoman armies and then, on 12 February 1833, taking Kütahya, only 240 kilometres from Istanbul, which so frightened Mahmut that he called on the Russians for help. Tsar Nicholas sent a fleet to Istanbul, and on 20 February Russian troops were landed on the Asian shore of the upper Bosphorus at Hünkâr Iskelesi. This led Ibrahim to come to terms with the Porte, and on 29 March 1833 he signed a peace treaty in Kütahya which gave him and Mehmet Ali control of the eastern Mediterranean and the

Middle East. Ibrahim thereupon evacuated his troops from Anatolia. Tsar Nicholas consolidated his gains at a treaty signed at Hünkâr Iskelesi on 8 July 1833, in which Russia and the Ottoman Empire agreed to an eight-year non-aggression pact, with Mahmut agreeing to close the strait to foreign warships in time of war. This agreement alarmed the British and French, who saw the prospect of the tsar taking control of the strait, and thenceforth they were determined to defend the Ottoman Empire against Russian encroachment.

Meanwhile there had been revolts against Ottoman rule in the Balkans, Anatolia and Iraq, which were difficult to put down because the sultan had not yet created a new army to replace the Janissaries. Thus Mahmut renewed his efforts to rebuild the army, but also considerably enlarged the scope of his reforms to include all areas of the Ottoman state and society. One result of his reforms was the creation of the first Turkish-language newspaper, the *Takvimi Vekayi*, or *Calendar of Events*, which began publication in Istanbul on 25 July 1831. Although its circulation was small and limited to high officials of the government, its effect was considerable and it led eventually to the establishment of a far more general press in the Ottoman Empire.

During the remaining years of Mahmut's reign the central government of the empire was reorganized under the successive direction of the grand vezirs Reşit Mehmet Pasha and Mehmet Emin Rauf Pasha. Mahmut personally supervised the work of rebuilding the empire's armed forces, which had again performed disastrously during Ibrahim Pasha's invasion. The reforms in both the government and the armed forces depended ultimately on the development of a proper educational system, for up until that time the only schools in Turkey aside from those of the minorities were the mekteps and medreses attached to the mosques and other foundations. Mahmut could not openly supplant these, so he built additional primary and secondary schools where promising youths could learn secular subjects that would prepare them for the military technical schools and other institutions of higher learning which he also established. These educational reforms laid the basis for the secularization that was to spread throughout Ottoman society after Mahmut's reign. The reorganization of the imperial administration also created the first municipal government in Istanbul, with regular police and firemen – the functions of these had previously been performed by the Janissaries.

The reforms also brought western ways to Istanbul, particularly in the sultan's court. Mahmut dressed like a European monarch rather than an Oriental potentate, appearing at public receptions and cultural events clad in trousers and the black frock-coat known as the Stambouline, wearing the red Moroccan fez rather than the elaborate and top-heavy turban of his predecessors. In 1829 he issued a decree forbidding the wearing of old-fashioned robes and turbans except by the clergy, and thenceforth the fez became the accepted head-dress. Stratford Canning, at the British Embassy in Pera, remarked on the

Mahmut II (1808–39), c. 1830; anonymous oil-painting. The sultan is wearing the fez and modern uniform he adopted after banning the turban and traditional Muslim clothing.

change in dress: 'Every person who has been absent and has now returned, notices the change, which has been most extraordinary. Very few years more, and not a turban will exist ... employees of every description now wear the red cap, Cossack trousers, black boots, and a plain red or blue cloak buttoned under the chin. No gold embroidery, no jewels, no pelisses.' The clothing reform infuriated conservatives, particularly in the religious establishment. One day, when Mahmut was riding through the streets of Istanbul in his phaeton, a dervish shouted at him, 'Infidel sultan, God will demand an accounting for your blasphemy! You are destroying Islam!' Nevertheless Mahmut continued with his reforms, among which was the equality before Ottoman civil law of people of all religions: as he insisted, 'I distinguish between my subjects Muslims in the mosque, Christians in the church, Jews in the synagogue, but there is no difference among them in any other way.'

European symphonies and opera had been brought to Istanbul by Giuseppe Donizetti, whom Mahmut had hired as his musical director in 1828, making him a pasha. Donizetti Pasha, elder brother of the famous Gaetano Donizetti, trained the imperial band in music *alafranga* – i.e. in the manner of the 'Franks', or Europeans – and wrote the Ottoman national anthem; later he built the first opera house in Istanbul, bringing foreign musical groups to perform there. The first theatre in the city was founded in 1840 with the financial support of the Ottoman government together with the foreign embassies; this was erected in Pera by a Genoese named Giustiani, whose successor, the Italian magician Bosco, put on his own magic shows as well as bringing in European plays and operas. Several other theatres soon opened, all of them catering principally to foreigners and the non-Muslim minorities, though the sultan often attended premier performances.

During the reign of Mahmut II many of the wealthy families of Istanbul built summer mansions along the Bosphorus – elegant wooden structures known as yalıs, of which only a few now survive. Julia Pardoe writes of these yalıs in *The City of the Sultan and the Domestic Manner of the Turks*, published in 1836:

To be seen in all its beauty, the Bosphorus should be looked upon by moonlight. Then it is that the occupants of the spacious mansions which are

*Yalıs, or waterfront houses, at Bebek on the European shore of
the middle Bosphorus, with the fortress of Anadolu Hisarı across
the way on the Asian shore.*

mirrored in its waters, enjoy to the fullest perfection the magnificence of the
scene around them. The glare of noonday reveals too broadly the features of
the locality; while the deep, blue, star-studded sky, the pure moonlight, and
the holy quiet of evening, lend to it, on the contrary, a mysterious indis-
tinctness, which doubles its attraction. The inhabitants of the capital are con-
scious of this fact; and during the summer months, when they occupy their
marine mansions, one of their greatest recreations is to seat themselves on
their seaward terraces, to watch the sparkling of the ripple, and to listen to
the evening hymn of the seamen on board the Greek and Italian vessels;
amused at intervals by a huge shoal of porpoises rolling past, gambolling in
the moonlight, and plunging amid the waves with a sound like thunder: while
afar off are the dark mountains of Asia casting their long dusky shadows far
across the water, and the quivering summits of the tall trees on the edge of
the channel sparkling like silver, and lending the last touch of loveliness to a
landscape perhaps unparalleled in the world.

Mehmet Ali had continued to make plans for the creation of a new empire, and on 25 May 1838 he declared his intention of founding a dynasty in Egypt independent of the Ottoman Empire. This led Mahmut to mount an expedition against him and Ibrahim Pasha. The Ottoman army invaded Syria, but Ibrahim's forces virtually annihilated them north of Aleppo on 24 June 1839. The news reached Mahmut just before he died on 1 July 1839, succumbing to the combined effects of tuberculosis and cirrhosis of the liver – the latter brought on by his love of champagne, another of his western innovations.

Mahmut was succeeded by his son Abdül Mecit, who was then sixteen years old. The new sultan's mother, Bezmialem, thereupon became valide sultan, while his younger half-brother, Abdül Aziz, was nominally confined to the Kafes, where he enjoyed considerable freedom, living with his mother, Pertevniyal. Abdül Mecit proved to be one of the most prolific of all the sultans. He is recorded to have had twenty-one wives, by whom he fathered nineteen sons and twenty-three daughters. Among his sons were the future sultans Murat V, Abdül Hamit II, Mehmet V Reşat and Mehmet VI Vahideddin, the last four rulers of the Ottoman Empire. The English traveller Charles MacFarlane was astonished by the sultan's procreative powers: as he writes, 'Before he was twenty years old, the puny stripling was the father of eight children, borne to him by different women in the imperial harem, in the course of little more than three years.' MacFarlane later noted the arrival of two more imperial offspring: 'Very early in the morning we were startled out of our sleep by a tremendous firing of salutes. The Sultan has another son. Only last week he had another daughter.'

As soon as Abdül Mecit came to the throne Mehmet Husrev Pasha seized the grand vezir's seals and forced the young sultan to appoint him as grand vezir. Bezmialem deeply distrusted Husrev, believing that he was in the pay of the Russians, and advised her son to rely upon his foreign minister, Mustafa Reşit. The grand admiral Ahmet Fevzi Pasha sailed the Ottoman fleet to Alexandria and surrendered it to Mehmet Ali, fearing that the grand vezir would turn over the ships to the Russians. Mustafa Reşit negotiated with the European powers – Britain, France, Russia, Austria and Prussia – to intervene, promising

Ladies in the Harem, by Thomas Allom.

that Abdül Mecit would institute far-reaching reforms. The five powers forced Mehmet Ali to accept the sultan's offer of the hereditary governorship of Egypt, thus ending the crisis for the time being.

Mustafa Reşit then returned to Istanbul to work with Abdül Mecit on the reforms that he had promised the western powers. These were embodied in a Hatti Şerif proclaimed by Abdül Mecit on 3 November 1839, meeting with his ministers and the European ambassadors at a pavilion in the lower gardens of Topkapı Sarayı known as Gülhane, the Rose Chamber. The Gülhane decree announced that Abdül Mecit intended to rule as an enlightened monarch, promising that he would protect the lives and property of all of his subjects – Muslims, Christians and Jews alike – and that he would create a government in which there would be equitable taxation, regular legislative councils, and a fair system of conscription to obtain manpower for a modern army and navy.

The British mounted an expedition against Ibrahim Pasha in 1840 and forced him to withdraw from Syria early the following year. A British fleet then bombarded Alexandria and prepared to land troops, which led Mehmet Ali to evacuate Crete and the Arabian peninsula. The Ottoman fleet that had been surrendered by Ahmet Fevzi Pasha was then allowed to sail back to Istanbul. Abdül Mecit thereupon issued a decree on 13 February 1841 confirming Mehmet Ali as the hereditary Ottoman governor of Egypt, thus settling the so-called Eastern Crisis. Both Mehmet Ali and Ibrahim Pasha died within a few months of one another in the winter of 1848–9. Mehmet Ali was succeeded by his grandson Abbas Hilmi, who in 1850 travelled to Rhodes to meet with Abdül Mecit, to whom he paid homage as sultan and caliph.

Abdül Mecit then began to implement the Tanzimat, or Reform Movement, which had been proclaimed in the Gülhane decree. The reforms embraced all areas of Ottoman society, including the creation of a Ministry of Education to develop secular education throughout the empire. The reforms also continued the reorganization of the municipal government of Istanbul that had begun under Mahmut II, founding modern police, fire, sanitation, transport and postal services, building new streets, sidewalks and squares, installing sewers, drains and street lighting, and generally transforming the old Ottoman city into a modern European metropolis, though at heart it remained a medieval labyrinth.

The old houses of Istanbul were virtually all built of wood, and consequently the city was constantly ravaged by fires. Edward Lear, in a letter to his sister Ann, described a fire that occurred in Pera when he was staying there in 1848:

I must now devote a word to conflagration general & especial. You know that nearly all the houses in Constantinople are of wood – and you may have heard of the frequency of fires, & their extent, but you will not be surprised to hear that since I came – (Aug 1st) there have been 8 dreadful burnings – the least of which destroyed 60, & the largest 5,000 houses – and reduced hundreds and thousands to wretchedness. If I had not seen these things, I could not have believed them . . . And now I come to the night of Wed, the 6th – when about 12 everybody was awakened by the waiters (throughout the hotel) with the news that a tremendous fire was raging in Pera, & advancing to the inn. But Miseri said there was no danger – as their [sic] was a stone house, & a church (Greek) between him and them, where the flames would stop, & as I guessed from his coolness – he was in the right. However, I packed up, & then joined everybody else on the house top – where wet carpets, & water were all in the fashion. A most horrible sight it was . . . The flames were tremendous – & all the city light as day. The houses fell crash, crash, crash, as the fire swept on nearer & nearer – and by four o'clock after midnight, it reached within 2 houses of the hotel – but there it stopped . . . As it was, only 300 houses were burnt! – no lives lost; they very seldom are! – & all the property is carried through the suburbs to the cemeteries etc. – & there the poor people live till another wooden suburb arises in less than a year's time. Such is life in Constantinople.

There was a fire-watch station on the Galata Tower, and when a blaze was spotted the local fire brigade rushed to put it out – a scene described by Edmondo de Amicis in his *Constantinople*, published in 1881:

Tulumbadgi! (firemen), cried one of the bridge-guards, and we drew to one side and watched them as they rushed by, a horde of swarthy half-naked savages with bare hands and hairy chests, streaming with perspiration, young and old, big and little, with faces of thieves and cutthroats, four of them bearing a small pump, that looked like a child's bier, on their shoulders, while the rest were armed with long hooked poles, coils of rope, axes, and picks. On they rushed, uttering hoarse cries, panting for breath, their eyes dilated, streaming hair, grim, determined, their rags fluttering in the wind and poisoning the sweet morning air with the close malodorous smell of wild beasts. Sweeping across the bridge, they finally disappear in the Rue de Galata, hence fainter and fainter came the cry 'Allah! Allah!' till at last profound silence reigned once more.

Abdül Mecit was a great builder, and he spent an enormous amount of money erecting palaces and mosques along the Bosphorus. The largest of these by far was Dolmabahçe Sarayı,[2] which was erected on

Dolmabahçe Sarayı, c. 1860, drawing by J. and A. Williams.

the European shore of the Bosphorus along with Çırağan Sarayı[3] and Yıldız Sarayı,[4] while Küçüksu Kasrı[5] (a kasır is a small palace) was built across the strait on the Sweet Waters of Asia. The valley beside the Küçüksu palace was a favourite gathering-spot for Ottoman women of the upper class, as Miss Pardoe notes in her *Beauties of the Bosphorus*.

All ranks alike frequent this sweet and balmy spot. The Sultanas move along in quiet stateliness over the greensward in their gilded arabas, drawn by oxen glittering with foil, and covered with awnings of velvet, heavy with gold embroidery and fringes; the light carriages of the Pasha's harems roll rapidly past, decorated with flashing draperies, the horses gaily caparisoned, and the young beauties within pillowed on satins and velvets, and frequently screened by shawls of immense value; while the wives of many of the Beys, the Effendis, and the Emirs, leave their arabas, and seated on Persian carpets under the leafy canopy of the superb maple-trees which abound in the valley, amuse themselves for hours, the elder ladies with their pipes, and the younger ones with their hand-mirrors; greetings innumerable take place on all sides; and the itinerant confectioners and water-vendors reap a rich harvest ...

Wallachian and Jewish musicians are common; and the extraordinary length of time during which they dwell upon a single note, with their heads thrown back, their mouths open, and their eyes fixed, and then follow it up with a whole sentence, rapidly and energetically uttered, is most singular. But these oriental troubadours are not without their rivals in their admiration of the veiled beauties who surround them; conjurors, improvvisatori, story-tellers, and Bulgarian dancers are there also, to seduce away a portion of their audience; while the interruptions caused by fruit, sherbet and water-vendors, are incessant. They are however the most popular of all; and a musician, whose talent is known and acknowledged, seldom fails to spend a very profitable day at the Asian Sweet Waters.

Another crisis arose in October 1853 when Russia refused to evacuate the Trans-Danubian Principalities. This gave rise to the conflict that came to be known as the Crimean War, beginning on 28 March 1854, in which the Turks were joined by the British and French in fighting against the Russians on the Crimean peninsula. The sick and wounded from the British forces were shipped back to Istanbul, where they were cared for by Florence Nightingale and her nurses at the Selimiye barracks, which had been converted into a hospital.

The Crimean War was settled by the Treaty of Paris, signed on 30 March 1856. The terms of the treaty left the map much as it had been before the war. Turkey was admitted to the Concert of Europe, the harmonious family of civilized European nations, and the other signatories undertook 'to respect the independence and the territorial integrity of the Ottoman Empire'. The tsar retained his right to act as protector of the subject Christians of the Ottoman Empire, while the sultan on his part pledged to respect the rights of all of his people regardless of their religion. This pledge had already been made by Abdül Mecit to his own subjects in February, when he had issued a rescript known as the Hatti Hümayun that reaffirmed the principles of the Gülhane decree in even greater detail.

The signing of the peace treaty was celebrated at a banquet given to mark the dedication of the new palace of Dolmabahçe Sarayı on 13 July 1856. Thenceforth Dolmabahçe became the principal imperial residence of the Ottoman sultans, leaving the old palace of Topkapı Sarayı virtually abandoned.

The Crimean War and its aftermath had a profound impact on the Ottoman Empire and Turkish society in general, particularly in Istanbul. The expense of the war, not to mention the extravagant palace-building of Abdül Mecit, placed a great burden on the new treasury established by the Tanzimat. This led the government to take out a series of foreign loans at very high interest rates, and the empire was soon saddled with a debt far beyond its power to pay. Refugees flocked to Istanbul from the war-torn European provinces of the empire, and the population of the city increased to 430,000 in 1856 – a total that did not include the large numbers of foreign soldiers and advisers and their families who were living in the capital. The presence of these foreigners made the people of Istanbul more familiar with European ways, making it easier for the Tanzimatcılar, or Men of the Tanzimat, to introduce their reforms, which were all based on western models.

Abdül Mecit died of tuberculosis on 25 June 1861. He was succeeded by his half-brother, Abdül Aziz, who was then thirty-one, and had spent the previous twenty-two years in nominal confinement in the Kafes. Abdül Aziz had fathered a son named Yusuf Izzeddin in 1857, four years before he succeeded Abdül Mecit as sultan – the first time in three centuries that the child of a non-reigning male of the Osmanlı was acknowledged and allowed to live. Yusuf's birth was not announced until after his father became sultan, when his mother, Dürrünev, became first kadın, while Pertevniyal became valide sultan. At first Abdül Aziz was content to have one wife – Dürrünev – but eventually he acquired six additional kadıns, by whom he had twelve more children: five sons and seven daughters. Yusuf, the first-born son, had the title of veliaht, or crown prince, until he took his own life on 1 February 1916.

Abdül Aziz was very different from his half-brother Abdül Mecit. The new sultan was a veritable bear of a man, weighing more than 100 kilograms and powerfully built – a physique that served him well in his favourite activity, wrestling, earning him the nickname of Güresçi, the Wrestler. He cared little for the cultural activities favoured by Abdül Mecit, preferring to spend his time wrestling with his favourites and watching cock-fights. Nor was he committed to the Tanzimat programme of his late brother, whose only quality he shared was extravagance.

Abdül Aziz's greatest single extravagance was his commissioning of Beylerbey Sarayı,[6] a new imperial palace across the Bosphorus from Ortaköy, built in the years 1861–5. Then in 1871 the sultan built an imperial mosque for his mother, Pertevniyal, in Aksaray, the ancient Forum Bovis, a rococo edifice known as Pertevniyal Valide Camii.[7]

Abdül Aziz was the first Ottoman sultan to travel abroad for pleasure, going to Paris in 1867 at the invitation of Napoleon III to see his Great Universal Exhibition. He was also received by Queen Victoria in Windsor, King Leopold in Brussels, Kaiser Wilhelm I at Koblenz, and the emperor Franz Josef in Vienna. After the sultan returned to Istanbul he received a number of royal guests, the first being the empress Eugénie of France, who stayed at Beylerbey Sarayı in October 1868, *en route* to the opening of the Suez Canal the following year. Abdül Aziz was very taken by Eugénie and presented her to his mother, the valide sultan Pertevniyal, who was outraged by the presence of a foreign woman in her harem and greeted the empress with a sharp slap across the face, almost provoking an international incident.

The new contacts with western Europe gave rise to a movement known as Yeni Osmanlılar Cemiyeti, the Young Ottomans Society, which was founded in Istanbul in 1865. The intellectuals of the Young Ottomans, most notably Ibrahim Şinasi and Namık Kemal, were themselves products of the Tanzimat movement, but they were impatient with the pace of the reforms, also feeling that western innovations were undermining traditional Turkish society without creating any viable substitutes, and in their writings they swayed public opinion in introducing the ideas of representative democracy, nationalism and patriotism in the empire.

The extravagances of Abdül Aziz, as well as enormously increased state spending on modernizing the armed forces and other institutions, forced the government into obtaining still more exorbitant foreign loans, until finally the empire was brought to the brink of bankruptcy. There was little continuity in the government to deal with this and other crises, for Abdül Aziz changed grand vezirs at the rate of one a year, the most outstanding of these transient ministers being Midhat Pasha, Hüseyin Avni Pasha and Mahmut Nedim Pasha. This political instability, together with the deepening financial crisis, allowed the conservative elements in Turkey, particularly the Ulema, to begin undermining the Tanzimat programme, claiming that the reforms were responsible for the present problems of the empire. The problems also included revolts and other crises in the Lebanon, Crete, Bosnia, Herzegovina, Montenegro, Moldavia, Wallachia and Bulgaria, where a revolt by Bulgarian nationalists in 1876 was put down by the Ottomans with great severity. The latter led the former British prime minister William Gladstone to denounce the Ottoman government, calling on the Turks to evacuate their provinces in Europe. The Bosnian and Bulgarian revolts had led to great loss of life among Muslims as well as Christians, but the former was not generally noted in Europe. The slaughter of Turks in the European provinces led to a feeling of outrage among the Muslims of the Ottoman Empire, and on 8 May 1876 the students of the medreses in Istanbul held a mass meeting to denounce the government for not taking action.

Abdül Aziz tried to appease the demonstrators by shuffling his cabinet. But his new minister of war, Hüseyin Avni, soon came into conflict with the sultan, who was showing signs of severe emotional instability. This led Hüseyin to confer with Süleyman Pasha, head of the Military Academy, and they decided to depose Abdül Aziz in favour of his nephew Murat – a plot they carried out successfully on 30 May 1876.

Abdül Aziz was at first confined in Topkapı Sarayı, but on the following day he was given more spacious quarters in the palace of Çırağan. Then on Sunday 4 June he was found dead, apparently a suicide, his wrists slashed by a pair of scissors. A committee of nineteen doctors, including foreigners and Turks, examined his body and issued a verdict of suicide, although the physician from the British Embassy disagreed, saying that the cuts could not have been self-inflicted.

Murat V was thirty-five when he became sultan. He had spent the previous fifteen years nominally confined to the Kafes, but in fact he had been given considerable freedom, he and his brother Abdül Hamit having accompanied Abdül Aziz on his grand tour in 1867. Murat seems to have developed a taste for champagne and cognac on that trip, for by the time he became sultan he was a hopeless alcoholic, aggravating his already serious mental instability. His condition was such that he was unable to go through with the traditional ceremony of being girded with the sword of Osman at Eyüp, which was postponed indefinitely and then in the end cancelled altogether, leaving the populace bewildered.

During the first three months of his reign Murat's mental condition deteriorated markedly, to the point where the cabinet decided that they must depose him. A fetva was obtained from the şeyhülislam, and on 31 August 1876 Murat was deposed on grounds of insanity. That same day he was succeeded by his brother Abdül Hamit, who was installed in the imperial apartments of Dolmabahçe Sarayı. Murat was then confined to Çırağan Sarayı along with his concubines and his children, beginning an imprisonment that would end only when he died of diabetes on 29 August 1904.

On the day that Murat began his long imprisonment, Abdül Hamit II was receiving the homage of his subjects in Dolmabahçe Sarayı, the third sultan in three months to occupy the imperial throne. Thus for long afterwards the people of Istanbul referred to 1876 as 'the year of the three sultans'. Though no one knew it at the time, the Age of Reform was coming to an end, along with the Ottoman Empire.

CHAPTER 23

The Fall of the Ottoman Empire
1876–1923

Abdül Hamit II was girded with the sword of Osman at Eyüp shortly before the noon prayer on Friday 7 September 1876. The new sultan then mounted a white charger and rode back at the head of a procession into the old city of Istanbul, where he paid his respects at the türbe of Mehmet II before returning to Dolmabahçe Sarayı.

Abdul Hamıt was nearly thirty-four when he became sultan, and had been nominally confined to the Kafes for the previous fifteen years. The sultan took up residence at Yıldız Sarayı, the Palace of the Star, which was rather a series of isolated pavilions in a wooded setting than a formal palatial residence like Dolmabahçe, which Abdül Hamit detested. The names of twelve of his concubines are known – those who bore his eighteen children, all but three of whom survived into their adult years. Abdül Hamit's younger brothers, the future sultans Mehmet V Reşat and Mehmet VI Vahıdeddın, were confined to their luxurious apartments in Dolmabahçe Sarayı, while his older brother, the former sultan Murat V, lived in primitive conditions in Çırağan Sarayı.

During the last months of the reign of Abdül Aziz there had been widespread discussion among all levels of society in Istanbul about creating a new constitution for the empire. The British ambassador to the Porte, Sir Henry Elliot, noted this in the spring of 1876: as he wrote, 'From the pashas down to the porters in the street and the boatmen on the Bosphorus no one thinks any longer of concealing his opinions. The word "constitution" is in every mouth and should the Sultan refuse to grant one, an attempt to depose him seems inevitable.'

As soon as Abdül Hamit came to the throne Midhat Pasha

pressured him to establish a Constitutional Commission. The commission, headed by Midhat, completed its work quickly and the new constitution was approved by the cabinet on 6 December 1876, with the sultan retaining the right to exile anyone whom he considered a threat to the state. Abdül Hamit appointed Midhat as grand vezir, and on 19 December the new Ottoman constitution was promulgated. The constitution provided for a bicameral legislature, with a popularly elected Chamber of Deputies and a Chamber of Notables appointed by the sultan.

Meanwhile the Great Powers had convened a conference in Istanbul on 4 November 1876. Their aim was to protect the territorial integrity of the Ottoman Empire, while calling on the sultan to consider reforms in governing the Bulgarian provinces. The conference was a complete failure, and on 20 January 1877 the delegates disbanded. The departure of the foreign delegates gave Abdül Hamit the freedom to rid himself of Midhat Pasha, whom he sent into exile on 5 February 1877.

Abdül Hamit formally opened the first Ottoman Parliament in a ceremony at Dolmabahçe Sarayı on 19 March 1877, after which the Chamber of Deputies convened in the Ministry of Justice on Aya Sofya Meydanı. The deputies comprised 71 Muslims, 44 Christians and 4 Jews, while the Chamber of Notables consisted of 21 Muslims and 5 Christians. The Parliament had little autonomy, for Abdül Hamit had made sure that all real power remained in his own hands.

Russia declared war on the Ottoman Empire on 16 April 1877, invading both the Balkans and eastern Anatolia. On 9 January 1878 the Russians broke through the Şipka Pass, and eleven days later they captured Edirne. They then advanced on Istanbul, forcing the Porte to sue for an armistice, which was concluded at Edirne on 31 January.

The first session of Parliament ended on 19 June 1877, and after new elections the second session opened on 13 December of that year with a speech from the throne by Abdül Hamit. The deputies replied to his speech by expressing their discontent with the handling of the Russian war and asking for the recall of Midhat Pasha. On 13 February 1878 the sultan convened a joint meeting of the two chambers to consult with him on whether to invite Britain to send a fleet to protect Istanbul from a possible Russian advance. After most of the members expressed their approval, a baker named Nacı Ahmet criticized the sultan for having delayed so long in consulting Parliament. That was the last straw for Abdül Hamit, and the following day he dissolved Parliament.

A peace conference of the Great Powers was convened at San Stefano, on the present site of the Istanbul airport, and on 3 March 1878 it essentially confirmed the armistice agreement at Edirne. The surrender of Ottoman territories created a flood of Turkish refugees into Istanbul, whose population by the end of 1878 increased to 547,527.

Britain insisted on revisions to the Treaty of San Stefano to protect the Ottoman Empire, and the Great Powers agreed to convene in Berlin to discuss the issue. According to the terms of the Treaty of Berlin, signed on 13 July 1878, part of Bulgaria became independent, along with all of Montenegro, Serbia and Romania, while a large area in north-eastern Anatolia was ceded to Russia, to whom the Porte agreed to pay a huge war indemnity. Aside from the financial losses, the Treaty of Berlin cost the Ottoman Empire 40 per cent of its territory and 20 per cent of its population, of whom almost half were Muslims.

Abdül Hamit had by then taken complete control of the government, appointing a series of grand vezirs who remained subservient to his will. The sultan ruled through a modern bureaucracy that he staffed with the graduates of the schools, both civil and military, which he had established or improved. He greatly expanded the two principal schools that had been already founded by the Tanzimat movement, namely the Mülkiye, a training-centre for civil servants, and the Harbiye, or War College, at Pangaltı. He founded eighteen new institutions, including schools of finance, law, fine arts, commerce, civil engineering, veterinary science, police and customs, as well as a university and a medical school.

Abdül Hamit also instituted important judicial, legal and financial reforms, reorganizing the Ministries of Justice and Finance. Faced with bankruptcy because of the enormous sums owed to foreign banks and Russia, he rescheduled the Ottoman debt in 1881. A Public Debt Commission was established independently of the Treasury Ministry, with delegates from the European countries to whom loans were due.

The sultan also ordered the building of paved roads and railways throughout the empire. This programme created a direct service from western Europe to Istanbul on the Orient Express, whose first through train reached the city on 12 August 1888. Soon afterwards the new Sirkeci Station was built on the shore of the Golden Horn, and the Wagons-Lits Company opened the luxurious Pera Palas Hotel on the heights above Galata. The last stretch of the railway line was laid along the Marmara shore of the old city, destroying much of the Byzantine sea walls as well as the Ottoman kiosks below Topkapı Sarayı. An ancient grove of boxwood trees was uprooted in the lower gardens of the palace, its loss bewailed by an old servant named Memiş Efendi, who lamented, 'Alas, in that grove of boxwood every Wednesday night the king of the jinns holds council. Where will he go now?'

The census of 1886 numbered the population of Istanbul as 851,494, an increase of over 110 per cent in forty years. This included 129,243 foreigners, among whom were Europeans resident in the city as well as refugees from the lost territories of the empire. Among the permanent residents of the city counted in this census, 53 per cent were Muslims, 21 per cent Greeks, 21 per cent Armenians, and 3 per cent Jews.

This increase in population had been accompanied by a programme of civic improvements in Istanbul. This included the widening and paving of streets and the construction of sidewalks, as well as the installation of water, sewage and gas pipes – the latter fuelling the street lights of the city. The first bridge across the Horn was built in 1836 between Azapkapı and Unkapanı, on the site of the present Atatürk Bridge. The present Galata Bridge between Eminönü and Karaköy in Galata is the fifth structure to have been built between those points, with the first one, a wooden structure, erected in 1845, and the first metal span in 1878. The Galata Bridge has been the main artery of Istanbul's pulsing daily life since then, and nowhere else can one better observe the passing parade of the city's populace than there. Edmondo de Amicis remarked on this in his *Constantinople* (1896):

Standing there, you can see all of Constantinople pass in an hour ... advancing among a mixed crowd of Greeks, Turks and Armenians may be seen a gigantic eunuch on horseback, shouting Vardah! (Make way!), and closely following him, a Turkish carriage decorated with flowers and birds filled with

*The first Ottoman bridge across the Golden Horn, with the
Süleymaniye Camii on the skyline to the left.*

the ladies of a harem . . . A Mussulman woman on foot, a veiled female slave,
a Greek with her long flowing hair surmounted by a little red cap, a Maltese
hidden in her black faletta, a Jewess in the ancient costume of her nation, a
negress wrapped in a many-tinted Cairo shawl, an Armenian from
Trebizond, all veiled in black – a funereal apparition; these and many more
follow in line as though it were a procession gotten up to display the dress of
the various nations of the world . . . Then there is the Syrian, clad in a long
Byzantine dolman, with a gold-striped handkerchief wrapped around his
head; the Bulgarian, in sombre-colored tunic and fur-edged cap; the
Georgian, with his casque of dressed leather and tunic gathered into a metal
belt; the Greek from the Archipelago, covered with lace, silver tassels, and
shining buttons. From time to time it seems as though the crowd were re-
ceding somewhat, but it is only to surge forward once more in great over-
powering waves of color crested with white turbans like foam, in whose midst
may occasionally be seen a high hat or umbrella of some European lady
tossed hither and thither by that Mussulman torrent . . . Every tint of human

skin can be found, from the milk-white Albanian to the jet-black slave from central Africa or blue-black native of Darfur ... brawny arms tattooed with outlines of leaves and flowers or rude representations of ships under full sail, and hearts transfixed by arrows ... While you are trying to make out the designs tattooed on an arm, your guide is calling your attention to a Serb, a Montenegrin, a Wallach, an Ukrainian Cossack of the Don, an Egyptian, a native of Tunis, a prince of Imerzi ... An expert eye can distinguish in that human torrent the distinctive features and costumes of Caramania and Anatolia, of Cypress [Cyprus] and Candia [Crete], of Damascus and Jerusalem – Druses, Kurds, Maronites, Telemans, Pumacs, and Kroats ... No two persons are dressed alike. Some heads are enveloped in shawls, others crowned with rags, others decked out like savages – shirts and undervests striped or particolored like a harlequin's dress; belts bristling with weapons, some of them reaching from the waist to the arm-pits; Mameluke trousers, knee-breeches, tunics, togas, long cloaks which sweep the ground, capes trimmed with ermine, waistcoats encrusted with gold, short sleeves and balloon-shaped ones, monastic garbs and theatre costumes; men dressed like women, women who seem to be men, and peasants with the air of princes.

Tramlines had been introduced in 1869, and in 1876 an underground funicular railway, known as Tünel, was built to take passengers from Galata to the heights of Pera. There was opposition to the funicular at first, with critics referring to it contemptuously as 'the mouse's hole'. But Tünel soon became very popular, sparing residents of Pera the long climb up the step-street known as Yüksek Kaldırım, though some old-timers still continued to make the ascent on foot, such as one ancient who said, 'Why should a man go underground before he dies?'

Istanbul's first public park was created beside Taksim Meydanı, where the western-oriented people of Pera took their ease on Sunday afternoons, a scene described by Edmondo de Amicis:

... on Sunday afternoons it is crowded with people and equipages, all the gay world of Pera pouring out to scatter itself among the beer-gardens, cafés and pleasure resorts ... It was in one of these cafés that we broke our fast – the café Belle Vue, a resort of the flower of Pera society, and well deserving its name, since from its immense gardens, extending like a terrace over the summit of the hill, you have, spread out before you, the large Mussulman village of Fundukli, the Bosphorus covered with ships, the coast of Asia dotted over with gardens and villages, Skutari with her glistening white mosques – a luxuriance of color, green foliage, blue sea, and sky all bathed in light, which forms a scene of intoxicating beauty.

Armenian terrorists known as Dashnaks seized the Ottoman Bank in Galata on Wednesday 26 August 1896, while a second group of them forced their way into the Sublime Porte, wounding several officials. Then on Friday a bomb was thrown at Abdül Hamit as he was going to attend the noon prayer at Haghia Sophia, killing a score of his guards. This led to reprisals in which some 6,000 Armenians were killed in Istanbul. The surviving Dashnak terrorists in the Ottoman Bank had by then negotiated their safe conduct from the city, having alerted the world to the cause of Armenian independence.

The new schools established by Abdül Hamit greatly increased the level of education in Ottoman society. This gave rise to the so-called Young Turks, people who were attracted by the liberal political ideas of western Europe and sought to apply these to the Ottoman state and society. The Young Turks formed a number of loosely knit coalitions, among which the Committee of Union and Progress (CUP) eventually came to the fore. The CUP attracted many young officers in the army, most notably Mustafa Kemal, later to be known as Atatürk. The Young Turks convened two congresses in Paris, the first in February 1902 and the second in December 1907, with their final declaration in the latter meeting calling for the overthrow of Abdül Hamit and the creation of a democracy using violence if necessary. On 23 July 1908 the leaders of the CUP sent a telegram giving their ultimatum to Abdül Hamit, informing him that unless the constitution was restored within twenty-four hours the army in Macedonia would march on Istanbul. Abdül Hamit got the message, and on the following day he restored the constitution and declared that Parliament would be reconvened.

The neighbours of the Ottoman Empire quickly took advantage of its disarray. On 6 October 1908 Austria annexed Bosnia-Herzegovina and Bulgaria declared its independence, and then on the following day Greece announced the annexation of Crete. Austria's action led the tsar to withdraw from his alliance with the Central Powers – Germany and its allies – and eventually to form the Triple Entente with Britain and France, thus creating the alignments that would face one another in the First World War.

Elections for the new Ottoman Parliament were held in the autumn of 1908, with the voters choosing electors who in turn elected the deputies – one for each 50,000 males in a sancak, or province (sanjak). The primary elections were held in an atmosphere of public euphoria, particularly in Istanbul, where the voting urns were carried in procession like trophies of victory – a scene described by H. G. Dwight in *Constantinople Old and New*, published in 1915:

Nothing, perhaps, filled the public eye quite so obviously as the primary elections for parliament. Symbolic of what the revolution had striven to obtain, this event was celebrated in each district with fitting ceremonies. One district in Stamboul brought its voting urn to the Sublime Porte on the back of a camel. Five villages on the Bosphorus, forming another district, made a water pageant that reminded one of state days in Venice. But the five great fishing caiques, with their splendid in-curving beaks, their high poops gay with flags and trailing rugs, their fourteen to twenty costumed rowers, were no imitation of other days, like the Venetian Bissone. Most imposing of all was the procession that carried the urns of Pera through the city in decorated court carriages, attended by music, banners, soldiers, school children, and other representative bodies to the number of several thousand. Two of these were peculiarly striking. Near the head of the procession, led by an Arab on a camel, rode a detachment of men representing the different races of the Empire, each in the costume of his 'country'. And later came a long line of carriages in which imams and Armenian priests, imams and Greek priests, imams and Catholic priests, imams and Jewish rabbis, drove two and two in the robes of their various cults.

The CUP won all but one of the 288 seats in the Chamber of Deputies. Muslim Turks were in a bare majority, with 147 seats, while Arabs had 60, Albanians 27, Greeks 26, Armenians 14, Slavs 10 and Jews 4. The Chamber of Notables was soon appointed by the Council of Ministers, whereupon the old Ministry of Justice on Aya Sofya Meydanı was restored to house the new Parliament. The Second Turkish Parliament opened on 17 December 1908, with Abdül Hamit marking the occasion with a speech from the throne.

Muslim fundamentalists demonstrated against the new constitution, declaring that the empire's decline was due to its rejection of Islamic values, demanding a return to the Şeriat, or Sacred Law. Under the leadership of Hafız Derviş Vahdeti, the fundamentalists formed the Society of Islamic Unity (SIU), which soon gained numerous supporters in the First Army Corps. During the night of 12–13 April 1909 the soldiers of the First Army joined the students of the medreses and marched to the Parliament building, killing two of the deputies, with the rest fleeing in terror. The minister of war refused to take action against the rebels, forcing the grand vezir to submit his resignation. Abdül Hamit then appointed Ahmet Tevfik as grand vezir, choosing his own men for all of the positions in the cabinet and the ministries. The CUP members who were still in Istanbul fled, leaving Abdül Hamit in complete control of the government once again.

The centre of opposition to the new regime was the headquarters of the Third Army in Thessalonica, commanded by Mahmut Şevket Pasha, with Mustafa Kemal serving as his chief of staff. Mahmut Şevket knew that the CUP was no longer effective and that the only course was direct military intervention. He was supported in this by Mustafa Kemal, who mustered the Macedonian troops and loaded them aboard a troop train bound for Istanbul. The train reached Sirkeci Station on 24 April, and before the day was over the Third Army had taken control of Istanbul, whereupon Mahmut Şevket declared martial law and set up courts-martial to try all of those responsible for the counter-revolution. The Parliament met three days later in Haghia Sophia as the National Public Assembly, under the chairmanship of Mehmet Sait Pasha. The assembly voted to depose Abdül Hamit in favour of his brother Mehmet Reşat, obtaining a fetva to that effect from the Şeyhülislam.

That evening Abdül Hamit was sent off by train to Thessalonica, along with two of his sons, two daughters, three kadıns, four concubines, four eunuchs and fourteen servants, as well as his Angora cats and his giant St Bernard. He remained in Thessalonica until 1912, when the Ottoman government brought him back to Istanbul, where he was sequestered in Beylerbey Sarayı. He died there on 2 July 1918, after which he was buried in the türbe[1] of his grandfather Mahmut II.

Mehmet V Reşat was sixty-four when he came to the throne, and had spent the previous forty-eight years confined to his luxurious apartment in Dolmabahçe Sarayı. Mehmet's inactive life in the Kafes made him extremely corpulent, as one can see from the size of his uniform now on display in Topkapı Sarayı. On the day he became sultan the şeyhülislam could not get his arms around Mehmet's waist to gird him and the sword of Osman almost fell to the ground; luckily Şerif Ali Haidar was able to catch it in time, preventing an accident.

The new government severely limited the authority of the sultan, so Mehmet V Reşat was largely a ceremonial figure. The two power centres in the new regime were the CUP, which controlled Parliament, and the military, dominated by Mahmut Şevket Pasha. The sultan had power to appoint only the şeyhülislam and the grand vezir, who in turn chose the cabinet.

Italy's designs on North Africa led it to declare war on the Ottoman Empire on 29 September 1911, putting Tripoli under blockade the following day. The Italians opened another front by occupying Rhodes and bombarding the forts at the entrance to the Dardanelles.

The Balkan states now sought to take advantage of the Tripolitanian War by forming alliances against the Ottomans in the summer and early autumn of 1912, their coalition comprising Greece, Bulgaria, Serbia and Montenegro. Meanwhile a new Ottoman cabinet had been formed under the grand vezir Ahmet Muhtar Pasha, who on 15 October 1912 ended the Tripolitanian War by signing a treaty with Italy.

The First Balkan War began when Montenegro invaded northern Albania on 8 October 1912, with the other allies beginning offensives against the Ottomans shortly afterwards. The war continued until an armistice was arranged on 30 May 1913, by which time the Bulgars were at Çatalca, less than forty kilometres from Istanbul, while the rest of the Ottoman possessions in Europe were occupied by the other allies. Ten days later the Treaty of London was signed, establishing the boundary of the Ottoman Empire in Europe as close as 100 kilometres from Istanbul.

The day after the signing of the Treaty of London Mahmut Şevket Pasha was assassinated in Beyazit Meydanı. The CUP then took control, forcing the sultan to appoint one of its leaders, Sait Halim Pasha, as grand vezir, with four other committee members, including Enver and Talat, assigned to key positions in the cabinet.

The Second Balkan War began on 29 June 1913, when the Bulgars launched surprise attacks on the Greeks and Serbs, who were soon aided by Romania and Montenegro. The four allies proved too much for the Bulgars and soon forced them to surrender. Enver seized the opportunity and led an army to recapture Edirne on 21 July. The war was officially ended by the Treaty of Bucharest, signed on 10 August 1913, in which Greece took most of western Thrace and Epirus.

The recapture of Edirne greatly enhanced the popularity of the CUP, particularly Talat, Cemal and Enver, who effectively controlled the government. Enver Pasha arranged for a German military mission headed by General Liman von Sanders, who was appointed inspector-general of the First Army in Istanbul in November 1913. With German assistance the Ottoman army was rapidly modernized and re-organized, its annual budget being doubled to purchase all of the necessary armaments.

Enver Pasha had been busy behind the scenes preparing the way for an alliance with Germany, for he knew that with Russia now entering the alliance known as the Triple Entente the Ottomans could expect no help from Britain or France. The treaty of alliance between the Ottoman Empire and Germany was signed secretly on 2 August 1914, just as the Triple Entente and the Central Powers were declaring war on one another. Three months later the Ottoman Empire entered the First World War as an ally of Germany.

During the First World War the Ottoman forces were engaged on several fronts: the Caucasus, eastern Anatolia, the Persian Gulf, Syria and Palestine, Thrace, and the Dardanelles, where the Turks drove back the Allies after an eight-month battle on the Gallipoli peninsula in which more than 100,000 men lost their lives on both sides. The CUP was in complete control of the government throughout most of the war, with Talat Pasha appointed as grand vezir on 3 February 1917, forming a triumvirate with Cemal and Enver.

Mehmet V Reşat died of heart failure on 2 July 1918. He was succeeded the following day by his brother Mehmet VI Vahideddin, who was then fifty, and had been confined to the Kafes since his infancy.

Meanwhile the Ottoman forces had suffered a series of defeats in both Iraq and Syria, where Mustafa Kemal Pasha commanded the Seventh Army. Damascus fell to the British on 1 October 1918, and the French took Beirut the following day, as the Ottoman army

Mehmet VI Vahideddin (1918–22), the last Ottoman sultan; anonymous oil-painting.

retreated to make a last stand in Anatolia. As they did so Kemal sent a cable to the sultan urging him to form a new government and sue for peace.

Talat Pasha resigned as grand vezir on 8 October, and soon afterwards he and Enver and Cemal fled from Turkey on a German warship, never to return. On 14 October the sultan appointed Ahmet Izzet Pasha as grand vezir, and he immediately began making overtures to the British for peace. An armistice was signed at Mudros to come into effect on 31 October 1918, eleven days before fighting stopped on the western front. The Mudros Armistice called for total and unconditional surrender of the Ottoman forces, with all strategic points in Turkey to be occupied by the Allied forces. A large Allied fleet sailed through the straits and reached Istanbul on 13 November, landing troops to begin the occupation of the city.

The princess Musbah, who was ten years old at the time, recalls this historic occasion in her autobiography, *Arabesque*; the account is

Allied warships moored off the European shore of the lower Bosphorus, 1919.

particularly poignant since she was with her mother, the princess Fatma, an Englishwoman who was married to Ali Haidar, the şerif of Mecca. Musbah writes of herself in the third person:

Everyone went to see the official entry of the Allies into Stamboul. The Princess Fatma, as a British woman, naturally rejoiced at the victory of her own people, but what of her husband's position and future?

She took the children to Pera to watch the march past. Musbah could feel the tense excitement of the crowds that lined the street. Allied flags hung everywhere, from every window and balcony. How had they managed to produce them and from where?

The Greeks were in an ecstasy of excitement; always volatile and quickly aroused, they saw in the defeat of the Turks a great future for their own country ... The Levantine population, always following the current of popular emotion, also made merry. But the Turk looked on dazed, hardly realizing that foreign soldiers were now flooding their streets; the Dardanelles in Allied hands; their Empire broken, with its provinces being formed into separate states.

At the Paris Peace Conference, which began in January 1919, the

Allies considered various plans for dividing up what was left of the Ottoman Empire. Greece, which had come in on the Allied side only late in the war, put in a claim for Izmir and its hinterland in Asia Minor. The Greek prime minister Eleutherios Venizelos received backing from Lloyd George and Clemenceau to send an expeditionary force to Asia Minor, and on 14 May 1919 an Allied armada landed a Greek division at Izmir. The Greek army then headed inland, and by early summer it had penetrated up the Menderes valley into western Anatolia.

The Ottoman government continued to function under the aegis of the Allied High Commissioners. Meanwhile a national resistance movement was developing in Anatolia under the leadership of Mustafa Kemal Pasha. On 19 March 1920 Kemal announced that the Turkish nation was establishing its own Parliament in Ankara, the Grand National Assembly. The new assembly met for the first time on 23 April 1920, choosing Kemal as its first president.

The Greeks renewed their offensive on 22 June 1920, and by mid-July they had captured Bursa. Another Greek army invaded eastern Thrace in July, and within a week it was within striking distance of Istanbul, from which it was held back only by Allied pressure.

The Allies agreed on the post-war boundaries of the Ottoman Empire at the Treaty of Sèvres, signed on 10 August 1920. The treaty greatly diminished the extent of the empire, putting the strait under international control, leaving Istanbul nominally under the sultan's rule.

The Greeks began another offensive in late October that threatened Ankara, leading Kemal to put Ismet Pasha in charge of the western front. The Greeks were halted early the following year in two battles on the river Inönü, which Ismet Pasha later took as his last name.

The final stage of the war began on 26 August 1922, when Kemal led the Nationalist forces in a counter-offensive that utterly routed the Greeks, who fled in disorder towards Izmir. The Turkish cavalry entered Izmir on 9 September, by which time the Greek army had been evacuated from Asia Minor. A fire broke out in Izmir on 13 September, destroying half of the city with great loss of life, just as the war ended.

An armistice was signed at Mudanya on 11 October, in which it was agreed that the Nationalists would occupy all of Thrace east of

*Mustafa Kemal Pasha (Atatürk) and Ismet Pasha (İnönü) before
the final Turkish offensive of the Graeco-Turkish War in 1922.*

the Mariza except for Istanbul and a zone along the strait, which
would continue to be held by the British until a final peace treaty was
signed.

On 1 November 1922 the Grand National Assembly in Ankara
enacted legislation separating the caliphate and the sultanate, with the
latter being abolished and the former reduced to a purely religious role
subservient to the state. The Allied High Commissioners were then
informed that henceforth Istanbul would be under the administration
of the assembly, and that Vahideddin was no longer sultan, though he
retained the title of caliph. On 4 November the grand vezir Ahmet
Tevfik Pasha resigned, along with his cabinet, delivering up his seals
of office to Vahideddin at Yıldız Sarayı. Vahideddin, alone and completely isolated, now felt that his life was in imminent danger; he con-
fided his fears to General Harington, the British high commissioner,
requesting safe passage out of Istanbul. Harington made the necessary arrangements, and on 17 November 1922 Vahideddin left

Istanbul aboard the British battleship HMS *Malaya* bound for Malta. He then went on to Italy and settled in San Remo, where he died on 15 May 1926, after which he was buried in Damascus. He was the last sultan in the Osmanlı dynasty – the thirty-sixth of his line to have ruled the Ottoman Empire.

The position of caliph was tentatively offered to the crown prince Abdül Mecit Efendi, eldest son of Abdül Aziz. Abdül Mecit indicated that he would accept this title if it was offered to him formally, and on 19 November 1922 he received a telegram from Kemal informing him that he had been chosen as caliph. His installation took place the following Friday, 24 November 1922, in a ceremony held in Topkapı Sarayı, which had been virtually abandoned for three-quarters of a century. The new caliph attended the Friday noon prayer at Fatih Camii, after which he paid a visit to the shrine of Eyüp and then returned to take up residence in Dolmabahçe Sarayı.

Abdül Mecit was fifty-four when he became caliph, and had been confined to the Kafes for the previous forty-six years. By all accounts he was a cultured gentleman, an amateur painter and musician of some talent, content with his ceremonial role as leader of Islam.

The final articles of the Treaty of Lausanne, signed on 24 July

Caliph Abdül Mecit (II), 1923; anonymous oil-painting.

1923, established the present boundaries of the Republic of Turkey, except for the province of Hatay, which was acquired after a plebiscite in 1939. A separate agreement between Greece and Turkey provided for a compulsory population exchange of their minorities, in which some 1.3 million Greeks and about half a million Turks were uprooted. The only exceptions to the exchange were the Turks of western Thrace and the Greeks of Istanbul and the islands of Imbros and Tenedos.

The Allied occupation of Istanbul came to an end on 2 October 1923, when the final detachment of British troops embarked from the quay at Dolmabahçe. Four days later a division of the Turkish Nationalist army marched into Istanbul. On 13 October the Grand National Assembly passed a law making Ankara the capital of Turkey. Then on 29 October the assembly adopted a new constitution that created the Republic of Turkey, and on that same day Kemal was elected as its first president, whereupon he chose Ismet as prime minister.

On 3 March 1924 the Grand National Assembly passed a law abolishing the caliphate, thus severing the last tenuous bond that linked Turkey with the Ottoman Empire. This same law deposed Abdül Mecit as caliph, and he and all of his descendants were forbidden to reside within the boundaries of the Turkish Republic.

Late in the evening of that day the governor of Istanbul, Haydar Bey, came to Dolmabahçe Sarayı to inform Abdül Mecit of the assembly's decision, telling him that he and his family would have to leave the country before dawn the following morning. Closed motor cars were waiting for the imperial family when they left the palace, driving them to Sirkeci Station, where a special carriage had been prepared for them on the Simplon Express. The princess Musbah and her two sisters had come to the palace that evening to say goodbye, and they accompanied the imperial family to the station to bid them a final farewell. Musbah described the scene, referring to herself and her sisters as the Sherifas:

It was a night of bitter cold and driving rain. When they reached Sirkirji, Musbah saw that the entrance to the station was guarded by troops and police. It seemed to be an unnecessary precaution in view of the apathetic attitude adopted by the public towards the banishment of the House of Osman from Turkey.

They passed through the double line of police onto the platform, where the Simplon Express stood waiting to carry the Imperial Family to exile. The platform was crowded with relatives, friends and retainers come to bid their last farewell.

Here, on the platform of Sirkirji station, a tragic end to the close of a chapter in Turkish history was being enacted.

A shrill whistle: the last embrace, the last words.

The Sherifas stood back. Behind them stood Akil Efendi, Medjid's faithful Greek steward, weeping bitterly. He had served his master since the latter was a boy.

The three sisters watched the train slowly move out and disappear into the darkness – a red light glimmered for a moment and then vanished. The Royal exiles had departed ...

Someone touched her on the shoulder. It was Akil Efendi.

'Come, Highness! They have gone ... It is all over.'

They never returned. Abdül Mecit died in Paris on 23 August 1944, after which he was buried in Medina. The remains of the last Ottoman sultan and the last caliph still lie in foreign soil far from Istanbul, where the Osmanlı dynasty ruled for 470 years.

CHAPTER 24

Istanbul under the Turkish Republic
1923–1995

The decision to make Ankara the capital of Turkey represented a clean break with the past, for Istanbul, the old imperial city on the Bosphorus, was linked with the traditions of two fallen empires. The Great Powers opened up new embassies in Ankara, while their palatial old residences on the Grande Rue de Pera – now renamed Istiklal Caddesi, the Avenue of Independence – were reduced to the status of consulates. When the Italian ambassador left Istanbul he sadly shipped his gondola back to Venice, where it is now displayed in the Naval Museum.

The abolition of the caliphate was part of a general secularization of the new Turkish state. This included the abolishment of the ancient office of the şeyhülislam and the Ministry of Şeriat, as well as closing the religious schools – the mekteps and medreses – all part of an anti-theocratic law passed by the Grand National Assembly on 20 April 1924. Legislation was also enacted banning all of the dervish orders in Turkey, closing their tekkes and forbidding them to practise their mystical rites, which many of them continued to do clandestinely. Kemal then went on to institute broader reforms designed to turn Turkey away from its Muslim ways towards the West. He seized on the fez as the symbol of Muslim backwardness, as he said in a speech in October 1927:

Gentlemen, it was necessary to abolish the fez, which sat on the heads of our nation as a symbol of ignorance, negligence, fanaticism, and hatred of progress and civilization, to accept in its place the hat, the headgear used by the whole civilized world, and in this way to demonstrate that the Turkish nation, in its mentality as in other respects, in no way diverges from civilized social life.

A law was enacted on 25 November 1925 banning the fez and other traditional clothing. A month later a law was passed abolishing the Muslim lunar calendar in favour of the Gregorian calendar. On 17 February 1926 the assembly adopted the Swiss civil code in place of the old Ottoman system that dated back to the time of Süleyman the Magnificent, superseding the Şeriat as well, so that time-honoured Muslim practices such as polygamy now became unlawful. Then on 9 August 1928 the assembly passed a law substituting the Latin alphabet for the Arabic script in which Turkish had always been written.

The next important reform came in December 1934, when women were for the first time given the right to vote. This was put into effect in the parliamentary elections of 1935, when seventeen women were elected to the assembly. That same year Sunday became the official day of rest instead of Friday, and all government offices were thenceforth closed from midday on Saturday until Monday morning. At the same time a law was passed requiring all Turks to take a second name, with Kemal himself adopting the surname Atatürk, 'Father of the Turks', by which he was thenceforth known. The new law had unexpected comic consequences, particularly when unlettered peasants were forced to register their new surnames at the local gendarmerie station, so that when an old man walked in and said, 'Gunaydın!', 'Good morning!', that became his family name.

Atatürk continued in office up until his last illness in 1938. He spent the summer of that year in Dolmabahçe Sarayı, becoming reacquainted with the city that he had fled from twenty years before to begin the struggle for national independence. One evening he left the palace and took a taxi up the Bosphorus to Arnavutköy, where his alarmed staff found him later that night drinking and dancing with the local fishermen in a Greek taverna. But that was his last foray, for he was diagnosed as having advanced cirrhosis of the liver, and from then on he was confined to bed. His illness became critical in the autumn of 1938, and shortly after nine in the morning on 10 November 1938 he died in his bedroom at Dolmabahçe Sarayı. His body lay in state at Dolmabahçe until all the people of Istanbul had

Atatürk, first president of the Turkish Republic, 1924.

paid their last respects, after which his remains were taken to Ankara for burial, while the Turkish nation mourned his passing.

On the day after Atatürk's death Ismet Inönü succeeded him as president, by unanimous vote of the assembly. Inönü served as president from then until 1950, when he was succeeded by Celâl Bayar, with Adnan Menderes as prime minister. Their government, representing the Democratic Party, lasted until 27 May 1960, when it was overthrown by a revolution led by General Cemal Gürsel, who then became president and governed through the power of the military. Charges of betraying Turkish democracy were brought against members of the previous Democratic Party government, and after a trial fifteen of the defendants were sentenced to death. Adnan Menderes and two of his ministers were hanged on 16 September 1961, while Celâl Bayar and eleven others had their sentences commuted to life imprisonment.

This was the first in a series of three military interventions in the Turkish government in the next two decades, the second coming in 1971 and the third in 1980. The third of the coups, which made General Kenan Evren president, had been preceded by violent political protest that caused great loss of life and resulted in the imprisonment of thousands of activists, particularly among the students and faculties of the universities. Evren continued as president until 1990, after which he was succeeded in turn by Turgut Ozal and Süleyman Demirel. In mid-June 1993 a new government was fored by Tansu Çiller, the first woman to become prime minister of Turkey. During the past decade there has been an extremely bloody civil war in eastern Anatolia between government forces and Kurdish separatist guerrillas of the Kurdistan Workers' Party (PKK). There has also been a revival of Islamic fundamentalism, represented in politics by the Refai ('Welfare') Party, which in June 1996 formed a new government led by Necmettin Erbakan, the first prime minister from the Islamic movement. The fundamentalist movement has reversed several of the reforms instituted by Atatürk, so that many children are now enrolled in religious schools, while a number of the dervish orders are meeting publicly in their old tekkes.

The first census ordered under the Republic, taken in June 1924, showed that Istanbul had a population of 1,165,866 – the highest in the history of the city. The actual population was even higher, for the census did not count some 100,000 refugees who had come to Istanbul during and immediately after the First World War, including 65,000 White Russians who had fled from the Bolsheviks. Nor did the census include 26,000 citizens of Greece resident in Istanbul. The population numbered in the census was made up of 61 per cent Muslim Turks, 26 per cent Greeks, 7 per cent Armenians and 6 per cent Jews. The total number of Greeks in the city, including those with Greek passports, was about 305,000.

The Greek population has declined steadily since then, and now there are less than 3,000 left in Istanbul, with many of those who remain being old people in retirement homes and hospitals. And so there are those who fear that the Greek presence in this city is coming to an end, after more than twenty-six centuries. But others are more hopeful, and one tends to agree with them after an evening spent at one of the very few remaining tavernas in the city, where Greeks and Turks sing and dance and drink together just as they did in times past. On such an evening one is reminded of what the late Todori Negroponte, last of the great Istanbul troubadours, said one night in Arnavutköy after singing a Greek love-song in the presence of a Turkish general: 'I sing Greek songs in Istanbul and Turkish songs in Athens; I am a hero of our times!'

During the last half-century of its existence the Ottoman government gathered antiquities from all over the rapidly shrinking empire. These were preserved in the Istanbul Archaeological Museum, founded by Osman Hamdi Bey, the first professional Turkish archaeologist. The Turkish Republic, through Atatürk's urging, early on established a policy of preserving the antiquities of Turkey and encouraging archaeological excavations. This has resulted in the restoration of the Byzantine and Ottoman monuments of Istanbul, many of which have been reopened to the public as museums, beginning with Topkapı Sarayı in 1927 and Haghia Sophia in 1934. New museums have been created, including the Museum of the Ancient Near East,[1] the Museum of Turkish and Islamic Art, the Military Museum,[2] the Naval Museum,[3] and the Sadberk Hanım Museum.[4] Archaeological excavations have uncovered parts of the ancient city and some of its lost monuments, including the Forum of Theodosius in Beyazit Meydanı, the church of St Polyeuktos in Saraçhane, the Theodosian church of Haghia Sophia, and some fragments of the Great Palace of Byzantium.

The city itself has changed almost beyond recognition during the years of the Turkish Republic, particularly in the second half of the twentieth century. The population in 1950 was only slightly over a million, less than it had been in 1924, but since then it has been increasing at an accelerating rate: 1,466,000 in 1960, 2,132,000 in 1970, and 4,433,000 in 1980, the latter number including twenty-five new municipalities that were added to the city, increasing its area by a factor of four. The population of Istanbul in 1990 was 7,500,000, and most estimates today, in 1996, put the number at more than 12,000,000. Most of the increase has been in the suburbs of the city, whose boundaries now stretch up both shores of the Bosphorus to within sight of the Black Sea, extending far along the European and Asian shores of the Marmara.

The new residents are mostly poorer people from the provinces who have come to the city in search of greater opportunity, moving into ramshackle structures known as *gecekondu*, or 'houses built by night', which now shelter more than half the population of Istanbul, creating vast slums behind the façade of the imperial city's Byzantine and Ottoman monuments. Latife Tekin (1957–) writes of these *gecekondu* in her novel *Tales from the Garbage Hills*:

One winter night, on a hill where the huge refuse bins came daily and dumped the city's waste, eight shelters were set up by lantern light near the garbage heaps. In the morning the first snow of the year fell, and the earliest scavengers saw these eight huts pieced together from materials bought on credit – sheets of pitchpaper, wood from building sites, and breezeblocks brought from the brickyards by horse and cart. Not even stopping to drop the sacks and baskets from their backs, they all ran to the huts and began a lively exchange with the squatters who were keeping watch. A harsh and powerful wind kept cutting short their words, and at one point almost swept the huts away. The scavengers pointed out that the ramshackle walls and makeshift roofs would never stand up to the wind, so the squatters decided to rope down the roofs and nail supports to the walls.

When the garbage trucks had come and gone, the simit [pretzel]-sellers on the way to the garbage heard that eight huts had been built on the slopes and spread the news through the neighbouring warehouses, workshops and coffee-houses. By noon people had begun to descend on the hillside like snow. Janitors, pedlars and simit-sellers all arrived with pickaxes, closely followed by people who had left their villages to move in with their families in the city, and by others roaming the city in the hope of building a hut. Men and women, young and old, spread in all directions. Kneeling and rising, they measured with feet and outstretched arms. Then with their spades they scratched crooked plans in the earth. By evening Rubbish Road had become a road of bricks and blocks and pitchpaper. That night in snowfall and lantern-light a hundred more huts were erected in the snow.

Next morning by the garbage-heaps – downhill from the factories which manufactured lightbulbs and chemicals, and facing a china factory – a complete neighbourhood was fathered by mud and chemical waste, with roofs of plastic basins, doors from old rugs, oilcloth windows and walls of wet breezeblocks. Throughout the day bits and pieces arrived to furnish the houses, and the remaining women and children, with sacks on their backs and babies in arms, entered their homes. Mattresses were unrolled and kilim-rugs spread on the earthen floors. The damp walls were hung with faded pictures and brushes with their blue bead good-luck charms and cradles were hung from the roofs and a chimney-pipe was knocked through the side wall of every hut.

Some attempts have been made in recent years to preserve what is left of Istanbul's faded beauty. Çelik Gülersoy, head of the Turkish Touring and Automobile Club (TTOK), tastefully restored a number of Ottoman buildings and put them to use as hotels, restaurants and cafés, a project that is now endangered by political developments following the municipal election in 1995. Bedrettin Dalan, mayor of Istanbul in the 1980s, instituted a programme of urban renewal that created new parks along the Bosphorus, the Marmara and the Golden Horn, so that the populace can enjoy the shores of the city's 'garland of waters'. One of these parks is on the promontory at Aşıyan, below the fortress of Rumeli Hisarı. At its centre is a bronze statue of the Turkish poet Orhan Veli (1914–50), who is shown seated there feeding a sea-bird, just as he did when in life. The memorial brings to mind one of his poems entitled 'Something's Up', translated thus by David Garwood:

> Is the sea this lovely every day?
> Do the skies look like this all the time,
> Are things, this window, for instance, always as lovely as this?
> No, certainly not,
> I swear it.
> There's something behind all this beauty.

Long-time residents of Istanbul bemoan the changes that have taken place here during the past generation, but those who really know the city feel that its character and spirit have remained essentially un-altered. The old city that one knew and loved half a lifetime ago is still there to be rediscovered, and so one seeks it out by venturing along venerable byways like the Street of a Thousand Earthquakes, the Avenue of the Bushy Beard, the Alley of the Chicken That Cannot Fly, the Dead End of Plato, the Street of Nafi of the Golden Hair, the Lane of the Poets, and the Street of Ibrahim of Black Hell. Then you make your way down a steep stepped street to the Golden Horn and find that you are on Fil Yokuşu, the Elephant's Path, and you remember that Evliya Çelebi walked this way when going from his father's house in Unkapanı to the school of Hamit Efendi. And in walking along the shore of the Golden Horn from Unkapanı to Zindan Kapı you come to the mosque of Ahi Çelebi, to which Evliya was transported in the fabulous dream in which the Prophet inspired him to become a traveller and to see 'the four quarters and seven climates of the world'. After his dream, when he went to see the interpreter of dreams Ibrahim Efendi, who lived in Kasım Pasha, Evliya would have taken a rowboat from Yağ Iskelesi, the Oil Pier, where boats still ferry passengers across the Golden Horn to the Galata shore.

Petrus Gyllius also crossed the Golden Horn by boat from Yağ Iskelesi, which he identified as the ancient Perama, a promontory that gave its name to the quarter of Pera on the other side of the Golden Horn, the ancient Sycae. Gyllius reckoned that Perama was the starting-point for ferries going from Constantinople both to Sycae and to Chrysopolis, the City of Gold, and also to Chalcedon, the 'Land of the Blind', where colonists from Megara settled a decade or so before Byzas founded Byzantium. Old rowboats, now equipped with outboard motors, still tie up at Yağ Iskelesi, waiting to take passengers across either the Golden Horn or the Bosphorus, following what must be the oldest civic ferry-routes in the world, ones that link modern Istanbul in time with medieval Constantinople and ancient Byzantium.

Two modern bridges now span the Bosphorus. The first of these, Boğaziçi Köprüsü,[5] which opened on 29 October 1973, the fiftieth anniversary of the founding of the Turkish Republic, crosses between Ortaköy on the European shore and Beylerbey in Asia. The second bridge, Fatih Sultan Mehmet Köprüsü,[6] crosses between Rumeli Hisarı and Anadolu Hisarı, just upstream from the Castles of Europe and Asia. This opened in the summer of 1988, exactly 2,500 years after the Persian king Darius built his bridge of boats on the Bosphorus across this same stretch of the Narrows.

Despite the opening of these two bridges the local fishermen in the Bosphorus villages still ferry passengers across the strait for a modest fee, one of the most popular crossings being from Bebek on the

*Fatih Sultan Mehmet Köprüsü, the second bridge across the
Bosphorus, opened in 1988. The bridge spans the strait between
Rumeli Hisarı* (left) *and Anadolu Hisarı* (right) *at the narrowest
point of the Bosphorus.*

European shore to Anadolu Hisarı. In times past the fishermen of
Bebek bided their time in a café known as Nazmi's, but that has long
since been replaced by an apartment house, and now they do their
drinking in a ramshackle wooden hut they have built down on the
shore where they beach their boats and sell their fish. Those of us who
see them there, and occasionally join them, feel a tug in our heart when
we pass the site of Nazmi's, for it was there that we learned the lore
of the Bosphorus. Our teacher was Kaptan Riza, who still works on
his boat at a little iskele opposite the site of Nazmi's, though he is now
approaching ninety, rising to his feet to salute old friends as they pass
on the quay.

Riza pointed out to us some of the old boats characteristic of the
Bosphorus, lineal descendants of the vessels that have sailed the strait
since the days of Jason and the Argonauts. The most common was the

taka, the workhorse of the Bosphorus, broad of beam, with peaked bow and high fantail, painted in the brightest colours of the sun's spectrum. Others were the *mauna*, a single-masted craft with lateen rig and raking stern; the *salapurga*, similar to the *mauna* but smaller and more snub-nosed; the *bombarda*, an old-fashioned caique from the Aegean isles, often seen loaded to the gunwales with wine from the Marmara islands; the *martika*, a sturdy Black Sea coaster; the *karavela*, or caravel, now almost extinct, the last surviving examples of the ships in which Columbus sailed; the *gagali*, another ancient craft, of which only one or two now remain, high poop-deck and transomed stern, bow curved like a parrot's beak and decorated with the sign of the oculus, or talismanic eye, by which sailors have warded off the evils of the deep since the days of the ancient Phoenicians. Riza also pointed out with pride the boats in which most of the Bosphorus fishermen make their living, the rowing *kayiks*, long, slim boats with heraldic carvings on metalwork decorating their upturned prows, each manned by a dozen rowers. The *kayiks* are towed in line behind powerful *maunas*, ready to dart out across the water like sea-swallows when a school of fish is sighted by the lookout, who is pinioned like a sailor-Christ on his cross-like perch atop the leading boat.

When the fish were not running we sat by the fire in Nazmi's back room and listened to Riza as he catalogued the winds and storms of the Bosphorus, each in its passing season. That fierce wind now howling outside Nazmi's, dashing salt spray on the windows and whistling through the cracks in the walls, is *Karayel*, the Black Wind, blowing from the cold north-eastern quarter of the compass. Later in the winter we feel the lash of *Yıldız*, the Star-Wind, as it shrieks in from due north and flays any fisherman foolhardy enough to be at sea in that icy season. Then in January we feel the wrath of *Poyraz*, the north-west storm-wind named after King Boreas, mythical ruler of the winds. *Poyraz* howls down the strait from the frigid Black Sea and whitens with snow the hillsides of the Bosphorus, lays white shrouds on the columnar cypresses, powders the leaden domes of village mosques, the roofs of yalıs and seaside palaces, the battlements of the Castles of Europe and Asia, tinting the teal-blue waters of the Bosphorus with the milky reflections of scudding clouds. In February the wind suddenly shifts to the south-east as *Keşişleme*, the Wind of

Mount Olympus, begins to blow moistly and the dismal winter rains begin. Cold rain pours down from louring grey clouds for weeks on end, soaking our overcoats, filling our shoes, dripping from our beards, fogging our spectacles and our minds, drowning the town in filthy mud and discolouring the Bosphorus in ugly brown streaks. We swear then to sail away from this dark and cheerless, cloud-shrouded town and never return, ending our exile from the century. But Kaptan Riza, ordering another raki at our expense, counsels us to be of good cheer, acquainting us with the winds that herald approaching spring and good weather. The worst of winter is done, he says, when you feel the fresh zephyr called *Hüzün Fırtınası*, the Agreeable Storm, which wafts in from the Marmara in early March. This harbinger is soon followed by another – *Kozkavuran Fırtınası* – the Storm of Roasting Walnuts, which blows across the Bosphorus from the greening hills of Anatolia. Then in rapid succession we see perennial vernal signs and feel the seasonal storm-winds that accompany them. Some of these are named for the birds they bring on the wing: *Çaylak Fırtınası*, the Storm of the Kites; *Karakuş Fırtınası*, the Storm of the Blackbirds; *Kırlangıç Fırtınası*, the Storm of the Swallows; *Kuğu Fırtınası*, the Storm of the Swans, *Kukulya Fırtınası*, the Storm of the Cuckoos. Others are named for the signs floral and celestial that mark their season: *Çiçek Fırtınası*, the Storm of Flowers; *Kabak Meltemi*, the Squash Breeze; *Ülker Fırtınası*, the Storm of the Pleiades; *Gündönümü Fırtınası*, the Storm of the Summer Solstice.

Then one day we look out of Nazmi's window and see a long and stately aerial procession of storks soaring across the Bosphorus, as they return to their ancestral nesting-places in the cemetery of Eyüp above the Golden Horn. Now the Bosphorus becomes azure blue again, flowering Judas-trees purple the hillsides and nightingales serenade us under the spring moon, giant plane-trees spread their dappled shade over Nazmi's courtyard and blossoming wisteria vines embower our seaside table, as the fishermen mend their nets on the cobble while one of them plays primitive melodies on a crude bagpipe.

Kaptan Riza then sits back and smiles with pleasure over his raki as he lists for us the fair winds that fill the sails of the boats skimming across Bebek Bay in late spring and early summer: *Çarkdönümü Fırtınası*, the Storm of the Turning Windmills; *Kara Erik Fırtınası* and

Kızıl Erik Fırtınası, the Storms of Red and Black Plums; *Kestane Harası Fırtınası*, the Storm of Ripening Chestnuts. But there are days when Riza is cross and uncommunicative, and we know that the evil wind *Lodos* is blowing from the south-west, filling the Bosphorus with garbage and sewage and clogging our sinuses with black phlegm, shrouding the city with a miasmatic haze and transforming it into an airless, sweating, seething, quarrelling Levantine hell. But never mind, the *Melteme* will soon come, sweeping in from the north-west to dispel all foul airs and bad feelings. Kaptan Riza soon becomes his old affable self once again and may even buy *you* a raki, while he recites a list of the storm-winds of late summer and early autumn, the most glorious season of all along the Bosphorus: *Turna Geçimi Fırtınası*, the Storm of the Passing Cranes; *Meryem Ana Fırtınası*, the Storm of Mother Mary; *Bağ Bozumu Fırtınası*, the Storm of the Vintage; and *Koç Katımı Fırtınası*, the Storm of the Mating Ram. And as they blow in turn the plane-trees turn gold over Nazmi's courtyard and the grapes ripen on the trellis that shades our table. Then the sky above the Asian hills begins to darken once again, as harsh winds blow down the strait from the Black Sea, rousing Kaptan Riza and his friends to set out in their boats as the various schools of fish make their appearance, most notably the palamut, or tunny, which they catch at night by the light of powerful lamps. As we watch from Nazmi's we see the fishing fleets drifting down the Bosphorus between the invisible continents like captive constellations, rivalling the stars in their beauty and luminosity. This reminds us that the tunny was one of the principal sources of income of ancient Byzantium, represented on some of the ancient city's coins. Then, as now, the tunny made its annual appearance in the Bosphorus only after that late-October squall that Kaptan Riza calls *Balık Fırtınası*, the Storm of Fish.

And so the year passes in the villages along the Bosphorus, a cycle of seasons and their ever-recurring winds that has implanted itself deep in the subconscious of the city, so that those of us exiled here have attuned ourselves to it in the same progression of blues and joys as those who dwelt here in times past, depressed by the *Lodos* and cheered by the *Melteme* in turn.

The village of Rumeli Hisarı has the oldest Turkish cemetery in Istanbul, dating back to 1452, its tombstones extending from the

Old Turkish tombstones.

lower walls of the fortress down to the Bosphorus. H. G. Dwight wrote of this cemetery in his *Constantinople Old and New*, reminiscing about life in Rumeli Hisarı in times past:

Another memento of that older time is to be seen in the cemetery lying under the castle wall to the south. It is perhaps the oldest Mohammedan burying-ground in Constantinople or at least on the European shore of the Bosphorus. It certainly is the most romantic, with its jutting rocks, its ragged black cypresses, its round tower and crenellated wall, overhanging a blue so fancifully cut by Asiatic hills. It too has a spicy odor quite its own, an odor compounded of thyme, of resinous woods, of sea-salt, and I know not what aroma of antiquity. But its most precious characteristic is the grave information it shares with other Mohammedan cemeteries. There is nothing about it to remind one of conventional mourning, no alignment of tombs, no rectilinear laying out of walks, no trim landscape gardening. It lies unwalled to the world, the gravestones scattered as irregularly on the steep hillside as the cyclamens that blossom there in February. Many of them have the same brightness of color. The tall narrow slabs are often painted, with the decorative Arabic lettering, or some quaint floral design, picked out in gold. It is another expression of the guardhouse soldiers who so often lounge along the water, of the boy who plays his pipe under a cypress while the village goats nibble among the graves, of the veiled women who preen their silks among the rocks on summer afternoons. The whole place is suffused with that intimacy of life and death, the sense of which makes the Asiatic so much more mature than the European. The one takes the world as he finds it, while the other must childlessly beat his head against stone walls; it is the source of the strength and weakness of the two stocks.

The scene described by Dwight has not really changed in its essentials, despite the fact that the fortress is now a museum, and that goatherds no longer graze their flocks there among the turbaned tombstones, where cyclamens still blossom in February. Among those buried here are dervishes who once lived in a Mevlevi tekke under the walls of the fortress, the most renowned being Durmuş Dede, one of the folk-saints that Evliya Çelebi writes of in his *Seyahatname*. Pilgrims still come to say prayers at the tomb of Durmuş Dede and other saints who are buried around the site of the tekke. The most notable of these is Sheikh Ismail Çelebi, who was executed along with ten of his disciples during the reign of Murat IV. Evliya tells the story of their death and subsequent burial:

Sheikh Ismail Çelebi and ten of his disciples were executed at the Hippodrome; their bodies were thrown into the sea at the Stable Gate, from which they miraculously floated up the Bosphorus against the current. The emperor [Murat IV] was then at Kandilli when he saw the remains of the sheikh and his ten followers floating by, dancing on the waves with their heads in their hands. The emperor's suite seeing this miracle, represented to him that they must have been unjustly executed. The emperor began to weep as he watched them floating against the current to the opposite shore of Rumeli Hisarı, where they were buried at the foot of Durmuş Dede's grave, and where, during ten nights, light was seen pouring down on their graves.

The Ottoman tombstones in the cemetery at Rumeli Hisarı and other Turkish burial-grounds are surmounted with representations of the head-dress that the deceased wore in life, those of Durmuş Dede and Sheikh Ismail Çelebi topped with the characteristic turbans of their dervish orders. Elsewhere, particularly in the great cemetery of Eyüp, one occasionally sees the huge turban of a pasha or the tiara of a princess. The funerary stelae of women are decorated in low relief with flowers, usually roses, each of which represents one of the children borne by the deceased. Tombstones topped by a turban date from before 1829, when Mahmut II introduced the fez, and the ones with a fez date from then until 1925, when Atatürk required Turks to wear a brimmed hat, a head-dress that has never been seen represented on a grave-marker – which says something about modern clothing reform.

The older tombstones at Eyüp and Rumeli Hisarı are engraved with epitaphs that are unique in the literature of death, as in the following collection translated by Cevat Şakir Kabaağaç, the great Turkish writer better known as the Fisherman of Halicarnassus. Cevat called these his Laughing Tombstones, for their light-hearted messages express cheerful farewells between the departed and their dear friends.

A pity to good-hearted Ismail Efendi, whose death caused great sadness among his friends. Having caught the illness of love at the age of seventy, he took the bit between his teeth and dashed full gallop to paradise.

Stopping his ears with his fingers, Judge Mehmet hied off from this beautiful world, leaving his wife's cackling and his mother-in-law's gabbling.

O passer-by, spare me your prayers, but please don't steal my tombstone!

I could have died as well without a doctor than with the quack that friends set upon me.

My name is Süleyman, not Süleyman the Magnificent but Süleyman the stoker. My greetings to you!

[On a tombstone with the relief of three trees: an almond, a cypress and a peach, the fruit of the latter being the Turkish metaphor for a woman's breasts] I've planted these trees so that people may know my fate. I loved an almond-eyed, cypress-tall maiden, and bade farewell to this beautiful world without savouring her peaches.

I have swerved away from you a long time. But in soil, air, cloud, rain, plant, flower, butterfly or bird, I am always with you.

There are particularly interesting tombstones in the Greek Orthodox shrine at Balıklı. The oldest tombstones there, which are set into the pavement of the church courtyard, have their epitaphs in Karamanlı, which is Turkish written in the Greek alphabet. The tombstones of the men are inscribed with representations of their profession or trade: the scissors of the tailor, the quilled pen of the scribe, the open book of the scholar or teacher, the hammer of the mason, the wine-barrel of the tavern-owner. The more recent tombstones are all inscribed in Greek, and on the stone there is invariably a colour photograph of the deceased, most of whom seem to have died in the fullness of their years, although here and there one sees the photo of a child or of a young bride, killed before their time by accident or sickness, their likenesses preserved in eternal youth in the graveyard of Balıklı.

Pilgrims, both Greeks and Turks, still come to Balıklı to drink the holy water of the ayazma, the sacred well of the Panayia Zoodochos Pege, the Virgin of the Life-Giving Spring, who has been performing miracles of healing here since late Roman times. This is one of the two most famous ayazmas in the city, the other being the sacred spring of the Virgin at Blachernae. Pilgrims, Christians and Muslims alike, also come to drink the holy water of the sacred spring at Blachernae, for they believe that the Virgin Blachernitissa will intercede with her divine Son to heal them or their ailing loved ones, just as in the past she protected Byzantine Constantinople during times of siege. The Blachernitissa saved Constantinople from the barbarian Avars in 626, and in commemoration of that miracle the hymn-cycle known as the Akathistos is sung here each year, beginning on the Feast of the Annunciation of the Virgin and continuing through Lent. Though there are fewer than 3,000 Greeks left in the city, some of them congregated here once again in the spring of 1995 to perpetuate the ritual of thanksgiving to the Blachernitissa. That was the one thousand three hundred and sixty-ninth year in succession that the Akathistos cycle had been sung at her shrine in Blachernae, where she drove away the barbarians from the walls of the once inviolable city.

The imperial city has fallen twice since then, to the Latins and to the Ottoman Turks, whose own empire has now vanished, leaving its monuments standing with those of Byzantium on the seven-hilled peninsula where Byzas the Megarian led his men ashore at the confluence of the Golden Horn and the Bosphorus. The Bosphorus still surges past the promontory where he landed, flowing eternally like time's river in the country of dreams, oblivious to all that has happened in the imperial city that its presence brought into being.

Now midway through the twenty-seventh century of its tumultuous existence, the City has survived sieges, sacks, conquests, civil wars, riots, plagues, fires, earthquakes, and modern construction projects; retaining its identity through successive changes of name, population, language, religion and political status; occupied in turn by Greeks, Macedonians, Romans, Byzantines, crusaders, Byzantines again and then Turks, followed by the Allied nations of Europe, with large minorities of Latins, Armenians, Jews, Arabs, Bulgars, Macedonians, Albanians, Russians and other ethnic groups during various eras of its history; its essential character and spirit enduring through the ages, almost as if it had an immortal soul. As Petrus Gyllius noted more than four centuries ago, when he set out to describe the topography of the imperial city on the Bosphorus, 'It seems to me that while other cities are mortal, this one will endure as long as there are men on earth.'

PART IV

NOTES ON
MONUMENTS AND
MUSEUMS

In the following notes items in small capitals are those which are described by themselves in separate notes. Bold figures in the index will guide the reader to the relevant note.

CHAPTER I

1. Petrus Gyllius identified one of the SYMPLEGADES as a huge rock off the fishing village of Rumeli Feneri, on the European side of the Bosphorus at its entrance on the Black Sea. Now joined to the shore by a concrete mole, the rock is about 20 metres high. The peak of the rock is surmounted by the remnants of the so-called Pillar of Pompey, of which only the base now remains. The base once had a Latin inscription that included the name Caesar Augustus, but this has long disappeared.

CHAPTER 2

1. The original WALLS OF BYZANTIUM included the fortifications around the periphery of the acropolis on the First Hill, along with a ring wall extending from the Golden Horn to the Marmara. According to Dio Cassius, there were twenty-seven defence towers between the Golden Horn and the Marmara. He also notes that 'The harbours within the walls and the chains and their breakwaters carried towers that jutted far out on either side, making approach impossible for the enemy.'

CHAPTER 3

1. The MILION, or Miliarium Aureum, the Golden Milestone, seems to have been a tetrapylon, i.e. a monumental gateway with four arched openings, one on each side, as in the Arch of Galerius at Thessalonica. The Milion disappeared shortly after the Turkish Conquest, probably demolished to provide building material for the suterazi, or water-control tower, which stands next to the surviving fragment of the Golden Milestone.

2. The ARCHAEOLOGICAL MUSEUM was founded in 1881, with a new wing added a century later, although the last of its exhibition halls did not open until June 1995. This last hall is devoted to Istanbul Through the Ages, an incomparable collection of antiquities from the ancient city of Byzantium and Byzantine Constantinople.

3. The GOTH'S COLUMN is a granite monolith 15 metres high surmounted by a Corinthian capital. The name of the column comes from the laconic Latin inscription on its base: FORTUNAE REDUCI OB DEVICTOS GOTHOS, meaning 'To Fortune, who returns by reason of the defeat of the Goths'. The column apparently stood in the centre of the Theatron Minor, erected by Septimius Severus soon after AD 200.

CHAPTER 4

1. The COLUMN OF CONSTANTINE stood in the centre of the emperor's forum. The column now consists of a masonry base about 10 metres high surmounted by a shaft of six porphyry drums, the joints between them hooped with iron bands; at the summit are ten courses of masonry topped by a marble block, giving the monument a total height of 34.8 metres. At the summit

The Goth's Column

The Column of Constantine

there was a large capital, presumably Corinthian, which was surmounted by the statue of Constantine as Apollo. The statue was destroyed during a storm in 1106; some fifty years later Manuel I Comnenus replaced the capital with the present masonry courses, on top of which he placed a large cross, removed at the time of the Turkish Conquest.

2. The HIPPODROME, as enlarged by Constantine the Great, was 480 metres long and 117.5 metres wide. The seats extended in tiers around the two long sides and the semi-circular southern end, the sphen done, which is today concealed behind the buildings at the south end of the At Meydanı. At the straight northern end of the arena there were great vaulted passageways. The royal enclosure known as the Kathisma was in the centre of the east side of the Hippodrome; this connected with the imperial apartments in the Great Palace, so that the emperor and his party could proceed to and from the arena in privacy. The race-track followed almost exactly the present street that borders the park in the At Meydanı. At the top of the

outer wall of the Hippodrome there was an arcade of columns with an epistyle in the classical manner. Many of these columns were still standing until 1550, when they were pulled down and used for building material. The final destruction of the Hippodrome occurred in 1609, when what remained of its superstructure was demolished by Ahmet I to make way for SULTAN AHMET I CAMII, after which it became a public square, the At Meydanı.

3. The COLOSSUS is a roughly built pillar of stone 32 metres high. Petrus Gyllius called it the Colossus, but most modern writers refer to it, incorrectly, as the Column of Constantine Porphyrogenitus. Both names refer to the Greek inscription on its base, where the monument is compared to the Colossus of Rhodes, and where it is recorded that the pillar was restored and sheathed in bronze (now vanished) by Constantine VII Porphyrogenitus. But the inscription also states that the pillar was decayed by time; thus it must date from an earlier period, perhaps the reign of Constantine the Great.

4. The SERPENT COLUMN takes its name from the three intertwined bronze serpents that form its shaft, their heads now missing. The column formed part of a monument that once stood in Apollo's temple at Delphi, dedicated by the men of the thirty-one Greek cities who defeated the Persians at the battle of Plataea in 479 BC. The column was brought from Delphi by Constantine the Great; it seems to have stood at first in the courtyard of HAGHIA SOPHIA and was erected in the HIPPODROME only at a later date. The base of the monument was uncovered in 1920, revealing the names of the cities inscribed on the lower coils of the serpents. The three serpent heads vanished during the Ottoman period, but one of them was found in 1847 and is now in the ARCHAEOLOGICAL MUSEUM.

5. The EGYPTIAN OBELISK is identified and dated by the hieroglyphics with which it is carved. The obelisk was commissioned by the pharaoh Thuthmose III (1549–1503 BC), who erected it at Deir el Bahri opposite Thebes in Upper Egypt to commemorate one of his campaigns in Syria and his crossing of the Euphrates. It was shipped to Constantinople at some time in the third quarter of the fourth century AD, probably by the emperor Julian. The obelisk was originally about 60 metres tall and weighed some 800 tonnes, but it broke apart during shipment to Constantinople and only the upper third survived. It is mounted on four brazen blocks resting on a marble base with sculptured reliefs. The scenes on the four sides of the base represent Theodosius I and his family in the Kathisma, as they look down at various events taking place in the HIPPODROME arena below. Inscriptions in Greek

and Latin on the base praise Theodosius and his prefect Proclus for erecting the obelisk; the Latin inscription records that thirty days were required to do the job, while the one in Greek says that it took thirty-two days. The total height of the monument, including the base, is about 26 metres; the bottom of the structure represents approximately the original level of the spina, some 4.5 metres below the present surface of the park.

6. ISA KAPI MESCIDI comprises two walls of a Byzantine church and the ruins of a medrese, or Islamic theological school. The church probably dates from the fourteenth century, but nothing is known of its history or identity. About 1560 the church was converted into a mosque by the grand vezir Hadım ('the Eunuch') Ibrahim Pasha, who added to it a handsome medrese built by the great architect Sinan.

7. SANCAKTAR MESCIDI has been dated variously from the eleventh century to the fourteenth, and it has been suggested that the little building was originally a funerary chapel, though its original name is unknown. The building has the form of an octagon on the exterior with a projecting apse at the east end; the interior is a domed cross in plan.

8. The MARTYRION OF SS. KARPOS AND PAPYLOS was discovered in 1935 under the Greek church of St Menas in Samatya. It is now used as a carpentry shop, with an entry to its ambulatory in the adjacent coffee-house. The two saints who were enshrined here were martyred in the persecution of Christians by the emperor Decius in 250–51. The crypt is a large circular domed structure reminiscent of the tholos tombs at Mycenae, only constructed of brick rather than stone, in the excellent late-Roman technique of the fourth to fifth century.

CHAPTER 5

1. KADIRGA LIMANI, or the Galley Port, has long been silted up. It is now buried beneath the quarter of Kadirga Limanı on the Marmara shore below the HIPPODROME. Anastasius I fortified the port, enclosing it on its landward side with a strong defence wall. Justin I had the harbour dredged and built a new pier, after which he commemorated the work by erecting statues of himself and his wife Sophia, for whom the port was thenceforth named.

2. The original harbour of KONTO-SKALION now comprises part of the Kumkapı quarter on the Marmara shore. Michael VIII made Konto-skalion the main base and arsenal for the Byzantine navy, but after the Turkish Conquest it silted up and was eventually filled in. A breakwater has recently been built to create a new harbour at Kumkapı, where the fishing fleet of Istanbul is based.

3. The VALENS AQUEDUCT was built by the emperor Valens *c*. 375. It was damaged at various times but was kept in good repair by both the Byzantine emperors and the Ottoman sultans, the last important restoration being that of Mustafa II in 1697. It continued in use until the late nineteenth century, when it was replaced by the modern water-distribution system. The length of the aqueduct was originally about a kilometre, of which some 625 metres remain standing; its maximum height, where it crosses Atatürk Bulvarı, is 18.5 metres. It consists of two superimposed series of arches, whose procession across the valley gives an imperial Roman aspect to the skyline of the old city.

4. The original HARBOUR OF THEODOSIUS was first built during the reign of Constantine the Great by a certain Eleutherius, by whose name it is sometimes known. The harbour soon filled up with silt carried by the Lycus river, which there empties into the Marmara. Theodosius I dredged the harbour and surrounded it with massive defence walls, of which those on the seaward side are now being rebuilt.

5. The FORUM OF THEODOSIUS was the largest of the public squares of Byzantine Constantinople, built on the site of the ancient Forum Tauri. Theodosius I dedicated the new forum in 393, and thenceforth it was known by his name. At the western end of the forum there was a monumental triumphal arch, and at its centre there was a commemorative column with a spiral band of reliefs showing the victories of Theodosius. The monumental remains of the forum were unearthed at the western end of Beyazit Meydanı in the 1950s, and colossal fragments of the triumphal archway are now arrayed there on either side of Ordu Caddesi. Two fragments of the reliefs of the column are built into the base of the bath of Beyazit II. Both fragments show ranks of marching Roman soldiers, with one of the reliefs set upside down, so that

The Valens Aqueduct

the troops seem to be standing on their heads.

6. The GOLDEN GATE is now part of YEDIKULE, the Castle of the Seven Towers. The two central towers of the four in the THEODOSIAN WALLS are huge marble pylons flanking the Golden Gate, a Roman triumphal arch erected *c.* 390 by Theodosius I. The name Golden Gate ('Porta Aurea') came from the fact that the gates themselves were covered with gold plate, and also from the now-vanished Latin inscription over its central arch: 'Theodosius ornaments this gate after the suppression of the Tyrant [presumably Maximus]. He who builds this Gate of Gold brings back the Golden Age.' The arch was of the usual Roman form, with a large central archway flanked by two smaller ones. The outlines of the arches can still be seen clearly, although the openings were bricked up in later Byzantine times. When Theodosius II decided to expand the city by building the walls that now bear his name, he incorporated the Golden Gate within his new line of fortifications.

CHAPTER 6

1. The COLUMN OF ARCADIUS was erected by Arcadius in honour of his father, Theodosius I. The shaft of the column was decorated with spiral bands of sculpture representing the victories of Theodosius and other important events of his life. At the top of the column, which was more than 50 metres high, there was a colossal statue of Arcadius, placed there in 421 by his son and successor, Theodosius II. The statue was destroyed by an earthquake in 704. The column itself remained standing until 1715, when it was demolished

The Golden Gate

because it appeared to be in imminent danger of collapsing on the surrounding houses. Now all that remains are the mutilated base and some fragments of sculpture from the column that are preserved in the ARCHAEOLOGICAL MUSEUM.

2. The THEODOSIAN WALLS comprise most of the present fortifications of the old city on its landward side, the work of Theodosius II. The main element in the defence system was the inner wall, which was about 5 metres thick at the base and rose to a height of 12 metres above the city. This wall was guarded by ninety-six towers, 18 to 20 metres high, at an average interval of 55 metres; these were mostly square but some were polygonal. Between the inner and outer walls there was a terrace called the peribolos, which varied from 15 to 20 metres in breadth, its level about 5 metres above that of the inner city. The outer wall, which was about 2 metres thick and 8.5 metres in height, also had ninety-six towers, alternating in position with those of the inner wall. Beyond this was an outer terrace called the parateichion, bounded on the outside by the counterscarp of the moat, a battlement nearly 2 metres high. The moat itself was originally about 10 metres deep and 20 metres wide, and may have been flooded when the city was threatened.

The Theodosian Walls were pierced by ten gates and a few small posterns. Five of the ten gates were public entryways and five were principally for the use of the military, the two types alternating with one another in position. Nearly all of the ancient gates continue in use.

The Theodosian Walls originally extended from the Marmara to the Golden Horn, which they reached just inside the Blachernae quarter, Region XIV of Byzantine Constantinople, which had its own separate fortifications. The northern stretch of the Theodosian Walls was subsequently demolished in order to include Region XIV within the city limits; the present walls in the Blachernae quarter date to several later stages of construction in the Byzantine era.

3. The CISTERN OF AETIUS is the oldest of the three Roman reservoirs in the city. Huge as it is, it is yet the smallest of the three open cisterns, measuring 224 by 85 metres, its original depth about 13 to 15 metres. Like the others, it was already disused in later Byzantine times and was turned into a kitchen garden. It is now used as a sports stadium.

4. The CISTERN OF ASPAR is on the summit of the Fifth Hill just to the south of the SELIM I CAMII. It is square in plan, 152 metres on a side and about 15 metres deep, making it somewhat larger than the earlier CISTERN OF AETIUS. Up until the early 1980s there was a picturesque village inside the cistern, a place called Çukur Bostan, or the Sunken Garden, but this has since been

demolished to make way for a municipal market, much diminishing the beauty of this historic quarter.

5. The CISTERN OF ST MOCIUS is the largest of the three Roman reservoirs, measuring 170 by 147 metres, its present depth ranging from 10 to 12 metres. The reservoir is now used as a public market.

6. The PALACES OF ANTIOCHUS AND LAUSUS were built in the first half of the fifth century. The grandest of these two contiguous edifices was the residence of Antiochus, a eunuch who served as grand chamberlain under Theodosius II. All that remains of the two palaces are the foundations and lower walls unearthed during the excavations, but these are so clearly delineated that one can make out the general plan. Early in the seventh century the palace of Antiochus was converted into a martyrion to enshrine the remains of St Euphemia of Chalcedon.

7. The CISTERN OF PHILOXENUS is known in Turkish as Binbirdirek Sarnıçı, the Cistern of a Thousand and One Columns. The cistern is believed to have been built underneath the palace of Philoxenus, one of twelve Roman senators who came to live in Constantinople during the reign of Constantine the Great. Some authorities believe that the structure was at least partially rebuilt in the fifth or sixth century. The dimensions are 64 by 56.4 metres, or

3,610 square metres, making it the second largest underground reservoir in the city after the BASILICA CISTERN, which is three times greater in area. The Binbirdirek cistern originally had a height of more than 19 metres, but mud solidifying on the floor has diminished this by 4.8 metres. The columns are in two tiers bound together by curious stone ties. There are 224 double columns in 16 rows of 14, with arches springing between their impost capitals to support little brick domes.

8. The CHURCH OF THE THEOTOKOS IN CHALKOPRATEIA was founded c. 450 by the empress Pulcheria, who built it to enshrine the Holy Girdle of the Virgin sent from Jerusalem by the empress's sister-in-law, the empress Eudocia. The building fell into ruins after the Turkish Conquest, and later a small mosque named Acem Ağa Mescidi was created in its apse. The mosque was destroyed early in the twentieth century, and today all that remains are the apse and the north wall.

CHAPTER 7

1. The original CHURCH OF THE VIRGIN AT BLACHERNAE was rebuilt on a larger scale by Justinian. After destruction by fire in 1434, the church was rebuilt on a smaller scale and subsequently restored on a number of occasions, most recently in 1960. The famous ayazma is housed in its own shrine below the

narthex, its healing waters still attracting pilgrims, both Christians and Muslims.

2. The base of the COLUMN OF MARCIAN is formed by a high marble pedestal decorated with reliefs of two Nikes, or Winged Victories, one of whom holds a basket ornamented with myrtle and a cross. Above this stands a Syenitic granite column 10 metres high, surmounted by a battered Corinthian capital and a plinth with eagles at the corners; this once supported a seated statue of Marcian. There is also on the base an elegaic couplet in Latin recording that the column was erected by the prefect Tatianus in honour of the emperor Marcian.

3. The CHURCH OF ST JOHN THE BAPTIST OF STUDIUS is known locally as Imrahor Camii, the Mosque of the Sultan's Equerry, after the notable who converted it to the service of Islam early in the sixteenth century. The building was badly damaged by an earthquake in 1894, after which it was abandoned and allowed to fall into ruins.

The church was preceded by an atrium, whose site is now occupied by the walled garden through which the building is approached. The nave is preceded by a narthex divided into three bays; the wider central bay has a very beautiful portal consisting of four columns *in antis*, with magnificent Corinthian capitals supporting an elaborate entablature with richly sculptured architrave, frieze and cornice. Two of the marble doorframes still stand between the columns. Five doors lead from the narthex into the church, which is a pure basilica in plan, with a nave flanked by side aisles separated from the sanctuary by two rows of seven columns each. Six of the columns on the north side still stand; they are of verd antique, with capitals and entablature as in the narthex. The nave ends in a single semicircular apse where there was once a

The Church of St John the Baptist of Studius (Imrahor Camii)

synthronon, with the altar in front of the tiers of seats. Above the entablature of the aisle colonnades there was a second row of columns, which supported the wooden roof, but this part of the building was destroyed in the 1894 earthquake.

4. The ruins of the PALACE OF BLACHERNAE form part of the land walls near their northern end. The first edifice built here by Anastasius I, the Triclinium Anastasiakos, would have been within the fortified enclosure of Region XIV. Later emperors added other edifices at Blachernae, which from the time of Alexius I Comnenus onwards became the principal imperial residence. The vast substructures of the palace are built up against the inside of the land walls where they are highest above the level of the terrain outside. All that can be seen of the palace from within the walls are two contiguous

towers and a stairway leading down into the great vaulted substructures. But from outside the city one can see the bricked-up windows and arches of twelve vaulted chambers in each of three storeys, rising up more than 20 metres from the exterior ground level.

CHAPTER 8

1. The CHURCH OF SS. SERGIUS AND BACCHUS was commissioned by Justinian soon after he came to the throne in 527, and was completed before 536. Theodora's name does not appear in the imperial monograms on the capitals, but she is mentioned in the dedicatory inscription on the architrave and so she must have been a co-founder of the church along with Justinian. The church was converted into a mosque in 1503 by Hüseyin Ağa, chief black eunuch of Beyazit II. Hüseyin Ağa

The Church of SS. Sergius and Bacchus (Küçük Aya Sofya Camii)

also added the six-bayed portico at the entrance to the building, as well as the medrese that forms the other three sides of the courtyard. SS. Sergius and Bacchus is known in Turkish as Küçük Aya Sofya Camii, the Little Mosque of Haghia Sophia, because of its supposed resemblance to the Great Church.

The church is in plan an irregular octagon inscribed off-axis in a very irregular rectangle. The dome is divided into sixteen segments, eight flat and eight concave sectors alternating with one another, the former rising from above the eight arches of the octagon and the latter from the pendentives in between. The octagon has eight polygonal piers with pairs of columns in between, alternately of verd antique and red Synnada marble, both above and below, arranged straight on the axes but curved out into the exedrae at each corner. The space between this brightly coloured curtain of columns and the exterior walls of the rectangle becomes an ambulatory below and a spacious gallery above. The capitals and the classic entablature are exquisitely carved and deeply undercut in the style of the sixth century, similar to those in HAGHIA SOPHIA. On the ground floor, the entablature is still basically classical, trabeated instead of arched, with the traditional architrave, frieze and cornice, but it is very different in effect from anything classical, giving the delicate impression of lace-work. The frieze consists of a long and

beautifully carved inscription in twelve Greek hexameters honouring Justinian and Theodora, the two founders, and also St Sergius, although for some reason St Bacchus is not mentioned.

2. HAGHIA SOPHIA was repaired and augmented on a number of occasions in both the Byzantine and the Ottoman periods, but the edifice that we see today is essentially Justinian's church. The building served as a church until 1453, when Mehmet II converted it into a mosque. The four minarets were added at various times in the century after the Conquest. Some of the buttresses are part of the original structure, while others were added in both the Byzantine and Ottoman periods. The building was restored in 1847–9 on orders of Sultan Abdül Mecit, who employed the Italian-Swiss architects Gaspare and Giuseppe Fossati. Haghia Sophia served as a mosque until 1934, when it was closed for restoration before being opened to the public as a museum.

The ground plan of the building is a rectangle, approximately 70 metres in width and 75 metres in length. At the centre of the east wall there is a projecting apse, semicircular within and three-sided on the exterior; to the west the church is preceded by an exonarthex and a narthex, each of nine cross-vaulted bays. Beyond the narthex to the south is a corridor of three cross-vaulted bays known as the Vestibule of the Warriors, where

Haghia Sophia

the troops of the imperial bodyguard waited while the emperor was attending service. At the north end of the narthex there is a labyrinthine ramp that ascends to the galleries.

Nine huge doors open from the narthex into the nave, the central one known as the Imperial Gate, since it was reserved for the use of the emperor and his entourage. Above the central part of the rectangular area of the nave there is an enormous dome, with smaller semidomes to east and west and conches over the apse and four corners. These cover the central area of the nave, which is flanked by side aisles with galleries above that extend around the west side of the church over the narthex. The main support for the dome is provided by four irregularly shaped piers standing in a square approximately 31 metres on a side. From these piers rise four great arches, between which four pendentives make the transition from the square to the slightly elliptical base of the

dome. The east–west diameter of the dome is approximately 31 metres and the north–south about 33 metres, with the crown soaring 56 metres above the floor – about the height of a fifteen-storey building. The dome has forty ribs that intersect at the crown, separated at the base by forty windows. To the east and west smaller pairs of subsidiary piers support the two great semi-domes, which give the nave its great length, each of them pierced by five windows. The central arches to the north and south are filled with tympanum walls, each pierced by twelve windows, seven in the lower range and five in the upper. Between the great piers on the north and south four monolithic columns of verd antique support the galleries, while above six columns of the same material carry the tympanum walls. At the four corners of the nave there are semicircular exedrae covered by conches, in each of which there are two massive columns of porphyry below and six of verd antique above. At the east, beyond the subsidiary piers, the semicircular apse projects beyond the east wall of the church, covered by a conch. To the north and south of the main piers there are lateral piers, which are joined structurally with the four main buttresses on those sides, consolidating the fabric of the church. These divide the side aisles and the galleries above into six large compartments on each floor, three on either side, joined to one another by great arches springing between the piers.

The capitals of the columns are unique and famous. There are several different types, but they are all alike in having the surface decoration of acanthus leaves and palm foliage so deeply undercut as to produce an effect of white lace on a dark ground. In the centre of the capitals there are imperial monograms of Justinian and Theodora. The brass-sheathed pillar at the north-west corner of the north aisle is the subject of legend, which has it that St Gregory the Miracle-Worker once appeared there, giving the stone miraculous powers.

A great variety of rare and beautiful marbles was used for the superb revetments of the piers and walls. Other types of decoration are also to be found in the church. The great square of *opus Alexandrinium* in the pavement towards the south-east of the nave is the most noteworthy of these. This is made up mostly of circles of granite, red and green porphyry, and verd antique. According to Antony of Novgorod, who visited Haghia Sophia in 1200, the emperor's throne stood upon this square at the time of his coronation, surrounded by a bronze enclosure.

Little remains of the figurative mosaics that once adorned the nave of Haghia Sophia. The largest and most beautiful of those that have survived is in the conch of the apse, a representation of the Virgin and Child that was unveiled on Easter Sunday 846. On the south side of the arch that frames the apse there is a colossal mosaic of the archangel Gabriel; the companion figure of the archangel Michael on the opposite side has now vanished except for a few feathers of his wings. Both of these mosaics are dated to the latter part of the ninth century. Three other mosaic portraits are located in niches at the base of the north tympanum wall and are visible from the nave. The figure in the first niche from the west is St Ignatius the Younger; in the central niche is St John Chrysostom; and in the fifth niche from the west is St Ignatius Theophorus of Antioch. The only other mosaics that are visible from the nave are the six-winged angels in the east pendentives. (Those in the west pendentives are imitations in paint done by the Fossatis during their restoration.) The east pendentives were probably destroyed when that side of the dome collapsed in 1346; the mosaics would therefore date to a restoration carried out in 1346–55.

There are four other mosaics in the galleries, which in the Byzantine era served as the gynaceum, or women's quarter. Three of the four surviving mosaics in the galleries are located at the far end of the south side, beyond the first bay. The first of these that one comes to is the Deesis, an iconographic type in which Christ is flanked by the Virgin and St John the Baptist, a superb work dating from the second half of the thirteenth century. Set into the pavement just opposite the Deesis there is a sarcophagus lid inscribed in Latin capital letters with the name of Henricus Dandolo, doge of Venice. The other two mosaics in the south gallery are located on the east wall of the church, at the far end of the last bay. The oldest of these is on the left, next to the apse, where Christ is shown between the figures of an emperor and empress of Byzantium. Inscriptions identify the empress as Zoë, daughter of Constantine VIII and one of the few women to rule Byzantium in her own right. The emperor is Constantine IX Monomachus, Zoë's third husband, and the mosaic is dated to the first year of his reign. The mosaic to the right of this, separated from it by a window, again represents Christ flanked by an imperial couple. Inscriptions identify the couple as John II Comnenus and his wife, Eirene, while their son Alexius is shown on the narrow panel of the side wall on the right. The mosaic is dated to the early years of John's reign.

The fourth of the surviving mosaics in the gynaceum is located in the north gallery, high on the east face of the north-west pier. This panel represents the emperor Alexander, who reigned from May 912 to June 913, and the mosaic is dated to the brief period of his reign.

There are two other mosaics on the ground floor: one in the narthex above the Imperial Gate, and the other in the Vestibule of the Warriors over the doorway leading into the narthex. The first of these shows Christ enthroned with a kneeling imperial figure, identified as Leo VI, dated to the late ninth century. The other mosaic shows the enthroned Virgin and Child flanked by two emperors. The figure on the right, identified by an inscription as 'Constantine, the great Emperor among the Saints', offers the Virgin a model of a walled town representing Constantinople. The figure on the left, identified as 'Justinian, the illustrious Emperor', offers her a model of a church symbolizing Haghia Sophia. The mosaic is dated to the last quarter of the tenth century, and is thought to have been commissioned by Basil II.

3. HAGHIA EIRENE is the second largest Byzantine church in the city, surpassed in size only by HAGHIA SOPHIA; it was restored in the 1970s and is now used as a concert hall. The church is a basilica, but one of a very unusual type. In plan the church is a rectangle, 42.2 metres

Haghia Eirene

long and 36.7 metres wide, with an apse projecting from the east end, five-sided on the exterior, semi-circular within, and to the west a narthex preceded by an atrium. The central nave is flanked by a pair of side aisles, above which there is a gallery that also extends over the narthex. The central area of the nave is covered by a dome of diameter 15.5 metres carried on a high drum. The dome is supported primarily by four huge piers standing on the corners of a square. Between these piers there are four great arches, with pendentives between them making the transition to the cornice of the drum carrying the dome. Around the periphery of the apse there is a synthronon – the only one in the city that has survived from the Byzantine period. This has six tiers of seats for the clergy, with doors at either side leading to an ambulatory that runs beneath the fourth tier. In the conch of the apse a mosaic cross in black outline stands on a pedestal of three steps, against a gold ground with a geometric border – a work that almost certainly is part of the original decoration of Justinian's period.

4. The CHURCH OF ST POLYEUK-TOS was excavated in the mid-1960s by Martin Harrison, whose work has established the plan of the edifice. The church was essentially basilical in form, divided into a nave and two side aisles by an arrangement of piers and columns. The church measured 52 by 58 metres, fronted by an atrium of 52 by 26 metres; a small apsidal building on the north may have been a baptistery, while a larger structure at the north-west corner of the site was probably the palace of Anicia Juliana.

5. The shrine of the PANAYIA ZOODOCHOS PEGE is known in Turkish as Balıklı, taking its name from the fish (in Turkish, 'balık') that swim in the pool of its holy spring. The church built by Justinian was destroyed by an earthquake and replaced by a smaller one, which was rebuilt on a number of occasions in

both the Byzantine and the Ottoman periods, with the present structure dating from 1833. The ancient ayazma is preserved in the shrine along with the sacred fish from which it takes its name. The Greek cemetery at Balıklı is one of the oldest around the city, and a number of patriarchs of Constantinople are buried there.

6. The BASILICA CISTERN is known in Turkish as Yerebatansaray, the Underground Palace. This is by far the largest underground cistern in the city. It is 139 metres long and 64.6 metres wide, with 336 columns, arrayed in 12 rows of 28 each, separated by 4 metres and with a height of 8 metres. Ninety of these columns near the north-western corner of the cistern were walled off at the end of the nineteenth century and are not visible today. At the north-western corner two of the columns are mounted on ancient classical pedestals in the form of Medusa heads, one of them upside down and the other on its side.

7. The GREAT PALACE of Byzantium was first built by Constantine the Great, and during the following eight centuries it was restored, adorned and augmented by many of his successors. The gardens and pavilions of the palace were laid out along the Marmara slope of the First Hill, where the scattered ruins of some of its buildings can still be seen here and there. The Great Palace was divided into at least five major parts – Chalke, Magnaura, Daphne, the Sacred Palace, and the PALACE OF BUCOLEON – whose locations have been the subject of specialized study for well over a century, with some sites still in question.

8. The exhibits in the MOSAIC MUSEUM were discovered during excavations made in 1935. These revealed extensive mosaic pavements as well as columns, capitals and other architectural fragments, all part of the GREAT PALACE. The ruins were identified as being the north-east portico of the Mosaic Peristyle, a colonnaded walkway which may have led from the imperial apartments of the palace to the Kathisma. There has been considerable discussion about the date of the mosaics, but current opinion is that they were done c. AD 500.

9. The PALACE OF BUCOLEON looked down upon the Harbour of the Bucoleon, a small port used by those living in the GREAT PALACE. All that remains of Bucoleon are its eastern loggia with its three marble-framed windows and the shell of a great vaulted room behind them. Below the tower to the west of the ruined façade of the palace are the remains of a beautifully carved lintel, part of the sea-gate of Bucoleon.

CHAPTER 9

1. The WALL OF HERACLIUS forms the inner circuit of the fortified

The Bucoleon Palace

enclosure at the northern end of the land walls, where they join up with the SEA WALLS on the Golden Horn. Heraclius built this wall after the Avar attack had been repelled in 626, replacing the original northern end of the THEODOSIAN WALLS. The fortification contains three hexagonal defence towers which are among the finest in the land walls.

CHAPTER 10

1. The CHURCH OF ST THEO-DOSIA is thought to have been built by Basil I. The building is a domed-cross structure with side aisles surmounted by galleries; the piers supporting the dome are disengaged from the walls, and the corners behind them form alcoves of two storeys. The central dome and the arches that support it are Ottoman reconstructions, as are most of the windows. It is now known locally as Gül Camii.

2. The edifice known as KILISE CAMI (Church Mosque) has been tentatively identified as the church of St Theodore Tyro. The inner narthex and the church itself, which is of the four-column type, are to be dated between the tenth century and the twelfth, when this type was common.

*Kilise Cami
(Church Mosque)*

336

But the very attractive brickwork on the façade of the outer narthex might suggest a later date. Constructed of stone, brick and marble, the elaborate design and decoration of the building proclaim it at once as belonging to the last great flowering of Byzantine architecture in the early fourteenth century. The narthexes contain some handsome columns, capitals and door-frames which appear to be reused material from an earlier building probably of the sixth century.

3. The CHURCH OF ST ANDREW IN KRISEI has been identified by some Byzantinists as Koca Mustafa Pasha Camii. The church is probably the one that chroniclers refer to as St Andrew of Crete in the quarter known as Krisis (in Greek, 'Agiou Andreou en Krisei'); this was dedicated c. 1284 by the princess Theodora Raoulina, probably using materials from an earlier edifice. The church was converted into a mosque early in the sixteenth century by Koca Mustafa Pasha, grand vezir of Selim I.

When the church was converted into a mosque the interior arrangements were reoriented by ninety degrees. Thus the mihrab and mimber

The Church of St Andrew in Krisei (Koca Mustafa Pasha Camii)

are under the semidome against the south wall, while the entrance is in the north wall, in front of which a wooden porch has been added. The interior now has a trefoil shape but was probably originally ambulatory; that is, there would have been a triple arcade supported by two columns to north and south, like the one that still exists on the west. This bay has a small dome supported by beautiful sixth-century capitals of the pseudo-Ionic type. The central portal opens into a sort of inner narthex or aisle, originally separated from the nave only by two verd-antique columns, but now obstructed by a large wooden gallery. To the east the conch of the apse is preceded by a deep barrel-vault; to the north and south the two later Ottoman semidomes open out. Even in its greatly altered form it is a very attractive building.

4. The WALL OF LEO forms the outer part of the fortified enclosure at the northern end of the land walls. This wall was built by Leo V in 813, after he had defeated an attack on the city in this area by Krum of the Bulgars. This wall stands 25 metres in front of the WALL OF HERA-CLIUS, running parallel to it for 80 metres before turning to meet the end of the SEA WALLS along the Golden Horn. Leo's wall was guarded by four towers: two along the Golden Horn and two facing westward into Thrace.

5. The SEA WALLS extended along the shores of both the Golden Horn and the Marmara. These walls were rebuilt and strengthened during the reign of Theophilus to protect Constantinople from a seaborne invasion by the Saracens. As rebuilt by Theophilus, the walls along the Golden Horn were 10 metres high and protected by 110 defence towers at regular intervals, and they had about a dozen gates. The walls along the Marmara were about 12 to 15 metres high, studded with 188 towers regularly spaced, and with 13 gates. The walls and towers are far better preserved on the Marmara shore, particularly below the First Hill. Numerous inscriptions on the walls and towers record repairs by various emperors from the ninth century to the fourteenth, the most numerous being those of Theophilus.

CHAPTER 11

1. The CHURCH OF THE MYRE-LAION was converted into a mosque late in the fifteenth century by Mesih Mehmet Pasha, grand vezir of Murat III. The mosque, known as Bodrum Camii, was for long in ruins, but it has since been restored after excavations by Professor Lee Striker. Striker also unearthed the substructure of the palace of Romanus, which has now been opened as a covered market under the terrace beside the mosque.

The excavation revealed that the building was actually a double church, with one on the level of the terrace and the other in a crypt below. The lower church was built by Romanus as a funerary chapel for his wife, Theodora, who was buried there in 922. The two superimposed churches were built during the years 919–22; both were of the same design, the four-column type so common in the tenth and eleventh centuries. The substructure of the palace is a rotunda, its roof supported by seventy-five columns; this was built in the fifth century AD as the reception hall of a late Roman palace but was apparently never completed. It was later roofed over and used as a cistern.

CHAPTER 12

1. The CHURCH OF ST SAVIOUR PANTEPOPTES, Christ the All-Seeing, was founded during the years 1085–90 by the empress Anna Dalassena, mother of Alexius I Comnenus. The church was converted into a mosque almost immediately after the Conquest. It served for a time as the imaret, or public kitchen, of the nearby Mosque of the Conqueror, and thus it came to be known as Eski ('Old') Imaret Camii.

The Pantepoptes is a typical Byzantine church of its period, with its twelve-sided dome, and its decorative brickwork in the form of blind arches and bands of Greek-key and swastika motifs, along with rose-like medallions. The interior plan is of the four-column type, with three apses and a double narthex, where most of the doors retain their magnificent frames of red marble. Over the inner narthex there is a gallery that opens into the nave through a charming triple arcade on two rose-coloured marble columns. The side apses preserve their original windows and their beautiful marble cornice. The dome, which has twelve windows between deep ribs tapering up towards the crown, rests on a cornice which still preserves its original decoration, a meander pattern of palmettes and flowers.

2. The CHURCH OF ST SAVIOUR PANTOCRATOR is known in Turkish as Molla Zeyrek Camii, and dominates the heights of the Fourth Hill above Atatürk Bulvarı. It is a composite building that originally consisted of a monastery with two churches and a chapel between them, the whole complex built within the period 1120–36. The monastery and the south church were founded by the empress Eirene, wife of John II Comnenus, and dedicated to St Saviour Pantocrator, Christ the Almighty. After Eirene's death in 1124 John erected another church just to the north of hers; this was dedicated to the Virgin Eleousa, the Merciful or Charitable. When this was finished John decided to join the two churches by another church, dedicated to the archangel Michael. This was designed to serve as a mortuary chapel for the imperial Comneni dynasty, with Eirene being

The Church of St Saviour Pantocrator (Molla Zeyrek Camii)

the first to be buried there. John himself was interred in the chapel after his death in 1143. The monastery, now vanished, was one of the most renowned in Byzantium, including a hospital, an insane asylum and a hospice for old men.

The south church is of the four-column type in plan, with a central dome, a triple apse, and a narthex with a gallery overlooking the nave. Excavations have brought to light its magnificent *opus-sectile* pavement. The central funerary chapel is a structure without aisles and with but one apse, covered by two domes; it is highly irregular in form to make it fit in between the north and south churches, which are not of exactly the same size. Parts of the walls of the churches were demolished so that all three sections opened widely into one another; however, in recent years they have been separated again by wooden partitions. The north church is essentially of the same type and plan as the one on the south.

Unfortunately it has retained none of its original decoration. John also added an outer narthex which must once have extended in front of all three structures, but which now ends awkwardly in the middle of the mortuary chapel.

3. The WALL OF MANUEL COMNENUS can be identified as the bow-shaped projection of the fortifications just north of TEKFURSARAYI, the Byzantine palace at the northern end of the present THEODOSIAN WALLS. Because of the steepness of the hill on which it for the most part stands, this section of the defence circuit was unprotected by a moat, but to compensate for this the wall was more massive, measuring nearly 5 metres in thickness at its summit, and it was protected by stronger towers than in other portions of the fortifications. Between the sixth and seventh towers from the north there is a gate known in Greek as Porta Kaligaria, the Gate of the Shoe-

makers, which in Turkish is called Egri Kapi, the Crooked Gate.

4. KIZ KULESI, is known in English as Leander's Tower, on the mistaken notion that it is associated with the myth of Hero and Leander, which is actually set on the Dardanelles. Manuel I Comnenus built a small fortress on the islet to guard the mouth of the Bosphorus. Since then the islet has served as the site of a lighthouse, a semaphore station, a quarantine post, a customs control point, and a home for retired naval officers. The present building dates from the eighteenth century; it is now used as an inspection station by the Turkish Navy.

CHAPTER 13

1. The CHURCH OF THE THEO-TOKOS KYRIOTISSA is known in Turkish as Kalenderhane Camii. Its identification was determined by Professor Lee Striker, who established that the church was dedicated to the Theotokos Kyriotissa, Our Lady the Mother of God, and that it dates from the late twelfth century, built on the ruins of earlier Byzantine structures.

The church is cruciform in plan, with deep barrel vaults over the arms of the cross and a dome with sixteen ribs over the centre. It originally had side aisles communicating with the nave, and galleries over the exonarthex and narthex. The building still preserves its elaborate and beautiful marble revetment and sculptured decoration, making it one of the most attractive Byzantine buildings in the city.

During a restoration in 1953 a number of mosaics and wall-paintings were discovered. These include a fresco cycle of the life of St Francis of Assisi painted during the Latin

The Church of the Theotokos Kyriotissa (Kalenderhane Camii)

occupation. The paintings were removed from the church after it was restored as a mosque, and some of them are now on display in the ARCHAEOLOGICAL MUSEUM.

CHAPTER 14

1. The CHURCH OF THE THEOTOKOS PANACHRANTOS is known in Turkish as Fenari Isa Camii. It is also known as Constantine Lips, after a high official in the reigns of Leo VI and Constantine VII, who in 907 built the first church and monastery on this site, dedicated to the Theotokos Panachrantos. The monastery was refounded by the empress Theodora, wife of Michael VIII Palaeologus, who added another church to the south of the original one, dedicating it to St John the Baptist. The new church served as a funerary chapel for the Palaeologus dynasty, beginning with Theodora herself, who was buried here in 1304. The church was converted into a mosque in 1496, while the monastery, now vanished, was given over to a community of dervishes.

The original north church constructed by Constantine Lips was of the four-column type, but quite unusually it had five apses, the extra ones to north and south projecting beyond the rest of the building. The northern apse is now demolished, while the southern one is incorporated into the south church. Another unusual, perhaps unique, feature is that there are four little chapels on

the roof, grouped around the main dome. The south church was of the ambulatory type; that is, its nave was divided from the aisles by a triple arcade to north, west and south, with each arcade supported by two columns. Of its three apses, the northern one was the southern supernumerary apse of the older church. Thus there were in all seven apses, six of which remain and make the eastern façade of the building exceedingly attractive.

2. The CHURCH OF ST MARY OF THE MONGOLS was either founded or rebuilt *c.* 1282 by the princess Maria Palaeologina, an illegitimate daughter of Michael VIII. The foundress had been sent off as a bride to the khan of the Mongols and built this church after her return. After the Conquest, Mehmet II gave the Greeks permission to retain the church as a favour to his Greek architect Christodoulos.

The plan of the church was originally quatrefoil internally and trefoil externally. That is, the small central dome on a high drum was surrounded by four semidomes along the axes, all but the western one resting on the outer walls of the building, which thus formed exedrae, with a narthex of three bays preceding the church to the west. But the entire southern side of the church was swept away in modern times and replaced by a narthex which is in every direction out of line with the original building. The effect is most disconcerting; nevertheless, the interior of the church is quite charming.

3. The so-called GENOESE CASTLE is known in Turkish as Yoros Kalesi. The fortress is actually Byzantine in construction, as is evident from the various Greek inscriptions still to be found in the walls. Early in the fourteenth century the fortress was taken over by the Genoese, who held it until the Turkish Conquest.

4. The GALATA TOWER is some 67 metres high, its base 35 metres above sea level. Originally known as the Tower of Christ, it was erected during the first expansion of the Genoese colony, in 1348. The final defence system consisted of six

walled enceintes, with the outer wall bordered by a deep ditch. Fragments of the fortifications can still be seen here and there in Galata, including two well-preserved towers just below the Galata Tower, as well as a Genoese postern that once led from the fourth enceinte to the fifth. Until the 1960s the Galata Tower was used as a fire-watch station, but now it has been restored as a tourist attraction. The walkway around the restaurant at the top commands extraordinary views of the city and its surrounding garland of waters.

5. The CHURCH OF SS. DOMENIC AND PAUL was built by the Dominicans during the years 1323–37.

The Galata Tower

Early in the sixteenth century it was converted into a mosque and given to the Moorish refugees who had settled in Galata; hence its Turkish name, Arap Camii, the Mosque of the Arabs. The interior has been partially destroyed by fire and rebuilt a number of times. Nevertheless, it remains a rather typical medieval Latin church, originally Gothic: a long hall ending in three rectangular apses, and with a campanile (now the minaret) at the east end.

6. The CHURCH OF ST SAVIOUR IN CHORA is just inside the THEODOSIAN WALLS on the Sixth Hill. The phrase 'in Chora' means 'in the country', because the original church and monastery on this site were out in the countryside. No trace remains of the original church, nor is anything certain known about its origin. The present building in its first form dates from the late eleventh century.

The church was founded by Maria Doucina, sister-in-law of Alexius I Comnenus, during the years 1077–81; it was probably of the four-column type so popular at that time. An elaborate remodelling of the church was carried out late in the twelfth century by Maria Doucina's grandson, the Sebastocrator Isaac Comnenus, third son of Alexius I. Then a third period of building activity two centuries later created the present church and its works of art, a project carried out in the years 1315–21 by Theodore Metochites. The Chora continued as a church until 1510, when it was converted to a mosque, known as Kariye Camii, by Atik Ali Pasha, grand vezir under Beyazit II. The mosaics and frescos were never obliterated, though in the course of time many of them were obscured by plaster, paint and dirt, and a number were shaken down by earthquakes. Restoration was begun

The Church of St Saviour in Chora (Kariye Camii)

in 1948 by Thomas Whittemore and Paul A. Underwood, a project directed by Ernest Hawkins, sponsored by the Byzantine Institute of America and the Dumbarton Oaks Center for Byzantine Studies.

The church is preceded by an exonarthex and a narthex, with a parecclesion to the south and a two-storeyed passageway to the north. The central area of the church is covered by a dome carried on a high drum; this is supported by four huge pilasters that stand at the corners of the nave, with great arches springing between them and with pendentives making the transition to the circular cornice. There are two smaller domes carried on lower drums above the first and fourth bays of the narthex (numbering from left to right), as well as above the western-most bay of the parecclesion.

The mosaics and frescos in the Chora are far and away the most important series of Byzantine paintings in the world. The paintings fall into seven quite distinct groups: six large Dedicatory or Devotional panels, in the inner and outer narthexes; the Ancestry of Christ, in the two domes of the inner narthex; the Cycle of the Life of the Blessed Virgin, in the first three bays of the inner narthex; the Cycle of the Infancy of Christ, in the lunettes of the outer narthex; the Cycle of Christ's Ministry, in the vaults of the outer narthex and the fourth bay of the inner narthex; Portraits of Saints; and the Mosaics in the nave. The

genealogy in the dome serves as a prelude to the narrative cycles of the Blessed Virgin and Christ, which comprise the major elements in the programme. The superb fresco decoration of the parecclesion was the last part of Theodore Metochites's work of decoration to be carried out, probably in 1320–21. The decoration of the chapel is designed to illustrate its purpose as a place of burial. Above the level of the cornice the paintings represent the Resurrection and the Life, the Last Judgement: Heaven and Hell, and the Mother of God as the Bridge Between Earth and Heaven. Below the cornice there is a procession of saints and martyrs, interrupted by four tombs, one of which is probably that of Theodore Metochites. There are four more tombs elsewhere in the church, one of them in the narthex and the others in the exonarthex.

7. The CHURCH OF THE THEO-TOKOS PAMMAKARISTOS, the All-Joyous Mother of God, was restored in the early 1960s by the Byzantine Institute of America. The main church was built in the twelfth century by a nobleman named John Comnenus and his wife, Anna Doucina. In form this church was of the ambulatory type, a triple arcade in the north, west and south dividing the central domed area from the ambulatory; at the east end were the usual three apses, and at the west a single narthex. Towards the end of the thirteenth century the church

The Church of the
Theotokos Pammakaristos
(Fethiye Camii)

was reconstructed by a general named Michael Doucas Glabas Tarchaniotes. Then, *c.* 1310, a parecclesion was added on the south side of the church by Michael's widow, Maria Doucina Comnena Palaeologina Blachena, serving as a funerary chamber for her departed husband. This chapel was of the four-column type and was preceded by a two-storeyed narthex carried by a tiny dome. In the second half of the fourteenth century the north, west and south sides of the church were surrounded by a perambulatory, which ran into and partly obliterated the south chapel. The church served as the Greek Orthodox Patriarchate during the years 1456–1586. Then in 1591 Murat III converted it to Islam, calling it Fethiye Camii, the Mosque of the Conquest, to celebrate his annexation of Georgia and Azerbaijan. At that time the building was radically altered so as to create a prayer-room with the maximum possible unobstructed space. After

the restoration the main prayer-room was separated from the side chapel and reconsecrated as a mosque, while the parecclesion was converted into a museum to exhibit the surviving mosaics.

The mosaic in the crown of the dome of the parecclesion is Christ Pantocrator, surrounded by twelve prophets of the Old Testament. The conch of the apse contains Christ Hyperagathos, the All-Loving; on the left wall of the bema is the Virgin; on the right wall is St John the Baptist; and in the domical vault above them are the Four Archangels. The Baptism of Christ is depicted in the east section of the domical vault in the side aisle. Seventeen saints are represented elsewhere in the chapel. The mosaics are dated to the early fourteenth century, undoubtedly done when Maria Doucina added the parecclesion *c.* 1310.

8. TEKFURSARAYI was probably built in the latter part of the thirteenth century, perhaps as an annexe of the nearby PALACE OF BLACHERNAE. It is a large three-storey building at the northern end of the THEODOSIAN WALLS, where they give way to the WALL OF MANUEL COMNENUS. On the ground floor an arcade with four wide arches opens into the courtyard, which is overlooked on the first floor by five large windows. The top floor has windows on all sides, seven of them overlooking the courtyard, with a curious bow-like apse on the

Tekfursarayı

opposite side, and a window with the remains of a balcony to the east. The palace is elaborately decorated with geometrical designs in red brick and white marble, typical of the later period of Byzantine architecture.

CHAPTER 15

1. ANADOLU HISARI originally comprised a keep and its surrounding wall together with a barbican guarded by three towers. Parts of the curtain wall were demolished to make way for the coastal road. It has

been suggested that only the keep and its wall were built by Beyazit, with the barbican and its towers added by Mehmet II.

2. RUMELI HISARI spans a steep valley with two tall towers on opposite hills and a third at the water's edge, where the sea-gate is guarded by a barbican. A curtain wall, protected by three smaller towers, joins the three major ones, forming an enclosure 250 metres long by 125 metres broad at its maximum. Mehmet II entrusted each of the

Rumeli Hisarı

347

three main towers to one of his vezirs: the north tower to Saruca Pasha, the sea tower to Halil Pasha, his grand vezir, and the south one to Zaganos Pasha. Rumeli Hisarı is now a museum, with a Greek-style theatre where theatrical performances are held during the summer months.

CHAPTER 16

1. YAVUZ ERSINAN CAMII is probably the oldest mosque in Istanbul, though restored on a number of occasions. It is of the simplest type: a square room covered by a dome, the walls built of stone. The tombstone of Yavuz Ersinan can be seen in the little graveyard beside the mosque, in what was once the garden of his house. The chronicler Evliya Çelebi was born in this house in 1611, and it was here that he had the fabulous dream that inspired him to write his *Seyahatname*.

2. The GREEK ORTHODOX PATRIARCHATE was established on its present site at the beginning of the seventeenth century. The present patriarchal church of St George dates only from 1720. It replaces an earlier church of St George described by an Italian traveller who saw it in 1615 as 'of moderate size, long in form, and with several aisles'.

3. YEDIKULE, the Castle of the Seven Towers, is partly Byzantine in structure and partly Turkish. The seven eponymous towers consist of

four in the THEODOSIAN WALLS, plus three additional towers built inside the walls by Mehmet II. The three inner towers are connected together and joined to the Theodosian Walls by heavy curtain-walls, forming a five-sided enclosure. The two central towers in the Theodosian Walls are marble pylons flanking the GOLDEN GATE, and are part of the original triumphal entryway, erected *c.* 390 by Theodosius I. Yedikule was garrisoned by the Janissaries, who used two of the towers as guardhouses for prisoners, the inmates including a number of foreign ambassadors to the Porte. Sultan Osman II was executed by the Janissaries here in 1622.

4. The main entrance to TOPKAPI SARAYI, the Imperial Gate, is beyond the north-east corner of HAGHIA SOPHIA. Outside the gate to the right is the street-fountain of Ahmet III, a magnificent rococo work dating from 1728. The Imperial Gate is one of the original structures from Mehmet II's time, erected in 1478, though it lost its second storey in 1856. The rooms in the gateway housed the Kapıcıs, or guards, of whom fifty were on watch at all times of the day and night.

The Imperial Gate leads to the First Court of the Saray. The First Court was in times past known as the Courtyard of the Janissaries, who once mustered there. The Janissaries stored their weapons in the former church of HAGHIA EIRENE, which

The Imperial Gate of Topkapı Sarayı

stands near the south-west corner of the courtyard. At the far end of the First Court is Bab-üs Selam, the Gate of Salutations, better known as Orta Kapı, or the Middle Gate. This was the entryway to the Inner Palace, through which only authorized persons could pass, and then only on foot. The gateway is typical of the military architecture of Mehmet II's time, with its twin octagonal towers capped with conical roofs. Between the two doorways there is a large central chamber that once housed the chief gatekeepers. One of the rooms was used by the chief executioner, a post held by the head gardener of the saray, with a tiny cell adjacent to it for the prisoner awaiting execution.

The enormous Second Court, some 130 metres long and 110 metres wide at its southern end, looks much as it did in Mehmet II's time. This was known in Ottoman times as the Court of the Divan, since it was used principally for meetings of the imperial council. The portal at the near left-hand corner of the courtyard is Meyyit Kapısı, the Gate of the Dead, because those who died in the Inner Palace were carried through it for burial outside. The gate leads to the Royal Stables, which at present are not open to the public.

The Divan complex projects from the north-west corner of the courtyard and is dominated by the square tower with a conical roof that forms the most conspicuous landmark of the saray. The complex dates in essentials from Mehmet II's time, though much altered in subsequent periods. The tower was originally lower and had a pyramidal roof; the present structure with its Corinthian columns was built by Mahmut II in 1820. The Divan complex consists of three contiguous chambers. The first on the left is the Council Chamber, followed by the Public Records Office and the Office of the Grand Vezir, with the first two rooms opening into one another under a great arch. Around three sides of the room there is a low couch covered with Turkish carpets – the divan from which the council took its name. Beyond the Divan complex at the corner of the courtyard is the Inner Treasury, a long chamber covered by eight domes in four pairs supported internally by three piers.

Around the corner from the Divan, directly under the south side of the Divan Tower, there is an entry-way known as the Carriage Gate. This is the starting-point for guided tours of the Harem, which most vis-itors defer until they have seen the rest of the palace.

Three gateways in the east portico of the Second Court lead to the Palace Kitchens, a series of ten spacious chambers, each with a high dome and a lofty conical chimney. The kitchens are used to house the saray's superb collection of Chinese porcelain and other china and glass-ware. The two rooms at the north end are outfitted with the cooking utensils that were used in the saray kitchens. The small building with three domes at the north end of the courtyard was the Confectioner's Mosque; it houses an interesting collection of glass made in Istanbul during the eighteenth and nineteenth centuries.

The entryway to the Third Court is known as Bab-üs Saadet, the Gate of Felicity, since it led to the Inner Palace, the House of Felicity. Just inside the gateway is the Arz Odası, or Throne Room, a small building with a widely overhanging roof sup-ported on a colonnade of antique marble columns. This is where the grand vezir and other members of the Supreme Council reported to the sultan after each meeting of the Divan. Here also the ambassadors of foreign powers were presented to the sultan upon their arrival and departure.

Behind the Throne Room and slightly to the left is the Library of Ahmet III, erected in 1719. It is an elegant little building of Procon-nesian marble, consisting of three domed areas flanked by loggias with sofas and cupboards for books. The library served the students in the Palace School, whose various branches were housed in the build-ings in and around the Third Court. The building to the left of the library, set at an angle in the corner of the courtyard, is Ağalar Camii, the Mosque of the Ağas. The mosque takes its name from the highest ranking of the white eunuchs who were in charge of the various branches of the Palace School, all of them having the rank of ağa, their chief holding the position of kapı ağası, or ağa of the gate. Ağalar Camii serves as the library of the Topkapı Sarayı Museum.

The first building on the right side of the courtyard's east side has a domed portico supported by a row of Byzantine columns in verd antique, while the hall itself is a long chamber divided into three aisles by two rows of pillars supporting barrel vaults. It houses the Imperial Wardrobe, a collection of imperial costumes worn by the sultans, of which only a few are on display at any given time.

The rest of the east side of the Third Court is taken up with the chambers that Mehmet II and his immediate successors used as reception halls, with the vaults below used as the Privy Treasury. The rooms now serve as the Treasury, an incomparable collection of precious objects that belonged to the Ottoman sultans. The central building at the far end of the courtyard houses the Collection of Miniatures and the Royal Portrait Gallery. The collection of miniatures is said to number 13,000, of which only a few are exhibited at any one time. This is the supreme treasure of the saray, with superb Turkish and Persian paintings done for albums belonging to the sultans. The Royal Portrait Gallery has portraits of all the Ottoman

sultans, although some of them are not authentic representations. The building at the north-west corner of the courtyard houses the Pavilion of the Holy Mantle and the Collection of Sacred Relics. These are relics of the Prophet Muhammad, of which his mantle is the most sacred.

The Fourth Court is not really a courtyard but a garden on several levels, in each of which there are one or more pavilions. The pavilion at the north-east corner of the court is the Mecidiye Köşkü, erected c. 1840 by Abdül Mecit. At the centre of the garden there is a structure known as Başlala Kulesi, the Tower of the Head Tutor. A short distance to the west of this there is a charming pavilion known as the Sofa Köşkü.

Steps lead up to a marble-paved terrace at the north-west corner of the Fourth Court, where there is a large marble pool with a cascade fountain at its centre. At the centre of the courtyard's balustrade, projecting over the lower gardens of the saray, there is a charming little balcony covered by a domed canopy in gilded bronze carried on four slim bronze pillars. An inscription on the canopy records that the balcony is called Iftariye and was made in 1640 for Sultan Ibrahim. The balcony takes its name from Iftar, the festive meal taken after sunset in the holy month of Ramazan, ending the daily fast.

The north end of the terrace is occupied by the Baghdad Köşkü, built in 1638 by Murat IV to commemorate his capture of Baghdad. At the south end of the terrace two kiosks face on to an L-shaped portico, formed by two colonnades around the north and west sides of the Pavilion of the Holy Mantle. The one to the east is the Rivan Köşkü, built in 1636 by Murat IV to commemorate his capture of Rivan (Erivan) in Armenia. The kiosk to the west is the Sünnet Odası, or Circumcision Room, built in 1641 for Sultan Ibrahim.

The itinerary now takes one to the Carriage Gate, to begin a tour of the Harem. The gateway leads to the long, narrow Courtyard of the Black Eunuchs. The left side of the courtyard is bordered by an arcade of ten marble columns with lotus capitals, above which hang wrought-iron lamps that once lighted the way to the Carriage Gate. The building to the rear of the porch was the barracks of the black eunuchs, built in three storeys around a courtyard. Beyond the barracks a flight of stairs leads up to the Schoolroom of the Princes, where the young sons of the sultan received their primary education. Just past the Schoolroom a door leads to the apartment of the chief black eunuch, who was in charge of the Harem and also supervised the primary education of the sultan's sons.

Beyond these apartments is Cümle Kapısı, the Main Gate, which leads into the Harem proper. This opens into a guardroom, from the left side of which a long, narrow corridor stretches to the open Courtyard of the Cariyelêr, or women servants. On the right side of this courtyard there are three suites of rooms for the chief women officials of the Harem: the head stewardess, the treasurer, and the chief laundress. The staircase just beyond the three suites leads down to a courtyard on a much lower level, once the site of the Harem hospital.

Just beyond Cümle Kapısı a gateway opens on to a wide corridor known as Altın Yol, or the Golden Way, which extends along the entire east side of the Harem. At the very beginning of the corridor an opening on the left leads to the large open Courtyard of the Valide Sultan. The Apartments of the Valide Sultan occupy most of the west side of the courtyard on two levels; the rooms are small but quite attractive, with tiled walls and painted ceilings. At the north-west corner of the courtyard a doorway opens into the Ocaklı Oda, the Room with a Hearth, a beautifully tiled chamber dominated by a splendid bronze chimney-piece. A door on the right leads into the suites of the birinci kadın and ikinci kadın, the first and second of the sultan's four wives. A door on the left opens into a smaller chamber called Çeşmeli Oda, the Fountain Room. This and Ocaklı Oda served as antechambers between the Harem and the sultan's own apartments.

A door leads from Çeşmeli Oda into Hünkâr Sofası, the Hall of the Emperor, the largest room in the palace. Divided by a great arch into two unequal sections, the larger section is domed and the smaller, slightly raised, has a balcony above. The upper part of the room – dome, pendentives and arches – has been restored to its original appearance, while the lower part retains the baroque decorations added by Osman III. Hünkâr Sofası was a reception room where the sultan gave entertainments for the women of the Harem, with the musicians playing on the balcony. This splendid chamber is believed to have been commissioned by Murat III, in which case the architect would surely have been Sinan, chief of the imperial architects under Suleyman and his two immediate successors.

A door at the north-east corner of Hünkâr Sofası leads into a small but lavishly tiled antechamber. This in turn leads into the Salon of Murat III, the most splendid room in the palace, dated by an inscription to 1578. Unlike Hünkâr Sofası, it has retained the whole of its original decoration. The walls are sheathed in superb Iznik tiles; the panel of plum blossoms surrounding the elegant bronze chimney-piece is especially noteworthy, as is the calligraphic frieze that extends around the room. Opposite the fireplace there is a three-tiered cascade fountain of carved polychrome marble set in a marble embrasure. The beauty of the decoration, as well as the perfect and harmonious form of the room, identify the salon as a work of Sinan.

Opening off the west side of the salon there is a small chamber known as the Library of Ahmet I, built in 1608–9. This is one of the most delightful rooms in the palace. The library is adorned with finely carved wooden bookshelves and cabinets inlaid with sea-tortoise shell and mother-of-pearl, and its walls are revetted with blue and green tiles almost as beautiful as those in the salon. The library is lit by windows on two sides, affording sweeping views out over the confluence of the Bosphorus and the Golden Horn.

A marble doorway in the south wall of the library leads to an even lovelier chamber, the so-called Dining-Room of Ahmet III, dated 1705. Its walls are panels of lacquered wood decorated with paintings of flowers and fruit. These decorations are characteristic of the Lale Devri, or Tulip Period, when European rococo art and architecture made their first appearance in Istanbul.

Returning through the salon and its anteroom, one comes to a corridor that leads along the north-east end of the Harem. At the beginning of the corridor on the left there are a pair of exceedingly handsome rooms known as the Double Kiosk; these date to c. 1600 and are revetted with the most beautiful Iznik tiles in the palace. The first room has a dome magnificently painted on canvas, while the ceiling of the inner room is flat but also adorned with superb painted designs. The second room has a wonderful brass-gilt fireplace, on each side of which, above, are two of the most gorgeous tile panels in existence.

The colonnaded corridor that runs past the Double Kiosk is called, for some unknown reason, the Consultation Palace of the Jinns. This leads out to an open courtyard known as Gözdeler Taşlığı, the Terrace of the Favourites, which overlooks the lower gardens of the palace. The right side of the terrace is formed by a long wooden building in two storeys that once housed the sultan's favourite women. The building has recently been restored, but its rooms are not yet open to the public.

At the far end of the colonnaded corridor the Golden Road leads off to the right, taking one along the eastern side of the Harem towards its main entryway in the inner palace, Kuşhane Kapısı, the Birdcage Gate. Guided tours of the Harem end at this point, leaving one in the Third Court of the Saray.

5. The ÇINILI KÖŞK, or Tiled Pavilion, stands on a terrace below the west side of TOPKAPI SARAYI, its colonnaded front facing the ARCHAEOLOGICAL MUSEUM. The kiosk is laid out in two almost identical storeys, cruciform in plan with chambers in the arms of the cross. It has a deeply recessed entrance alcove on the main floor entirely revetted in ceramics of various kinds, most of them tile mosaic in turquoise and dark blue. It now serves as a museum of Turkish ceramics, with tiles ranging in date from Selcuk work of the twelfth century to Ottoman tiles of the nineteenth century.

Çinili Köşk

6. FATIH CAMII, the Mosque of the Conqueror, was built during the years 1463–71 by an architect known as Atik ('Old') Sinan, who may have been a Greek named Christodoulos. This was the largest and most extensive mosque complex ever built in the Ottoman Empire, laid out on a vast, nearly square area – about 325 metres on a side – with almost rigid symmetry. The original mosque was completely destroyed by an earthquake on 22 May 1766. Mustafa III immediately undertook its reconstruction, and the present mosque, designed on a wholly different plan, was completed in 1771. The hospital and the caravansarai have disappeared, and all of the other buildings in the külliye were badly damaged in the earthquake. But all of the other structures survive from their restoration by Mustafa III, presumably in their original form.

7. MAHMUT PASHA CAMII was erected in 1462 – the first large mosque to be built in Istanbul after that of Mehmet II himself, FATIH CAMII. Aside from its great age, it is also interesting because it is a very fine example of the so-called Bursa style of mosque architecture.

The mosque is preceded by a porch of five domed bays, in which the original columns have been replaced by octagonal piers. The entryway leads into a narthex, an unusual feature found in only one other mosque in Istanbul, the BEYAZIDIYE. The mosque itself consists of a long rectangular room divided in the middle by an arch, thus

Fatih Camii

forming two square chambers each covered by a dome of equal size. On each side of the hall there is a narrow barrel-vaulted passage that communicates both with the hall and with three small rooms on either side. The side chambers were called tabhanes and were used as hospices by travelling dervishes, a feature found only in early Ottoman mosques.

The tomb of the founder is just behind the mosque. This magnificent türbe is dated by an inscription to 1474, the year Mahmut Pasha was executed by Mehmet II.

8. The KAPALI ÇARŞI, or Covered Bazaar, is probably the largest market of its kind in the world, a small city in itself. According to a survey made in 1976, there are more than 3,000 shops of various kinds, along with storehouses, workshops, stalls, and hans, as well as several restaurants and numerous lunch-counters, cafés and tea-houses, altogether employing more than 20,000 people. The market has expanded since Mehmet II's reign and it has been rebuilt several times after catastrophes, the most recent being an earthquake in 1894 and a fire in 1954. Nevertheless, the plan and structure of the bazaar and its buildings are essentially the same as they were in early Ottoman times.

At first the Kapalı Çarşı seems a veritable labyrinth, but its central area forms a regular grid, with shops selling the same kind of merchandise congregated in their own streets, the names of which come from the various market guilds that originally had their establishments in those places. The grid is centred on the Old Bedesten, one of the original structures surviving from the time of Mehmet II. Then, as now, it was used to house the most precious wares, for it can be securely locked and guarded at night. It is rectangular in plan, covered by fifteen domes in three rows of five each, sorted by four pairs of massive pillars. A short way to the east of the Old Bedesten there is another building of similar type known as the Sandal Bedesten, a lofty hall covered with twenty domes in four rows of five each. The Sandal Bedesten was probably built during the reign of Beyazit II, when the great increase of Ottoman trade and commerce required the expansion of the Kapalı Çarşı.

9. The mosque of EYÜP is approached through a picturesque outer courtyard with two great baroque gateways. Another gateway leads into the inner court, shaded by venerable plane-trees and bordered by an unusually tall and stately colonnade along three sides. The plan of the mosque is an octagon inscribed in a rectangle. The interior is singularly attractive, with its pale honey-coloured stone, its decoration picked out in gold, the elegant chandelier hanging from the centre of the dome, and the magnificent turquoise carpet that covers the entire floor.

The side of the building opposite the mosque is a blank wall, most of it covered with tiles without an overall pattern and of many different periods, some of them of great individual beauty. A door in the wall leads to the vestibule of Eyüp's türbe. The türbe is sumptuously decorated, though with work largely of the baroque era, while the vestibule is revetted with Iznik tiles of the best period.

10. The BEYAZIDIYE was the second great mosque complex to be erected in Istanbul, after that of Mehmet II, FATIH CAMII. The külliye, built in the years 1501–6, consists of the mosque itself along with a medrese, primary school, public kitchen, public bath and several türbes.

Beyazit I Camii is entered through what is perhaps the most charming of all the mosque courtyards in Istanbul. A peristyle of twenty ancient columns – porphyry, verd antique, and Syenitic granite – upholds an arcade with red-and-white or black-and-white marble voussoirs. The pavement is of polychrome marble, and in the centre there is a beautifully decorated şadırvan, or ablution fountain.

An exceptionally fine portal leads into the mosque, which in plan is a greatly simplified and much smaller version of HAGHIA SOPHIA. As there, the great central dome and the semidomes to east and west form a kind of nave, beyond which to north and south are side aisles. The arches supporting the dome spring from four huge rectangular piers standing on the corners of a square. The central area of the building is approximately 40 metres on a side, and the diameter of the dome is about 17 metres. There are no galleries over the aisles, which open wide into the nave, separated only by the piers and a single antique

Beyazit I Camii

granite column between them. At the west a side corridor, divided into domed or vaulted bays and extending considerably beyond the main body of the mosque, creates the effect of a narthex. At each end of the corridor rise the two minarets, their shafts picked out with geometric designs in terracotta; they stand far beyond the main part of the building in an arrangement that is unique and gives a very grand effect. The sultan's loge is to the right of the mimber, supported on columns of very rich and rare marbles.

11. The GALATA MEVLEVIHANE was established *c.* 1492 by Şeyh Mohammed Semai Sultan Divani, a descendant of Mevlana Celaludin Rumi, the great divine and mystic poet who in the thirteenth century founded the religious brotherhood known as the Mevlevi, famous in the West as the 'Whirling Dervishes'. At

the rear of the courtyard is the semahane, the dancing-room of the tekke, an octagonal structure splendidly restored in the 1970s. The semahane and its surrounding chambers now house the Museum of Turkish Court Literature, a form inspired by the mystical poetry of Mevlana. The collection includes manuscripts and calligraphy as well as musical instruments and memorabilia of the Mevlevi dervishes.

12. SELIM I CAMII stands on a high terrace of the Fifth Hill, overlooking the Golden Horn. The mosque, with its great dome and cluster of little domes on either side, is impressive and worthy of the site. The courtyard is one of the most vivid in the city, with its columns of various marbles and granites, the polychrome voussoirs of the arches, the very beautiful tiles of the earliest Iznik period in the lunettes above the

Selim I Camii

windows – turquoise, deep blue, and yellow – and the pretty şadırvan surrounded by tapering cypress trees.

The plan of the mosque interior is very simple: a square room, 24.5 metres on a side, covered by a shallow dome 32.5 metres in height under the crown, with the cornice resting on the outer walls through smooth pendentives. The dome is significantly less than a hemisphere. This gives a very spacious and grand effect, recalling to a certain extent the beautiful shallow dome of the Roman Pantheon. The room itself is vast and empty, but saved from dullness by its perfect proportions and by the exquisite colour of the Iznik tiles in the lunettes of the windows. The border of the ceiling under the loge is an exceptionally beautiful example of the painted and gilded woodwork of the early sixteenth century. The main prayer-room of the mosque is flanked to north and south by annexes, each consisting of a domed cruciform passage giving access to four small domed rooms. These, as in other early mosques elsewhere in the city, served as hospices for travelling dervishes.

CHAPTER 17

1. IBRAHIM PASHA SARAYI was the grandest private residence ever built in the Ottoman Empire – far greater in size than any of the buildings of TOPKAPI SARAYI itself. After Ibrahim Pasha's execution the palace for a time housed the High Court of Justice; later it seems to have been used as a barracks for the Janissaries and also as a prison. After being abandoned it fell into ruins, with its north-west wing demolished in 1939 to make way for a new law-court. Then in 1965 a programme of restoration was begun to save the remainder of the palace, which now houses the Museum of Turkish and Islamic Art.

The surviving part of the palace is a huge structure in two storeys around three sides of a courtyard. The ground floor consists of a series of vaults supported internally by pillars. The second floor on the north and west sides consists of a series of domed cubicles opening off a corridor along the side of the courtyard, while on the south side two large rooms form an ante-chamber to the former audience chamber of the grand vezir, a great hall that on its far end overlooks the HIPPODROME. The works of Turkish and Islamic art in the museum are arranged chronologically on the second floor, beginning in the north wing, while the area on the ground floor of the south wing is used for the ethnological collection, principally objects belonging to the Yürük, the nomadic Türkoman tribespeople of Anatolia.

2. The TÜRBE OF BARBAROSSA is one of the earliest works of Sinan, dated by an inscription over the door to 1541–2. The structure is octagonal with two rows of windows.

The bronze statue of Barbarossa in the park facing the türbe is by the sculptor Zühtü Müridoğlü; it was unveiled in 1946, the fourth centennial of the admiral's death.

3. HASEKI HÜRREM CAMII is Sinan's earliest work in Istanbul. Aside from the mosque, the külliye includes a medrese, an imaret, a hospital and a primary school. All of the buildings are in good repair, with the hospital once again serving its original purpose.

The mosque originally consisted of a small square room covered by a dome on stalactited pendentives, preceded by a porch of five bays that overlapped the building at both ends. It may perhaps have had a certain elegance of form and detail in its original design. But in 1612 a second and identical room was added on the north, requiring the removal of the original north wall and its replacement by a great arch supported on two columns. The mihrab was then moved to the middle of the new extended east wall, so that it stands squeezed behind one of the columns – a distinctly unpleasing arrangement.

4. ŞEHZADE CAMII is surrounded by an outer courtyard wall that encloses the mosque and the other institutions of the külliye, which include a medrese, a hospice, an imaret, a primary school and five türbes, the most beautiful of the tombs being that of Prince Mehmet.

The mosque is preceded by a handsome inner courtyard whose area is equal to that of the building itself, with entryways on all three sides. The courtyard is bordered by a portico with five domed bays on each side, with the voussoirs of the arches in alternating pink and white marble. The two minarets rise from the corners of the building just outside the courtyard wall. The stonework of the minarets is particularly beautiful: notice the elaborate geometrical

Şehzade Camii

sculpture in low relief, the intricate tracery of the şerefes, and the occasional use of terracotta inlay. The minarets are a superb frame for the mosque, with its cluster of domes and semidomes, many of them with fretted cornices and bold ribbing. It was in this mosque that Sinan first adopted the bold expedient of placing colonnaded galleries along the entire length of the north and south façades in order to conceal the buttresses.

The interior is covered by a dome surrounded on all four sides by semidomes. The vast and empty prayer-hall is very unusual among the imperial mosques, for it has not a single column, nor are there any balconies. Nevertheless, the general effect of the interior is of an austere simplicity that is not without charm.

5. ISKELE CAMII is very imposing because of its dominating position high above Iskele Meydanı, and also because of its great double porch, a curious projection of which covers a charming fountain. The interior is perhaps less satisfactory, for the central dome is supported by three instead of the usual two or four semi-domes, which gives the mosque a rather truncated appearance.

The medrese of the külliye is to the north, a pretty building of the rectangular type, now used as a clinic. The primary school is behind the mosque, built on sharply rising ground so that it has very picturesque supporting arches; it has recently been restored and is now a children's library. At the foot of the steps below the mosque terrace is the very handsome Fountain of Ahmet III, dated 1726.

6. MIHRIMAH CAMII stands on the peak of the Sixth Hill, just inside the THEODOSIAN WALLS, south of the Edirne Gate. Besides the mosque, the külliye includes a medrese, a primary school, a double hamam, two türbes and a long row of shops in the substructure of the terrace on which the complex was built.

The mosque is strong and dominant, as befits its position on the highest point in the old city. The square of the dome base with its multi-windowed tympana, identical on all sides, is given solidity and boldness by the four great weight-towers at the corners, prolongations of the piers that support the dome arches. Above this square rises the dome itself on a circular drum pierced by windows. The mosque is preceded by a great courtyard, three of its sides formed by the porticoes and cells of the medrese, with an attractive şadırvan in the centre. Most of the fourth side is taken up by the mosque porch, which has seven domed bays supported by eight marble and granite columns.

The central area of the interior is square, covered by a great dome 20 metres in diameter and 32 metres high under the crown, resting on smooth pendentives. High triple arcades to north and south open into

Mihrimah Camii

side aisles with galleries above; each of these has three domed bays, reaching only to the springing of the dome arches. The tympana of all four dome arches are filled with three rows of windows, flooding the mosque with light. The mimber is a fine original work of white marble perforated like an iron grille. The voussoirs of the gallery arches are fretted polychrome of verd antique and Proconnesian marble.

7. The SÜLEYMANIYE is the second largest imperial mosque complex in the city, surpassed in size but not in grandeur by the külliye of FATIH CAMII. The mosque stands in the centre of a vast outer courtyard surrounded on three sides by a wall with grilled windows. On the north side, where the land slopes sharply down to the Golden Horn, the courtyard is supported by an elaborate vaulted substructure. Around this courtyard on three sides the other buildings of the külliye are arranged with as much symmetry as the site would permit. These include four medreses and their preparatory school, a school for reading the Koran, a school of Sacred Tradition, a primary school, a medical school, a hospital with an insane asylum, a public kitchen, a caravansarai, a market street, a public bath, the türbes of Süleyman and Roxelana, and the tomb of Sinan, the architect of the Süleymaniye.

The mosque is preceded by a

Süleymaniye Camii

porticoed courtyard of exceptional grandeur, with columns of the richest porphyry and granite. At the four corners of the courtyard rise four great minarets.

The vast prayer-room of the mosque is almost square in plan, measuring 58.5 by 57.5 metres, surmounted by a dome 27.5 metres in diameter, with its crown 47 metres above the floor. The dome is flanked to east and west by semidomes and to north and south by arches with tympana filled with windows. The dome arches rise from four irregularly shaped piers. Between the piers, to the north and south, triple arcades on two enormous porphyry monoliths support the tympana of the arches. There are no galleries here,

nor can there really be said to be aisles, since the great porphyry columns are so high and so far apart that they do not in any way form a barrier between the central area and the walls. The general effect of the interior is of a severely simple grandeur. Only the east wall is enlivened by some touches of colour; here the lovely stained-glass windows are by the glazier known as Sarhoş ('the Drunkard') Ibrahim. The tiles, used with great restraint, are the earliest known examples of the new technique of the Iznik kilns, deep blue and red on a pure white ground. The mihrab and mimber in Proconnesian marble are of great simplicity and distinction, as is also the woodwork, inlaid with ivory and mother-of-pearl, of the doors, the window-shutters and the preacher's chair. Throughout the building the inscriptions are by the most famous of Ottoman calligraphers, Ahmet Karahisarı, and his pupil Hasan Çelebi.

The tombs of Süleyman and his wife Roxelana are in the walled garden behind the mosque; his türbe is open to the public, while hers is not. Süleyman's türbe is octagonal in form, surrounded by a pretty porch on columns. It has a double dome, with the inner cupola supported by columns in the interior. The inner dome preserves its gorgeous painting in wine-red, black and gold. The walls of the interior are covered with Iznik tiles, twice as many in this small room as in all the vastness of the mosque itself. Catafalques cover the graves of Süleyman and his daughter Mihrimah, as well as those of Süleyman II and Ahmet II.

8. HASEKI HÜRREM HAMAMI was built by Sinan in 1556. After having long been closed, it has recently been restored and is now used to display Turkish carpets. It is thus the only Ottoman hamam in the city where one can easily examine the entire structure, both the men's and women's baths, which in this case are virtually identical, with their entrances at opposite ends of the building.

Ordinarily, a hamam has three distinct sections. The first is the camekan, which is used as a reception and dressing-room. Next comes the soğukluk, a chamber of intermediate temperature, which serves as an anteroom to the bath. Finally, there is the hararet, or steam-room. In Turkish baths like this one, built for Roxelana, the first of these areas, the camekan, is the most monumental. Here, as typically, it is a large square room covered by a dome, with a fountain pool in the centre and around the periphery a gallery with private changing-booths. The soğukluk is almost always a mere passageway, which usually contains

The Türbe of Süleyman

Haseki Hürrem Hamami

the lavatories; here it is a narrow transverse corridor with a small dome at the centre and vaults on either side. The hararet is usually the most elaborate chamber. Here, where the plan is typical, the hararet is a domed cruciform area with cubicles for private bathing in the diagonals. In the centre there is a large hexagonal marble platform, the göbek taşı, or belly-stone, which is heated from the subterranean kulhane, or furnace room. The patrons lie on the belly-stone to sweat and be massaged before bathing in one of the private cubicles.

9. RÜSTEM PASHA CAMII was erected by Sinan in 1561 in the market quarter of Eminönü down by the Golden Horn, built on a high terrace over an interesting complex of vaulted shops. Interior flights of steps lead up from the corners of the platform to a spacious and beautiful courtyard, unique in the city. The mosque is preceded by a curious double porch. The inner part of the portico is the usual type of porch consisting of five domed bays, and then, projecting from this, a deep and low-slung penthouse roof, its outer edge resting on a colonnade.

The plan of the mosque is an octagon inscribed in a rectangle. The dome is flanked by four small semi-

Rüstem Pasha Camii

365

domes in the diagonals of the building. The arches of the dome spring from four octagonal pillars, two on the north, two on the south, and from piers projecting from the east and west walls. To north and south there are galleries supported by pillars and by small marble columns between them.

The mosque is especially famous for the superb tiles that almost cover the walls, not only on the interior, including the galleries, but also on the façade of the porch. Like all of the great Turkish tiles, those of Rüstem Pasha came from the kilns of Iznik in its greatest era, showing the tomato red or 'Armenian bole' which is characteristic of that period. These exquisite tiles, in a wide variety of floral and geometric designs, cover not only the walls, but also the columns, the mihrab and the mimber. Altogether they make this one of the most beautiful and striking mosque interiors in the city.

CHAPTER 18

1. SOKOLLU MEHMET PASHA CAMII, one of the most beautiful of the vezirial mosques of Sinan, was built in 1571–2 below the HIPPO-DROME on the First Hill. The mosque is preceded by a courtyard whose periphery is formed by the cells of a medrese, with the dershane, or lecture hall, built above a stairway that enters the cloister from the street below. The seven-bayed porch of the

Sokollu Mehmet Pasha Camii

mosque forms the fourth side of the court, the lunettes in its windows decorated with striking inscriptions in blue and white faience.

The plan of the mosque is a hexagon inscribed in an almost square rectangle, its central area covered by a dome, balanced at the corners by four small semidomes. There are no side aisles, but around three sides there is a low gallery supported on slender marble columns with typical Ottoman lozenge capitals. The polychrome of the arches, with voussoirs of alternate red and green marble, is characteristic of the period. The tile decoration of the mosque has been used with singularly charming effect. Only selected areas of the walls have been sheathed in tiles: the pendentives below the dome, a frieze of floral design, and the exquisite central section of the east wall. The latter panel frames the mihrab with tiles decorated in vine and floral motifs in turquoise on a background of pale green, interspersed with panels of fine calligraphy with white letters on a deep-blue field. The elegant marble mimber is surmounted by a tall conical cap, sheathed in the same turquoise tiles that frame the mihrab. Above the mihrab the framed arch in the east wall is pierced by elegant stained-glass windows, whose bright spectrum of warm colours complements the cool tones of the faience flowers below. Above the entrance portal a small specimen of the wonderful painted decoration of the classical period can be seen. It consists of very elaborate arabesque designs in rich and varied colours.

2. The TÜRBE OF SELIM II is the earliest of the imperial Ottoman tombs in the garden south of HAGHIA SOPHIA, completed in 1577. Superb Iznik tiles adorn both the entrance façade and the whole of the interior. The building is square, with an outer dome resting directly on the exterior walls, while a circlet of columns supports the inner dome. Selim II is buried here beside his wife Nurubanu. Arrayed around them are tiny coffins covering the graves of five of Selim's sons, three of his daughters, and thirty-two children of his son and successor, Murat III.

3. KILIÇ ALI PASHA CAMII was built in 1580–81 on the European shore of the Bosphorus just beyond Galata. The külliye includes the great mosque, a medrese, a hamam and the türbe of the founder, the admiral Kılıç Ali Pasha. The mosque is preceded by a very picturesque double porch. The outer porch has a deeply sloping penthouse roof, supported by twelve columns on the west façade and three on each side, all with lozenge capitals. The inner porch is of the usual type: five domed bays supported by columns capped with stalactite capitals.

The central area of the mosque interior is covered by a great dome, supported by semidomes to east and west. The main area is separated from the side aisles by the piers that support the dome and by a pair of columns between them to north and south. The mihrab is in a square projecting apse, where there are some fine Iznik tiles of the best period. At the west end there is a kind of pseudo-narthex of five cross-vaulted bays separated from the central area by four rectangular pillars.

4. ŞEMSI AHMET PASHA CAMII was built in 1580–81 in a very picturesque position at the mouth of the Bosphorus in Üsküdar. The founder was the vezir Şemsi Ahmet Pasha, who traced his descent to the imperial Selcuk dynasty. The mosque is of the simplest type, a square room covered by a dome with conches as squinches. Şemsi Pasha's türbe opens into the mosque itself, from which it is divided by a green grille, a most unusual and pretty feature. An elegant medrese forms two sides of the courtyard, while the third side consists of a wall with grilled windows opening directly on to the Bosphorus quay.

5. ATIK VALIDE CAMII was erected by Sinan in 1583 on the hill above Üsküdar. The founder was the valide sultan Nurubanu, wife of Selim II and mother of Murat III. Besides the great mosque, the külliye consists of a medrese, a hospital, an imaret, a school for reading the Koran, a caravansarai and a hamam, all of which are still standing.

The mosque courtyard is one of the most beautiful in the city, a grandly proportioned cloister with domed porticoes supported on marble columns; in the centre are the şadırvan and a copse of ancient plane-trees and cypresses. The mosque is entered through an elaborate double porch, the outer one with a penthouse roof, the inner domed and with handsome tiled inscriptions over the windows.

The prayer-hall is a wide rectangular room with a central dome supported by a hexagonal arrangement of pillars and columns; to the north and south there are side aisles, each with two domed bays. There are galleries around three sides of the room, and the wooden ceilings under some of them preserve that rich painting typical of the period, with floral and arabesque designs in black, red and gold. The mihrab is in a square projecting apse entirely revetted in magnificent tiles of the best Iznik period; notice also the window-frames of deep-red conglomerate marble with shutters richly inlaid with mother-of-pearl. The mihrab and mimber are fine works in carved marble.

6. RAMAZAN EFENDI CAMII was Sinan's last mosque, built in 1586 on the Seventh Hill in Samatya. The founder was a court official named Hoca Hüsrev, but the mosque is usually called Ramazan Efendi Camii, after the first şeyh (sheikh) of the dervish tekke which was part of the original foundation. The mosque is of the simplest type, a small rectangular room with a wooden roof and porch. It is believed that it was originally covered by a wooden dome, and that it had a porch with three domed bays supported by four marble columns. The present porch and flat wooden ceiling are botched restorations after an earthquake. The minaret is an elegant structure both in proportion and detail, while the small şadırvan in the courtyard is exquisitely carved. The great fame of the mosque comes from the magnificent panels of faience with which it is adorned. These are from the Iznik kilns at the height of their artistic production, and are thus some of the finest tiles in existence; the borders of tomato red are especially celebrated.

7. The TÜRBE OF MURAT III was completed in 1599. It is hexagonal in plan, with a double dome, and it is revetted with Iznik tiles comparable to those in the TÜRBE OF SELIM II. Murat is buried here beside his wife Safiye, and around them are the coffins of four of his concubines, twenty-three of his sons, and twenty-five of his daughters. Built up against Murat's tomb is the little Tomb of the Princes, which contains the catafalques of five infant sons of Murat IV, all of whom died of the plague in 1640.

8. The TÜRBE OF MEHMET III was completed in 1607. The türbe is octagonal in plan, with a double dome, and it too is revetted with superb Iznik tiles. Mehmet is buried here beside his wife Handan, and around them are the coffins of nine of his children. The türbe also contains the graves of sixteen daughters of Murat III, all of whom died of the plague in 1598.

9. SULTAN AHMET I CAMII is thought by many to have the most splendid exterior of the imperial mosques of Istanbul, with its graceful cascade of domes and semi-domes, and its six slender minarets rising from the corners of the building and its forecourt.

The courtyard is as large as the

Sultan Ahmet I Camii

mosque itself, with monumental entryways at each of the three sides. The courtyard is in the classic style, bordered by a peristyle, or peripheral colonnade, of twenty-six columns forming a portico covered by thirty small domes. At the centre of the courtyard there is a handsome octagonal şadırvan, which now only serves a decorative purpose. The ablutions are today performed at water taps beneath the graceful arcade which forms part of the north and south walls of the courtyard. The four minarets at the corners of the mosque each have three şerefes, while the other two have two each. The minarets are fluted and the şerefes have sculptured stalactite parapets.

The interior of the mosque is 51 metres long and 53 metres wide, covered by a dome 23.5 metres in diameter, resting on four pointed arches and four pendentives, with its crown 43 metres above the floor. The dome is supported on all four sides by semidomes, each of which is flanked by smaller semidomes at the corners. The main support for the great dome comes from four colossal free-standing columns, 5 metres in diameter, divided in the middle by a band and ribbed above and below with convex flutes.

The mosque is flooded with light from its 250 windows. These were once filled with Turkish stained-glass of the early seventeenth century. The painted arabesques in the domes and the upper parts of the building are modern works, feeble in design and crude in colouring. Here the predominant colour is an overly bright blue, from which the building derives its popular name of the Blue Mosque. Iznik tiles of the best period are used to decorate the lower part of the walls, especially in the galleries. The magnificent floral designs display the traditional lily, carnation, tulip and rose motifs, as well as cypresses and other trees; these are all in exquisite colours, subtle blues and greens predominating. The mihrab and mimber, of white Proconnesian marble, are fine examples of the carved stonework of the early seventeenth century. The woodwork of the doors and window-shutters of the mosque are also notable, encrusted as they are with ivory, mother-of-pearl and sea-tortoise shell. Under the sultan's loge, which is in the upper gallery to the left of the mihrab, the wooden ceiling is painted with floral and geometrical arabesques in that exquisite early style in rich and gorgeous colours, of which so few examples remain.

Sultan Ahmet's külliye was extensive, including, besides the mosque, a medrese, a hospital, a caravansarai, an imaret, a primary school, a market and a türbe. The hospital, caravansarai and market were destroyed in the nineteenth century, and the imaret is now incorporated into the modern buildings at the south end of the HIPPODROME. The primary school is elevated above the north wall of the outer precinct. The medrese is just outside the precinct wall towards the north-west, near the large square türbe, which has recently been restored and opened to the public. Ahmet I is buried here, along with his wife Kösem and three of his sons, Osman II, Murat IV and Beyazit.

A ramp at the north-east corner of the mosque leads up to the hünkâr kasrı, the imperial pavilion, a suite of rooms used by the sultan whenever he came here for services, with an internal passageway leading to the royal loge within the mosque. The hünkâr kasrı is now used to house the Kilim Museum, a remarkable collection of Turkish carpets that includes several that were made for the sultan's use.

Beneath the east end of the mosque there are huge vaulted chambers that once served as storerooms and stables; these have been restored to serve as a Rug Museum, exhibiting works ranging from the fifteenth century to the eighteenth, including rare and beautiful examples.

CHAPTER 19

1. AHI ÇELEBI CAMII stands beside the Golden Horn just above the Galata Bridge, one of the few remnants of the old quarter known as Zindan Kapı, the Prison Gate. The quarter takes its name from the ancient tower close to the mosque, which served as a prison in both Byzantine and Ottoman times. The

mosque was founded in the early sixteenth century by Ahi Çelebi ibni Kemal, chief physician at the hospital of Fatih's külliye. The mosque was restored by Sinan, but it is now abandoned and beginning to deteriorate.

2 ALAY KÖŞKÜ, the Kiosk of the Processions, is a large polygonal gazebo set into the outer defence wall of TOPKAPI SARAYI opposite the Sublime Porte. The sultans used the kiosk to review parades and also to keep an eye on those entering and leaving the Sublime Porte, the head-quarters of the grand vezir. The present kiosk dates only from 1819, when it was rebuilt by Mahmut II, but there has been a Kiosk of the Processions here since much earlier times, probably from the reign of Fatih.

CHAPTER 20

1. YENI CAMI was completed in 1663 by the architect Mustafa Ağa. The mosque is preceded by a courtyard as large as the mosque itself, bordered by a portico supported by a peristyle of twenty columns, with a pretty octagonal şadırvan in the centre. The two minarets rise from the corners of the building outside the courtyard wall, each of them having three şerefes adorned with superb stalactite carvings. The north and south façades of the building have two storeys of porticoed galleries. At the north-east corner of

Yeni Cami

the building is the hünkâr kasrı, which is approached by a ramp that passes over the street behind the mosque in a great arch.

The floor plan of the mosque is a square 41 metres on a side. The central area is covered by a great dome supported by semidomes on all four sides. The central area of the interior is defined by the four huge piers that are the main support of the dome. Four great arches rise between the piers, and between them four squinches make the transition to the circular cornice of the dome, which has a diameter of 17.5 metres, its crown 36 metres above the floor. A colonnade of slender marble columns supports the gallery, which has a fine marble parapet. The royal loge is at the north-east corner of the gallery.

The original külliye of Turhan Hadice included the mosque, a medrese, a hospital, a primary school, a hamam, two fountains, a türbe and the Egyptian Market. The hospital, the primary school and the hamam have vanished, but the other structures survive. The türbe is the domed octagonal building at the east end of the garden beside Yeni Cami. Buried there with Turhan Hadice are her son Mehmet IV, as well as five later sultans: Mustafa II, Ahmet III, Mahmut I, Osman II and Murat V.

2. MISIR ÇARŞISI, the SPICE BAZAAR, is the handsome L-shaped building that borders two sides of the park beside YENI CAMI. It is called Mısır Çarşısı, or the Egyptian Market, because it was endowed with the Cairo imposts, while its English name comes from the fact that it was famous for its spices and medicinal herbs. There are eighty-eight vaulted shops in all, along with a tiny mosque at the inner corner of the L, and a restaurant – Pandelis –

in the chambers above the main gateway.

3. YENI VALIDE CAMII was built in the years 1708–10, during the very last phase of the classical period, and just before the baroque influence had come to enliven it. In plan the mosque is a variant of the octagon-in-the-square theme, decorated with inferior tiles of later date. The mektep is built over the main gate of the mosque courtyard. Outside the gate stands the large imaret, with a çeşme or fountain at the corner; this is of later date than the rest of the külliye and is fully in the baroque style. At the corner is the valide sultan's handsome open türbe, looking like a large aviary, and next to it a grand sebil.

CHAPTER 21

1. The CAĞALOĞLU HAMAMI, built in 1741, is the most famous and beautiful Turkish bath in Istanbul. The layout of the men's section is conventional, in that the bathers pass from the camekan through the rather small soğukluk into the hararet, with all three chambers laid out in a straight line. But in the women's baths the camekan is not in line with the other two chambers but set off to one side, with one of its corners joining a corner of the soğukluk. As in most Turkish baths, the most elaborate chamber is the hararet, which here has the same form in both the men's and women's sections. This is an open cruciform chamber, with its central dome supported by a circlet of columns and with domed side chambers in the arms of the cross.

2. NURUOSMANIYE CAMII stands on the Third Hill just to the east of the KAPALI ÇARŞI. The mosque was begun in 1748 by Mahmut I and completed in 1755 by Osman III. The architect seems to have been a Greek by the name of Simeon, who had probably studied in the West, for the mosque is the first large Ottoman building to exemplify the

Nuruosmaniye Camii

new baroque architectural style then prevalent in western Europe.

The mosque is erected on a low terrace to which irregularly placed flights of steps give access. It is preceded on the west by a five-bayed porch, enclosed by a very unusual courtyard with nine domed bays arranged in a semicircle. The two minarets rise from outside the ends of the porch. At the north-east corner of the mosque an oddly-shaped ramp supported on wide circular arches leads to the sultan's loge.

The mosque interior is essentially a square room covered by a large dome resting on four circular arches in the walls. The form of the dome arches is strongly emphasized, particularly on the exterior, where the great wheel-shaped arcs form the most characteristic feature of the building. There are a semicircular apse for the mihrab at the centre of the east wall and side chambers at the north-east and south-east corners. The sultan's loge, screened off by a gilded grille, is in the gallery above the north-east corner.

3. AYAZMA CAMII was built in 1760–61 by Mustafa III, who dedicated it to his mother, Rabia Gülnus. This is one of the more successful of the baroque mosques, especially on the exterior. A handsome entrance portal opens on to a courtyard from which a pretty flight of semicircular steps leads up to the mosque porch; on the left is a large cistern and

beyond, an elaborate two-storeyed colonnade gives access to the imperial loge. The upper structure is also diversified with little domes and turrets, and many windows give light to the interior.

4. LALELI CAMII, the Mosque of the Lily, was built in the years 1759–63. Besides the mosque, the külliye originally included an imaret, which has since disappeared, and a caravansarai known as the Büyuk Taş Hanı, which is still in use. It also includes the türbe of Mustafa II, who is buried there along with his son Selim III.

The plan of the mosque interior is an octagon inscribed in a rectangle. All but the west pair of supporting columns are engaged in the walls; those at the west support a gallery along the west wall. All the walls are revetted in variegated marbles, which give a gay if somewhat gaudy effect. The west wall of the gallery has medallions of *opus sectile* which incorporate not only rare marbles but also semi-precious stones such as onyx, jasper and lapis lazuli. A rectangular apse contains the mihrab, which is made of sumptuous marbles. The mimber is fashioned from the same materials, while the Kuran kursu, from which the imam reads the Koran, is a rich work of carved wood heavily inlaid with mother-of-pearl.

5. The MIHRIŞAH KÜLLIYESI includes the türbe of the foundress together with an imaret and a splendid sebil. The türbe is round, but the

façade undulates so as to transform it into a polygon, the various faces being separated by slender columns of dark-grey marble.

CHAPTER 22

1. NUSRETIYE CAMII was built by Kirkor Balyan, the first of a family of Armenian architects who served the sultans through most of the nineteenth century. Balyan had studied in Paris, and his mosque shows a curious blend of baroque and French Empire motifs, highly un-Turkish, but not without charm. Here he abandoned the traditional arrangement of a monumental courtyard and substituted an elaborate series of palace-like apartments on two storeys; these form the western façade of the building, a feature that became a characteristic of all the

Balyan mosques. One particularly notices the bulbous weight towers, projections of the dome piers, the jutting dome arches, and the slender minarets. Other distinctive features are the ornate bronze grilles on the exterior, and in the interior the abundance of marble garlands in the French Empire style, and the elegant mimber, a marvellous baroque creation.

2. DOLMABAHÇE SARAYI is by far the most imposing monument on the European shore of the lower Bosphorus, its seaside façade of white marble measuring 248 metres, and its gardens and auxiliary buildings extending along a quay some 600 metres in length.

The palace was built by Karabet Balyan (son of Kirkor Balyan) and his son Nikoğos. It was completed in

Nusretiye Camii

Dolmabahçe Sarayı

1853, whereupon the sultan and his household moved in, abandoning Topkapı Sarayı. After the end of the Ottoman Empire, Dolmabahçe served as a presidential residence for Atatürk, who died here on 10 November 1938. The palace has since been restored and is now a museum.

The core of the palace is a great imperial hall flanked by two main wings containing the state rooms, with the selamlık, or male quarters, on the south side and the harem on the north. The apartment of the valide sultan is in a separate wing linked to the sultan's harem through the apartment of the crown prince. In addition, there was another harem for the women of the other princes, and still another residence at the north-west corner of the palace for the chief black eunuch. All in all, there was a total of 285 rooms, including 43 large salons and 6 hamams.

The palace interior was the work of the French decorator Sechan, designer of the Paris Opera, and thus the décor of Dolmabahçe is strongly reminiscent of French palaces of a somewhat earlier period. A number of European artists were commissioned to do paintings for Dolmabahçe, including Boulanger, Gérôme, Fromentin, Ayvazovski and Zonaro, whose works still hang in the palace or in the Exhibition Hall, which has a separate entrance off the coast road. The world's largest chandelier hangs in the State Room, comprising four and a half tonnes of Bohemian glass with 750 lights. A great showpiece is the ornate stairway that leads up from the Salon of the Ambassadors, its balusters made of Baccarat crystal and its upper landing framed with monoliths of variegated marble. Two-thirds of the palace is taken up with the Harem, the most notable chambers of which are the valide sultan's apartment; the

Mavi (Blue) Salon, the Pembe (Pink) Salon, the School Room, the apartment of Abdül Aziz, and Atatürk's bedroom.

3. ÇIRAĞAN SARAYI was begun by Abdül Mecit I and completed in 1874 by his successor, Abdül Aziz, who died there on 4 June 1876. Murat V was confined to Çırağan after he was deposed in 1876, and he died there on 29 August 1904. Çırağan served as the seat of the Second Turkish Parliament from October 1909 until 19 January 1910, when the palace was destroyed by fire. The structure has recently been rebuilt as a luxury hotel, the Çırağan Palace.

4. YILDIZ SARAYI first began to take form during the time of Mahmut II, with the present buildings ranging in date from his reign through that of Abdül Hamit II, who preferred to live here rather than at the DOLMABAHÇE SARAYI. The various buildings and pavilions of Yıldız Sarayı have been restored in recent years and most of them are open to the public, most notably Malta Köşkü, Çadır Koşkü, Lale Sera (the Tulip Conservatory), and Yeşil Sera (the Green Conservatory). The most palatial of the surviving buildings at Yıldız Sarayı is Şale Köşkü, so called because of its resemblance to a Swiss chalet.

5. KÜÇÜKSU KASRI is named for the stream that flows into the Bosphorus just beside the palace, one of the two little rivers that together are known as the Sweet Waters of Asia. This little rococo palace, erected on the site of several imperial pavilions constructed in succession by earlier sultans, was built in 1856–7 by Nikoğos Balyan. Thenceforth it was used by the sultans whenever they and their entourage came to enjoy a holiday at the Sweet Waters of Asia, which in late Ottoman times was a favourite resort for the Ottoman *beau monde*. The palace has recently been restored and is now open as a museum. Just north of the palace on the seashore is the baroque fountain of the valide sultan Mihrişah, mother of Selim III, built in 1796.

6. BEYLERBEY SARAYI was built in 1861–5 by Sarkis Balyan, brother of Nikoğos Balyan. It was used mostly as a summer residence and also for the use of visiting royalty. The deposed Abdül Hamit II lived out his last years in Beylerbey, dying here on 10 February 1918. The palace has been restored and is now a museum.

The palace is divided into the usual selamlık and harem. The building is in three storeys, although the two upper floors are visible only along the Bosphorus façade. The ground floor houses the kitchens and the other service departments of the palace; the state rooms and imperial apartments are on the two upper floors, a total of twenty-six elegantly appointed chambers, including six grand salons, with a magnificent winding staircase leading upwards from the reception hall that divides the selamlık from the harem. The palace is decorated with murals and framed paintings by European artists, most notably Ayvazovski.

7. PERTEVNIYAL VALIDE CAMII was built in 1871 for Pertevniyal Valide Sultan, mother of Sultan Abdül Aziz. The mosque was designed by Hagop and Sarkis Balyan, who combined elements from Moorish and Turkish, Gothic, Renaissance and French Empire styles in a garish rococo hotchpotch. The white marble türbe of Pertevniyal stands behind her mosque.

CHAPTER 23

1. The TÜRBE OF MAHMUT II stands on the north side of Divan Yolu at its intersection with Babıali Caddesi. The türbe was completed in 1840, the year after the death of Mahmut II, who is buried there along with his son Abdül Aziz and his grandson Abdül Hamit II. The tomb is in the French Empire style.

CHAPTER 24

1. The MUSEUM OF THE ANCIENT NEAR EAST is housed in the former Institute of Fine Arts, erected in 1883. The collections include antiquities from the ancient Egyptian, Sumerian, Akkadian, Babylonian, Hittite, Urartian, Aramaic and Assyrian civilizations, as well as unique objects from Arabia and Nabatea in the pre-Islamic period.

2. The MILITARY MUSEUM is in Harbiye, just beyond the Hilton Hotel. The museum has an interesting collection of antiquities from all periods of Ottoman history as well as items concerning the Republic of Turkey. The array of cannon outside the museum includes many that were captured by the Ottomans in their campaigns in Europe.

3. The NAVAL MUSEUM is on the Bosphorus shore in Beşiktaş. The museum has exhibits associated with the naval history of the Ottoman Empire and modern Turkey, as well as a unique collection of pazar caiques, the beautiful boats in which the sultan was rowed to his summer palaces along the Bosphorus and the Golden Horn. The most famous exhibit in the museum is a map made by the sixteenth-century Turkish mariner Piri Reis, showing the Atlantic coast of North America.

4. The SADBERK HANIM MUSEUM is housed in an old yalı on the Bosphorus shore road in Sarıyer. The museum was founded by the industrialist Vehbi Koç in memory of his wife, Sadberk Hanım. The collections include works from the prehistoric civilizations of Anatolia as well as the Graeco-Roman, Byzantine, Selcuk and Ottoman eras.

5. BOĞAZIÇI KÖPRÜSÜ is the seventh longest suspension bridge in the world. Its span is 1,074 metres in length between the two great piers on the opposing continental shores,

with its roadway 64 metres above the Bosphorus at the middle of the span.

6. FATIH SULTAN MEHMET KÖPRÜSÜ is the sixth longest suspension bridge in the world, the span between its two piers measuring 1,090 metres. The bridge presents a stirring sight for those sailing through the Narrows of the Bosphorus, flanked as it is by the towers of RUMELI HISARI and ANADOLU HISARI, the Castles of Europe and Asia.

Fatih Sultan Mehmet Köprüsü

APPENDICES

Glossary

The following are some Turkish words and technical terms in architecture and archaeology that are used frequently in the text. Turkish words enclosed in parentheses are the form that they take when they are modified by a preceding noun; e.g. Yeni Cami = the New Mosque, whereas Sultan Ahmet Camii = the Mosque of Sultan Ahmet.

antae: projecting side walls; columns *in antis* are between these walls
atrium: the court of a Roman house or basilica
ayazma: a holy well or spring
bedesten: a multi-domed building, usually in the centre of a Turkish market, where valuable goods are stored and sold
bema: the elevated area containing the altar and the seats of the clergy
beylik: a Türkoman principality
bulvar (*bulvarı*): boulevard
büyük: big
cadde (*caddesi*): avenue
camekan: the reception or dressing-room of a Turkish bath
cami (*camii*): mosque
caravansarai: a Turkish inn for travellers
çarşı (*çarşısı*): market or bazaar
çeşme (*çeşmesi*): a Turkish fountain
conch: the semidome of an apse
darülhadis: a college of advanced studies in the religious law of Islam
darülkura: a school for learning the Koran
darüşşifa: an Ottoman hospital
dershane: the lecture hall of an Islamic school of theology
devşirme: the periodic levy of Christian youths inducted into the Ottoman army and converted to Islam

entablature: the superstructure carried by a colonnade, comprising the architrave, frieze and cornice; also called the *epistyle*
epistyle: see *entablature*
eski: old
exedra (pl. *exedrae*): a semicircular niche
exonarthex: the outer vestibule of a Greek church
eyvan: a vaulted alcove open at outer end
fetva: a legal opinion in Islamic law
frieze: the middle element of an entablature, often with reliefs
Gazi: Warrior for the Faith
hamam (*hamamı*): a Turkish bath
han (*hanı*): a Turkish commercial building, sometimes a *caravansarai*
hararet: the steam-room of a public bath
harem: the women's quarters of a Turkish home or palace
haseki: the favourite woman of the sultan
hisar (*hisarı*): castle or fortress
hücre: a student's cell in a medrese
hünkâr kasrı: a royal pavilion attached to an imperial mosque
hünkâr mahfili: a royal loge in a mosque
imam: the cleric who presides over public prayers in a mosque
imaret: the public kitchen in an Ottoman mosque complex
iskele (*iskelesi*): quay
kadın: woman, the wife of a sultan
kale (*kalesi*): castle or fortress
kapı (*kapısı*): gate or door
kapıcı: a gateman or guard
kible: the direction of Mecca
kilise (*kilisesi*): church
köprü (*köprüsü*): bridge
köşk (*köşkü*): a Turkish kiosk or pavilion
köy (*köyü*): a village
küçük: little
kule (*kulesi*): tower
külliye (*külliyesi*): an Ottoman religious complex, usually including a
 mosque and all of its associated pious and philanthropic foundations
kursu or *Kuran kursu*: the throne on which the imam sits when he is reading
 the Koran to the congregation
kütüphane (*kütüphanesi*): a Turkish library
liman (*limanı*): harbour
mahalle (*mahallesi*): a local neighbourhood or quarter in a Turkish city
medrese (*medresesi*): an Islamic school of theology

mektep (*mektebi*): an Ottoman primary school, also called *sibyan mektebi*

mescit (*mescidi*): a small mosque

meydan (*meydanı*): a village square or town centre

mihrab: the niche in a mosque indicating the direction of Mecca

mimber: the pulpit in a mosque

müezzin: the cleric who chants the responses to the prayers of the imam in a mosque and gives the call to prayer from the minaret

müezzin mahfili: the raised platform from which the müezzins chant their responses to the prayers of the imam

narthex: the inner vestibule of a Greek church

nymphaeum: a monumental fountain or a reservoir; also in Byzantine Constantinople an edifice in which weddings were celebrated

oda (*odası*): room or chamber

opus Alexandrinium: a mosaic in which geometrical patterns are found in combination with large circular slabs of coloured marbles

opus sectile: a mosaic in which geometrical patterns are formed with straight lines

parecclesion: a side chamber in a Greek church, often used as a funerary chapel

pazar (*pazarı*): bazaar or market

pendentive: the triangular spherical surface between the circular cornice of a dome and the four arches beneath it

portico: a colonnaded space, with a roof supported on at least one side with columns; also called a *stoa*

propylon (pl. *propylaea*): a monumental gateway

revetment: the facing on a wall, usually to provide a smoother or more decorative surface

şadırvan: a mosque fountain for ritual ablutions

saray (*sarayı*): a Turkish palace

sebil: an Ottoman fountain or fountain-house

selamlık: the male quarters of an Ottoman home or palace

selsebil: an Ottoman cascade fountain

şerefe: the balcony of a minaret

Şeriat: the Sacred Law in Islam

şeyhülislam: the head of the Islamic religious hierarchy

soğukluk: the chamber of intermediate temperature in a Turkish bath

sokak (*sokağı*): street

squinch: a small arch or bracket across each angle of a polygonal structure to support it over a square or polygonal base

stoa: see *portico*

synthronon: tiers of seats for the clergy in the apse of a church *tabhane*: a hospice for travelling dervishes

tekke: a dervish monastery

timarhane: an Ottoman insane asylum

tip medrese: an Ottoman medical school

trabeated: arranged with beams and lintels rather than arches

türbe (türbesi): an Ottoman mausoleum

tympanum: the wall that fills in an arch

Ulema: the Islamic religious hierarchy

valide sultan: the mother of a reigning sultan

verd antique: a compact variety of serpentine used as a marble, often variegated with veins of calcite or magnesium carbonates, iron oxides, etc., the prevailing colour being green

voussoirs: the truncated wedge-shaped blocks forming an arch

yalı: a Turkish mansion on the Bosphorus

yeni: new

yol (yolu): road

Emperors and Sultans

BYZANTINE EMPERORS

Constantine the Great, 324–37
Constantius, 337–61
Julian, 361–3
Jovian, 363–4
Valens, 364–78
Theodosius I, 379–95
Arcadius, 395–408
Theodosius II, 408–50
Marcian, 450–57
Leo I, 457–74
Leo II, 474
Zeno, 474–91
Anastasius I, 491–518
Justin I, 518–27
Justinian I, 527–65
Justin II, 565–78
Tiberius II, 578–82
Maurice, 582–602
Phocas, 602–10
Heraclius, 610–41
Constantine II, 641
Heraclonas, 641
Constantine III, 641–68
Constantine IV, 668–85
Justinian II (1st reign), 685–95
Leontius, 695–8
Tiberius III, 698–705

Justinian II (2nd reign), 705–11
Philippicus Vardan, 711–14
Anastasius II, 714–15
Theodosius III, 715–17
Leo III, 717–41
Constantine V, 741–75
Leo IV, 775–80
Constantine VI, 780–97
Eirene, 797–802
Nicephorus I, 802–11
Stauracius, 811
Michael I, 811–13
Leo V, 813–20
Michael II, 820–29
Theophilus, 829–42
Michael III, 842–67
Basil I, 867–86
Leo VI, 886–912
Alexander, 912–13
Constantine VII Porphyrogenitus, 913–59
Romanus I Lecapenus, 919–44
Romanus II, 959–63
Nicephorus II Phocas, 963–9
John I Tzimisces, 969–76
Basil II, 976–1025
Constantine VIII, 1025–8

Romanus III Argyrus, 1028–34

Michael IV, 1034–41

Michael V, 1041–2

Theodora (1st reign) and Zoë,
1042

Constantine IX, 1042–55

Theodora (2nd reign), 1055–6

Michael VI, 1056–7

Isaac I Comnenus, 1057–9

Constantine X Doucas, 1059–67

Eudocia Macrembolitissa, 1067

Romanus IV Diogenes, 1068–71

Michael VII Doucas, 1071–8

Nicephorus III Botaneiates,
1078–81

Alexius I Comnenus, 1081–1118

John II Comnenus, 1118–43

Manuel I Comnenus, 1143–80

Alexius II Comnenus, 1180–83

Andronicus I Comnenus, 1183–5

Isaac II Angelus (1st reign),
1185–95

Alexius III Angelus, 1195–1203

Isaac II Angelus (2nd reign),
1203–4

Alexius IV Angelus, 1203–4

Alexius V Doucas Mourtzouphlos,
1204

* Theodore I Lascaris, 1204–22

* John III Vatatzes, 1222-54

* Theodore II Lascaris, 1254–8

* John IV Lascaris, 1258–61

Michael VIII Palaeologus,
1259–82

Andronicus II Palaeologus,
1282–1328

Michael IX Palaeologus,
1294–1320

Andronicus III Palaeologus,
1328–41

John V Palaeologus, 1341–91

John VI Cantacuzenus, 1347–54

Andronicus IV Palaeologus,
1376–9

John VII Palaeologus, 1390

Manuel II Palaeologus,
1391–1425

John VIII Palaeologus, 1425–48

Constantine XI Dragases,
1449–53

LATIN EMPERORS OF CONSTANTINOPLE

Baldwin I of Flanders, 1204–5

Henry of Hainault, 1206–16

Peter of Courtenay, 1217–18

Yolanda, 1218–19

Robert of Courtenay, 1221–8

Baldwin II, 1228–61

John of Brienne, 1231–7

OTTOMAN SULTANS

† Osman Gazi, c. 1282–1326

† Orhan Gazi, 1326–62

† Murat I, 1362–89

† Beyazit I, 1389–1402

(Interregnum)

† Mehmet I, 1413–21

* ruled in Nicaea only

† ruled before the Turkish capture of Constantinople

† Murat II, 1421–51
Mehmet II, 1451–81
Beyazit II, 1481–1512
Selim I, 1512–20
Süleyman I, the Magnificent,
   1520–66
Selim II, 1566–74
Murat III, 1574–95
Mehmet III, 1595–1603
Ahmet I, 1603–17
Mustafa I (1st reign), 1617–18
Osman II, 1618–22
Mustafa I (2nd reign), 1622–3
Murat IV, 1623–40
Ibrahim, 1640–48
Mehmet IV, 1648–87
Süleyman II, 1687–91
Ahmet II, 1691–5

Mustafa II, 1695–1703
Ahmet III, 1703–30
Mahmut I, 1730–54
Osman III, 1754–7
Mustafa III, 1757–74
Abdül Hamit I, 1774–89
Selim III, 1789–1807
Mustafa IV, 1807–8
Mahmut II, 1808–39
Abdül Mecit I, 1839–61
Abdül Aziz, 1861–76
Murat V, 1876
Abdül Hamit II, 1876–1909
Mehmet V Reşat, 1909–18
Mehmet VI Vahideddin, 1918–22
Abdül Mecit (II) (Caliph only),
   1922–4

Bibliography

Alderson, A. D., *The Structure of the Ottoman Dynasty*. Oxford, 1956

Allom, Thomas, and Walsh, Robert, *Constantinople and the Scenery of the Seven Churches of Asia Minor*. London, 1839

Amicis, Edmondo de, *Constantinople*, trans. Maria Horner Lansdale. Philadelphia, 1896

Ammianus Marcellinus, *Res Gestae*, trans. John C. Rolfe. Cambridge, Mass., 1935

Angold, Michael, *A Byzantine Government in Exile*. Oxford, 1975

Angold, Michael, *The Byzantine Empire, 1025–1204*. London, 1984

Apollonius of Rhodes, *The Argonautica*, trans. E. V. Rieu. London, 1959

Appian, *Roman History*, trans. Horace White. London, 1913

Athenaeus, *The Deiphnosophists*, trans. C. B. Gulick. London, 1927

Atil, Esin, *The Age of Süleyman the Magnificent*. New York, 1987

Babinger, Franz, *Mehmet the Conqueror and his Time*, trans. Ralph Manheim, ed. William C. Hickman. Princeton, 1978

Baker, G. P., *Justinian*. New York, 1931

Balfour, Patrick, (Lord Kinross), *Atatürk*. London, 1964

Balfour, Patrick, (Lord Kinross), *The Ottoman Centuries*. London, 1987

Barker, John W., *Justinian and the Later Roman Empire*. Madison, Wisconsin, 1966

Barker, John W., *Manuel II Palaeologus (1391–1425): A Study in Late Byzantine Statesmanship*. New Brunswick, New Jersey, 1968

Baynes, Norman H., *Constantine the Great and the Christian Church*. London, 1929

Benjamin of Tudela, *The Oriental Travels of Benjamin of Tudela*, in *Contemporaries of Marco Polo*, ed. Manuel Komroff. New York, 1928

Borowski, Miroslav, *Pulcheria, Empress of Byzantium, AD 414–453*. Ann Arbor, Michigan, 1975

Bowder, Diana, *The Age of Constantine and Julian*. London, 1978

Brand, Charles M., *Byzantium Confronts the West, 1180–1204*. Cambridge, Mass., 1968

Browning, Robert, *The Emperor Julian*. Berkeley, California, 1972

Bury, J. B., *History of the Later Roman Empire*. London, 2nd edn, 1923

Byron, Lord, *Byron's Letters and Journals*, ed. Leslie A. Marchand. Vol. 2: *Famous in My Time, 1810–1812*. London, 1973

Cahen, Claude, *Pre-Ottoman Turkey*. New York, 1968

Cameron, Averil, and Herrin, Judith, (eds.), *Constantinople in the Early Eighth Century*. Leiden, 1984

Cantemir, Demetrius, *The History of the Growth and Decay of the Othman Empire*, trans. N. Tindal. London, 1734–5

Cary, M., *A History of the Greek World from 323–146 BC*. London, 1932

Coles, Paul, *The Ottoman Impact on Europe*. London, 1968

Comnena, Anna, *The Alexiad*, trans. Elizabeth Dawes. London, 1928

Dallaam, Thomas, *The Diary of Thomas Dallaam in Constantinople, 1599–1600*, in *Early Voyages and Travels in the Levant*, ed. J. T. Bent, Hakluyt Society. London, 1893

Davis, Fanny, *The Palace of Topkapi*. New York, 1970

Dawes, Elizabeth, and Baynes, Norman H., *Three Byzantine Saints*. Oxford, 1948

Diehl, Charles, *Byzantine Empresses*, trans. Harold Bell and Theresa de Kerpely. New York, 1963

Dio Cassius, *Roman History*, trans. E. Cary. London, 1914

Diodorus Siculus, *The Library of History*, trans. C. H. Oldfather et al. Cambridge, Mass., 1960

Diogenes Laertius, *Lives of the Eminent Philosophers*, trans. R. D. Hicks. London, 1958

Downey, Glanville, *Constantinople in the Age of Justinian*. Norman, Oklahoma, 1960

Ducas, *Decline and Fall of Byzantium to the Ottoman Turks*, trans. Harry S. Magoulias. Detroit, 1975

Dwight, H. G., *Constantinople Old and New*. New York, 1915

Evliya Efendi (Evliya Çelebi), *Narrative of Travels in Europe, Asia and Africa* [the *Seyahatname*], trans. Joseph von Hammer. London 1834–46

Freely, John, *Stamboul Sketches*. Istanbul, 1974

Freely, John, *Blue Guide Istanbul*. London, 3rd edn, 1991

Freeman, Kathleen, *Greek City-States*. London, 1950

Gardner, Alice, *The Lascarids of Nicaea*. London, 1912

Geanakoplos, Deno John, *Emperor Michael Palaeologus and the West*. Cambridge, 1959

Geanakoplos, Deno John, *Byzantium: Church, Society and Civilization Seen through Contemporary Eyes*. Chicago, 1984

Gibbon, Edward, *The History of the Decline and Fall of the Roman Empire*, ed. David Womersley. Harmondsworth, 1994

Gilles, Pierre, (Petrus Gyllius), *The Antiquities of Constantinople*, based on the translation by John Ball in 1719 of the *Four Books on the Topography of Constantinople and its Antiquities*, ed. Ronald G. Musto. New York, 1986

Goodwin, Godfrey, *A History of Ottoman Architecture*. London, 1971

Goodwin, Godfrey, *The Janissaries*. London, 1994

The Greek Anthology, trans. W. R. Paton. London, 1917

Grelot, Guillaume-Joseph, *Relation nouvelle d'un voyage de Constantinople, 1680*. Paris 1681 (The quote from Grelot was translated by Hilary Sumner-Boyd and appears in our *Strolling through Istanbul*.)

Grierson, Philip, *Tombs and Obits of the Byzantine Emperors*, Dumbarton Oaks Proceedings, Vol. 16, pp. 1–63. Washington, D C, 1962

Haidar, H R H Princess Musbah, *Arabesque*, London, 1944

Haldon, J. F., *Byzantium in the Seventh Century*. Cambridge, 1990

Hammond, N. G. C., *A History of Greece*. London, 1959

Haslip, Joan, *The Sultan: The Life of Abdül Hamit II*. London, 1958

Head, Constance, *Justinian II of Byzantium*. London, 1972

Head, Constance, *Imperial Twilight, The Palaiologos Dynasty and the Decline of Byzantium*. Chicago, 1977

Head, Constance, *Imperial Byzantine Portraits, A Verbal and Graphic Gallery*. New Rochelle, New York, 1982

Herodotus, *The Histories*, trans. Aubrey de Sélincourt. Harmondsworth, 1954

Hobhouse, John Cam, (Baron Broughton), *A Journey through Albania and the Other Provinces of Turkey in Europe and Asia to Istanbul during the year 1809 and 1810*. London, 1813

Hussey, J. M., *The Byzantine World*. London, 1957

Imber, Colin, *The Ottoman Empire, 1300–1481*. Istanbul, 1990

Inalcik, Halil, *The Ottoman Empire: The Classical Age, 1300–1600*, trans. Norman Itzkowitz and Colin Imber. London, 1973

Inalcik, Halil, *The Ottoman Empire: Conquest, Organization and Economy*. London, 1978

Janin, Raymond, *La géographie ecclésiastique de l'empire byzantin: Constantinople, Les églises et les monastères*. 2nd edn, Paris, 1969

Jenkins, Romilly, *Byzantium, The Imperial Centuries, AD 610–1071*. London, 1966

Jones, A. H. M., *The Cities of the Eastern Roman Provinces*. London, 1937

Jones, A. H. M., *The Later Roman Empire, 284–602.* Oxford, 1964

Jones, A. H. M., *Constantine and the Conversion of Europe.* London, 1948

Jones, A. H. M., *The Decline of the Ancient World.* New York, 1966

Kazhdan, Alexander, and Constable, Giles, *People and Power in Byzantium.* Cambridge, Mass., 1982

Kritovoulos of Imbros, *History of Mehmed the Conqueror*, trans. Charles T. Riggs. Princeton, 1954

Kuran, Aptullah, *Sinan, the Grand Old Man of Ottoman Architecture.* Washington, D C, 1986

Laiou, Angeliki E., *Constantinople and the Latins: The Foreign Policy of Andronicus II, 1282–1328.* Cambridge, Mass., 1972

Lethaby, William R., and Swainson, Harold, *The Church of Sancta Sophia, Constantinople.* London, 1894

Lewis, Bernard, *The Emergence of Modern Turkey.* Oxford, 1961

Lewis, Bernard, *Istanbul and the Civilization of the Ottoman Empire.* Norman, Oklahoma, 1963

Lewis, Geoffrey L., *Turkey.* New York, 1964

Lewis, Raphaela, *Everyday Life in the Ottoman Empire.* London, 1971.

Lithgow, William, *The Total Discourse of the Rare Adventures and Painful Peregrinations of Long Nineteene Yeares Travayles from Scotland to the Most Famous Kingdomes in Europe, Asia, and Africa, 1645.* Glasgow, 1905

Liutprand of Cremona, *The Works of Liutprand of Cremona*, trans. F. A. Wright. London, 1930

Lybyer, A. H., *The Government of the Ottoman Empire in the Time of Süleyman the Magnificent.* Cambridge, Mass., 1913

McCormick, Michael, *Eternal Victory.* New York, 1986

MacFarlane, Charles, *Istanbul in 1828.* London, 1829

Magdalino, Paul, *Tradition and Transformation in Medieval Byzantium.* Brookfield, Vermont, 1991

Magie, David, *Roman Rule in Asia Minor.* Princeton, 1950

Majeska, George P., *The Journey of Ignatius of Smolensk to Constantinople (1389–93).* Bloomington, Indiana, 1963

Mango, Cyril A., *The Brazen House: A Study of the Vestibule of the Imperial Palace of Constantinople.* Copenhagen, 1954

Mango, Cyril A., *Byzantium, The Empire of the New Rome.* London, 1980

Mango, Cyril A., *Byzantium and its Image.* London, 1984

Mansel, Philip, *Constantinople, City of the World's Desire, 1453–1924.* London, 1995

Marsh, Frank Burr, *A History of the Roman World from 146–30 BC.* London, 2nd edn, 1953

Millingen, Alexander Van, *The Walls of the City and Adjoining Historical Sites,* London, 1899

Millingen, Alexander Van, *Byzantine Churches in Constantinople.* London, 1912

Montagu, Lady Mary Wortley, *The Complete Letters of Lady Mary Wortley Montagu,* ed. Robert Halsband. Vol. 1: 1708–1720. Oxford, 1965

Necipoğlu, Gülru, *Architecture, Ceremonial and Power: The Topkapı Palace in the Fifteenth and Sixteenth Centuries.* New York, 1991

Nicol, Donald M., *The Last Centuries of Byzantium, 1261–1453.* Cambridge, 1972

Norwich, John Julius, *Byzantium: The Early Centuries.* Harmondsworth, 1988

Norwich, John Julius, *Byzantium: The Apogee.* Harmondsworth, 1991

Norwich, John Julius, *Byzantium: The Decline and Fall.* Harmondsworth, 1995

Odo of Deuil, *The Journey of Louis VII to the East,* trans. V. G. Berry. New York, 1948

Ostrogorsky, George, *History of the Byzantine State,* trans. Joan Hussey. Oxford, 1956

Palmer, Alan, *The Decline and Fall of the Ottoman Empire.* London, 1992

Pardoe, Julia, *The City of the Sultan and the Domestic Manners of the Turks.* London, 1836

Pardoe, Julia, *The Beauties of the Bosphorus.* London, 1839

Parker, H. M. D., *A History of the Roman World from AD 138 to 337.* London, 1935

Penzer, N. M., *The Harem.* London, 1965

Pierce, Leslie P., *The Imperial Harem.* Oxford, 1993

Polybius, *The Histories,* trans. W. R. Paton. London, 1922

Procopius of Caesarea, *Works,* trans. H. B. Dewing. London, 7 vols., 1914–40

Psellus, Michael, *Chronographia,* trans. E. R. A. Sewter. London, 1953

Rice, Tamara Talbot, *Everyday Life in Byzantium.* New York, 1967

Robert de Clari, *The Conquest of Constantinople,* trans. Edgar Holmes McNeal. New York, 1936

Runciman, Steven, *The Emperor Romanus Lecapenus and his Reign.* Cambridge, 1929

Runciman, Steven, *Byzantine Civilization.* London, 1933

Runciman, Steven, *A History of the Crusades.* Cambridge, 1952–4

Runciman, Steven, *The Last Byzantine Renaissance.* Cambridge, 1971

Salmon, E. T., *A History of the Roman World, 30 BC–AD 133.* London, 1957

Shaw, Sanford, *History of the Ottoman Empire and Modern Turkey. Vol. I: Empire of the Gazis: The Rise and Decline of the Ottoman Empire, 1280–1808*. Cambridge, 1976

Shaw, Sanford, and Shaw, Ezel Kural, *History of the Ottoman Empire and Modern Turkey. Vol. II: Reform, Revolution, and Republic, 1808–1975*. Cambridge, 1977

Stoneham, Richard, *A Literary Companion to Travel in Greece*. Harmondsworth, 1984

Stoneham, Richard, *Across the Hellespont, Travellers in Turkey from Herodotus to Freya Stark*. London, 1987

Sumner-Boyd, Hilary, and Freely, John, *Strolling through Istanbul*. Istanbul, 1972

Tacitus, *The Histories*, trans. John Jackson. Cambridge, Mass., 1972

Tekin, Latife, *Tales from the Garbage Hills*. Istanbul, 1993

Thucydides, *History of the Peloponnesian Wars*, trans. Rex Warner. Harmondsworth, 1951

Toynbee, Arnold J., *Constantine Porphyrogenitus and his World*. Oxford, 1973

Vasiliev, A. A., *Justin the First*. Cambridge, Mass., 1950

Walsh, Robert, *A Residence at Constantinople*. London, 1836

Wittek, Paul, *The Rise of the Ottoman Empire*. London, 1938

Wolff, Robert Lee, *Studies in the Latin Empire of Constantinople*. London, 1976

Xenophon, *Anabasis*, trans. Carleton L. Brownson. London, 1922

Zosimus, *Historia Nova*, trans. J. J. Buchanan and H. T. Davis. San Antonio, Texas, 1967

Index

Numbers in **bold** type indicate principal entries in the Notes on Monuments and Museums section.

Abbas Hilmi I, Ottoman governor of Egypt, 273
Abdül Aziz, sultan, 271, 277–81, 296, 377–8
Abdül Hamit I, sultan, 255–7
Abdül Hamit II, sultan, 271, 280–83, 287–9, 377–8
Abdül Mecit I, sultan, 271, 273, 275, 277–8, 330
Abdül Mecit (II) Efendi, caliph, 275, 296–8
Adair, Robert, British ambassador, 261
Adrianople (Edirne), 54, 164, 173, 187–8, 191, 193, 208, 242, 247–9, 258, 282, 291
Agathius Scholasticus, poet, 86–7
Ahmet I, sultan, 214–17, 219, 221, 238, 240, 322, 353
Ahmet II, sultan, 238–9, 247, 353, 364
Ahmet III ('the Tulip King'), sultan, 230, 242–3, 248–52, 254, 348, 350, 372
Ahmet Fevzi Pasha, grand vezir, 271–3
Ahmet Izzet Pasha, grand vezir, 292
Ahmet Muhtar Pasha, grand vezir, 290
Ahmet Tevfik Pasha, grand vezir, 289, 295

Alans, 68, 126
Alay Köşkü, 229, 231–5, 240, 371
Alcibiades, 19
Alemdar Mustafa Pasha, 259
Alexander, emperor, 116–17, 333
Alexander the Great, 20–21
Alexis, patriarch of Constantinople, 125
Alexius I Comnenus, emperor, 132–4, 329, 344, 339
Alexius II Comnenus, emperor, 135, 141–2
Alexius III Angelus, emperor, 144–7, 149–50
Alexius IV Angelus, emperor, 143–4, 146–7
Alexius V Doucas Mourtzouphlos, emperor, 146–7
Alexius I Comnenus, emperor of Trebizond, 142
Alexius IV, emperor of Trebizond, 169
Alexius, son of John II, 333
Alexius Apocaucus, 160
Alexius Strategopoulos, general, 151–2
Ali Haidar, şerif of Mecca, 290, 293
Allied occupation of Istanbul (1919–22), 292, 295, 297
Alp Arslan, Selcuk sultan, 131

Anadolu Feneri, 6, 9
Anadolu Hisarı, 6, 9, 17, 167, 173,
    270, 306–8, 347
Anastasius I, emperor, 41, 75–6, 88,
    323, 329
Anastasius II, emperor, 100
Anatolicus, patriarch of
    Constantinople, 71
Anaxabius, Spartan general, 20
Andrew, St, of Crete, 107
Andrew, St, the Fool, 103–6
Andronicus I Comnenus, emperor,
    141–2
Andronicus II Palaeologus, emperor,
    155–9
Andronicus III Palaeologus, emperor,
    156–60
Andronicus IV Palaeologus, emperor
    164–5
Anemodoulion, 103
Anicia Juliana, princess, 82, 334
Ankara: battle of (1402), 168–9;
    capital of Turkey, 297, 299
Anna, sister of Basil II, 121
Anna (née Agnes), wife of Alexius II
    and Andronicus I, 141–2
Anna Comnena, daughter of Alexius I,
    133–4
Anna Dalassena, mother of Alexius I,
    130, 132–3, 339
Anna Doucina, founder of church of
    Theotokos Pammakaristos, 345
Anna of Hungary, wife of Andronicus
    II, 156
Anna of Savoy, second wife of
    Andronicus III, 159–61
Anthemius, praetorian prefect, 61–2
Anthemius of Tralles, architect of
    Haghia Sophia, 81, 86
Antiochus II, Seleucid king, 21
Antiochus, grand chamberlain, 65
Antiochus, Palace of, 65, 327
Antiphilus of Byzantium, poet, 15–16
Antonina, wife of Belisarius, 79–80,
    85, 88

Apocaucus, Alexius, see Alexius
    Apocaucus
Arabs (Saracens), 96–7, 101, 109,
    111, 114, 118, 120, 122, 338
Arcadius, emperor, 55, 58–61, 325
Ariadne, daughter of Leo I, wife of
    Zeno and Anastasius I, 73–6
Arian heresy, 31, 50, 67, 68
Ariston, tyrant of Byzantium, 17
Armenians, 100, 115, 122, 126, 140,
    184, 188, 234, 239, 245, 284–5,
    287, 288, 315
Arsenius, patriarch of Constantinople,
    153
Artemius, St, 104
Aspar the Alan, magister militum, 63,
    68, 69, 71, 73
Atatürk (Mustafa Kemal Pasha), first
    president of Turkey, 287, 289,
    291–2, 294–7, 299–303, 376–7
Athenians, 18–21
Atik Ali Pasha, grand vezir, 344
Atik Sinan (Christodoulos?), architect,
    355
Attila the Hun, 62, 68–9
Augustaeum, 38, 40, 61, 64
Augustus, Roman emperor, 22
Avars, 90–92, 95–6
ayazmas (holy wells), 70, 82–3, 244–5,
    314, 327–8

Balat quarter, 184, 191
Baldwin I of Flanders, Latin emperor of
    Constantinople, 144, 148–9
Baldwin II, Latin emperor of
    Constantinople, 151–2
Balkan Wars: First (1912), 290;
    Second (1913), 290–91
Balyan family, architects: Hagop, 378;
    Karabet, 375; Kirkor, 375; Nikoğos,
    375, 377; Sarkis, 377–8
Barbarossa (Hayrettin Pasha), 198–9,
    359–60
Bardas, Caesar, 114
Bardas Sclerus, 121

Basil I ('the Macedonian'), emperor, 115–16, 127

Basil II ('Bulgaroctonus' – 'the Bulgar-Slayer'), emperor, 120–22

Basil, patriarch of Constantinople, 120

Basil the Bogomil, 134

baths, Turkish (hamam): Çağaloğlu Hamamı, 255, 373; Haseki Hürrem Hamamı, 202, 364–5

Bayar, Celâl, president of Turkey, 301

Bayram Pasha, 226

Bekri ('the Drunkard') Mustafa, 237

Bela III, king of Hungary, 139

Belgrade Forest, 254

Belisarius, general, 7, 79–80, 85, 88

Bellini, Gentile, 182, 188

Benjamin of Tudela, chronicler, 41, 137–8

Berlin, Treaty of (1878), 283

Beşir Ağa, chief black eunuch, 254

Bessarion, cardinal, 169

Beyazit I ('Yıldırım' – 'Lightning'), sultan, 166–9

Beyazit II, sultan, 189–92, 324, 344, 356

Beyazit, brother of Osman III, 255

Beyazit, son of Ahmet I, 371

Beyazit, son of Süleyman I, 194, 199, 204

Beylerbey Sarayı, 7, 278, 289, 377–8

Beyoğlu, see Pera

Bezmialem, valide sultan, 271

Blachernae Palace, 77, 137–8, 142, 144, 146–7, 151, 153, 159, 161–2, 175, 177, 329

Blachernae quarter, 28, 63, 77, 95–6, 110, 326

Black Ali, chief executioner, 239

boats, 307–8

Bohemund of Taranto, Count, 134

Boniface of Montferrat, Marquis, 145, 148

Book of Ceremonies, 42, 53, 56, 74, 119

Book of the Prefect, 104–6

Bosphorus, 3–9, 11, 28, 34, 76, 152, 167, 173, 188, 239, 258, 270, 276, 281, 299–300, 303, 305–12, 314–15, 319, 341, 367–8, 375, 377–80

Boucicaut, Marshal, 167–8

bridges: Boğaziçi Köprüsü, 306–7, 378–9; Fatih Sultan Mehmet Köprüsü, 306–7, 379; Galata, 183, 284–5, 371

Bucoleon, Palace of, 84, 148, 153, 335

Bucharest, Treaty of (1913), 291

Bulgars, 75, 95, 99, 107, 109–10, 114, 121, 143, 160, 279, 290

Bursa, see Prusa

Byron, George Gordon, Lord, 261–2

Byzantium, city-state of: setting, 3; founded by Byzas (c. 660 BC), 10; advantages of the site, 11–12; defences, 13; cultural traditions, religion and political system, 14; daily life and morals, 14–16; poets, 15–16; dominated by Persians, 16–18; Darius crosses Bosphorus (512 BC), 17; joins Ionian Revolt (499 BC), 18; city abandoned after Persians crush Ionian Revolt (494 BC), 18; contributes ships to Persian fleet (481 BC), 18; Persian garrison surrenders to Pausanias (477 BC), 18; Pausanias expelled (470 BC), 18; Byzantium joins Athenian League, 18; revolt against Athens fails, 19; alliance with Sparta (413 BC), 19; Athenians take city (409 BC), 19; Spartans take city (403 BC), 20; Ten Thousand pass through (400 BC), 20; Athenians take city (390 BC), 20; democratic faction ends alliance with Athens (363 BC), 20; joins anti-Athenian coalition (357 BC), 20; resists siege by Philip II of Macedon (340–339 BC), 21; withstands invasion by Gauls (279 BC), 21;

resists siege by Antiochus II
(246 BC), 21; resists siege by
Rhodians and Bithynians (220 BC),
21; alliance with Rome, 21;
incorporated into Roman Empire
(AD 73), 22; destroyed by Septimius
Severus (196), 22–4; rebuilt by
Septimius Severus (c. 200), 25–8;
resists attack by Goths (257), 28;
resists attack by Goths (268), 28;
surrenders to Constantine I after his
victory over Licinius (324), 30;
rebuilt by Constantine to be his new
capital (325–30), 30–31
Byzas the Megarian, 10–11, 34, 306,
314

caliphate, 192
Canning, Stratford, (later Viscount
Stratford de Redcliffe), 268–9
Cantacuzenus, Manuel, see Manuel
Cantacuzenus
Cantacuzenus, Matthew, see Matthew
Cantacuzenus
Cantemir, Demetrius, see Demetrius
Cantemir
Capitulations, 187, 198, 213
Capsali, Moshe, chief rabbi, 184
Caracalla, Roman emperor, 25
Carthage, Exarchate of, 90–91
Catalans, 157
Catherine the Great, empress of Russia,
256
Cem Sultan, son of Mehmet II, 190
Cemal Pasha, 291–2
cemeteries and tombstones, 31–4,
310–14
Cerularius, Michael, see Michael
Cerularius
Cervantes, Miguel, 207
Cevri Khalfa, 259
Chalcedon (Kadıköy), 10, 13–14, 18,
28, 52–3, 91–2, 95, 145, 258, 306
Chalke, the 38, 101
Chalkoprateia (Copper Market), 65

Charlemagne, emperor of the West, 109
Charles V, Holy Roman Emperor, 197,
198, 207
Charles I of Anjou, king of Sicily and
Naples, 155
Charles VI, king of France, 167–8
Choniates, Nicetas, see Nicetas
Choniates
Chosroes II, Persian king, 96
Christopher, son of Romanus I, 118
Chronicon Paschale, 27
Chrysaphus, grand chamberlain, 67, 69
Chrysopolis (Üsküdar), 19, 30, 159,
368
Chrysostom, St John, see John
Chrysostom, St
Church Councils (synods): First
(Nicaea, 325), 31; Third (Ephesus,
431), 67; Fourth (Chalcedon, 451),
69–70; Sixth (Constantinople,
680–81), 97–8; Quinisextum
(Constantinople, 691), 98–9;
Seventh (Nicaea, 787), 108;
Constantinople (815), 110;
Constantinople (845), 112;
Constantinople (1054), 127;
Ferrara-Florence (1438–9), 169–70
churches (see also Haghia Sophia):
Haghia Eirene, 37, 44, 50, 64, 80,
82, 333–4, 348–9; Holy Apostles,
42–6, 55, 61, 68, 70, 74–6, 82, 89,
96, 110, 122–3, 184; Isa Kapı
Mescidi, 44, 323; Myrelaion
(Bodrum Camii), 117–18, 338–9;
Panayia Zoodochos Pege (Balıklı),
82–3, 313–14, 334–5; Peribleptos,
123; St Andrew in Krisei (Koca
Mustafa Pasha Camii), 107, 337–8;
SS. Constantine and Helena, 47; SS.
Domenic and Paul (Arap Camii),
157, 343–4; St Euphemia, martyrion
of, 70, 102, 108, 327; St George
(Greek Orthodox Patriarchate), 70,
184, 348; St George of the
Mangana, 126–7, 162–3; St John

the Baptist of Studius (Imrahor
Camii), 74, 110–11, 113, 124,
130–31, 152, 328–9; SS. Karpos
and Papylos, martyrion of, 47, 323;
St Mary of the Mongols, 154,
342–3; St Polyeuktos, 82, 300, 334;
St Saviour in Chora (Kariye Camii),
159, 344–5; St Saviour Pantepoptes
(Eski Imaret Camii), 133, 339;
St Saviour Pantocrator (Zeyrek
Camii), 134, 169, 171, 339–40;
SS. Sergius and Bacchus (Küçük Aya
Sofya Camii), 79, 82, 329–30;
St Theodore Tyro (Kilise Cami),
104–5, 336–7; St Theodosia
(Gül Camii), 100, 336; Sañcaktar
Mescidi, 46–7, 323; Theotokos in
Chalkoprateia, 65, 327; Theotokos
Kyriotissa (Kalenderhane Camii),
149, 341–2; Theotokos
Pammakaristos (Fethiye Camii),
159, 184, 345–6; Theotokos
Panachrantos (Fenari Isa Camii),
154, 342; Virgin at Blachernae
(Blachernitissa), 70, 77, 95, 161,
313, 327
Cihangir, son of Süleyman I, 194, 199,
20
Çiller, Tansu, prime minister of
Turkey, 302
Cinci Hoca, 238
Çinili Köşk, 184, 354
Çırağan Sarayı, 276, 280, 377
cisterns: of Aetius, 63, 326; of Aspar,
63, 326; Basilica (Yerebatansaray),
84, 201, 327, 335; of St Mocius
(Altımermer), 63–4, 327; of
Philoxenus (Binbirdirek), 65, 327
Claudius II Gothicus, Roman emperor,
28–9, 34
Clearchus, Spartan general, 20
Clemenceau, Georges, French prime
minister, 294
Clement IV, pope, 155
Codex Theodosianus, 65–6

Columns and obelisks: of Arcadius, 61,
325–6; Colossus, 40, 322; of
Constantine, 37–9, 46, 320–21;
Egyptian, 40, 55–6, 322–3; Goth's,
33–4, 320; of Marcian, 70–71, 328;
Serpent, 40, 322
Committee of Union and Progress
(CUP), 287, 289–91
Comnena, Anna, see Anna Comnena
Comnena, Maria, see Maria Comnena
Comnenus, David, see David
Comnenus
Comnenus, Isaac, see Isaac Comnenus
Comnenus, John, see John Comnenus
Conrad, king of the Romans, 135
Constans, son of Constantine I, 44–5,
48
Constantine I ('the Great'), emperor, 4,
29–32, 37–8, 42, 44–6, 48, 57, 65,
83, 320–22, 324, 333
Constantine II, emperor, 96
Constantine III, emperor, 96–7
Constantine IV, emperor, 97, 98
Constantine V ('Copronomous' –
'Called from Dung'), emperor,
102–3, 106–7, 110
Constantine VI, emperor 107–9
Constantine VII Porphyrogenitus,
emperor, 42, 116–19, 322, 342
Constantine VIII, emperor, 120–22
Constantine IX Monomachus,
emperor, 125–7, 333
Constantine X Doucas, emperor,
130–31
Constantine XI Dragases, emperor,
170–76, 189
Constantine, prefect, 62
Constantine, son of Constantine I, 44
Constantine, son of Romanus I, 118
Constantine, uncle of Michael V, 124
Constantine Lips, 342
Constantinople (see also Byzantium,
Istanbul): dedicated as new Rome by
Constantine I (330), 4; setting, 5;
topography, 37; population, 37–8;

monuments 38–9; Constantius erects church of Haghia Sophia, 44; Constantius massacres orthodox partisans in Haghia Eirene, 50; death and burial of Constantine (337), 44–6; Julian the Apostate attempts to re-establish paganism (362), 50–51; Valens puts down revolt (365), 52; Goths attempt to capture city (378), 54; Theodosius I prohibits paganism (391–2), 55; Goths seize city but are slaughtered by populace (400), 60; supporters of John Chrysostom riot and Haghia Sophia is burned down (404), 60; Theodosius II erects new church of Haghia Sophia (414), 61; Theodosius II builds new line of defence walls (413), 62; Theodosian Walls destroyed by earthquake and rebuilt as double line of walls (447), 62, 67; fire (465), 71; insurrection by Isaurian troops (471), 73; riot in Hippodrome (501), 76; revolt led by Count Vitalian (515), 76; Nika Revolt, destruction of Haghia Sophia (532), 80; Justinian builds new church of Haghia Sophia (532–7), 81; plague (542), 84–5; besieged by Huns (559), 88; Persians twice penetrate as far as Chalcedon (608, 615), 91, 92; Avars penetrate as far as Theodosian Walls (617), 92; siege by Avars and Persians (626), 95; siege by Arabs (668–9), 97; siege by Arabs (674–8), 97; Justinian II captures city and regains throne (705), 99; siege by Arabs (717–18), 101; Iconoclastic Crisis begins (726), 101; plague (747), 102; siege by Bulgars (813), 110; end of Iconoclastic Crisis (845), 112; attack by Russians (860), 114–15; populace revolts and restores Zoë to throne (1042), 124; populace revolts (1044), 126; schism between Greek and Roman churches (1054), 127; besieged by Patzinaks and Turks (1090), 133; arrival of First Crusade (1096), 133–4; taken by Andronicus I (1182), 142; arrival of Third Crusade (1187), 143; coup by Alexius III (1195), 144; arrival of Fourth Crusade in Venetian fleet, Latins attack city (1203), 145–6; Latins capture and sack city (1204), 147–8; Greeks recapture city (1261), 151–2; rebuilding of city by Michael VIII, 153–4; Genoese fortify Galata, 157; city taken by Andronicus III and John Cantacuzenus, beginning civil war (1328), 158; Black Plague (1347), 161; besieged by Beyazit I (1394–1402), 167–8; ruined state of city (1400), 168; Mehmet II builds fortress of Rumeli Hisarı (1452), 173; Mehmet II begins siege of city (5 April 1453), 174; city captured by Mehmet II (29 May 1453), 175–7

Constantius, emperor, 43, 45, 48–50
Constantius Chlorus, Roman emperor, 29
Copper Market, *see* Chalkoprateia
Cosmidion, 28, 152
Covered Bazaar *see* Kapalı Çarşı
craft guilds, 41–2, 64, 104–6, 131–8
Crimean War (1854–6), 276–7
Crusades: First (1096), 133–4; Third (1187–90), 143; Fourth (1203–4), 144–8
Cumans, 133, 143
Cyril (née Constantine), St, 114

Dalan, Bedrettin, mayor of Istanbul, 305
Dalassena, Anna, *see* Anna Dalassena
Dalgıç Ahmet Çavuş, architect, 213, 215–16

Dallaam, Thomas, organ-maker, 213–14
Dalmata, John, *see* John Dalmata
Dandolo, Enrico, doge of Venice, 144–5, 147–8, 333
Daniel, St, the Stylite, 71, 73
Darius I, Persian king, 16–17, 306
David Comnenus, emperor of Trebizond, 187–8
David Comnenus, brother of Alexius I of Trebizond, 142
Davut Ağa, architect, 212
Demetrius Cantemir, historian, 237–9, 248–9
Demetrius Palaeologus, son of Manuel II, 170–72, 187
Demirel, Süleyman, president of Turkey, 302
dervishes, 190–91, 299, 358
Diocletian, Roman emperor, 29, 31
Dionysius Byzantius, historian, 27–8
Divan, Council of the, 192–3, 211, 229, 240, 264, 350
Dolmabahçe Sarayı, 275, 277, 280–82, 290, 296–7, 300–1, 375–7
Donizetti Pasha, Giuseppe, 269
Dorino Gattilusio, second wife of Constantine XI, 172
Doucas, John, *see* John Doucas
Doucina, Anna, *see* Anna Doucina
Doucina, Eirene, *see* Eirene Doucina
Dragas, Helena, *see* Helena Dragas
Dürrünev, wife of Sultan Abdül Mecit, 278

Edirne, *see* Adrianople
Eirene, empress, wife of Leo IV, 107–9
Eirene, daughter of Isaac II, 143–4
Eirene (née Adelaide), first wife of Andronicus III, 157, 161
Eirene (née Priska), wife of John II, 134, 333, 339
Eirene Doucina, wife of Alexius I, 132–3

Elisabeth, St, the Miracle-Worker, 73
Elizabeth I, queen of England, 213
Elliot, Sir Henry, British ambassador, 281
Eminönü quarter, 213, 241, 284, 365
Enver Pasha, 290–92
Epirus, Despotate of, 149
Erbakan, Necmettin, prime minister of Turkey, 302
Eski Saray (the Old Palace), 184, 212, 214, 243, 253, 257
Esmahan, daughter of Selim II, 206, 208
Eudocia (Athenais), wife of Theodosius II, 62, 66–8
Eudocia Macrembolitissa, empress, second wife of Constantine X, 130–31
Eudoxia, wife of Arcadius, 58, 60–61
Eugene of Savoy, Prince, 248
Eugénie, empress of France, 278
Eugenius III, pope, 135
Eugenius IV, pope, 169–71
eunuchs, 49, 51, 58, 67, 69, 209, 254, 259, 329, 352
Euphemia of Chalcedon, St, 69–70, 90–91, 102, 108
Euphemia (Lupacina), wife of Justin I, 77
Euphrosyne, wife of Alexius III, 144
Eusebius, grand chamberlain, 49, 51
Eusebius of Caesarea, historian, 28, 45–6
Euthemius I, patriarch of Constantinople, 116
Eutropius, grand chamberlain, 58, 60
Evliya Çelebi, chronicler, 56, 64, 181–3, 189–93, 206, 219, 221–36, 243–6, 312, 348
Evren, Kenan, president of Turkey, 302
Eyüp (*see also* Cosmidion), 28, 186–7, 189, 208, 225, 231, 238, 243, 250, 253, 280–81, 312–13

Fatma, Princess, daughter of Ahmet III, 254

Fener quarter, 70, 184

Ferdinand of Hapsburg, Archduke, 187, 207

folk-saints, Muslim, 243–4

forums: Amastrianum, 43, 105; of Arcadius, 43, 61; Bovis, 43, 278; of Constantine, 38, 43, 103, 105; Tauri, 43, 103–5, 324; of Theodosius, 55, 147, 190, 304, 324

Fossati, Gaspare, architect, 330, 332–3

Fossati, Giuseppe, architect, 330, 332–3

fountains (çeşme): Ahmet III (First Hill), 348; Ahmet III (Üsküdar), 361; Mihrişah (Küçüksu), 377

François I, king of France, 198, 200

Franz Josef I, emperor of Austria and king of Hungary, 278

fratricide, Ottoman code of, 208, 211, 214, 219, 255

Frederick I Barbarossa, German emperor, 141

Gainas, Gothic general, 60

Gaiseric, king of the Vandals, 74

Galata, 4, 28, 63, 145, 155–7, 184, 188, 190–91, 198, 202, 245, 274, 284, 286, 343

Galata Bridge, 183, 284–5, 371

Galata, Castle of, 145

Galata Mevlevihane, 190–91, 358

Galata Tower, 157, 184, 274, 343

Galerius, Roman emperor, 29, 31

Galla Placidia, daughter of Theodosius I, 62, 65

Gallipoli campaign (1915–16), 291

Gallus, Caesar, 48–9

Gattilusio, Dorino, see Dorino Gattilusio

gecekondu (illegal housing), 304–5

Gedik Ahmet Pasha, 189

Gelimer, king of the Vandals, 85

Gennadius, patriarch of Constantinople, 78, 173, 184

Genoese, 140, 150, 155–7, 162, 164, 167, 174, 176, 184, 188, 343

Genoese Castle (Yoros Kalesi), 155, 343

George Muzalon, regent for John IV, 150

Germanus III, patriarch of Constantinople, 153

Giustiniani Longo, Giovanni, 174, 176

Giyaseddin Keyhüsrev I, Selcuk sultan, 150

Gladstone, William, British statesman, 279

Godfrey of Bouillon, Count, 134

Golden Gate, 54, 56–7, 101, 115, 152, 325, 348

Golden Horn, 3, 4, 28, 34, 44, 62–3, 76, 95–6, 112, 145–7, 155, 162, 174, 183, 205, 241, 250, 251, 260, 285, 305–6, 314, 319, 326, 338, 362, 371, 378

Goths, 28–9, 34, 54

Grand National Assembly of Turkey (GNA), 294–5, 297, 299

Grande Rue de Pera (Istiklal Caddesi), 187, 198, 299

Gratian, emperor of the West, 53, 55

Great Palace of Byzantium, 10, 38, 41–2, 44, 60, 64, 84, 109, 111–12, 124, 163, 177, 303, 321, 335

'Greek fire', 76, 97, 101

Greek minority in Istanbul, 182–4, 210, 234, 245, 263, 284–5, 288, 293, 297, 302–3, 314

Greek Orthodox Patriarchate, 70, 184, 346, 348

Greek–Turkish population exchange (1923), 297

Greek–Turkish War (1919–21), 294

Greek War of Independence (1821–30), 262–3, 266

Gregoras, Nicephorus, see Nicephorus Gregoras

Gregory III Mammes, patriarch of Constantinople, 173
Gregory V, patriarch of Constantinople, 263
Guiscard, Robert, 130, 133–4
Gülbahar, valide sultan, mother of Beyazit II, 189–90
Gülbahar, wife of Süleyman I, 194
Gülersoy, Çelik, 305
Gülhane decree (1839), 273
Gürsel, General Cemal, president of Turkey, 301
Gyllius, Petrus, (Pierre Gille), 4, 5, 7, 8, 11, 26, 51, 200–202, 306, 315, 319
gypsies, 188

Habsburgs, 196–8, 204, 207, 247
Hadice (Mahfiruze), valide sultan, 215, 218
Hadice, sister of Süleyman I, 196
Hadrian, Roman emperor, 22
Hafise, valide sultan, 195
Haghia Sophia (Aya Sofya), 10, 38, 41, 44, 60–61, 64–5, 80–83, 89, 101, 105–6, 110, 122, 125, 131–2, 137, 144, 146, 148–9, 152–3, 159, 161, 165, 173, 175, 177–8, 181–3, 185, 201, 205, 208, 239, 255, 287, 289, 303, 322, 330–3, 348, 367
Halil Çandarlı Pasha, grand vezir, 173, 348
Handan, valide sultan, 214–15, 369
Harbours: of Julian (Kadirga Limanı), 51, 323; Kontoskalion (Kum Kapı), 51, 323; Neorion, 23; Prosphorion, 23; of Theodosius (Eleutherius), 4, 55, 105, 324
Harem of Topkapı Sarayı, 207–9, 212–14, 238–9, 352–4
Harington General Sir Charles ('Tim'), 295
Hasan Pasha, Gazi, grand admiral (later grand vezir), 257
Hatti Hümayun (1856), 277
Hawkins, Ernest, 345

Haydar Bey, mayor of Istanbul, 277
Hebdomon (Bakırköy), 52–4, 56, 71, 91
Helena, St, mother of Constantine I, 38–9, 46–7
Helena, daughter of John VI, 161
Helena, daughter of Romanus I, 117
Helena Dragas, wife of Manuel II, 165, 171
Henry VI, German emperor, 143
Henry IV, king of England, 168
Henry of Hainault, Latin emperor of Constantinople, 149
Heraclius, emperor, 91–3, 95–6, 121, 336
Heraclius, exarch of Carthage, 91
Heraclonas, emperor, 96
Hippodrome, 25–6, 37, 40–41, 46, 64, 70, 76, 79–80, 85, 88, 93, 100, 111, 137, 142, 196–8, 202, 209–10, 216, 312, 321–2, 359, 366, 370
Hobhouse, John Cam, (Baron Broughton), 261–2
Hodegetria, the Virgin, icon of, 101, 152, 175
Holy League, 207, 242
Honorius, emperor of the West, 55, 58
Hovakim Armenian patriarch, 184
Humbert of Silva Candida, cardinal, 127
Hünkar Iskelesi, Treaty of (1833), 267
Huns, 62, 68–9, 88, 95
Hunyadi, John, 171
Hüseyin Avni Pasha, grand vezir, 279–80
Hüseyin Ağa, chief black eunuch, 329
Husrev Pasha, grand admiral, 261
Hypatius, nephew of Justin I, 77, 80

Ibrahim ('the Mad'), sultan, 215, 217, 219, 238–9, 243, 351–2
Ibrahim Müteferrika, printer, 250
Ibrahim Pasha, grand vezir and favourite of Süleyman I, 196–8, 359

Ibrahim Pasha, Nevşehirli Damat, grand vezir, 249–52

Ibrahim Pasha, son of Mehmet Ali of Egypt, 263, 266–7, 271, 273

Ibrahim Pasha Sarayı, 196, 198, 359

Ibrahim Şinasi, 279

Iconoclastic Crisis, 101–2, 106–10, 112–13

Innocent III, pope, 144

Innocent XI, pope, 244

İnönü, Ismet, president of Turkey, 294–5, 297, 301

Isa, son of Beyazit I, 169

Isa Kapı Mescidi, 46, 323

Isaac I Comnenus, emperor, 129–30

Isaac II Angelus, emperor, 142–4, 146–7

Isaac Comnenus, Sebastocrator, 344

Isaurians, 73

Ishak Pasha, grand vezir, 176

Isidore I, patriarch of Constantinople, 161

Isidore of Kiev, cardinal, 173

Isidorus of Miletus, architect of Haghia Sophia, 81, 89

Isidorus the Younger, architect of Haghia Sophia, 89

Istanbul (see also Byzantium, Constantinople) Mehmet II enters city in triumph (29 May 1453), 181; Haghia Sophia converted to mosque, 182; Mehmet II rebuilds and repopulates city, erecting an imperial mosque and the palace of Topkapı Sarayı, 182–6; plague (1466), 203; first Ottoman census (1477), 188; Beyazit II welcomes Sephardic Jewish refugees (1492), 191; plague (1526), 203; census of 1535, 202; the architect Sinan completes the Süleymaniye for Süleyman I (1557), 202; smallpox epidemic (1543), 199; plague (1561), 203; Janissaries revolt (1589), 210–11; Sipahis revolt (1593), 211; Janissaries depose and assassinate Osman II (1622), 219; Janissaries and Sipahis revolt (1631), 226; procession of guilds (1638), 229–36; Janissaries depose and execute Sultan Ibrahim (1648), 239; Janissaries and Sipahis revolt (1656), 240; Janissaries run amok in city (1688), 246; Janissaries revolt (1730), 251–2; revolt by Kara Ali (1731), 253–4; Janissaries and medrese students revolt (1807), 259; Janissaries revolt and assassinate Selim III, replacing him with Mustafa IV (1808), 259; Alemdar Mustafa Pasha puts down Janissaries and deposes Mustafa IV in favour of Mahmut II (1808), 159–60; civil war led by Janissaries (1808), 260–61; Mahmut II annihilates Janissary Corps (1826), 263–4; clothing reform by Mahmut II (1829), 268–9; Ottoman reforms (Tanzimat) proclaimed by Sultan Abdül Mecit in Gülhane decree (1839), 273; opening of first Ottoman Parliament (1877), 282; Parliament dissolved by Abdül Hamit II, 283; census of 1886, 284; Orient Express begins service to city (1888), 284; Armenian terrorist attack leads to massacre of Armenians (1896), 287; Parliament reconvened (1908), 287–8; Abdül Hamit II deposed (1909), 289; Committee of Union and Progress (CUP) takes control of government (1913), 290; Turkey enters First World War as ally of Germany (1914), 291; Allied army occupies Istanbul (13 November 1918), 292; Kemal Pasha (Atatürk) begins Turkish Nationalist movement, 292–3; Grand National Assembly (GNA) in Ankara abolishes sultanate, Mehmet VI leaves Istanbul

for exile (November 1922); 295;
Allied occupation of Istanbul ends
(2 October 1923), 297; Ankara
replaces Istanbul as the capital of
Turkey (13 October 1923), 297;
GNA adopts constitution creating
the new Republic of Turkey, with
Atatürk as president (29 October
1923), 297; GNA abolishes
caliphate, Abdül Mecit (II) leaves
Istanbul for exile (3 March 1924),
297; republican reforms, 299–300;
death of Atatürk in Istanbul (10
November 1938), 300–1;
restoration of historic monuments
and opening of museums, 303;
population explosion 1950–95 and
associated civic problems, 303–5;
first Bosphorus bridge (1973), 306;
second Bosphorus bridge (1988),
306; survivals of the old Istanbul in
the modern metropolis, 306–15
Ismail Ağa, 258–9
Ivan IV ('the Terrible'), tsar of Russia,
207

Janissaries, 176, 191, 199, 203,
210–11, 219, 226, 239–40, 246–8,
251–3; 258–9, 263–5
Jason and the Argonauts, 8, 9
Jews (see also Karaite Jews), 65, 105,
126, 138, 183–4, 188, 191, 202,
213, 234, 245, 269, 273, 276, 282,
284–5, 288, 315
John I Tzimisces, emperor, 118,
120–21
John II Comnenus, emperor, 134–5,
333, 339–40
John IV Lascaris, emperor, 150, 153
John V Palaeologus, emperor, 159–62,
164–5
John VI Cantacuzenus, emperor,
158–63
John VII Palaeologus, emperor, 165
John VIII Palaeologus, emperor, 169–71

John XIV Kalekas, patriarch of
Constantinople, 160
John Chrysostom, St, Patriarch of
Constantinople, 59–61, 132, 152
John Comnenus, brother of Isaac I, 130
John Comnenus, patron of the
Pammakaristos church, 345
John Dalmata, 176
John Doucas, Caesar, 133
John the Orphanotrophus, 123–4
John Tzetzes, poet, 138–9
John Xiphilinus, patriarch of
Constantinople, 131
Joseph II, patriarch of Constantinople,
153, 170
Jovian, emperor, 52
Juan of Austria, Don, 207
Julian ('the Apostate'), emperor, 48–52
Justin I, emperor, 77–9, 323
Justin II, emperor, 90
Justinian I ('the Great'), emperor, 7,
10, 45–6, 55, 77, 79–90, 168,
201–2, 205, 329–30, 333
Justinian II ('Rhinometus' – the
'Noseless'), emperor, 98–100

Kabaağaç, Cevat Şakir, 313
Kadıköy, see Chalcedon
Kafes (the Cage), 217–20, 238, 239,
242–3, 246–9, 252, 255–7,
259–60, 271, 281, 290–91, 296
Kalojan, Bulgar tsar, 149
Kapalı Çarşı (Covered Bazaar), 186,
190, 356, 373
Kara Ahmet Pasha, 203
Kara Ali, 254
Kara Mustafa Pasha of Merzifon,
grand vezir, 242
Karaite Jews, 213
Karlowitz, Peace of (1699), 248
Kemankes Ali Pasha, grand vezir, 219
Khazars, 99
Kılıç Ali Pasha, 207–8
Kız Kulesi (Maiden's Tower), 135–6,
341

Koca Mustafa Pasha, grand vezir, 337
Koca Sinan Pasha, grand vezir, 210
Köprülü Amcazade Hüseyin Pasha,
    grand vezir, 248
Köprülü Fazıl Ahmet Pasha, grand
    vezir, 241–2
Köprülü Fazıl Mustafa Pasha, grand
    vezir, 242, 247
Köprülü Mehmet Pasha, grand vezir,
    240–41
Kösem, valide sultan, 215, 217–19,
    225, 238–40, 371
Kossova, battle of: first (1389), 166;
    second (1448), 171
Kritovoulos of Imbros, historian, 177,
    184
Krum, khan of the Bulgars, 109–10
Küçük Kaynarca, Treaty of (1774),
    256
Küçüksu Kasrı, 276, 377
Kulhan Beyler (Men of the Stoke-
    Hole), 264–5
Kurds, 302
Kynegion, 27, 69

Ladislas III, king of Poland and
    Hungary, 171
Lala Mustafa Pasha, 207
Lausanne, Treaty of (1923), 296
Lausus, Palace of, 65, 327
Lazar, prince of Serbia, 166–7
Lear, Edward, 274
Leo I, emperor, 71–4
Leo II, emperor, 74
Leo III, emperor, 100–2
Leo IV, emperor, 107
Leo V ('the Armenian'), emperor,
    110–11
Leo VI ('the Wise'), emperor, 116–17,
    326, 342
Leo IX, pope, 127
Leo the Mathematician, 114
Leontius, emperor, 99–100
Leopold I, king of Belgium, 278
Lepanto, battle of (1571), 207–8

Levant Company, 213
Licinia Eudoxia, daughter of Arcadius,
    62, 66
Licinius, Roman emperor, 27–8
Lips, Constantine, see Constantine Lips
Lithgow, William, 215–16
Liutprand of Cremona, 112, 119
Lloyd George, David, British prime
    minister, 294
London, Treaty of (1913), 290
Louis VII, king of France, 135, 137
Lycus river, 4, 68, 324

Magdalena Tocco, first wife of
    Constantine XI, 172
Magnaura, Palace of, 112, 119, 126
Mahmut I, sultan, 248, 253–5, 372–3
Mahmut II, sultan, 256–7, 259–64,
    266–9, 271, 273, 289, 350, 375,
    377–8
Mahmut, son of Mehmet III, 214
Mahmut Nedim Pasha, grand vezir,
    279
Mahmut Pasha, grand vezir, 356
Mahmut Şevket Pasha, grand vezir,
    289–90
Maiden's Tower, see Kız Kulesi
Malta, siege of (1565), 204
Mandrocles of Samos, military
    engineer, 17
Manuel I Comnenus, emperor,
    135–41, 321, 341
Manuel II Palaeologus, emperor, 164–9
Manuel Cantacuzenus, son of John VI,
    162
Manuel Palaeologus, son of Michael
    IX, 158
Manzikert, battle of (1071), 131
Marcian, emperor, 69–73, 328
Maria (née Margaret), second wife of
    Isaac II, 143
Maria (née Rita), wife of Michael IX,
    156
Maria (née Martha) of Alania, wife of
    Michael VII, 131–2

Maria of Antioch, second wife of
Manuel I, 135, 141–2
Maria Comnena, third wife of John
VIII, 169–70
Maria Doucina Comnena Palaeologina
Blachena, 346
Maria Palaeologina, illegitimate
daughter of Michael VIII, 154, 342
Marinus, praetorian prefect, 76
Martin V, pope, 169
Martina, wife of Emperor Heraclius,
96
Matthew Cantacuzenus, son of John
VI, 162
Maurice, emperor, 90–91, 94
Maxentius, Roman emperor, 29
Maximian, Roman emperor, 29
Maximinus Daia, Roman emperor,
29–30
Maximus, usurper, 55, 325
Megara, 10–11, 13–14, 306
Mehmet I, sultan, 169
Mehmet II ('Fatih' – 'the Conqueror'),
sultan, 4, 171, 173–7, 181–9, 243,
281, 330, 342, 348–50, 355–6
Mehmet III, sultan, 209, 211, 213–15,
241
Mehmet IV, sultan, 239–43, 247, 372
Mehmet V Reşat, sultan, 271, 281,
289–91
Mehmet VI Vahideddin, sultan, 271,
281, 291–6
Mehmet, Şehzade, son of Süleyman I,
194, 197, 199–200, 360
Mehmet Ağa, architect, 216
Mehmet Ali Pasha, Ottoman governor
of Egypt, 263, 266, 271, 273
Mehmet Emin Rauf Pasha, grand vezir,
267
Mehmet Husrev Pasha, grand vezir,
271
Mehmet Sait Pasha, grand vezir, 289
Mehmet Tahir Ağa, architect, 256
Melek Ahmet Pasha, grand vezir, 221,
227–8

Menderes, Adnan, prime minister of
Turkey, 301
Menes, patriarch of Constantinople, 81
Mese (the Middle Way), 26, 29, 38,
43–4, 192
Mesih Pasha, 189
Methodius, St, 114
Metochites, Theodore, see Theodore
Metochites
Michael I Rhangabe, emperor, 109–10
Michael II ('the Amorian'), emperor,
111
Michael III ('the Sot'), emperor,
111–12, 114–16
Michael IV ('the Paphlagonian'),
emperor, 122–4
Michael V ('Calaphates' – 'the
Caulker'), emperor, 123–4
Michael VI, emperor, 127, 129
Michael VII Doucas, emperor,
130–31
Michael VIII Palaeologus, emperor,
150–55, 157, 342
Michael IX Palaeologus, emperor, 156,
158
Michael Cerularius, patriarch of
Constantinople, 127
Michael Doucas Glabas Tarchaniotes,
346
Michael Psellus, chronicler, 116,
122–7
Midhat Pasha, grand vezir, 279, 281–2
Mihrimah Sultan, daughter of
Süleyman I, 194, 197, 199–200,
364
Mihrişah, valide sultan, 257
Mihrişah Sultan, külliye of, 257,
374–5
Miletus, 9, 18
Miliareum Aureum (Milion), 26, 38,
40, 52, 319
Milion, see Miliareum Aureum
millet system, 183, 198
Mısır Çarşısı (Spice Bazaar), 241,
372–3

Moero of Byzantium, poetess, 16
Mohács, battle of (1526), 196
Monophysite heresy, 69, 76
Monothelete heresy, 97–8
Montagu, Lady Mary Wortley, 251
Morea, Despotate of the, 162
Morosini, Thomas, Latin patriarch of Constantinople, 149
Moryson, Fynes, 212–13
mosques (see also churches for converted buildings): Ahi Çelebi Cami, 222, 371; Atik Valide Camii, 210, 368; Ayazma Camii, 256, 374; Beyazidiye, 190–92, 354, 357–8; Eyüp Camii, 186–7, 356–7; Fatih Camii, 185, 189, 202, 296, 339, 355, 362; Haseki Hürrem Camii, 199, 360; Iskele Camii, 200, 361; Kılıç Ali Pasha Camii, 210, 367–8; Laleli Camii, 256, 374; Mahmut Pasha Camii, 185, 355–6; Mihrimah Camii, 200, 361–2; Nuruosmaniye Camii, 256, 373–4; Nusretiye Camii, 266, 375; Pertevniyal Valide Camii, 278, 378; Ramazan Efendi Camii, 210, 368–9; Rüstem Pasha Camii, 202, 365–6; Şehzade Camii, 185, 199–200, 360–61; Selim I Camii, 193, 326, 358–9; Şemsi Ahmet Pasha Camii, 210, 368; Sokollu Mehmet Pasha Camii, 208, 366–7; Süleymaniye, 195, 202, 210, 362–4; Sultan Ahmet I Camii (Blue Mosque), 10, 216–17, 238, 240, 322, 369–71; Yavuz Ersinan Camii, 183, 221, 348; Yeni Camii (New Mosque), 213–14, 241, 255, 371–2; Yeni Valide Camii, 250, 373
Muawiya, caliph, 97
Mudanya Armistice (1922), 294
Mudros Armistice (1918), 292
Muhammed, the Prophet, 96, 187, 223–4
Murat I, sultan, 164–6
Murat II, sultan, 169, 171, 173

Murat III, sultan, 206, 208–12, 346, 367–9
Murat IV, sultan, 215, 217, 219, 221–2, 225–34, 236–8, 312, 351–2, 369, 371
Murat V, sultan, 271, 280–81, 372
Müridoğlu, Zühtü, sculptor, 362
Musa Çelebi, 226, 228
Musa, son of Beyazit I, 169
Musbah, Princess, 292–3, 297–8
Museums: Ancient Near East, 303, 378; Archaeological, 31, 41, 303, 320, 326, 342; Military, 303, 378; Mosaic, 84, 335; Naval, 303, 378; Sadberk Hanım, 303, 378; Turkish and Islamic Art, 303, 359
Mustafa I, sultan, 217, 219–20, 239
Mustafa II, sultan, 242–3, 247–9, 253, 324, 372
Mustafa III, sultan, 255–8, 355
Mustafa IV, sultan, 256–7, 259–61
Mustafa, son of Süleyman I, 194, 196, 203
Mustafa Reşit Pasha, grand vezir, 271, 273
Muzalon, George, see George Muzalon

Nakşidil, valide sultan, 260
Namık Kemal, 279
Napoleon III, emperor of France, 278
Nasi, Joseph, 207
Negroponte, Todori, cabaret singer, 303
Nestorian heresy, 67
New Order, see Nizamı Cedit
Nicaea (Iznik), 31, 52, 108, 149–50, 153, 159
Nicaea, Byzantine empire of, 149–50, 160
Nicephorus I, emperor, 109
Nicephorus II Phocas, emperor, 118–20
Nicephorus III Botaneiates, emperor, 131–3
Nicephorus Gregoras, historian, 34, 102, 153–4, 159

Nicetas Choniates, historian, 105–6, 135, 139, 141, 147–8
Nicholas V, pope, 173
Nicholas I, tsar of Russia, 268–9
Nicholas, patriarch of Constantinople, 116
Nicopolis, battle of (1396), 167
Nightingale, Florence, 277
Nika Revolt (532), 80, 84
Nizamı Cedit (New Order), 258–9
Normans, 130–31, 133, 140, 142–3
Notitia urbis Constantinopolitanae, 62, 64, 86
Nurubanu, valide sultan, 206–8, 367–8
Nymphaeum, Treaty of (1261), 150

Orhan Gazi, sultan, 157, 159–61, 164, 284
Orient Express, 284
Osman II, sultan, 215, 217–19, 348, 371–2
Osman III, sultan, 248, 255–6, 373
Osman Gazi, founder of the Osmanlı dynasty, 157, 187, 238, 252–3, 280–81, 290
Osman Hamdi Bey, 303
Ottoman Parliament, 282, 287–90, 377
Ozal, Turgut, president of Turkey, 302

Palaeologina, Maria, see Maria Palaeologina
Palaeologus, Demetrius, see Demetrius Palaeologus
Palaeologus, Manuel, see Manuel Palaeologus
Palaeologus, Thomas, see Thomas Palaeologus
Paris Peace Conference (1919), 293–4
Paris, Treaty of (1856), 277
Parliament, see Ottoman Parliament
Partitio Romanum (1204), 148
Passarowitz, Treaty of (1718), 249
Patrona Halil, 252–3

Patzinaks, 133–5
Paul the Silentiary, poet, 86–7
Paulinus, master of offices, 67
Pausanias, Spartan general, 18
Pera (Beyoğlu), 286
Pera Palas Hotel, 284
Persians (Iranians), 16–18, 50, 52, 75–6, 80, 90–95, 192, 226, 237
Pertevniyal, valide sultan, 271, 278
Pescinnius Niger, Roman emperor, 22
Pezevenk ('the Pimp'), 238
Philadelphaeum, 29, 43–4, 117
Philiki Hetairia, 262
Philip II, king of Macedon, 20–21
Philip of Swabia, German king, 143–4
Philippicus Vardan, emperor, 100
Philon of Byzantium, military engineer, 13
Phocas, emperor, 91–2, 94
Photius, patriarch of Constantinople, 114–15
Piyale Pasha, 207
Polyeuktos, patriarch of Constantinople, 120
Pompeius, nephew of Anastasius I, 77, 80
Portico of Severus, 26–7, 38
Princes' Isles, 28, 109–11, 118, 120, 124, 131
Probus, nephew of Anastasius I, 77
procession of the guilds (1638), 229–36
Proclus, prefect, 323
Procopius, usurper, 52–3
Procopius of Caesarea, historian, 5, 79–86, 88
Prusa (Bursa), 159
Prusias I, king of Bithynia, 21
Psellus, Michael, see Michael Psellus
Ptochoprodromos, Theodorus, see Theodorus Ptochoprodomos
Public Debt Commission, 283
Pulcheria, sister of Theodosius II and wife of Marcian, 61–2, 65, 67, 68–9

Rabia Gülnus, valide sultan, 242–3, 247, 249–50
Ravenna, Exarchate of, 90
Refai (Welfare) Party, 302
reforms in the early Turkish Republic, 299–300
Reis, Piri, 378
Reşit Mehmet Pasha, grand vezir, 267
Robert de Clari, historian, 57
Roger de Flor, 157
Romania, Latin kingdom of, 148–52
Romans, 21–3
Romanus I Lecapenus, emperor, 117–18, 339
Romanus II, emperor, 119–20
Romanus III Argyrus, emperor, 122–3
Romanus IV Diogenes, emperor, 131
Romulus Augustus, emperor of the West, 69
Roxelana (Haseki Hürrem), wife of Süleyman I, 194–7, 199, 202–5
Rufinus, praetorian prefect, 58, 60
Rumeli Feneri, 6, 9, 319
Rumeli Hisarı, 6, 17, 305–8, 310, 312–13, 347–8
Russia and the Russians, 114–15, 121, 256, 271, 282
Rüstem Pasha, grand vezir, 199, 202–3

Sa'adabat, Palace of, 250–52, 254
Sahye, valide sultan, 208, 213–15, 241, 369
Sait Halim Pasha, grand vezir, 290
Saliha, valide sultan, 253
Samatya quarter, 28, 46–7, 74, 107, 368
Samuel, tsar of the Bulgars, 121
San Stefano (Yeşilköy), Treaty of (1878), 283
Sancaktar Mescidi, 46–7, 323
Sanders, General Liman von, 291
Saracens, see Arabs
Sclerina, mistress of Constantine IX, 126–7
Sclerus, Bardas, see Bardas Sclerus

Scythians, 17, 95
Şehsuvar, valide sultan, 255
Selcuk Turks, 130, 133–4, 140, 142, 144, 150
Selim I ('Yavuz' – 'the Grim'), sultan, 191–3, 337
Selim II ('the Sot'), sultan, 194, 203–4, 206–8, 221
Selim III, sultan, 256–9, 374, 377
Selim Pasha Benderli, grand vezir, 264
Selimiye Barracks, 258
Senate of Constantinople, 38, 51, 64
Septimius Severus, Roman emperor, 22–4, 25–7, 34, 37, 320
Sergius, patriarch of Constantinople, 95
Sèvres, Treaty of (1920), 294
Sigismund, king of Hungary, 167
Sinan, architect, 199–200, 202, 208, 210
Sinan, Atik, see Atik Sinan
Sipahis, 211, 226, 240, 258
Siyavuş Pasha, grand vezir, 210
Skanderberg, 171
slave-market, Istanbul, 215–16
Slavs, 95, 109, 114
Sobieski, John, 242
Sokollu Mehmet Pasha, grand vezir, 203–8, 241
Sophia, first wife of John VIII, 169
Sophia, wife of Justin II, 90
Sophia of Monteferrat, second wife of John VIII, 169
Spartans, 18–20
Sphrantzes, George, historian, 169, 173, 175
Spice Bazaar, see Mısır Çarşısı
Stauracius, emperor, 109
Stephen II, king of Hungary, 135
Stephen, son of Romanus I, 118
Stephen the Younger, St, 106–7
Stilicho, magister militum, 58, 60
Stoa Basilica (see also cisterns: Basilica), 40, 51, 64, 201
Strategion, 27, 31, 104

Strategopoulos, Alexius, *see* Alexius
　Strategopoulos
street names, 305–6
Striker, Professor Lee, 338, 341
Studius, Roman patrician, 74
Sublime Porte, the, 240, 256, 281,
　283, 287
Süleyman I ('the Magnificent'), sultan,
　194–206, 221, 285, 364
Süleyman II, sultan, 238–9, 242–3,
　246–7, 364
Süleyman, son of Beyazit I, 169
Süleyman Pasha, head of the Military
　Academy, 280
Svyatoslav, prince of Kiev, 121
Sweet Waters of Asia, 6, 250, 377
Sweet Waters of Europe, 4, 250, 276
Symeon, tsar of the Bulgars, 117
Symeon, grand duke of Moscow,
　161
Symplegades, the 8, 9, 319

Tabani Yassı Arnavut Mahmut Pasha,
　grand vezir, 226
Taksim Meydanı, 255, 287
Talat Pasha, grand vezir, 290–92
talismans, 64
Tamerlane, 168–9
Tanzimat (Reform Movement), 273,
　277–9, 283
Tekfursarayı, 162, 212, 340, 346–7
Ten Thousand, the, 20
Terval, khan of the Bulgars, 99
Tetrastoon, 26, 38
Theodora, empress, daughter of
　Constantine VIII, 124–8
Theodora, daughter of John VI, 161
Theodora, wife of Justinian I, 79–82,
　85, 87, 89, 329
Theodora, wife of Justinian II, 99
Theodora, wife of Michael VIII,
　153–4, 342
Theodora, wife of Emperor
　Theophilus, 111–12, 114
Theodora, wife of Romanus I, 339

Theodore I Lascaris, emperor, 149–50
Theodore II Lascaris, emperor, 150
Theodore Metochites, 159, 344–5
Theodore the Studite, St, 110–11
Theodore of Sykeon, St, 94–5
Theodore Tyro, St, 104
Theodorus Ptochoprodromos, poet,
　139–40
Theodosia, St, 101
Theodosia, wife of Leo V, 111
Theodosius I ('the great'), emperor, 40,
　54–7, 65–8, 70, 322–5, 348
Theodosius II, emperor, 4, 59, 61–3,
　103, 325–6
Theodosius III ('the Reluctant'),
　emperor, 100
Theodotus, patriarch of
　Constantinople, 111
Theophano, wife of Romanus II,
　119–20
Theophilus ('the Unfortunate'),
　emperor 111–12, 338
Thomas Palaeologus, son of Manuel II,
　171–2, 187
Thracians, 13
Thrasybulus, Athenian general, 20
Tiberius II, emperor, 90
Tiberius III (Apsimar), emperor,
　99–100
Tiberius, son of Justinian II, 100
Tocco, Magdalena, *see* Magdalena
　Tocco
tombs (türbe): Ahmet I, 216, 219, 238,
　240, 371; Barbarossa (Hayrettin
　Pasha), 198–9; 359–60; Beyazit II,
　191–2; Gülbahar, wife of Mehmet
　II, 199; Laleli Camii, 256, 374;
　Mahmut II, 289, 378; Mahmut
　Pasha, 356; Mehmet II, 189, 281;
　Mehmet III, 215, 369; Murat III,
　212, 369; Roxelana, 205, 362–3;
　Selim I, 193; Selim II, 208, 367,
　369; Sinan, 210, 362–3; Süleyman I,
　205, 362–3; Yeni Cami, 243, 252,
　255, 372

tombstones, *see* cemeteries and
tombstones
Topal Recep Pasha, grand vezir, 226
Tophane (Artillery Corps
headquarters), 258
Topkapı Sarayı, 10, 184, 188, 192,
194, 198, 206–15, 217–20, 225–9,
238–40, 259–60, 273, 277, 284,
290, 296, 303, 348–54, 359, 371,
276
Tott, Baron François de, 257–8
Trajan, Roman emperor, 22
Trebizond, Byzantine empire of, 142,
149
Tribonian, jurist, 86
Tripolitanian War (1911–12), 290
Tulip Period, 251, 254, 353
Tünel, 286
Turhan Hadice, valide sultan, 238–41,
243, 371
Turkish Republic, founding of,
296–7
Tzachas, emir of Smyrna, 133
Tzetzes, John, *see* John Tzetzes
Tzycanisterion (polo grounds), 44, 64

Ulema, 217, 219, 239, 261, 279
Ulubatlı Hasan, 176
Underwood, Paul, 345
University of Constantinople, 65, 114
Urban V, pope, 164
Üsküdar, *see* Chrysopolis
Uzun Süleyman Ağa, chief black
eunuch, 239

Vahdeti, Hafız Derviş, 289
Valens, emperor, 52–4, 149, 324
Valens Aqueduct, 53, 149, 324
Valentinian I, emperor of the West,
52–3
Valentinian II, emperor of the West,
53, 55
Valentinian III, emperor of the West,
62, 66
Vandals, 74, 85

Varangarians, 121
Varna, battle of (1444), 171
Veli, Orhan, 307
Venice and the Venetians, 135, 140,
144–9, 156–7, 162, 164, 167, 171,
176, 187–8, 198, 206–8, 210, 242,
253, 333
Venier, Maffeo, Venetian bailo, 210
Venizelos, Eleutherios, 294
Verina, wife of Leo I, 70, 73, 75
Vespasian, Roman emperor, 22
Via Egnatia, 21, 26, 46
Victoria, queen of Great Britain, 278
Vienna, first Ottoman siege (1529),
196–7; second Ottoman siege
(1683), 242
Vitalian, Count, 74
Vladimir, prince of Kiev, 89, 121
Vlanga quarter, 105

Walls: of Anastasius (Long Walls), 75,
88; of Byzantium, 13, 31, 319;
Constantinian, 37, 43 4, 46; of
Heraclius, 96, 110, 335 6, 338; of
Leo V, 110, 338; of Manuel I
Comnenus, 135–6, 340; Sea, 110,
338; Theodosian, 4, 44, 46, 62–3,
65, 67–8, 92, 95, 97, 101, 113,
161, 169, 174–6, 262, 325, 326,
336, 344
Whittemore, Thomas, 345
Wilhelm I, king of Prussia and emperor
of Germany, 278
winds, 308–10
World War, First (1914–18), 291

Xenophon, 20
Xerxes, Persian king, 16, 18

Yazid, son of Caliph Muawiya, 97
Yeats, William Butler, 112
Yedikule (Castle of the Seven Towers),
184, 219, 325, 348
Yermisekiz Mehmet Çelebi, 249
Yıldız Sarayı, 281, 295, 377

Young Ottomans, 279

Young Turks, 287

Yusuf Izzeddin, Prince, son of Sultan
Abdül Aziz, 278

Zeno ('the Isaurian'), emperor, 73–5,
96

Zeuxippus, Baths of, 23–4, 40, 64, 87,
98

Zoë, empress, daughter of Constantine
VIII, 122–6, 333

Zoë Carbonopsina, fourth wife of Leo
VI, 116–17